C000277808

1 MONTH OF
FREE
READING

at

www.ForgottenBooks.com

By purchasing this book you are eligible for one month membership to ForgottenBooks.com, giving you unlimited access to our entire collection of over 1,000,000 titles via our web site and mobile apps.

To claim your free month visit:

www.forgottenbooks.com/free1118445

* Offer is valid for 45 days from date of purchase. Terms and conditions apply.

ISBN 978-0-331-39933-2
PIBN 11118445

This book is a reproduction of an important historical work. Forgotten Books uses state-of-the-art technology to digitally reconstruct the work, preserving the original format whilst repairing imperfections present in the aged copy. In rare cases, an imperfection in the original, such as a blemish or missing page, may be replicated in our edition. We do, however, repair the vast majority of imperfections successfully; any imperfections that remain are intentionally left to preserve the state of such historical works.

Forgotten Books is a registered trademark of FB &c Ltd.
Copyright © 2018 FB &c Ltd.
FB &c Ltd, Dalton House, 60 Windsor Avenue, London, SW19 2RR.
Company number 08720141. Registered in England and Wales.

For support please visit www.forgottenbooks.com

OFFICIAL REPORTS

OF THE

TOWN OF WAYLAND,

FOR ITS

ONE HUNDRED AND FOURTEENTH MUNICIPAL YEAR,

FROM

MARCH 1, 1893, TO MARCH 1, 1894.

BOSTON:
THE ROCKWELL AND CHURCHILL PRESS.
1894.

OF THE

OWN OF WAYLAND,

FOR ITS

ONE HUNDRED AND FOURTEENTH MUNICIPAL YEAR,

FROM

RCH 1, 1893, TO MARCH 1, 1894.

BOSTON:

THE ROCKWELL AND CHURCHILL PRESS.

1894.

LIST OF TOWN OFFICERS, 1893–4.

The following is a list of the officers of the Town of Wayland, and when their term of office expires.

Town Clerk.

Term expires.

RICHARD T. LOMBARD 1894

Treasurer.

HERBERT C. WELLS 1894

Auditor.

ARTHUR G. BENNETT 1894

Collector of Taxes.

WILLARD B. WARD 1894

Treasurer of Library Funds.

HERBERT C. WELLS 1894

Selectmen.

THOMAS W. FROST 1894
ISAAC DAMON 1894
EDWARD P. BUTLER 1894

Assessors.

HORATIO G. HAMMOND 1896
EDWARD CARTER 1895
RICHARD T. LOMBARD 1894

School Committee.

Term expires.

LIZZIE E. MITCHELL 1896
L. ANNA DUDLEY 1895
JOSEPH CANDLIN 1894

Water Commissioners.

HENRY G. DUDLEY 1896
CHAS. H. BOODEY 1895
WILLIAM H. BENT 1894

Overseers of Poor.

DAVID P. W. LOKER 1894
DANIEL W. RICKER 1894
WILLARD B. WARD 1894

Trustees Public Library.

JOHN CONNOLLY 1896
RICHARD T. LOMBARD 1896
ELLEN M. BRAMAN 1895
HENRY D. PARMENTER. 1895
ISAAC DAMON 1894
EMILY A. HEARD 1894

Constables.

CLINTON E. HIBBARD 1894
JOHN E. LINNEHAN 1894
LAWRENCE H. McMANUS 1894
WILLIAM C. NEAL 1894
JOHN WOODWORTH 1894
[*Two vacancies.*]

Fence Viewers.

ALBION F. PARMENTER 1894
HORATIO G. HAMMOND. 1894
EDWARD CARTER 1894

5

Trustees Allen Fund.

Term expires.

LUTHER H. SHERMAN 1894
DANIEL G. GRIFFIN 1894
THEO. S. SHERMAN 1894

Measurers of Wood and Bark.

L. K. LOVELL 1894
EDWARD CARTER 1894
ERNEST E. BUTLER 1894

Superintendent of North and Centre Cemeteries.

THEO. S. SHERMAN 1894

Committee in charge of Lakeview Cemetery.

WM. W. LOVEJOY 1894
HENRY B. PHALEN 1894
DAVID P. W. LOKER 1894

Field Driver.

IRA S. DICKEY 1894

Sealer of Weights and Measures.

RICHARD T. LOMBARD 1894

Surveyor of Lumber.

EDWIN W. MARSTON 1894

Finance Committee.

H. B. BRAMAN 1894
R. T. LOMBARD 1894
C. W. DEAN 1894
L. H. SHERMAN 1894
A. H. BRYANT 1894

Committee on Decoration Day.

Term expires.

E. P. BUTLER 1894

ELBRIDGE J. CARTER 1894

WM. H. JAMESON 1894

Registrars of Voters.

LUTHER H. SHERMAN . . . . April 30, 1896

DELOSS W MITCHELL . . . " 1895

THEO. L. SAWIN . . . . " 1894

RICHARD T. LOMBARD . . Town Clerk *ex officio.*

Superintendent of Streets.

THEODORE S. SHERMAN.

TOWN WARRANT.

MIDDLESEX, SS.

To WILLIAM C. NEAL *or either of the Constables of the Town of Wayland,*

GREETING : In the name of the Commonwealth of Massachusetts, you are hereby required to notify and warn the inhabitants of the town of Wayland qualified to vote in elections and town affairs, to meet at the Town House, Wayland, on Monday, the 26th day of March, Inst., at 8 o'clock in the forenoon, then and there to act upon the following articles, viz. :

ARTICLE 1. To choose a Moderator to preside in said meeting.

ART. 2. To choose a Town Clerk, Treasurer, Collector of Taxes, Auditor, three Selectmen, three Overseers of the Poor, Treasurer of the Library Funds, and Seven Constables, all of the above for the term of one year ; and one School Committee, one Assessor, one Water Commissioner, two Trustees of the Public Library, all for the term of three years ; also to vote upon the question, " Shall licenses be granted for the sale of intoxicating liquors in the town of Wayland for the year ensuing?" All of which must be voted for in accordance with Chapter 368 of the Acts of the year 1890, and all names appear upon the official ballot.

ART. 3. To choose all other necessary Town Officers, Agents, and Committees.

ART. 4. To hear reports of Town Officers, Trustees, Agents, and Committees, and act thereon.

ART. 5. To appropriate such sums of money as may be necessary to defray town charges, or other purposes for the year ensuing, and order the same to be assessed, or do or act.

Art. 6. To provide for the payment of any part of the Town debt, or do or act.

Art. 7. To appropriate the license money on dogs, refunded by the County Treasurer, or do or act.

Art. 8. To authorize the Treasurer to borrow money in anticipation of taxes for the current year, or do or act.

Art. 9. To act upon the Jury List as prepared by the Selectmen.

Art. 10. To authorize the Selectmen to consult counsel on important Town cases.

Art. 11. To see if the Town will accept a gift of money from James Sumner Draper, Esq., for the benefit of the Wayland Public Library, subject to the conditions contained in the " Offer of Gift," or do or act.

Art. 12. To see if the Town will appropriate the sum of nine thousand dollars to build a School House at Wayland Centre in accordance with plans and specifications procured by the Committee, by virtue of the vote of Town, at a meeting held June 24, 1893, or do or act.

Art. 13. To see if the Town will continue the appropriation of five hundred dollars, for rebuilding Stone bridge, so called, for another year, or do or act.

Art. 14. To see if the Town will appoint a committee to apply to the Legislature for authority to refund its debt, or do or act.

Art. 15. To see if the Town will authorize the Selectmen to contract for Electric Lights for two years or more, or do or act.

Art. 16. To see if the Town will authorize its Selectmen to petition the Massachusetts Highway Commission that the Commonwealth should acquire any of its roads as a State highway, or do or act.

ART. 17. To see if the Town will authorize its Selectmen to establish one or more drinking-fountains within the Town, or do or act.

ART. 18. To see if the Town will order and direct the sale of the North and Centre High School buildings. Also order and direct the sale of the Centre Primary School building and land, the Rutter School building and land, and the Thomas School building and land, and that the Treasurer of the Town be authorized and empowered to sign and execute a deed or deeds of said premises to the purchaser or purchasers for and in behalf of the Town, or do or act.

And you are required to serve this warrant by posting up attested copies thereof at each of the post-offices and Town House in said Town, seven days at least before the time appointed for said meeting.

Hereof fail not and make due return of this warrant with your doings thereon, to the Town Clerk, at the time and place appointed for holding said meeting.

Given under our hands this third day of March, in the year of our Lord one thousand eight hundred and ninety-four.

THOMAS W. FROST,
ISAAC DAMON,
EDWARD P. BUTLER,
Selectmen of Wayland.

A true copy. Attest:

Constable.

LIST OF JURORS.

For the Town of Wayland, 1894, as prepared by the Selectmen.

WILLARD B. WARD.

MICHAEL W. HYNES.

EDWARD CARTER.

ALBION F. PARMENTER.

WILLIAM W. LOVEJOY.

GRANVILLE L. LOKER.

JAMES A. DRAPER.

SIDNEY LOKER.

DELOSS W. MITCHELL.

THEO. L. SAWIN.

WILLIAM H. CAMPBELL.

JOHN E. LINNEHAN.

EDWARD A. ATWOOD.

ISAAC C. DAMON.

HENRY B. PHALEN.

LUTHER H. SHERMAN.

HORATIO G. HAMMOND.

ROSCOE C. DEAN.

GEORGE B. FOLSOM.

ERNEST F. LAWRENCE.

GEORGE E. SHERMAN.

THEO. S. SHERMAN.

EDGAR B. LOKER.

NAPOLEON PERADEAU.

SELECTMEN'S REPORT.

MARCH 1, 1894.

The Selectmen hereby submit their annual report for the year ending Feb. 28, 1894.

We have appointed the following officers during the year, as required by the Statutes:

Special Police Officer.
JOHN LAMARINE.

Auctioneer.
GEORGE E. SHERMAN.

Registration of Voters for Three Years.
LUTHER H. SHERMAN.

Forest Fire Wardens.
RALPH BENT, LAWRENCE H. McMANUS.

Undertakers.
DAVID P. W. LOKER, ANDREW S. MORSE.

Inspector of Cattle and Provisions.
THOMAS W. FROST.

Superintendent of Streets.
THEODORE S. SHERMAN.

Engineers.

RALPH BENT, HENRY B. PHALEN,
EDWIN W. MARSTON.

ELECTION OFFICERS.

Precinct 1.

Warden. — ALBION F. PARMENTER.
Clerk. — JAMES A. DRAPER.
Inspectors. — MICHAEL W. HYNES,
THEO. S. SHERMAN,
PETER ZIMMERMANN,
WM. H. CAMPBELL.

Precinct 2.

Warden. — HENRY B. PHALEN.
Clerk. — DANIEL D. GRIFFIN.
Inspectors. — EDWARD B. SMITH,
RUSSELL E. FRYE,
GEORGE A. LEACH,
LEONARD A. LOKER.

By vote of the Town we have divided the Town into two voting-precincts, and at the State election held Nov. 7, 1893, the voting took place under conditions so favorable to the people that it has given very general satisfaction.

During the year we have settled the suit of Wayland *v.* Folsom by the payment to the Town of $768.00, which we considered a desirable settlement.

Also the suits of Heard *v.* Wayland and Egan *v.* Wayland. In the settlement of these cases the parties have conveyed to the town two parcels of land between the old and new roads, which will save any future controversy as to the right of the town and abutters. At our request the Boston & Maine Railroad has erected gates at the principal crossings in town, adding greatly to the safety of travel at these points.

The town of Framingham not making any provision to rebuild Stone bridge, we were unable to carry into effect the vote of the town in reference to this bridge.

The reinsurance of the town hall, library, and school-house, Cochituate, dividing the town into voting-precincts, and the payment of attorney's fees in the settlement of the cases named, has caused a heavy draft on our Incidental Expense account during the year.

During the year there have been destroyed by fire buildings to the value of $5,920. At Wayland centre there is absolutely no protection against fire. We think something should be done by giving some means to meet this want.

In accordance with the vote of the town we have rebuilt the dry bridge on Sudbury causeway, and rebuilt the bridge on Mill street, using hard-pine lumber and making them more substantial. The Town having elected a Committee on Finance, we make no recommendations for the various town departments, as those matters seem to come under the duties of that committee.

THOMAS W. FROST,
ISAAC DAMON,
EDWARD P. BUTLER,
Selectmen of Wayland.

REPORT OF TOWN CLERK AND REGISTRAR.

WAYLAND, Jan. 1, 1894.

To the Inhabitants of the Town of Wayland:

I hereby transmit the Annual Report of the Clerk and Registrar for the year ending Dec. 31, 1893.

BIRTHS.

Whole number registered during the year is twenty-seven, being four more than in 1892. Of the number twelve were males, and fifteen were females.

Born of native parents 13
" foreign parents 7
" native and foreign parents 7

MARRIAGES.

Whole number registered during the year is eleven, being three less than in 1892.

Of native birth of both parties 6
Of foreign " " 2
Of native and foreign birth 3
First marriage of both parties 7
First of one and second of the other party . . . 4

DEATHS.

Whole number registered during the year is thirty-eight, being thirteen more than in 1892.

CONDITION.

Married	. . . .	10
Widowed	. . . .	10
Single	. . . .	18
Native born	. . . .	32
Foreign born	. . . .	6

NAMES AND AGES OF PERSONS DECEASED OVER SEVENTY YEARS OF AGE.

	Years.	Months.	Days.
Benjamin M. Folsom	70	9	17
Caroline A. Reeves	80	9	19
Phebe C. Underwood	79	. .	15
Henry B. Fischer	74	11	
Bathsheba Holt	86		
George Gleason	77	4	15
Ellen Linnehan	80		
David Spofford	74	1	3
Charles Moulton	83		
Anna Adams	81	1	
Mary M. Loker	72	7	
Mary J. Whitney	78	4	
Sophia W. Mellen	84	4	6
Susan C. Reed	82	6	18

NOSOLOGICAL TABLE.

Inanition	3
Typhoid fever	1
Peritonitis	1
Mitral insufficiency	3
Old age	3
Diphtheria	2
Suicide	1
Phthisis	4

Cancer	1
Heart disease	3
Apoplexy	2
Stillborn	1
Consumption	2
Pneumonia	2
Drowned	1
Inflammation of bowels	1
Alcoholic poisoning	1
Bronchitis	1
Scrofula	1
Influenza	2
Urinal poisoning	1
Suppurative bastate	1

DOGS.

Whole number of persons licensed to keep dogs, for the year ending Nov. 30, 1893, 116.

101 male dogs at $2		$202 00
15 female dogs at $5		75 00
		$277 00
116 licenses at 20 cents each		23 20
		$253 80

Paid County Treasurer, June 1, $78.00.
    "   "   "   December 1, $175.80.

Number of registered voters Nov. 7, 1893		412
Number registered, Precinct 1	151	
Number registered, Precinct 2	261	
		412
Number ballots cast, Precinct 1	117	
Number ballots cast, Precinct 2	231	
Total number of ballots cast in the town		348

The vote for Governor is as follows :

Louis A. Banks 9
George H. Cary 12
Frederic T. Greenhalge 176
John C. Russell 144
Blanks 7

The vote for Senator, Fourth Middlesex District :

Joseph W. Barber 15
Maurice F. Coughlin 134
Francis C. Curtis 182

The vote for Representatives, Twenty-eighth Middlesex District :

Walter Adams 130
Henry E. Bullard 166
Frank Cass 102
William C. Wight 169

The following was the vote for Representative in the District :

	Framingham.	Holliston.	Sherborn.	Wayland.	Total.
Walter Adams...................	859	254	44	130	1,287
Henry E. Bullard...............	626	288	81	166	1,161
Frank Cass.....................	694	385	70	102	1,251
William C. Wight	787	173	54	169	1,183

Respectfully submitted,

RICHARD T. LOMBARD,
Town Clerk.

ASSESSORS' REPORT.

For the Year ending Feb. 28, 1893.

Value of real estate, May 1, 1893	$1,190,750 00
" personal estate, May 1, 1893	318,915 00
Total value, May 1, 1893	$1,509,665 00
" " 1892	1,457,830 00
Increase	$51,835 00
Taxes assessed for town purposes	$15,852 42
Overlayings	5 84
State tax	1,825 00
County tax	1,490 22
Polls assessed	1,058 00
Total amount of taxes assessed	$20,231 48
Number of polls, May, 1892	522
" " May, 1893	529
Increase	7
Additional polls assessed	10
Total increase of polls	17
Number of persons assessed	799
" residents assessed on property,	402
" non-residents assessed on property	139

Total value of land $471,905 00
"   "   buildings 718,845 00
"   "   church property . . . 29,740 00
"   "   town property . . . 86,100 00

Number of horses 343
"   cows 795
"   neat cattle other than cows . 120
"   swine 32
"   sheep 88
"   acres of land . . $9,145\frac{25}{100}$
"   dwelling-houses . . . 402
Rate of taxation, 1892 . . . . $16 00
"   "   1893 . . . . 12 70

Additional assessments 33 33

Abatements, 1890 . . . . . 2 30
"   1891 . . . . . 990 32
1892 . . . . . 22 00
1893 . . . . . 55 88

                                    $1,070 50

Respectfully submitted,

RICHARD T. LOMBARD,
EDWARD CARTER,
HORATIO G. HAMMOND,
          · *Assessors of Wayland.*

COLLECTOR'S REPORT.

TAXES FOR 1890.

Balance due March 1, 1893	. . . .	$98 78
Paid Treasurer .	. . . . .	98 78

TAXES OF 1891.

Balance due March 1, 1893	. . . .	$6,379 31
Paid Treasurer	. . . . .	5,904 13
		$475 18

TAXES OF 1892.

Balance due March 1, 1893	. . . .	$9,914 60
Paid Treasurer .	. . . . .	3,608 98
		$6,305 62

TAXES OF 1893.

Town tax	. . . . . .	$16,910 42
County tax	. . . . . .	1,490 22
State tax	. . . . . .	1,825 00
Overlayings	. . . . . .	5 84
		$20,231 48
Additional assessments	. . . . .	33 33
		$20,264 81
Paid Treasurer	. . . .	11,957 98
		$8,306 83

WILLARD B. WARD,
Collector.

REPORT OF THE OVERSEERS OF THE POOR.

The following is the report of the Overseers of the Poor of the town of Wayland for the year ending Feb. 28, 1894.

The Almshouse has been in charge of Mr. and Mrs H. P. Parker: The inmates supported at the almshouse during the year are as follows :

Mrs. Sarah Puffer, invalid, aged 78 years.

Mr. James Burk, aged 67 years.

Mr. Charles Moulton, aged 84 years ; died Aug. 10, 1893.

Mrs. Bathsheba Holt, aged 87 years ; died April 6, 1893.

Mr. Benj. Nealey, admitted March 1, 1893, aged 70 years.

Mr. Geo. F. Bond, admitted Nov. 24, 1893, aged 72 years.

Mr. Chas. W. Moore, admitted Jan. 10, 1894, aged 57 years.

Annie Burrill, aged 11 years ; at Eunice Bemis'.

Mr. James A. Wing, aged 59 years ; Worcester Insane Asylum.

Mr. Chas. W. Bemis, aged — years ; Worcester Insane Asylum ; released March 31, 1893.

Miss Addie Moore, aged 31 years ; Worcester Insane Asylum ; died Aug. 12, 1893.

Miss Ellen Burk, aged 65 years ; Taunton Insane Asylum.

Miss Carrie A. Davis, aged 33 years ; admitted Westboro' Insane Asylum ; Oct. 2, 1893.

Number of tramps during year 427
Number of meals furnished tramps 761

Number of persons receiving outside aid during the year and amount rendered to each family were as follows :

Nelson Normandin, wife and 11 children, at No.
Brookfield $213 00
Elijah Roberts, wife and 2 children, at No. Brook-
field 28 00
Alex. Benoit, wife and 3 children, at Brockton .   30 00
Mrs. L. Lucier and 2 children 83 69
Frank Daviere, wife and 7 children . . .   53 06
Louis Cormier, wife and 9 children . . .   14 75
Frank Byron, wife and 4 children . . .   3 93
John Shenett, wife and 2 children . . .   55 05
Geo. A. Chalmers, aged 73 years, rent . .   36 00
Annie Burrill, at Mrs. E. H. Bemis', board and
clothes 140 00
Ann Painter, at C. Randolph's 52 00

Total number of persons receiving outside aid, 58.

The resources for the support of the poor of the year were
as follows :

March 1, 1893. Balance in treasury . . . $0 01
1893
March 27. Appropriation 2,000 00
Extra appropriation . . .   500 00
Received from estate of Phebe C.
Underwood 250 00
Received from town of Natick . .   18 25
Returned by Overseers of Poor . .   14 87
1894
Feb. 28. Receipts at farm 307 65
                                                  ‾‾‾‾‾‾‾‾
                                                  $3,090 78

Expenditures at farm . $307 65
   "   "   orders,   416 36
Outside aid and bills due
   March 1, '93 . .   2,327 15
Unexpended balance .   39 62
                              ‾‾‾‾‾‾‾‾ $3,090 78

DETAILED STATEMENT.

RECEIPTS AT FARM.

Eggs	$62 27
Poultry	30 91
Calves	37 77
Cows	95 00
Wood	13 00
Corn	16 37
Beans	6 00
Onions	15 83
Pork	10 50
Corn stover	15 00
Work	5 00
Total receipts	$307 65

EXPENDITURES AT FARM.

H. F. Lee & Co., grocéries and grain	$84 02
S. Russell, meat	43 43
Blacksmithing	20 00
Two shoates	13 25
Clothing for Burk and Neeley	11 25
Fertilizer	8 75
Wagon, wheels, and axle	7 50
Grain	18 40
Stone drag	7 65
Work	5 00
Repairing harnesses	6 05
Paint and paper	10 00
Incidentals	64 81
A. H. Parker	7 53
	$307 65

EXPENDITURES AT FARM, ORDERS.

T. S. Shearman	$3 00
H. F. Lee & Son	167 02
E. P. Butler	38 96
W. D. Parlin	2 40
S. Russell	112 20
F. W. Pousland	34 07
J. McAulliffe	12 53
L. K. Lovell	31 68
W. Stearns	5 50
Cleeland, Healey & Underwood	9 00
Total expenditures at farm	$416 36

ORDERS APPROVED FOR OUTSIDE AID AND BILLS DUE MARCH 1, 1893.

H. P. Parker, salary	$300 00
A. H. Parker, salary	108 00
Worcester Insane Asylum	468 23
Taunton Insane Asylum	212 81
Westboro' Insane Asylum	42 25
Commonwealth of Massachusetts	94 25
H. F. Lee and Co.	93 26
J. R. Moore	12 36
J. F. Sawin	30 00
D. W. Ricker	16 50
Mrs. T. Steele	10 00
J. H. Immick	5 00
W. H. Bent	6 00
E. H. Bemis	143 00
M. J. Maloney	37 00
B. W. Smith	4 84
C. H. Boodey	77 50
Carried forward,	$1,661 00

Brought forward,		$1,661 00
Robinson and Jones		99 95
E. A. Atwood		38 36
F. E. Hooker		18 00
North Brookfield		96 09
W. Lovejoy		5 00
D. P. W. Loker		66 50
W. B. Ward		89 67
R. T. Lombard		12 00
C. Randolph		52 00
Elijah Hollway		26 00
E. P. Loker		36 00
Ray Bros.		15 00
Town of Pepperell		83 75
J. M. Moore		12 83
John Lamarine		3 00
W. F. Garfield		12 00
		$2,327 15

NOTE. — Of the above amount there was paid .the sum of $817.54 for the insane in hospitals.

OUTSTANDING CLAIMS, MARCH 1, 1894.

Robinson & Jones		$24 36
Commonwealth of Massachusetts . . .		255 36
H. P. Parker		250 00
A. H. Parker		34 47
E. A. Atwood		77 78
Dr. C. H. Boodey		29 00
Town of North Brookfield		213 00
City of Brockton		30 00
M. J. Maloney		24 77
W. H. Bent, clerk		9 00
		$947 74

Carried forward, $947 74

Brought forward,	$947 74
H. F. Lee & Son	56 62
S. Russell	12 55
E. P. Butler	17 05
J. B. Charbonier	8 00
Total	$1,041 96

APPRAISED VALUE OF TOWN PROPERTY.

Real estate	$5,000 00
Personal property	1,502 40

We would respectfully recommend an appropriation of twenty-five hundred dollars ($2,500.00) to pay outstanding claims, and for the support of the poor for the ensuing year.

Respectfully submitted,

DANIEL W. RICKER,
DAVID P. W. LOKER,
WILLARD B. WARD,
Overseers of the Poor of the Town of Wayland.

REPORT OF SUPERINTENDENT OF HIGHWAYS.

GENTLEMEN : The total amount of appropriations for highways for the past year was two thousand seven hundred and
fifty dollars ($2,750.00), including a special appropriation of
two hundred and fifty dollars ($250.00) for German Hill
street, and an appropriation of five hundred dollars ($500.00),
made at a special town meeting held Dec. 22. The total
amount expended was two thousand seven hundred and forty-
two dollars and seventy-nine cents ($2,742.79), leaving an un-
expended balance of seven dollars and twenty-one cents
($7.21). The snow bills for the past year were seven hundred
and ninety-nine dollars and eighty-eight cents ($799.88).
The guide-boards are in fair condition, and in their proper
places. Expended on guide-boards, twelve dollars and eighty-
five cents ($12.85). Itemized bills for the above amounts are
on file in the Selectmen's office.

MARCH.

Geo. B. Folsom, 27 days, 8½ hours .	$55 70
Geo. B. Folsom, horses, 6 days, 8 hours	11 89
Geo. W. Videon, 9 hours . . .	1 80
W. A. Jessop, 1 day	2 00
E. Eagan, 1 day, 8 hours . . .	3 60
E. F. Lawrence, 5 hours . . .	1 00
C. H. Richardson, 1 day, 5 hours . .	3 00
C. F. Dickey, 9 hours . . .	1 80
Thos. Dowey, 6 days, 1½ hours . .	12 30

T. F. Maynard, 9 days	$18 00
T. L. Hynes, 5 days, 5½ hours	11 10
M. W. Hynes, 6 days, 4½ hours	12 90
M. W. Hynes, horses, 11 days, 7 hours,	20 46
Geo. L. Baker, 4 days, 1 hour	8 20
J. W. Zimmerman, 3 days, 5½ hours	7 10
L. J. Bemis, 6 days, 4½ hours	12 90
J. S. Dickey, 5 days, 5 hours	11 00
P. S. Zimmerman, 3 days	6 00
M. W. Hynes, horses, 11 days, 7 hours,	20 46
W. H. Campbell, 3 days	6 00
W. H. Campbell, horses, 5 days, 6 hours,	9 80
E. Ellms, 3 days, 1 hour	6 20
A. B. Sherman, 3 days, 4½ hours	6 92
James Fox, 5 days, 2½ hours	9 50
Melvin Sherman, 4 days, 1 hour	8 20
T. B. Smith, 3 days, 7½ hours	7 50
Geo. E. Sherman, 11 days, 5 hours	23 00
Geo. E. Sherman, 6 days, 4½ hours	11 20
T. Maloy, 6 days, 2 hours	12 40
H. Haynes, 2 days, 9 hours	5 80
W. Halpin, 3 days, 8 hours	7 60
H. F. Imminck, 2 days, 7 hours	5 40
P. Tatro, 5 hours	1 00
H. E. Carter, 5 hours	1 00
N. Latour, 11 days, 5 hours	23 00
John Banks, 1 day, 5 hours	3 00
M. Hurley, 1 day	2 00
John Hurly, 6 days, 1 hour	12 20
N. Latour, 4 days, 3 hours	8 60
M. Caswell, 1 day, 6 hours	3 20
C. A. Roak, 10 days	20 00
Ted. Tatro, 3 days	6 00
Samo. Lee, 2 hours	40
F. F. Holten, 6 hours	1 20

M. O. Rouke, 6 days, 3 hours . . $12 60
W. C. Neal, 13 days, 9½ hours . . 27 90
W. C. Neal, horses, 8 days, 7½ hours . 15 24
C. H. Morse, 2 days 4 00
H. Erwin, 2 days, 3 hours . . . 4 60
T. S. Sherman, 15 days, 8½ hours . 31 70
A. Spear, 1 day 2 00
J. F. Loker, 1 day 2 00
———— $502 53

APRIL.

D. W. Lewis, drain-pipe for culverts . $24 00
Geo. Tyler & Co., knife for road-scra-
per 8 50
Chas. Jacobs, 6½ hours . . . 1 30
Tim. Maloy, 5 hours 1 00
W. C. Neal, 5 days, 1½ hours . . 9 26
W. C. Neal, horses, 13 days, 6½ hours . 23 93
W. C. Neal, painting road-scraper . 2 75
John Yarward, 3 days, 1 hour . . 6 30
A. Moran, 4 days, 1 hour . . . 8 30
C. A. Roak, 4 days, 3½ hours . . 8 86
C. A. Roak, horse, 4 days, 3½ hours . 7 58
J. Woodworth, 4 days, 8½ hours . . 9 95
N. Latour, 4 days, 3½ hours . . 8 86
Mass. Central R.R., freight on pipe . 1 41
American Ex. on knife for road-scraper . 25
T. S. Sherman, 3 days, 5 hours . . 7 01
———— $127 66

MAY.

W. C. Neal, 6 days, 8 hours . . $13 80
W. C. Neal, horses, 22 days, 1¼ hours . 38 70
C. A. Roak, 7 days, 3 hours . . 14 67

C. A. Roak, horses, 6 days, 3 hours .	$11 00
A. Morrow, 4 days	8 00
N. Latour, 5 days, 6 hours . .	11 34
John Woodworth, 1 day, 7 hours .	3 57
Henry Mathews, 4 days, 3 hours .	8 67
J. Yarward, 4 days	8 00
J. R. Hawkins, 3 days, 4 hours . .	6 88
J. R. Hawkins, horse, 2 days, 4 hours .	4 17
T. S. Sherman, 7 days, 3 hours . .	14 66
T. S. Sherman, horse, 2 days, 3 hours	4 00
Thos. L. Hynes, 2 days, 5 hours .	5 00
Thos. L. Hynes, horse, 4½ hours .	88
T. F. Maynard, 1 day . . .	2 00
W. C. Neal, 3 days	6 00
W. C. Neal, horse, 10 days . .	17 00
Geo. Whitney, 4 days . . .	8 00
H. Mathews, 4 days	8 00
H. Neal, 3 days	6 00
C. A. Roak, 3 days	6 00
C. A. Roak, horse, 3 days . . .	5 25
T. S. Sherman, 4 days, 4 hours . .	8 80
T. S. Sherman, horse, 6 hours . .	1 00
L. J. Bemis, 14 days, 7 hours . .	29 40
L. J. Bemis, horses, 21 days, 4 hours	37 46
E. P. Butler	2 27
R. H. Hawkins, 4 days, 4½ hours .	9 00
Henry Neal, 4 days	8 00
Geo. Whitney, 3 days, 4 hours . .	6 88
Nap. Latour, 2 days, 5 hours . .	5 10
W. C. Neal, 4 days, 3 hours . .	8 66
W. C. Neal, horses, 12 days, 3 hours .	21 57
Francis Shaw, 350 loads of gravel .	16 50
T. S. Sherman, 3 days, 1 hour . .	6 20

————— $372 43

JUNE.

W. C. Neal, 7 days, 3½ hours	. .	$15 45
W. C. Neal, horses, 17 days, 2½ hours .		30 16
Henry Neal, 6 days, 6½ hours	. .	13 45
E. N. Philips, 1 day, 5 hours	. .	3 12
Geo. Whitney, 5 days, 6½ hours .	.	11 45
N. Latour, 8 days, 5 hours .	. .	16 99
C. A. Roak, 7½ hours	. . .	1 72
C. A. Roak, horse, 7½ hours	. .	1 42
Richard Hawkins, 7 days	. . .	14 00
C. H. Richardson, 2 days	. . .	4 00
T. S. Sherman, 4 days, 2½ hours .	.	8 48
T. S. Sherman, horse, 1 day .	. .	1 75
L. J. Bemis, 24 days, 6⅛ hours	. .	49 46
L. J. Bemis, horses, 49 days, 6¼ hours .		86 72
T. S. Sherman, 2 days, 1⅓ hours .	.	4 24
T. S. Sherman, horse, 1 day .	. .	1 75
J. R. Hawkins, 5 days .	. . .	10 00
W. C. Neal, 6 days, 6½ hours	. .	13 50
W. C. Neal, horses, 13 days, 7½ hours .		24 00
W. C. Neal, 26 loads of gravel	. .	2 60
Henry Neal, 8 days, 5⅓ hours	. .	17 12
E. N. Philips, 5 days, 1¼ hours	. .	10 24
Geo. Whitney, 6 days, 5¼ hours .	.	13 12
W. C. Neal, 2 days	. . . .	4 00
W. C. Neal, horses, 5 days, 4½ hours	.	9 57
N. Latour, 8 days, 5½ hours .	. .	17 12

––—— $385 33

AUGUST.

C. A. Roak, 1 day, 4 hours .	. .	$2 86
C. A. Roak, horse, 1 day	. . .	1 75
John McLory, 2 days .	. . .	4 00
Wood, Barker, & Co., lumber, fence	.	10 67

T. S. Sherman, 3 days, 1½ hours . .	$6 30	
T. S. Sherman, 20 chestnut posts . .	4 00	
	——	$29 58

SEPTEMBER.

Geo. E. Sherman, horses, 9 days . .	$15 75
Ed. Eagan, 1 day, 4½ hours . . .	3 00
M. Guelfoil, 3 days, 2½ hours . .	6 50
D. W. Lewis, 72 feet of drain-pipe .	11 88
James Murphy, 1 day	2 00
John Woodworth, 4 hours . . .	86
L. J. Bemis, 18 days, 2 hours . .	36 40
L. J. Bemis, horses, 36 days, 4 hours .	63 60
W. F. Guelfoil, 5 days, 4½ hours . .	11 00
James Cooledge, 113 loads of gravel .	11 30
D. W. Lewis, 44 feet of drain-pipe .	10 02
M. W. Hynes, 25 days, 2 hours . .	50 44
M. W. Hynes, horses, 13 days, 1 hour .	22 94
T. F. Maynard, 22 days, 2 hours . .	44 44
T. F. Maynard, horses, 17 days, 2¼ hours	29 94
T. F. Maynard, 102 loads gravel .	6 12
T. L. Hynes, 12 days, 6½ hours . .	25 33
T. L. Hynes, horses, 12 days, 1¼ hours .	21 49
N. H. Chesman, 38 feet drain-pipe .	2 34
Chas. Keys, 1 day, 4½ hours . .	3 00
T. S. Sherman, 7 days, 2 hours .	14 40
T. S. Sherman, horse, 2 days . .	3 50
T. S. Sherman, cash paid for dynamite .	4 88
Frank Haynes, plank	1 75
M. B. Sherman, 9 days . . .	18 00
M. B. Sherman, horse, 8 days . .	14 00
Geo. E. Sherman, 21 days . . .	42 00

L. H. Sherman, 77 loads gravel .   . $4 62
Robinson, laying drain-pipe .   .   .   11 90

                      ———— $492 10

OCTOBER.

L. J. Bemis, 8 days $16 00
L. J. Bemis, horses, 6 days   .   . 10 50
D. W. Lewis, 52 feet drain-pipe .   .   9 00
Frank Haynes, to stock and labor on fence, 12 39
T. S. Sherman, 4 days, 6½ hours .   . 9 40
Mass. Central R.R., freight on drain-pipe, 1 25
T. S. Sherman, horse, 4½ hours .   .   87
C. A. Roak, 1 day 2 00
C. A. Roak, horse, 1 day .   .   . 1 75
John McLory, 4 days 8 00
C. A. Roak, 3 days 6 00
C. A. Roak, horse, 3 days .   .   . 5 24
C. A. Roak, gravel   45

                      ———— $82 85

NOVEMBER.

L. J. Bemis, 19 days, 5 hours   .   . $39 10
L. J. Bemis, horses, 31 days, 5 hours . 54 95
J. R. Hawkins, 5 days   .   .   . 2 00
P. A. Leary, to repairing tools .   . 4 37
D. W. Lewis, drain-pipe .   .   . 6 75
T. S. Sherman, 3 days   .   .   . 6 00
T. S. Sherman, 25 chestnut posts . 5 00
American Ex.   50
Horse, American Ex., 1 day   .   . 1 75
W. C. Neal, 4 hours   88
W. C. Neal, 2 loads gravel .   .   .   20
W. C. Neal, horse, 8 hours .   .   . 1 52
N. Latour, 8 hours 1 76
W. C. Neal, 5 days, 1 hour   .   . 13 88

W. C. Neal, horses, 9 days, 3 hours . $16 26
N. Latour, 5 days, 8 hours . . . 11 78
John Hurly, 3 days, 3 hours . . 6 80
————— $181 51

JANUARY.

W. C. Neal, 8 hours $1 80
W. C. Neal, horse, 8 hours . . . 1 57
Union Lumber Co., lumber for fence . 6 80
T. S. Sherman, 2 days, 4½ hours . . 5 00
T. S. Sherman, horse, 1 day . . 1 75
E. W. Marston, building snow-plough . 3 22
E. P. Butler, nails 1 31
——— $21 45

FEBRUARY.

Geo. W. Whitney, 6½ hours . . $1 40
John B. McLlory, 6½ hours . . 1 45
Henry Neal, 8 hours 1 78
P. C. More, 6½ hours . . . 1 40
H. F. Bond, 8 hours 1 78
W. Gerald, 3½ hours . . . 68
E. N. Philips, 6½ hours . . . 1 40
F. P. Hannon, 4½ hours . . . 1 00
Geo. Jennison, 3½ hours . . . 78
E. A. Carter, 6 hours . . . 1 35
W. C. Neal, 4 days, 5 hours . . 9 23
N. Latour, 2 days, 6 hours . . . 5 49
W. C. Neal, horses, 4 days, 1 hour . 7 20
A. S. Bowles, 8 hours . . . 1 60
A. S. Bowles, horses, 3 days, 5 hours . 5 60
C. H. Richardson, 6½ hours . . 1 30
Thos. Bowles, 7½ hours . . . 1 65
C. F. Dickey, 7 hours . . . 1 54
J. H. McMannus sharp pick-drills . 2 85
Frank Amnot, 8 hours 1 76

W. C. Neal, 1 day, 8 hours . .	$3 79
W. C. Neal, horses, 1 day, 4 hours .	2 53
William Halpin, 6½ hours . . .	1 30
A. S. Booles, horses, 3 days, 4 hours .	11 50
A. S. Booles, 1 day, 6 hours . .	3 00
Albert Tatro, 1 day	2 00
John Yarward, 1 day	2 00
W. H. Gerald, 1 day . . .	2 00
C. S. Smith, 7 hours	1 55
J. Morrisy, 1 day	2 00
Bert Ward, 1 day . . .	2 00
F. Lemay, 1 day	2 00
F. T. Hannun, 1 day	2 00
N. Tatro, 1 day	2 00
H. F. Bond, 1 day	2 00
N. Latour, 2 days, 7 hours . . .	4 56
Ted. Tatro, 2 days, 7 hours . . .	4 56
Chas. May, 6 hours	1 35
W. C. Neal, 4 days, 8 hours . .	9 80
W. C. Neal, horse, 1 day . . .	1 75
C. A. Roak, 2 days, 1 hour . .	4 22
C. A. Roak, horse, 2 days, 6 hours .	4 86
Chas. May, horses, 3 days, 3 hours .	5 85
Thos. Bowles, 1 day, 5 hours . .	2 80
Geo. E. Sherman, 5 days, 4 hours .	10 80
Geo. E. Sherman, horses, 5 days, 5½ hours	9 80
E. A. Carter, 1 day	2 00
J. B. McLlory, 1 day . . .	2 00
C. H. Dunham, 2 hours . . .	44
William Bowles, 2 days, 5 hours . .	5 00
Geo. L. Baker, 1 day, 2½ hours . .	2 50
Geo. L. Baker, horses, 2 days . .	3 40
J. F. Hawkins, 1 day, 2½ hours . .	2 75
A. H. Gleason, 2 days, 5 hours . .	5 00

L. J. Bemis, 3 days, 5¼ hours . .	$7 04
L. J. Bemis, horses, 3 days, 3½ hours .	5 89
M. W. Hynes, 5. days, ⅓ hour . .	10 14
M. W. Hynes, horses, 5 days, 2 hours .	9 14
T. L. Hynes, 4 days, 3½ hours . .	8 81
T. L. Hynes, horse, 3 days, 2 hours .	5 63
T. F. Maynard, 9 days, 4 hours . .	18 96
T. F. Maynard, horses, 7 days, 2 hours,	12 59
T. S. Sherman, 6 days . . .	12 00
W. H. Campbell, 2 days, 7¾ hours .	5 72
W. H. Campbell, horses, 2 days, 2¼ hours	3 99
W. Stearns, building snow-plough .	5 50
T. Damon, 1 day	2 00
P. Zimmerman, 1 day . . .	2 00
T. B. Hams, 1 day, 6 hours . .	3 55
A. B. Sherman, 1 day, 4½ hours . .	3 00
A. B. Sherman, horses . . .	5 25

$297 35

JUNE.

German Hill Street — Special.	*Expended.*
W. C. Neal, 4 days, 4 hours . .	$8 88
W. C. Neal, horses, 13 days, 3 hours .	23 30
Henry Neal, 4 days, 4 hours . .	8 88
E. N. Phillips, 5 days, 4 hours . .	10 88
N. Latour, 4 days, 4 hours . .	8 88
C. A. Roak, 4 days	8 00
C. A. Roak, horse, 4 days . . .	7 00
Geo. Whitney, 4 days, 1½ hours . .	8 33
J. F. Elliot, 4 days	4 00
John B. McLlory, 4 days . . .	8 00
D. W. Lewis, drain-pipe . . .	24 85
Mass. Central R.R., freight . .	1 50
J. F. Elliot, 4 days, 1 hour . .	4 10

C. A. Roak, 4 days	$8 00
C. A. Roak, horse, 4 days . . .	7 19
Henry Neal, 5 days, $\frac{1}{2}$ hour . .	10 11
E. N. Phillips, 4 days, $6\frac{1}{3}$ hours . .	9 45
J. B. McLlory, 4 days, $1\frac{1}{3}$ hours .	8 24
W. C. Neal, gravel, 175 loads . .	17 50
W. C. Neal, 7 days, $1\frac{1}{2}$ hours . .	14 27
W. C. Neal, horses, 13 days, 8 hours .	24 29
N. Latour, 5 days, $4\frac{1}{2}$ hours . .	11 00
Geo. Whitney, 5 days, $\frac{1}{2}$ hour . .	10 11
Robinson Jones, cement . . .	3 00
	——— $250 00

THEO. S. SHERMAN,
Superintendent of Streets.

SUPERINTENDENT WAYLAND WATER-WORKS REPORT.

MAINTENANCE ACCOUNT.

1893.

March 13.	Cash paid C. C. Ward, labor and materials	$4 25
March 24.	Cash paid W. Porter, labor and materials	55 67
March 24.	Cash paid Brown Bros., labor and materials	11 00
May 1.	Cash paid W. Porter, labor and materials	8 80
June 27.	Cash paid W. Porter, labor and materials	28 96
Sept. 7.	Cash paid H. G. Dudley, labor and materials	81 50
Sept. 7.	Cash paid P. A. Leary, labor and materials	9 00
Sept. 20.	Cash paid Robinson & Jones, labor and materials	5 24
Sept. 20.	Cash paid C. K. Barker, labor and materials	3 50
Oct. 18.	Cash paid J. Carey, labor and materials	10 39
Oct. 18.	Cash paid Fiske & Co., labor and materials	62 08
Dec. 19.	Cash paid Walworth M'f'g Co., labor and materials . . .	24 25

1894.

Jan. 2.	Cash paid H. G. Dudley, labor and materials	16 45

Feb. 28. Cash paid E. W. Marston, labor and
materials $19 41
Feb. 28. Cash paid W. D. Parlin, labor and
materials 32 96

              $373 46

NOTE. — One hundred and five dollars ($105) of the maintenance account is for bills contracted before I was appointed superintendent.

Gentlemen, in this my first report as Superintendent of Water Works, I will say that when I was placed in charge of same, I found there was not a tool of any kind to work with. I have purchased what tools I needed.

I found the gate-house in bad repair. Have had the same put in good shape and painted, and have also had the hydrants painted, as they needed it very much. I have also had quite a lot of repairs to make on the works, most important of which was the lowering of main pipes on King street.

The water in reservoir is in poor condition, and is growing worse every year. The cause of same is overflow of water from upper pond. I would recommend that the Town appropriate a sum of money sufficient to carry water of upper pond around lower pond, so that no water from upper pond could flow into the lower pond. The water is used by the following:

Families 229
Manufactories 7
Public Buildings 4
Miscellaneous 12
Horses 85
Cows 78

    Respectfully submitted,
      HENRY G. DUDLEY,
       Superintendent.

WAYLAND WATER

WAYLAND WATER COMMISSIONERS *in account*

DR.

1893.   Orders drawn on Town Treasurer :

March 13.	To order No. 1, C. C. Ward,	$4 25
March 24.	To order No. 2, W. Porter,	55 67
March 24.	To order No. 3, Brown Brothers	11 00
May 1.	To order No. 4, W. Porter,	8 80
June 27.	To order No. 5, W. Porter,	28 96
Sept. 7.	To order No. 6, H. G. Dudley	81 50
Sept. 7.	To order No. 7, P. A. Leary,	9 00
Sept. 20.	To order No. 8, Robinson & Jones	5 24
Sept. 20.	To order No. 9, C. K. Barker,	3 50
Oct. 18.	To order No. 10, J. Carey,	10 39
Oct. 18.	To order No. 11, Fiske & Co.,	62 08
Dec. 19.	To order No. 12, Walworth Manufacturing Company,	24 25
1894.		
Jan. 2.	To order No. 13, H. G. Dudley	16 45
Feb. 28.	To order No. 14, E. W. Marston	19 41
Feb. 28.	To order No. 15, W. D. Parlin	32 96
	Interest on water bonds	1,450 00
Feb. 28.	To order No. 16, on Town Treasurer for balance of water funds	632 79
	To balance carried down	46 00
		$2,502 25

COMMISSIONERS' REPORT.

with HERBERT C. WELLS, *Town Treasurer.*

1893.		CR.	
	By appropriation for hydrants . .	$384 00
April 1.	By water rates from Jan. 1, 1893, to Jan. 1, 1894	
April 1.	Paid to Town Treasurer . . .	133 00
May 16.	" " . . .	100 00
Oct. 6.	. . .	643 00
Dec. 4.	. . .	424 50
1894.		
Feb. 3.	. . .	286 50
Feb. 28.	" " . . .	485 25
Feb. 28.	By Town order received for water-rates of 1893	46 00

$2,502 25

Balance brought down $46 00

NOTE. — On account of the appropriation for incidentals being exhausted, payment on Town order for $46.00 was refused.

The proceeds of this order when paid will be invested for a water works sinking-fund.

CHAS. H. BOODY,

WM. H. BENT,

HENRY G. DUDLEY,

Water Commissioners of Wayland.

WAYLAND, Feb. 28, 1894.

NOTE. — The Water Commissioners recommend that the water rates for horses be changed to $2 for each horse, instead of $4 for one horse and $2 for each horse more than one.

WAYLAND WATER WORKS SINKING-FUND.

1894.

Feb. 28. Amount deposited in Natick Five Cent
Savings Bank $3,645 74
Interest on above deposit to Nov. 1,
1893 . . . . . . 1,400 56
Amount deposited in Suffolk Savings
Bank 1,000 00
Interest on above deposit to Oct 1, 1893, 234 80
Amount deposited in Home Savings,
Bank 2,292 38
Interest on above deposit to Oct. 1, 1893, 281 04
Amount deposited in Framingham Sav-
ings Bank 1,205 21
Interest on above deposit to Nov. 1,
1893 . . . . . . 73 74
Amount deposited in North End Sav-
ings Bank 826 61
Interest on above deposit to June 1,
1894 . . . . . . 24 94
Amount deposited in North End Sav-
ings Bank, March 5, 1894 . . 632 79
Proceeds of town order, when paid to
be invested for water works sinking-
fund 46 00
_____
$11,663 81

CHARLES H. BOODY,
WILLIAM H. BENT,
HENRY G. DUDLEY,
Commissioners Wayland Water-Works Sinking-Funds.

WAYLAND, Feb. 28, 1894.

REPORT OF ENGINEERS OF THE FIRE DEPARTMENT.

The Department has responded to three alarms during the year.

April 1. Woods fire (Hammond).
Aug. 31. Mrs. Carroll's house.
Oct. 22. Woods fire (Shaw).

The Engineers have received a request for an extension of the fire-alarm system to Simpson's corner. The large amount of property located on the proposed extension that would be better protected makes it seem to the Engineers that the request should be granted, and for that purpose, and to make some necessary repairs in the present system, we would ask the town to appropriate the sum of two hundred dollars.

The Department is in excellent condition as regards apparatus, buildings, and membership.

RALPH BENT, *Chief*,
E. W. MARSTON,
HENRY B. PHALEN,
Engineers.

REPORT OF SUPERINTENDENT OF NORTH AND CENTRE CEMETERIES.

FROM MARCH 1, 1893, to MARCH 1, 1894.

Appropriated	$50 00	
Unexpended balance of 1892 . .	23 77	
		$73 77

EXPENDED.

Frank Haynes, labor and lumber on Hearse House	$18 98	
To labor, at 20 cents per hour . .	40 39	
Unexpended balance	14 40	
		$73 77

CASH RECEIVED, AND PAID TOWN TREASURER.

Lots	$10 00	
Grass	6 00	
Refuse wood	3 00	
		$19 00

T. S. SHERMAN,
Superintendent.

REPORT OF THE LAKEVIEW CEMETERY COMMITTEE.

For the Year ending Feb. 28, 1894.

Appropriated	$50 00	
Rec. from sale of lots and paid Treas .	35 00	
		$85 00

Orders drawn :

No. 1, Wm. C. Neal . . .	$14 75	
No. 2, Wm. Parlin . . .	16 50	
No. 3, W. W. Wight . . .	35 00	
		66 25

Balance	$18 75

WM. W. LOVEJOY,
Treasurer.

When the committee took charge of the cemetery, they found the condition of many lots such that it was decided to establish permanent bounds, make a plan, number, and make a record of them. The committee have made a record of six sections, and would have bounded them with stone bounds and numbered each lot, a work that is to be demanded by all future lot-owners. Owing to the appropriation not being large enough, the work could not be done. The committee ask for an appropriation of one hundred and fifty dollars for the ensuing year, that the work may be satisfactorily done, and save life-long differences in regard to ownership.

H. B. PHALEN,
DAVID P. W. LOKER,
WM. W. LOVEJOY,
Town Committee.

REPORT OF THE TREASURER FOR THE YEAR ENDING FEB. 28, 1894.

APPROPRIATIONS.

1893.

March 27. For schools, care of rooms and fuel . $5,700 00
School supplies   .   .   .   450 00
Highways and bridges   .   .   2,000 00
Incidentals 1,200 00
Firemen's pay 224 00
Support of poor   .   .   .   2,000 00
Salaries 1,200 00
Collection of taxes 300 00
Abatement of taxes .   .   .   200 00
Hydrants 384 00
Repairs on school buildings   .   200 00
Lakeview Cemetery 50 00
North and Centre Cemeteries   .   50 00
Library 300 00
Decoration Day   .   .   .   100 00
Rebuilding stone bridge   .   .   500 00
Electric lights 250 00
Suppress on of illegal sale of in-
toxicating liquors, and special
police 200 00
Repairs on German Hill road   .   250 00
Interest 3,000 00
Repairs on Centre School-house .   88 80
Contingent fund   .   .   .   31 77
Highways and bridges   .   .   215 22

1893.

March 27.	For Abatement of taxes . . .		$16 63
	Repairs on Town Hall . .		70 63
	Moderator		5 00
	Steam for fire-alarm . .		150 00
	Committee on school-house alterations		100 00
June 24.	For electric lights		100 00
	Rebuilding culverts . . .		250 00
Dec. 22.	For Highways		500 00
	Incidentals		500 00
	Support of poor . . .		500 00
1894.			
Jan. 15.	For settlement of Egan claim . .		2,000 00

$23,086 05

1893.

March 27.	From contingent fund .	$2,000 00	
	" " .	70 63	
		5 00	
	.	150 00	
	.	100 00	
June 24.	.	100 00	
	" " .	250 00	
Aug. 4.	Town tax assessed . .	16,910 42	
Dec. 22.	From contingent fund .	500 00	
	" " .	500 00	
	.	500 00	
1894.			
Jan. 15.	.	2,000 00	

$23,086 05

SCHOOLS, CARE OF ROOMS AND FUEL.

1893.	Amount expended .	.	.	.	$5,878 77
March 1.	Balance unexpended	.	$602 78		
" 27.	Appropriation	.	. 5,700 00		
1894.					
Jan. 15.	Treasurer donation fund .		12 00		
" 25.	School fund (State) . .		206 84		
Feb. 3.	Dog licenses (half)	.	119 28		

$6,640 90

SCHOOL SUPPLIES.

	Amount expended .	.	.	.	$467 49
March 1.	Balance unexpended	.	$33 27		
" 27.	Appropriation	.	.	450 00	

$483 27

REPAIRS ON SCHOOL BUILDINGS.

	Amount expended .	.	.	.	$156 39
March 1.	Balance unexpended	.	$3 27		
" 27.	Appropriation	.	.	200 00	

$203 27

WESTON ROAD LEADING TO BOSTON.

March.	Paid Emily A. Heard, in settlement of award, and for land acquired by the town	$450 00
June 1.	Transferred to contingent fund . .	1,159 62

$1,609 62

March 1.	Balance unexpended	. $1,609 62

CASE OF WAYLAND *v.* FOLSOM.

1893.
June 1. Transferred to contingent fund . . $300 00
March 1. Balance unexpended . $300 00

CEMETERY ACCOUNT.

June 1. Transferred to contingent fund . . $78 30
March 1. Balance unexpended . $78 30

REPAIRS ON CENTRE SCHOOL-HOUSE.

March 1. Expenditures over appropriation ,, $88 80
" 27. Appropriation . . . $88 80

DECORATION DAY.

June 1. Transferred to contingent fund . . $85 85
Paid Robinson & Jones, labor, Lake-
view Cemetery . . . 1 00
Marston & Wells, flags . . 1 65
M. D. Jones & Co., badges . 13 75
W. F. Garfield, team to Way-
land 1 50
1894.
Feb. R. T. Lombard, 34 baskets flow-
ers 13 60

$117 35
1893.
March 1. Balance unexpended . $85 85
" 27. Appropriation . . 100 00

$185 85

ELECTRIC LIGHTS.

1893–4. Paid Natick Electric Company . .		$334 98

1893.			
March 1.	Balance unexpended .	$52 50	
" 27.	Appropriation . .	250 00	
June 24.	" . . .	100 00	
		$420 50	

PUBLIC LIBRARY.

1893–4. Paid treasurer of library funds . .		$594 68

1893.			
March 1.	Balance unexpended .	$175 39	
" 27.	Appropriation . .	300 00	
1894.			
Feb. 3.	Dog licenses (half) .	119 29	
		$594 68	

BOARD OF WAYLAND WATER COMMISSIONERS.

1893.			
June 1.	Transferred to "Interest" . . .		$1,450 00
1893–4.	Paid Wm. H. Bent, clerk . .		1,006 25
			$2,456 25
1893–4.	Received from Wm. H. Bent, clerk . . .	$2,072 25	
Feb. 28.	Transferred from hydrants,	384 00	
			$2,456 2

DEFICIT.

1893.			
March 1.	Amount as per auditor's report . .		$771 22
Nov. 4.	Received in settlement of case Wayland v. Folsom	$768 00	
Feb. 28.	Anonymous . . .	3 22	
			$771 22

REPAIRS ON TOWN HALL.

1893.

June.	Paid Frank Haynes, labor and materials	$15 93
	D. O. Frost, labor and materials,	7 90
Sept.	Frank Amnot, labor on plastering,	1 50
	T. W. Frost, labor and materials,	31 81
1894.		
Feb.	Wm. Stearns, labor and materials,	13 49
1893.		$70 63
March 27.	Appropriation . . . $70 63	

MODERATOR.

April 1.	Paid Henry G. Dudley .	$5 00
March 27.	Appropriation . . $5 00	

REPAIRS ON GERMAN HILL ROAD.

June 26.	Amount expended . .	$250 00
March 27.	Appropriation . . $250 00	

REBUILDING CULVERTS.

Aug. 28.	Paid Frank Haynes, work on bridges . . .	$195 00
Sept. 25.	Paid John Hurley, work on bridges . . .	26 00
	Paid C. A. Roak, work on bridges . . .	29 00
		$250 00
March 27.	Appropriation . . $250 00	

EGAN CLAIM.

1894.

Jan. 17.	Paid Allin & Mayberry, attorneys for Mrs. Egan . . .	$2,000 00
Jan. 15.	Appropriation . .	$2,000 00

MISCELLANEOUS APPROPRIATIONS UNEXPENDED.

1893.

March 27.	Rebuilding stone bridge .	$500 00
	Steam for fire-alarm .	$150 00
	Committee on School-House Alterations . .	$100 00

HYDRANTS.

1894.

Feb. 28.	Paid Water Commissioners for year 1893 .	$384 00

1893.

Mar. 27.	Appropriation . .	$384 00

LAKEVIEW CEMETERY.

1893–4.	Amount expended		$49 79

1893.

March 1.	Balance unexpended .	$8 00	
March 27.	Appropriation . .	50 00	
		$58 00	

NORTH AND CENTRE CEMETERIES.

1893–4.	Amount expended . .		$59 37

1893.

March 1.	Balance unexpended .	$23 77	
March 27.	Appropriation . .	50 00	
		$73 77	

STATE TAX.

Dec. 11.	Paid State Treasurer .		$1,825 00
Aug. 4.	Levied and assessed .	$1,825	

COUNTY TAX.

1893.

Nov.	Paid County Treasurer .		$1,490 22
Aug. 4.	Levied and assessed .	$1,490 22	

HIGHWAYS AND BRIDGES.

March 1.	Excess of expenditure over appropriation		215 22
	Amount expended		2,492 78
			$2,708 00
March 27.	Appropriation . .	215 22	
" "	" . .	2,000 00	
Dec. 22.	. .	500 00	
	.	$2,715 22	

SUPPORT OF POOR.

1893–4.	Amount expended		$2,743 51
1893.			
March 1.	Balance unexpended . . .	01	
March 27.	Appropriation . . .	2,000 00	
April 18.	Est. Phœbe C. Underwood,	250 00	
Dec. 6.	Town of Natick, aid refunded . . .	9 15	
Dec. 22.	Appropriation . . .	500 00	
1894.			
Feb. 26.	Aid refunded . . .	14 87	
" "	" " town of Natick	9 10	
			$2,783 13

FIREMAN'S PAY.

1893.

April	Paid J. M. Bent Hose Co. and C. H. Boodey Hook & Ladder Co. .	$224 00
March 1.	Balance unexpended .	224 00
March 27.	Appropriation . .	224 00
		$448 00

SUPPRESSION OF ILLEGAL SALE OF INTOXI-
CATING LIQUORS, AND SPECIAL POLICE.

1893.

May.	Paid John Lamarine, fees in case of Ward, Brown & Bill . . .	$5 00
June 1.	Trans. to Contingent Fund . .	150 20
Aug.	W. B. Ward, travelling ex., Richards case	16 00
Sept.	· John Woodworth, services as special police	9 00
Oct.	L. H. McManus services as constable	2 00
	L. H. Wakefield, legal services .	5 00
	John Lamarine, team to So. Framingham	1 00
	W. F. Garfield, team-hire . .	10 00
	John Lamarine, use of horse and wagon	1 50
Nov.	John Linnehan, time and team .	9 50
1894.		
Feb.	John Lamarine, services as police officer six mos. to Jan. 1, 1894 .	45 10
	John Lamarine, paid detective liquor case	18 00
	L. H. Wakefield, legal services .	5 00
		$277 30

1893.

March 1.	Balance unexpended .	$155 20
" 27.	Appropriation . .	200 00
		$355 20

COLLECTION OF TAXES.

April	Paid W. B. Ward . . .	$300 00
June 1.	Transferred to Contingent Fund. . . .	600 00
		$900 00
March 1.	Balance unexpended .	$900 00
" 27.	Appropriation . . .	300 00
		$1,200 00

ABATEMENT OF TAXES.

March 1.	Balance, Excess of Abatement over Appropriation	$16 63
	Abatements . . .	1,070 50
		$1,087 13
March 27	Appropriation . .	$16 63
	"	200 00
		$216 63

TAXES OF 1890.

March 1.	Amount due from Collector	$98 78
	Abatements . . . $2 30	
	Received from collector . 96 48	
		$98 78

TAXES OF 1891.

1893.

March 1.   Amount due from Collector $6,379 31

        Abatements .   .   . $990 32

        Received from Collector .   4,913 81

                             $5,904 13

TAXES OF 1892.

March 1.   Amount due from Collector $9,914 60

        Abatement   .   .   . $22 00

        Received from Collector .   3,586 98

                             $3,608 98

TAXES OF 1893.

        Amount as assessed due

           from Collector   .   . $20,264 81

        Abatements   .   . $55 88

        Received from Collector .   11,902 10

                             $11,957 98

SALARIES OF TOWN OFFICERS.

March.   Paid W. H. Bent, services as Water Com-

           missioner and Clerk, 1892–3   . $95 00

        Est. B. M. Folsom, services as

           Treasurer 10 months   .   .   125 00

        N. Perodeau, services as Overseer

           of the Poor, 1892–3   .   .   20 00

        T. W. Sawin, services as Registrar

           of Voters, 1892–3   .   .   .   15 00

        Est. B. M. Folsom, services on

           School Committee, 1892–3   .   60 00

        J. Candlin, services on School Com-

           mittee, 1892–3   .   .   .   47 00

1893.

March. Paid E. W. Marston, services as Selectman and Engineer Fire Dept.,
1892–3 . . . . . $35 00

R. T. Lombard, services as Town
Clerk, Assessor, and Registrar,
1892–3 . . . . 77 25

H. B. Phalen, services as Engineer
Fire Dept., 1892–3 . . . 10 00

Ralph Bent, services as Engineer
Fire Dept. and Supt. Water
Works, 1892–3 . . . 60 00

L. Flanders, services as Selectman,
1892–3 . . . . . 40 00

T. W. Frost, services as Selectman,
1892–3 . . . . . 25 00

C. H. Boodey, services as Water
Commissioner, 1892–3 . . 20 00

W. B. Ward, services as Overseer
of the Poor, 1892–3 . . . 20 00

D. W. Ricker, services as Overseer
of the Poor, 1892–3 . . 20 00

H. C. Wells, services as Treasurer,
bal. of 1892–3 . . . 50 00

April. Edw. Carter, services as
Assessor 2½ days . . . 8 75

J. C. Butterfield, services as Supt.
Lakeview Cem., 1892–3 . . 15 00

D. W. Mitchell, services as Registrar, 1892–3 . . . . 15 00

A. H. Bryant, services as Water
Commissioner, 1892–3 . . 20 00

L. K. Lovell, services as Auditor,
1892–3 . . . . . 50 00

A. F. Parmenter, services as Ballot
Clerk, 1892–3 . . . . 4 00

1893.

August. Paid H. G. Hammond, services as Assessor $53 75

Edw. Carter, services as Assessor . 63 00

R. T. Lombard, services as Assessor 61 25

October. Nellie Rice Fiske, care of Pump-
house to Apr., '93 . . . 52 00

1894.

Feb. R. T. Lombard, services as Assessor, 8 75

Edw. Carter, services as Assessor . 7 00

H. G. Hammond, services as Assessor 5 25

D. W. Mitchell, services as Registrar 21 50

T. S. Sawin, services as Registrar, 21 50

Wm. H. Bent, services as Water
Commissioner and Clerk, 1893–4 95 00

C. H. Boodey, serices as Water
Commissioner, 1893–4 . 20 00

H. B. Phalen, services as Asst.
Engineer, 1893–4 . . . 10 00

D. P. W. Loker, services as Overseer of Poor, 1893–4 . . 25 00

W. B. Ward, services as Overseer
of Poor 1893–4 . . . 25 00

E. P. Butler, services as Selectman,
1893–4 . . . . . 50 00

I. Damon, services as Selectman,
1893–4 . . . . . 50 00

H. B. Phalen, services as care of
fire alarm, 1893–4 . . . 25 00

D. W. Ricker, services as Overseer
of Poor, 1893–94 . . . 25 00

H. C. Wells, services as Treasurer,
1893–4 . . . . . 200 00

1894.

Feb. Paid R. T. Lombard, services as Town
        Clerk, Registrar and Clerk,
        1893–4 . . . . . . $75 00
      L. H. Sherman, services as Regis-
        trar, 1893–4 . . . .   20 00
      T. W. Frost, services as Selectman,
        1893–4 . . . . .   75 00
      Ralph Bent, services as Engineer,
        1893–4 . . . . .   10 00

1893.

March 1. Balance unexpended . $659 69
          Appropriation . . 1,200 00
                                _____
                                $1,859 69

INCIDENTALS.

1893.

March. Paid H. B. Phalen, services rendered . $4 00
        R. T. Lombard, recording, express-
          age, etc. 32 50
        E. W. Marston, services Town Hall
          repairs 16 75
        Robinson & Jones, coal and wood,   19 16
        T. W. Frost, expenses — travelling,
          etc. 9 12
        T. W. Frost, services as Inspector
          of Cattle 75 00
        W. B. Ward, expenses — pauper
          cases 29 81
        D. W. Ricker, use of team to Way-
          land 11 00
April. D. W. Ricker, distributing reports
          and posting warrants . .   9 00
        H. B. Phalen, services as ballot
          clerk 4 00
        M. W. Hynes, services rendered
          March 27 . . . .   4 00

1893.

April.	Paid J. C. Butterfield, services, returning " deaths "	$2	25
	J. Candlin, travelling expenses, etc.	1	05
	J. M. Forbush & Co., fire insurance policy	3	00
	G. W. Gregerson, premium Treasurer's bond	100	00
	Wright & Potter Printing Company, ballots	10	00
	Thomas Groom & Co., assessors' notices	3	75
	L. H. Loker, services as ballot clerk	4	00
	J. M. Bent Hose Company, labor at fires	5	00
	J. C. Butterfield, care of hearse, two years	12	00
	C. H. Boodey Hook and Ladder Company, labor at fires . .	7	50
	J. M. Forbush & Co , fire insurance policies	150	00
	Rockwell & Churchill, 550 copies Town Report	98	45
	L. K. Lovell, sundries for Town Hall	5	32
May.	C. H. Boodey, services, returning " Births "	3	75
	American Express Company, expressage		55
	Knights of Labor Association, rent of hall	8	00
	E. P. Butler, oil for engine-house .		90
June.	W. B. Ward, expenses, cleaning hall, etc.	13	50
	J. Candlin, travelling expenses .	1	10

1893.

June.	Paid E. W. Marston, labor and materials	$12 06
August.	Town of Natick, aid of poor .	86 95
	James M. Forbush, fire insurance policy	45 00
	Ernest E. Butler, fire insurance policy	22 50
	C. Callahan Company, repairing hose pipe	1 00
	G. M. Stevens, material for fire alarm	15 60
	J. M. Bent, Hose Company, repairs on coats	3 93
	H. B. Phalen, expressage paid .	75
	Thomas Groom & Co., town books,	13 75
	H. H. Rutter, printing posters .	2 00
	Boston Woven Hose & Rubber Co., repair fire hose . . .	16 00
	E. L. Barry, printing tax bills .	4 00
Sept.	C. H. Roak, work on bridges .	4 50
	L. J. Bemis, carting stone . .	3 00
	Frank Amnot, repairing furnace .	15 05
	T. W. Frost, repairs on engine-house	14 52
	Wm. Stearns, labor and materials, and care of clock . . .	33 54
	James Devine, coffee-boiler . .	2 50
	American Express Company, express on hose	80
	J. Mullen, labor	1 00
	L. K. Lovell, sundries, Town Collector	15 20
	Fiske & Co., faucet . . .	55
October.	L. H. McManus, expenses on town reports, warrants, etc. .	26 00

1893.

October.	Paid Thos. Groom & Co., town books, etc.	$51	00
	Gilbert & Barker Mfg. Co., gasolene,	28	26
	Wm. Jessops, wood, Town Hall .	6	00
	H. H. Rutter, 50 posters . .	2	50
	W. B. Ward, care of Town Hall to November, '93	65	00
Nov.	P. H. Cooney, legal services, Wayland *vs.* Folsom . . .	68	00
	Commonwealth of Massachusetts Corporation Tax	10	35
	J. Lamarine, for fees in case of John Yarwood	8	30
	L. H. McManus, for fees in case of Chas. Doyle	5	37
	A. Coolidge, for fees in case of Chas. Doyle	7	46
	T. S. Sherman, guide boards .	12	85
	Frank Haynes, labor and materials	31	55
	American Express Company, express on voting-boxes . .	1	60
	G. M. Stevens, repairs, fire alarm .	15	15
	Howe's Express, account on fire alarm		35
	J. F. Burke, labor on fire alarm .		90
	S. E. Underwood, labor and stock,	2	00
	Pay-roll elections, officers . .	67	50
	W. B. Ward, postage and envelopes, 1887–1893	90	00
	W. B. Ward, expenses on Doyle case	9	00
Dec.	J. W. Parmenter, 2 cords wood .	12	00
	R. E. Farwell & Son, fire insurance policies	255	00
	W. C. Neal, posting warrants .	4	00

1893.

Dec.   Paid W. C. Neal, posting warrants   . $4 00

F. W. Barry, Beale & Co, ink-
stands, Town Hall   .   .   .   4 53

1894.

Jan.   H. Howard, for fees in case of Wes-
ley A. Rowell, Herbert Osborne,
Ernest Harrington, William Mer-
rill 15 02

E. W. Marston, labor and materials,   3 36

A. S. Morse, returning deaths   .   4 50

W. C. Neal, insurance road machine 1 00

W. B. Ward, sawing and splitting
wood, etc. 10 65

L. H. McManus, printing and posting town warrants   .   .   .   7 00

Thos. Groom & Co., printing
notices 2 00

C. C. Coakley, one day's service   .   3 00

E. P. Butler, stationery, etc.   .   6 65

R. E. Farwell & Son, fire insurance
policies 112 50

E. E. Butler, fire insurance policies,   67 50

D. P. W. Loker, returning deaths   5 25

J. T. & R. E. Joslin, legal services,   40 25

T. W. Frost, sundry expenses   .   13 70

D. P. W. Loker, use of team one
year, to March 1, 1894   .   .   9 00   .

D. W. Ricker, team to Wayland,
three times 3 00

L. K. Lovell, sundry supplies   .   3 50

W. F. Garfield, team hire, school
committee 9 50

$2,064 71

1893.
March 1. Balance unexpended . . $364 86
      Appropriations . . . 1,700 00

                           $2,064 86

CONTINGENT FUND.

March 1.	Excess of expenditures over receipts .	$31 77
1893–4.	Paid State aid on general order .	7 57
1893.	Military aid on general order . .	320 00
March 27.	Appropriation	2,000 00
	"	70 63
	. . . . .	5 00
	. . . . .	150 00
	. . . . .	100 00
June 24.	. . . . .	100 00
	. . . . .	250 00
Dec. 22.	. . . . .	500 00
	. . . . .	500 00
1894.	. . . . .	500 00
Jan. 15.	. . . . .	2,000 00

                           $7,284 40

1893.
March 27. Appropriation . . $31 77
Recd.
Apr. 29. Wayland town scales . 19 50
" 1. Fines, First District Court, 20 00
" 29. Sale of lot, Lakeview Cemetery 5 00
March 27. Auctioneer's license . 2 00
June 1. Unexpended appropriations:
    Collection of taxes . . 600 00
    Weston road . . . 1,159 62

1893.

June 1. Case of Wayland *v.* Fol-
          som $300 00
          Decoration Day   .   .   85 85
          Suppression illegal sale, etc.,   150 20
          Cemetery account .   .   78 30
June 30. Fines, First District Court   5 99
Aug. 4. Overlayings .   .   .   5 84
  "   4. Additional assessments .   4 44
              "   "   8 89
              "   "   .   20 00
Oct. 6. Fines, First District Court,   2 61
     27. Rent, Town Hall .   .   30 50
Dec. 11. Corporation tax   .   ·   1,855 54
          National Bank stock tax .   847 75
          State aid   .   .   ·   620 00
          Military aid .   .   .   191 00
Dec. 30. Fines, First District Court,   5 85
     1894.
Jan. 20. Middlesex County :
          Account of " Weston road,
              etc.,"   .   .   .   1,500
Feb. 26. Interest, taxes of 1890 .   8 35
          Dynamite   .   .   .   1 00
          North and Centre cemeteries :
          Sale of lots and grass   .   19 00
          Cochituate town scales · .   12 73
     28. Lakeview Cemetery :
          Sale of lots and grass   .   30 00
          Rent of Town Hall .   .   17 00
          Sale of grass, Town Hall
              lot 1 00
                                      ─────────
                                      $7,639 73

INTEREST.

TEMPORARY LOANS.

1893-4. Paid on notes, taxes of 1891 . .		$210 00
" " 1892 to Jan. 1, 1894 . .		434 34
" 1893 to Nov. 29, 1893 . .		199 33

TOWN DEBT.

Paid coupons town bonds . . .		$2,225 00
Coupons water bonds . . .		1,410 00
Interest " (18 months) .		60 00
" Note with Allen Fund .		60 00
" " " Donation Fund,		78 00
" " " Loker Fund .		100 00
		$4,776, 67

1893.

March 1.	Balance unexpended . . .	$331 50
March 27.	Appropriation	3,000 00
June 1.	Transferred from Water Account .	1,450 00
		$4,781 50

TEMPORARY LOANS.

July 29.	Paid Waltham National Bank note of May 28, 1892 . . .	$3,000 00
Oct. 2.	Paid Waltham National Bank note of May 2, 1893	2,000 00
Oct. 16.	Paid Waltham National Bank note of March 27, 1893 . . .	3,000 00
Nov. 18.	Paid Waltham National Bank note of Nov. 29, 1891 . . .	4,000 00
		$12,000 00

1893.
March 1. Notes outstanding . .$13,000 00
" 27. Borrowed in anticipation of
    taxes 3,000 00
May 2. Borrowed in anticipation of
    taxes 2,000 00
July 29. Borrowed in anticipation of
    taxes . . . . 5,000 00 .
1894.
Jan. 16. Borrowed in anticipation of
    taxes 2,000 00
Feb. 26. Borrowed in anticipation of
    taxes 2,000 00

$27,000 00

OBLIGATIONS OUTSTANDING.

Dated.
April 3, 1892. Anticipation of taxes of
    1892, demand, 4 % . $4,000 00
Aug. 27, 1892, Anticipation of taxes of
    1892, demand, 4 % . 2,000 00
July 29, 1893. Anticipation of taxes
    of 1893, demand, 4 % . 5,000 00
Jan. 16, 1894. Anticipation of taxes
    of 1893, demand, 4 % . 2,000 00
Feb. 26, 1894. Anticipation of taxes
    of 1893, demand, 4 % . 2,000 00
    $15,000 00
Nov. 3, 1863. Draper Library Fund,
    demand, 6 . $500 00
Jan. 1, 1875. Allen Fund, demand,
    6 % . . . 1,000 00
Aug. 1, 1878. Water bonds, due
    August 1, 1898, 5 % . 25,000 00

Oct. 1, 1878. Town Bonds, due Oct.
1, 1898, 5% . . . $44,500 00
Jan. 1, 1881. Mrs. Child's Library
Fund, demand, 6 % . 100 00
Oct. 1, 1882. Water Bonds, due Oct.
1, 1902, 4 % . . 4,000 00
July 27, 1888. Water Bond, due July
27, 1898, 4% . . 1,000 00
Jan. 1, 1889. Donation Fund, de-
mand, 6 % . . . 1,300 00
April 1, 1891. Loker Fund, demand,
5 % 2,000 00
————— $79,400 00

HERBERT C. WELLS,
Treasurer.

HERBERT C. WELLS, Treasurer, in

1893.   Dr.

March 1. To balance as per Audit . . . $1,091 68
1893–4.

G. E. Sherman, auctioneer's license .	2 00
Wayland town scales . . .	19 50
Cochituate town scales . . .	12 73
Settlement of case, "Wayland *vs.* Folsom"	768 00
Commonwealth of Massachusetts :	
Corporation tax	1,855 54
National bank tax . . .	847 75
Military aid	191 00
State aid	620 00
Income school fund . . .	206 84
County Treas., for " Weston-road leading, etc."	1,500 00
County Treas., for dog licenses .	238 57
Treas. "Donation fund" for schools,	12 00
Supt. Lakeview Cemetery, sale of lots and grass	19 00
Supt. North and Central Cemeteries, sale of lots and grass . . .	35 00
T. H. Sherman, for sale of dynamite,	1 00
T. H. Sherman, for sale of grass, town-hall lot	1 00
—— to balance " Deficit " . .	3 22
First District Court, fines . .	34 45
Rent of town hall	47 50
Aid refunded, " Support of Poor" .	283 12
Borrowed in anticipation of taxes .	14,000 00
W. B. Ward, collector, account taxes 1890, '91, '92, '93 . . .	20,499 37
W. B. Ward, collector, interest taxes of 1890	8 35
Wm. H. Bent, clerk, water-rates, 1893	2,072 25
	$44,369 87

ACCOUNT WITH TOWN OF WAYLAND.

1893–4.   CR.

By Commonwealth of Massachusetts :

Corporation tax	$10 35
J. Lamarine, constable fees . .	8 30
L. H. McManus, constable fees .	5 37
Andrew Coolidge, constable fees .	7 46
H. H. Howard, constable fees . .	15 02
County tax paid	1,490 22
State tax paid	1,825 00
State and military aid paid . .	1,077 00
Interest paid	4,776 67
Notes paid	12,000 00
Water Commissioners' orders paid .	1,006 25
*Selectmen's orders paid . . .	20,335 20

Feb. 28. Balance in Waltham National Bank,	1,813 03
	$44,369 87

* The unexpended balances of the appropriations not being sufficient, payment was re-
fused on orders to the amount of $203.30 " Incidentals," and $50 " Salaries."

AUDITOR'S REPORT.

Town officers from whom bonds are required have given them, and the same are on file.

Vouchers are on file for all orders drawn on the Treasurer by the Selectmen, and the Treasurer's vouchers agree with all sums expended, and his various accounts are correct.

Books of the Water Commissioner and Treasurer of Sinking Fund, are accurate in all particulars.

Balances shown by reports from other departments, agree with Treasurer's balances, with the exception of a variation of one cent in Supt. of Highways Report, and one dollar and ninety-five cents in financial statement of School Report.

If it were possible to specify one department of the town's business as more important than another, it would seem as if that of the Collector of Taxes might stand first. The report of this department is submitted, as received from the Collector, which, in its totals, agrees with the Treasurer's books. Beyond that it has been impossible to verify figures, as no books or vouchers (though requested) have been furnished, except a book which the Collector receives from the Assessors at the time taxes are levied on which are various marginal entries.

TRIAL BALANCE.

Schools, balance unexpended		$762 13
School supplies, balance unexpended . . .		15 78
Highways and bridges, balance unexpended .		7 22
Incidentals, " " . .		15
Support of poor, . .		39 62
Salaries, . .		28 69
Fireman's pay, . .		224 00
Collector of Taxes, ⸱ . .		300 00
Repairs on school buildings, " " . .		46 88
Rebuilding stone bridge, " . .		500 00
Lakeview Cemetery, ⸱ . .		8 21
North and Centre Cemetery, " . .		14 40
Decoration day, " . .		68 50
Electric lights, . .		67 52
Illegal sale of liquor, . .		77 90
Interest,		4 83
Contingent, . .		355 33
Miscellaneous, . .		250 00
		$2,771 16
Temporary loans		15,000 00
		$17,771 16

Abatement of taxes	$870 50	
Due from Collector of Taxes, 1891 .	475 18	
" " " " " 1892 .	6,305 62	
" " " " " 1893 .	8,306 83	
Cash balance	1,813 03	
		$17,771 16

A. G. BENNETT,
Auditor.

ANNUAL REPORT

OF THE

SCHOOL COMMITTEE

OF THE

TOWN OF WAYLAND.

FOR THE YEAR 1893-94.

FINANCIAL STATEMENT.

SCHOOL EXPENSES.

Balance	. .	$602 78	Teachers' sal-		
Appropriation	.	5,700 00	aries	. .	$4,923 00
Baldwin fund	.	12 00	Conveying		
State Treasurer,			scholars.	.	149 50
school fund	.	206 84	Fuel.	. .	481 10
County Treas-			Car-fare and		
urer, dog			telegrams	.	4 70
license	. .	119 28	Care of buildings,		320 47
			Balance	. .	762 13
Total	. .	$6,640 90	Total	. .	$6,640 90

AMOUNT PAID TEACHERS.

Nellie M. Roundy	. . . .	$130 00
Annie B. Brown	. . .	130 00
Grace W. Berry	. . .	130 00
Dora M. Wiggins	. . .	130 00

George A. Andrews	$60 00
Helen G. Cutter	10 00
Lillian M. Adams	133 00
Harriet O. Rolfe	66 50
H. L. Wilbur	200 00
Alice Draper	61 00
Wm. B. Andrews	260 00
Martha E. Dodge	20 00
Christine O. White	210 00
Nellie D. Hill	340 00
Grace E. Loker	280 00
Edith P. Stratton	353 50
James H. Hefflon	440 00
Ida Elden	220 00
Blanche Townsend	220 00
Mary J. Kaufman	216 00
Leila S. Taylor	460 00
Clara E. Dunham	230 00
Louise G. White	245 00
Lucy E. Morgan	135 00
Elizabeth Coolidge	73 00
Edith I. Gale	170 00

$4,923 00

CONVEYING SCHOLARS.

John T. Dunn	$58 50
Temple	91 00

149 50

Car-fare and telegrams 4 70

FUEL.

Robinson & Jones	$348 49
J. W. Parmenter	34 70
A. E. Adams	97 91

481 10

CARE OF BUILDINGS.

A. D. Collins	$144 35
Lizzie Lucier	74 75
L. K. Lovell	18 27
Herbert Parmenter	13 00
Bills paid by committee . . .	6 45
Wilson Porter	5 00
Elizabeth Poole	9 38
H. P. Sherman	47 50
E. P. Butler	1 77
	$320 47

$5,878 77

SCHOOL SUPPLIES.

Receipts.

Balance	$33 27
Appropriation	450 00
Total	$483 27

Expenditures.

Boston School Supply	$307 85
American Book Company	66 21
Carter Rice Company	10 00
Bills paid by committee	14 86
American Express	9 75
Postage	3 38
Lee & Company	60
Houghton, Mifflin Company	2 30
Ginn Company	40 20
Silver, Burdett & Company	12 34
Balance	15 78
	$483 27

REPAIRS.

Balance	$3 27
Appropriation	200 00
Total	$203 27

Expenditures.

W. D. Parlin	$43 69
Wilson Porter	8 99
Bills paid by committee	1 35
James Devine	8 50
George Folsom	3 10
T. W. Frost	17 16
S. Zimmerman	3 25
Charles F. Dickey	20 40
Fred F. Brance	2 00
Waterhouse	1 85
Charles F. Koff	2 85
Champion Flue Scraper Company . . .	4 50
A. D. Collins	2 70
John Hurley	3 75
W. F. Choate	8 00
Howe's Express	1 48
H. G. Dudley	2 75
Frank C. Healey	1 00
Boles	3 50
E. W. Marston	13 62
Balance	48 83
	$203 27

REPORT OF COMMITTEE.

One of the greatest glories of our national life is to be found in the public-school system. The bulwark of our nation's strength, in its superior citizenship, is in the compulsory and systematic education of our youth. In no land has there been a more-rapid advance in civilization than in ours, and one of the greatest factors in this wonderful progress is the public-schools system of our land. The crowning excellency of this method of instruction is that it is entirely secular, without any religious dictation. Dr. McKenzie, of Cambridge, recently said: "In this country we have no great cathedrals, but we have big school-houses; and big school-houses where characteristic men and women are formed are the grandest of all cathedrals." A good liberal education is a richer bestowment to any child than a large fortune in gold or property.

Let the child be well educated, then, with good health and a fair amount of push, life will be successful. Wayland, according to her wealth, has been quite as liberal in providing for the education of her children as other towns of the same size in the county.

WAYLAND CENTRE.

The retaining of a district school in Wayland Centre and the Rutter-district school has long since been a questionable policy with the committee. For some years it has been a troublesome problem how to gather these scholars in one building, and let them have the advantage of a good system of grading. Centralization was strongly recommended by the committee in last year's report.

At a special town meeting held June 24, 1893, it was voted: "That R. T. Lombard, H. B. Braman, L. K. Lovell, Edward Carter, and S. M. Thomas be a committee, and instructed to procure plans and specifications for a four-room school-building, to be heated by steam (or by any other system which the committee may deem best), the whole expense not to exceed nine thousand dollars, and to report to the next annual town meeting."

In view of this decision, and in consideration of repairs necessary at the two district school-houses, the committee decided to make some changes in the high school building, so as to accommodate all the children except those from the North School. By removing stoves from the other buildings we were able to fix up the first floor and make two very comfortable rooms. By this method the upper room has been very much warmer. This change was not brought about without consulting the parents. In nearly every case there was a hearty approval of the plan, because there was a feeling that it would be greatly to the advantage of their children.

When this general consent was obtained and the plan was deemed a practicable one, the committee carefully considered the matter of principal. It was felt desirable, if possible, not only to have a competent teacher, but also one of experience, who would thus be thoroughly fitted for the position, and one who would probably be willing to stay more than one year. We believe that a woman capable of doing, as efficiently, the same amount of work as a man should receive the same pay; but as long as that is not the rule, we decided to take advantage of the prevailing custom, hoping by this means to avoid an annual and sometimes a semi-annual change. The committee therefore decided to employ an experienced lady principal. Miss Taylor has proved to be very competent for the position. The disciplinary condition of the school has been very satisfactory. All the pupils, from the primary to the high-school students, have been carefully classified, and with the good corps of teachers under the principal's direction, the whole school, under this new departure, has had a very prosperous opening. The arrangement is now so good that when the new school-building is ready for occupancy, everything will be in good order to bring the best possible results.

NORTH SCHOOL.

The children attending this school are scattered over such a wide territory, and are all of them such a great distance from the centre, that it was found impossible to make arrangements for their transportation to the central building, so the school has been conducted on the old district plan. Miss White, the present teacher, has been very enthusiastic and devoted to her work.

COCHITUATE SCHOOLS.

The same teachers that were employed at the writing of the last report held their positions till the close of the school year in June. The year closed with good results. There were five graduates from the grammar school. Quite a satisfactory per cent. of scholars from each room received promotion, and in very many cases there was good proof that the scholars had been very thorough in their work.

It is important to cultivate, in all our children, a true spirit of patriotism. One very pleasant feature of our spring term was the day given in commemoration of our fallen heroes. Each teacher provided a separate entertainment. There was an unusually large number of visitors, who went into every room, as it was arranged to have the exercises follow each other. The scholars did great credit to themselves and their teachers. This custom is becoming very widespread in our schools, and we esteem it a very wise one. Too much cannot be done to foster the true spirit of patriotism and especially in the line of honorable remembrance of the brave men who gave their lives for the salvation of their country.

The committee, as usual, had to spend much time during vacation period in looking up new teachers. This year there were more than usual left for new fields. Only two came back at the opening of the school term in September, and one of them was soon taken sick and obliged to give up her school, so that, at the present time, we have only one teacher in the building that was employed last year. In nearly every case the teachers who left us did so because of offers of larger salaries. Of course teachers are always ready to receive better pay, and we rejoice in the prosperity of teachers on this line; but it makes a great deal of extra work for the committee and is usually harmful to schools. From this cause chiefly we have had twenty-six different teachers during the year.

At the beginning of the present school year it seemed as though there might not be any who desired to pursue high-school studies, so the committee tried to do without an assistant in the principal's room. But as soon as school opened several presented themselves, so that it was soon found to be altogether impracticable to do without an assistant, and after a little delay an excellent teacher was secured; but sickness soon compelled her to leave her work. In a few days a teacher in every way thoroughly adapted for the position was found, who is still doing good service. The committee was very fortunate in securing the services of Mr. Hefflon for the principalship in September. He has held the school in excellent condition, is doing faithful work, and the classes, under his immediate instruction, are making very commendable progress.

Having only six rooms for nine grades besides students in high-school work, we found great difficulty in arranging them so as best to equalize the work of the teachers. The primary classes are always much larger than the higher grades. Because of this fact the scholars of the seventh, eighth, and ninth years' studies must all be in the principal's room. This, with a few high-school students, makes the room full, and, on account of having so many grades, makes the work heavy for two teachers.

As regards the present teachers in the building, we feel it is unnecessary to speak of them separately. We believe that they are all doing their work honestly, and are having admirable success. We would earnestly recommend the parents to visit the schools where their children are, and see for themselves.

LOKERVILLE.

This building is still used as a primary school, principally for those who are not able to walk to the village. It is still in the hands of Mrs. Grace E. Loker, who is giving excellent satisfaction. There is quite an improvement here on all lines.

GENERAL REMARKS.

The committee has endeavored to make the course of study as perfect as possible, according to the means in their hands. It has long been felt very desirable to have better music-teaching in our schools; but the great difficulty has been that we were not able to employ a competent music-teacher. The matter being left with each teacher could not be perfectly carried on, as the instruction could not be systematic. An effort is being made to remedy this trouble. The matter of drawing is also under very careful consideration. The committee is also making arrangements for properly graded text-books on physiology.

SCHOOL SUPPLIES.

The committee finds that it requires very rigid economy (and sometimes it is a question if it be wise economy) in order to make the appropriation hold out. The time has certainly come when some text-books that are out of date must be replaced. The committee, as far as they had means, have commenced this work, and therefore feel that less money will not suffice. If business were better we should ask for more. The present appropriation only gives about one dollar for each scholar.

The expense of fuel at the present time is a serious consideration. Since the change in the Cochituate building, the coal bill has greatly increased. In order to bring the cost to the lowest possible figure, the committee asked for bids, with the understanding that the coal was to be weighed on the town scales. Robinson & Jones offered for 25c. a ton less than others, and received the order.

APPROPRIATIONS.

We recommend for teachers' salaries, fuel, care of buildings, and transportation of scholars, $5,700. For school supplies, $450.

For repairs and new seats, $200.

JOSEPH CANDLIN,
LIZZIE E. MITCHEL,
L. ANNA DUDLEY,
School Committee.

LIBRARY TRUSTEES' REPORT.

The Trustees of the Public Library herewith present their annual report for the year ending Feb. 28, 1894.

On the first of the present year the Library was inspected by the Trustees, and found in commendable condition, as far as the care and duties of the Librarian were concerned.

It has been difficult to warm the library room in the most inclement weather of the winter season for only one day in the week, after the rooms and the books they contain have been thoroughly chilled through the remaining six days.

We have had the present wood-furnace put in complete repair to improve its heating capacity, and the result seems to be but a partial success.

Six years have elapsed since the fourth supplement to the library catalogue was printed, and another should be printed to give the readers the full benefit to be derived from the accessions to the library during that period.

This is a longer time than has elapsed between the issuing of either two of our previous consecutive supplements.

An appropriation for this object is necessary.

For details of our purchases, reference may be made to the Librarian's report and to the list printed in the town reports.

HENRY D. PARMENTER,
JOHN CONNELLY,
EMILY A. HEARD,
ELLEN M. BRAMAN,
R. T. LOMBARD.

WAYLAND, March 1, 1894.

LIBRARIAN'S REPORT.

To the Library Trustees:

Statistical information for the year 1893 is submitted as follows:

ACCESSIONS.

	Books.
By purchase	151
By gift	64
Bound and transferred from the pamphlet department .	33
Total	248
Whole number of volumes in the Library . . .	11,962
Pamphlets presented	334

CIRCULATION.

In Cochituate village	1,774
In Wayland centre	3,712
Total	5,486

DONORS OF BOOKS AND PAMPHLETS.

	Books.	Pamphlets.
Apsley, Mr. L. D.	4	8
Atwood, Mr. E. A.	1	
Blake and McIntire, Misses, agricultural papers, etc.		12
Clement, Mr.		
Cutting, Mrs. Chas. A.		72
Draper, Mr. J. S.		
Dudley, Miss Anna, " Nations," etc. . .		16

	Books.	Pamphlets.
Dudley, Mrs. Wm.		13
Editors of " Science "		27
Fowler, Mr. F. H.	1	
Heirs of Rev. Samuel Robbins . . .	1	
Hill, Mr. N. P.	1	
Heard, Misses M. and L.		15
Heard, Mrs. J. A.	1	12
Lombard, Mr. R. T.		1
Massachusetts Woman's Suffrage Association		1
Merrill, Mrs. Caroline	3	
Packard, Mrs. Ellis, " Christian Register."		
Rice, Mrs. Chas. A.	9	
Reeves, Miss Caroline	23	
Reeves, Miss M. L.		12

Reports :

	Books.	Pamphlets.
Bridgewater Normal	1	
Brooklyn Library		1
Chicago Library		1
Children's Hospital, Boston . . .		1
Cleveland Public Library . . .		2
Fall River Public Library . . .		1
Harvard College Library . . .		1
Harvard University Catalogue . .	1	
Lawrence Public Library . . .		1
Maimonides, New York . . .		1
Newton Public Library		1
Public Library Commission . . .		1
Salem Public Library		1
School for Feeble Minded . . .		1
St. Louis Mercantile		1
Taunton Public Library . . .		1
Trustees of Public Reservation . .	1	2
University of Pennsylvania . . .		2
Roby, Mrs. Warren G. . . .		72

	Books.	Pamphlets.
Seaver, Mr. Edwin P.	1	
Sent to the Reading-room . . .		20
State Government in its different departments	7	1
Thomas, Mrs. J. " New Nations."		
University Extension	1	
U. S. Government	6	33

CLASSES OF READING.

Art . . .	.04	Juvenile . . .	.17
Biography . .	.03	Religion and morals .	.05
Fiction . . .	.57	Science . . .	.04
History . . .	.07	Travels . . .	.03

To the foregoing statistics, which give a fairly good account of the Library workings for the year ending Dec. 31, 1893, it is hardly necessary to append any lengthy written statement. While our Library has not done the work which might be expected of it in an unusually intelligent community, it is steadily accomplishing some good work in the generation which is growing up. The schools are hampered in the obtaining of books by the fact that the Library is closed on the days when the schools are in session, but, with a little consultation and a few book-lists of such as are needed, it is certain that broader work could be done, and our deficient departments more speedily filled with books specially useful to the teachers.

The want of a supplement is more keenly felt as each year adds lists attainable only from the tablets, at present crowded with six years' accessions. The perusal of the catalogue at home, at one's leisure, is the only way to insure a decided increase in circulation.

Our magazine literature is gradually assuming substantial proportions. By Mrs. Charles A. Cutting's generous gift of " Harper's Monthly " for six years, and Mrs. Warren G. Roby's valuable contribution of " North American," " Century," and " Scribner's," six years combined, it is essentially strengthened.

The Reading-room has received regularly "The Christian Register," "Rural Home," "Free Russia," "Travellers' Record," "The Tablet," "Home Market Bulletin," "Student's Journal," with "Nations," "New Nations," and agricultural papers from time to time. Magazines and pamphlets have been sent treating of the questions prominent in the minds of people of advanced thought. Still the need of regular reading is very apparent by the absence of constant readers. I have emphasized this want in several reports, and still hope I shall see it acted upon.

The subjects of heating, lighting, and insufficient room are trite subjects, but their conditions work irreparable injury to the welfare of the Library, and to the health and comfort of those who have the charge in trust.

The gift to the Library-room of a bust of Cicero by the late Miss Caroline Reeves is a great addition, but the space on the opposite side of the room is very suggestive, and we hope it will appear so to some other generous and kindly donor. A welcome addition to our coins was a silver florin from Mr. J. S. Abbott. Appended to this statement is a list of the books, in numerical order, added to the Library this year.

Received for fines	$6 31
" " cards	1 94
" " catalogue	1 50
Paid to the Library treasurer	$9 75
Received for incidental expenses	$12 00
Paid out for incidentals	10 19
In the hands of the Librarian	$1 81

Respectfully,

SARAH E. HEARD,
Librarian.

March 1, 1894.

HERBERT C. WELLS, Treasurer, in

1893.	Dr.		
	To town of Wayland, unexpended appropriation of 1892	$175	39
	To town of Wayland, appropriation of 1893,	300	00
June 26.	Cochituate Branch, fines, etc. . . .	2	76
1894.			
Feb. 28.	Wayland Library, fines, etc. . . .	9	75
26.	Town of Wayland, dog licenses (half) .	119	29

$607 19

ACCOUNT WITH LIBRARY FUNDS.

1893.	Cr.		
April 1.	By S. E. Heard, salary, 3 months to date,	$50	00
29.	Wayland Book Club, magazines . .	13	00
	J. M. & H. Parmenter, wood . .	17	49
	De Wolfe, Fiske & Co., books . .	24	71
	Wayland Book Club, magazines and papers	7	00
May 29.	S. E. Heard, incidental expenses . .	12	00
June 21.	Estes & Lauriat, books . . .	22	00
26.	J. D. F. Brooks, binding . . .	4	40
	S. E. Heard, salary 3 months, to July 1,	50	00
	N. R. Gerald, salary 12 months, to April 1, 1893	40	00
Aug. 28.	H. H. Rutter	3	75
Sept. 28.	S. E. Heard, salary 3 months, to Oct. 1,	50	00
Oct. 30.	Wm. Jessop, 1 cord wood . . .	6	00
Nov. 27.	T. E. Jennings, labor on wood . .	1	00
Dec. 7.	J. D. F. Brooks, binding . . .	9	55
22.	S. E. Heard, salary 3 months, to Jan. 1,	50	00
26.	J. W. Parmenter, 4 cords wood . .	24	00
	A. E. Adams, ½ cord wood . . .	3	50
1894.			
Jan. 17.	Frank Haynes, labor and stock . .	6	67
Feb. 15.	F. E. Healey, Jr., repairs on clock .	1	00
20.	Am. Ex. Co., carting books between Wayland and Cochituate . . .	40	00
28.	De Wolfe, Fiske, & Co., books . .	65	30
28.	Balance	105	82
		$607	19

ACCESSION OF TITLES IN 1893.

OFFICIAL REPORTS

OF THE

TOWN OF WAYLAND,

FOR ITS

ONE HUNDRED AND FIFTEENTH MUNICIPAL YEAR,

FROM

MARCH 1, 1894, TO MARCH 1, 1895.

WAYLAND:

H. H. RUTTER, PRINTER.

1895.

OFFICIAL REPORTS

OF THE

TOWN OF WAYLAND,

FOR ITS

ONE HUNDRED AND FIFTEENTH MUNICIPAL YEAR,

FROM

MARCH 1, 1894, TO MARCH 1, 1895.

WAYLAND:

H. H. RUTTER, PRINTER.

1895.

LIST OF TOWN OFFICERS, 1894-95.

The following is a list of the officers of the Town of Wayland and when their term expires.

Town Clerk.

Term expires.

RICHARD T. LOMBARD, ... 1895

Treasurer.

HENRY F. LEE, ... 1895

Auditor.

DANIEL BRACKETT, ... 1895

Collector of Taxes.

WILLARD B. WARD, ... 1895

Treasurer of Library Funds.

HENRY F. LEE, ... 1895

Selectmen.

EDWARD P. BUTLER, ... 1895
THOMAS W. FROST, ... 1895
DAVID P. W. LOKER, ... 1895

Overseers of Poor.

DAVID P. W. LOKER, ... 1895
WILLARD B. WARD, ... 1895
WILLIAM H. JAMESON, ... 1895

School Committee.

L. ANNA DUDLEY, ... 1895
LIZZIE E. MITCHELL, ... 1896
CHARLES H. BOODEY, ... 1897

Assessors.

EDWARD CARTER, ... 1895
HORATIO G. HAMMOND, ... 1896
RICHARD T. LOMBARD, ... 1897

4

Water Commissioners.

CHARLES H. BOODEY,	1895
HENRY G. DUDLEY,	1896
WILLIAM H. BENT,	1897

Trustees Public Library.

ELLEN M. BRAMAN,	1895
HENRY D. PARMENTER,	1895
JOHN CONNOLLY,	1896
RICHARD T. LOMBARD,	1896
EMILY A. HEARD,	1897
LIZZIE E. MITCHELL,	1897

Constables.

CLINTON E. HIBBARD,	1895
JOHN E. LINNEHAN,	1895
LAWRENCE H. McMANUS.	1895
FRANK P. QUACKENBUSH,	1895
THOMAS E. GLENNAN,	1895

[*Two vacancies.*]

Trustees Allen Fund.

ISAAC DAMON,	1895
WILLIAM H. CAMPBELL,	1895
LUTHER H. SHERMAN,	1895

Fence Viewers.

ALBION F. PARMENTER,	1895
ISAAC DAMON,	1895
EDWARD CARTER,	1895

Field Driver.

IRA S. DICKEY,	1895

Sealer of Weights and Measures.

RICHARD T. LOMBARD,	1895

Measurers of Wood and Bark.

EDWARD CARTER,	1895
GEORGE B. HOWE,	1895

Surveyor of Lumber.

FRANK HAYNES,	1895

Superintendent North and Centre Cemetries.
THEO. S. SHERMAN, ... 1895

Committee in Charge of Lakeview Cemetery.
WILLIAM W. LOVEJOY, . - . . . 1895
DAVID P. W. LOKER, ... - 1895
HENRY B. PHALEN, ... 1895

Committee on Finance.
H. B. BRAMAN, ... 1895
R. T. LOMBARD, ... 1895
ALFRED H. BRYANT, ... 1895
LUTHER H. SHERMAN, ... 1895
LLEWELLYN FLANDERS, ... 1895

Committee on Decoration Day.
CHARLES H. MAY, ... 1895
CHARLES H. THING, ... 1895
E. P. BUTLER, ... 1895
D. W. RICKER, ... 1895
EDWARD CARTER, ... 1895

Engineers of Fire Department.
RALPH BENT, ... 1895
EDWIN W. MARSTON, . . . , . . 1895
HENRY B. PHALEN, ... 1895

Forest Fire Wardens.
RALPH BENT, ... 1895
HENRY B. PHALEN, ... 1895

Inspector of Cattle and Provisions.
THOMAS W. FROST, ... 1895

Superintendent of Streets.
LEONARD A. LOKER, ... 1895

Registrars of Voters.
DELOSS W. MITCHELL, ... 1895
LUTHER H. SHERMAN, ... 1896
THEODORE L. SAWIN, ... 1897
RICHARD T. LOMBARD, Town Clerk *ex-officio*, . . 1895

RICHARD T. LOMBARD,
Town Clerk.

TOWN WARRANT.

To CLINTON E. HIBBARD, *or either of the Constables of the Town of Wayland,*

GREETING: In the name of the Commonwealth of Massachusetts, you are hereby required to notify and warn the inhabitants of the Town of Wayland qualified to vote in elections and town affairs to meet at the Town House, Wayland, on Monday, the twenty-fifth day of March inst., at 8 o'clock in the forenoon, then and there to act upon the following articles, viz. :

ARTICLE 1. To choose a Moderator to preside in said meeting.

ART. 2. To choose a Town Clerk, Treasurer, Collector of Taxes, Auditor, three Selectmen, three Overseers of the Poor, Treasurer of the Library Funds, and seven Constables, all of the above for the term of one year; and one School Committee, one Assessor, one Water Commissioner, two Trustees of the Public Library, all for the term of three years. Also to vote upon the question, " Shall Licenses be granted for the sale of intoxicating liquors in the Town of Wayland for the year ensuing," and that the polls will be open at 8 o'clock and fifteen minutes A. M., and may be closed at 12 o'clock and fifteen minutes P. M." All of which must be voted for in accordance with Chapter 386 of the acts of the year 1890, and all names appear upon the Official Ballot.

ART. 3. To choose all other necessary Town Officers, Agents and Committees.

ART. 4. To see if the Town will accept Section 271 of the Acts of the General Court of the year 1893 relating to the election of Road Commissioners in Towns.

ART. 5. To see if the Town will determine that after the present year the names of Candidates for Road Commissioner be placed on the Official Ballot.

ART. 6. To hear reports of Town Officers, Trustees, Agents and Committees, and act thereon.

ART. 7. To appropriate such sums of money as may be necessary to defray town charges, or other purposes for the year ensuing, and order the same to be assessed, or do or act.

ART. 8. To provide for the payment of any part of the Town debt, or do or act.

ART. 9. To appropriate the license money on dogs, refunded by the County Treasurer, or do or act.

ART. 10. To authorize the Treasurer to borrow money in anticipation of taxes for the current year, or do or act.

ART. 11. To act upon the Jury List as prepared by the Selectmen.

ART. 12. To authorize the Selectmen to consult counsel on important Town cases.

ART. 13. To see if the Town will vote to pay Mrs. Michael Hurley two hundred and sixty-two dollars, or do or act.

ART. 14. To provide for the payment of " one hundred dollars," appropriated for Lakeview Cemetery, in 1894.

ART. 15. To see if the Town will appropriate the sum of three hundred dollars for sidewalks, or do or act.

ART. 16. To see if the Town will appropriate the sum of five hundred dollars for Special Police service in Cochituate village, or do or act.

ART. 17. To see if the Town will appropriate the sum of five hundred dollars for paying military aid and assisting poor soldiers, sailors and their families, or otherwise act thereon.

ART. 18. To appropriate six hundred dollars to fill and grade a parcel of land in front of the house of Samuel D. Reeves, in accordance with a vote of the Town passed at the last Annual Town Meeting, or do or act.

ART. 19. To see if the Town will appropriate the sum of one hundred and fifty dollars to build a shed at the Poor Farm, or do or act.

ART. 20. To see if the Town will instruct the School Committee to employ a Superintendent of Schools, as provided in Chapter 200 of the Acts of the General Court of the year 1893, or do act.

ART. 21. To see if the Town will discontinue a highway from the land of Mrs. Sarah E. Heard to land of J. M. and H. D. Parmenter, said highway running in an easterly and westerly direction between the land of said Parmenters and H. B. Braman, or do or act.

And you are required to serve this warrant by posting up attested copies thereof at each of the Post Offices and Town House in said Town seven days at least before the time appointed for said Meeting.

Hereof fail not, and make due return of this warrant with your doings thereon to the Town Clerk, at the time and place appointed for holding said Meeting.

Given under our hands this eighth day of March, in the year of our Lord one thousand eight hundred and ninety-five.

EDWARD P. BUTLER, ⎫ *Selectmen*
THOMAS W. FROST, ⎬ *of*
DAVID P. W. LOKER, ⎭ *Wayland.*

LIST OF JURORS

For the Town of Wayland, 1895, as prepared by the
Selectmen.

WILLIAM T. DUDLEY.

JOHN J. MCCANN.

EDWARD CARTER.

ALBION F. PARMENTER.

WILLIAM W. LOVEJOY.

GRANVILLE L. LOKER.

JAMES A. DRAPER.

SIDNEY LOKER.

ARTHUR J. RICKER.

DELOSS W. MITCHELL.

THEO. L. SAWIN.

PETER S. ZIMMERMAN.

JOHN E. LINNEHAN.

ERNEST E. BUTLER.

ISAAC C. DAMON.

ADONIRAN J. PUFFER.

FRANK LUPEIN.

LUTHER H. SHERMAN.

HORATIO G. HAMMOND.

ISAAC S. WHITTEMORE.

ROSCOE C. DEAN.

COLIN C. WARD.

EDWARD B. SMITH.

ELIJAH H. ATWOOD.

GEORGE E. SHERMAN.

THEO. S. SHERMAN.

EDGAR B. LOKER.

LEONARD A. LOKER.

EDWARD P. BUTLER, *Selectmen*
THOMAS W. FROST, *of*
DAVID P. W. LOKER, *Wayland.*

SELECTMEN'S REPORT.

MARCH 1, 1895.

The Selectmen hereby submit their annual report for the year ending February 28, 1895.

We have appointed the following officers during the year, as required by the Statutes :

Engineers of Fire Department.

RALPH BENT.   EDWIN W. MARSTON.   HENRY B. PHALEN.

Forest Fire Wardens.

RALPH BENT.   LAWRENCE H. McMANUS.

Undertakers.

ANDREW S. MORSE.   DAVID P. W. LOKER.

Inspector of Cattle and Provisions.

THOMAS W. FROST.

Registrar of Voters.

THEO. L. SAWIN.

Superintendent of Streets.

LEONARD A. LOKER.

Auctioneer.

GEORGE E. SHERMAN.

11

Precinct 1.

Warden.— ALBION F. PARMENTER.
Clerk.— JAMES A. DRAPER.
Inspectors.— M. W. HYNES.
THEO. S. SHERMAN.
PETER S. ZIMMERMAN.
WILLIAM H. CAMPBELL.

Precinct 2.

Warden.— HENRY B. PHALEN.
Clerk.— DANIEL D. GRIFFIN.
Inspectors.— EDWARD B. SMITH.
RUSSELL E. FRYE.
LEONARD A. LOKER.
NOAH A. CHESSMAN.

Officer to Prosecute the Illegal Sale of Intoxicating Liquors.
JOSEPH M. MOORE.

At the commencement of the fiscal year it was found necessary as well as convenient to change our bank of deposit, and also to make arrangements with some bank whereby our treasurer could borrow money from time to time, as the needs of the town might require. We accordingly changed our business from the Waltham Bank to the Natick National Bank, which has filled the requirements very acceptably.

Our treasurer has taken up the small and scattered obligations of the town, and we now have the floating temporary debts of the town concentrated in one bank, where they are much easier to look after, and where they may be paid in part or in full, as the collections of the town may admit.

Main Street through Cochituate Village has been regraded, and the street railway company has laid a new track, substituting macadam for paving stone, now making the grade of the track conform to the grade of street, thereby preventing the water from standing between the tracks, as it has formally done.

In conjunction with the Selectmen of Weston we have perambulated the bounds between Wayland and Weston and found them in their proper places.

Heretofore the central part of the town has had no adequate protection against fire, and it has been deemed advisable by the Selectmen to furnish hand fire extinguishers, and they have been placed in the Town House and in the house on the Town Farm, where they are easily accessible in case of fire.

Respectfully submitted,

EDWARD P. BUTLER,
THOMAS W. FROST,
DAVID P. W. LOKER,
Selectmen of Wayland.

REPORT OF TOWN CLERK AND REGISTRAR.

WAYLAND, JAN. 1, 1895.

To the Inhabitants of the Town of Wayland:

I hereby transmit the Annual Report of the Clerk and Registrar for the year ending Dec. 31, 1894.

BIRTHS.

Whole number registered during the year is thirty-four, being seven more than in 1893. Of the number fourteen were males and twenty were females.

Born of native parents, ...	16
" foreign parents, ...	6
" native and foreign parents, ...	12

DEATHS.

Whole number registered during the year is twenty-nine, being nine less than in 1893.

CONDITION.

Married, ...	10
Widowed, ...	3
Single, ...	16
Native born, ...	25
Foreign born, ...	4

NAMES AND AGES OF PERSONS DECEASED OVER SEVENTY YEARS OF AGE.

	Years.	Mos.	Days.
Caroline G. Merrill, ...	80	8	..
Mary Butterfield, ...	77	9	20
Oliver Cormier, ...	78	8	..
Sarah W. Dickey, ...	71	8	3
Chas. H. Campbell, ...	70	7	..
Joseph S. Abbott, ...	72	9	17

NOSOLOGICAL TABLE.

Influenza,	1
Tuberculosis,	1
Inanition,	2
Still-born,	2
Old age,	1
Cancer,	2
Meningitis,	1
Diphtheria,	2
Gangrene,	1
Phthisis,	3
Heart disease,	3
Apoplexy,	1
Marasmus,	1
Abscess,	1
Cholera infantum,	1
Paralysis,	1
Pneumonia,	2
Hemorrhage of Lungs,	1
Aneurism,	1
Uterine tumor,	1

MARRIAGES.

Whole number registered during the year is sixteen, being five more than in 1893.

Native birth of both parties,	11
Foreign " "	3
Native and foreign birth,	2
First marriage of both parties,	11
First of one and second of the other,	4
Second marriage of both parties,	1

DOGS.

Whole number of persons licensed to keep dogs for the year ending Nov. 30, 1894 is eighty-nine.

82 males at $2,	$164.00
7 females at $5,	35.00
	$199.00
89 licenses at 20 cts. each,	17.80
Balance paid over,	$181.20

Number of registered voters, Nov. 6, 1894, . . . 413
   " in precinct 1, ... 148
   " in precinct 2, ... 265

Ballots cast in precinct 1, ... 119
Ballots cast in precinct 2, ... 214

Total, ... 333

Vote for Governor:

	Precinct 1.	Precinct 2.
Frederic T. Greenhalge, ...	62	133
Alfred W. Richardson, ...	1	5
John E. Russell, ...	51	64
David Taylor, ...	..	1

Vote for Senator, Fourth Middlesex District:

	Precinct 1.	Precinct 2·
Wm. H. Horendon, ...	1	8
Geo. A. Reed, ...	67	132
Wm. H. Walsh, ...	46	59

Vote for Representative, 28th Middlesex District:

	Precinct 1.	Precinct 2.	Total.
Walter Adams, ...	63	51	114
Thos. W. Frost, ...	57	58	115
John Heffron, ...	..	7	7
Geo. A. Leach, ...	34	141	175
E. Lewis Moore, ...	50	69	119
Luther H. Sherman, ...	1	..	1

VOTE IN THE 28TH MIDDLESEX DISTRICT.

	Walter Adams.	Thomas W. Frost.	John Heffron.	Geo. A. Leach.	E. Lewis Moore.	Luther H. Sherman.
Framingham, ...	802	573	99	674	763	......
Holliston, ...	224	188	45	251	231	......
Sherborn, ...	35	33	2	85	63	......
Wayland, ...	114	115	7	175	119	1
Total, ...	1,175	909	153	1,185	1,176	1

Respectfully submitted,
      RICHARD T. LOMBARD *Town Clerk.*

ASSESSORS' REPORT.

For Year ending Feb. 28, 1894.

Value of real estate, May 1, 1894, . .	$1,203,460.00
" personal estate, May 1, 1894, . .	292,660.00
Total valuation, May 1, 1894, . . .	$1,496,120.00
" " " 1893, . . .	1,509,665.00
Decrease, ...	$13,545.00
Taxes assessed for town purposes,. . .	$18,948.00
Overlayings, ...	31.08
Additional assessments, ...	5.60
State tax,.	1,460.00
County tax, ...	1,596.67
Total amount assessed, ...	$22,041.35

No. polls assessed May 1, 1894, . .	559	
" " " 1893, . .	529	
Increase, ...	30	
Additional polls assessed, . . .	5	
Total increase of polls . . .	35	

Number of persons assessed, . .	830	
" residents assessed on property,	397	
" non-residents, assessed on property, . . .	131	

Total value of land, ...	$478,815.00
" " buildings, ...	724,645 00
" " church property, . . .	30,240.00
" " town property, . . .	104,413.00

Number of horses,	. . .	. 354		
" cows,	. . .	. 808		
" sheep,	. . .	. 102		
" neat cattle other than cows,	.	90		
" swine,	. . .	. 125		
" acres of land,	. .	9,145$\frac{9}{10}$		
" dwelling houses,	.	. 404		

Rate of taxation, 1893, ... $12.70

  "   "   1894, ...   14.00

Additional assessments, ...   8.40

Abatements of tax of 1891, ...   17.05

    "   "   1892, ...   23.40

    "   "   1893, ...   6.35

             "   1894, ...   169.90

                                 ——————

Total abatements, ... $216.70

Respectfully submitted,

RICHARD T. LOMBARD,
EDWARD CARTER,
HORATIO G. HAMMOND,
Assessors of Wayland.

COLLECTOR'S REPORT.

TAXES OF 1891.

Balance due March 1, 1894, ...	$475.18
Paid Treasurer, ...	15.98
	$459.20

Interest paid on tax of 1891, ...	$142.21

TAXES OF 1892.

Balance due March 1, 1894, ...	$6,305.62
Paid Treasurer, ...	5,433.92
	$ 871.70

Interest paid on tax of 1882, ...	$200.00

TAXES OF 1893.

Balance due March 1, 1894, ...	$8,306.83
Paid Treasurer, ...	3,277.72
	$5,029.11

TAXES OF 1894.

Amount assessed, ...	$22,041.35
Paid Treasurer, ...	13,336.43
	$ 8,704.92
Additional Assessments, ...	18.40
	$8,723.32

WILLARD B. WARD,
Collector.

REPORT OF THE OVERSEERS OF THE POOR.

The following is the report of the Overseers of the Poor of the Town of Wayland for the year ending February 28, 1895.

The Almshouse has been in charge of Mr. and Mrs. H. P. Parker. The inmates supported at the Almshouse during the year are as follows:

Mrs. Sarah Puffer, invalid, aged 79 years.
Mr. James Burk, aged 68 years.
Mr. Benj. Nealey, aged 71 years.
Mr. George F. Bond, aged 73 years.
Mr. Charles W. Moore, admitted November 20, aged 58 years.
Annie Burrill, aged 12 years ; at Eunice Bemis'.
Mr. James A. Wing, aged 60 years ; at Worcester Insane Asylum.
Mrs. Ellen Burk, aged 66 years, Taunton Insane Asylum.
Miss Carrie E. Davis, aged 34 years ; at Westboro Insane Asylum.

Number of tramps during the year, ...	510
Number of meals furnished tramps, ...	838

Number of persons receiving outside aid during the year and amunt rendered each family were as follows:

Nelson Normandin and wife and 10 children, at North Brookfield, ...	$95.17
Elijah Roberts, wife and 2 children, at North Brookfield,	29.39
S. Luciar and 2 children, ...	32.37
Frank Davieu, wife and 8 children, ...	32.00
John Chinett, wife and 2 children, ...	13.13
George A. Chalmus, aged 74, for rent, . . .	36.00
Annie Burrill, at E. H. and C. W. Bemis'. . . .	146.00
Ann Painter, at C. Randolph's, ...	52.00
Joseph A. Sumpter, at Lowell, ...	10.10
William H. Mullen, at Boston, ...	14.00

Mrs. Sumpter, in Hudson (bills not received).
Mrs. Hardy, in Boston (bills not received).

The resources for the support of the poor for the year were as follows :

March	1, 1894.	Balance in treasury,	. . . .	$39.62

1894.

March 26.	Appropriation, ...	2,500.00
	Extra appropriation, ...	500.00
	Received from Town of Natick, . .	133.64
	Received from Town of Lexington, .	52.00

1895.

Feb. 28.	Receipts from Town Farm for milk, .	625.71
	Receipts from Town Farm for hoop poles,	20.52
	Receipts at Town Farm, . . .	170.73

$4,042.22

Expenditures at Town Farm,	$170.73	
Expenditures at Town Farm, orders, ...	1,342.82	
Outside aid and bills due March 1, 1894, ...	2,360.16	
Unexpended balance, . .	168.51	
		$4,042.22

DETAILED STATEMENT.

RECEIPTS AT FARM.

Eggs, ...	$22.74
Wood, ...	3.00
Potatoes, ...	1.50
Poultry, ...	28.22
Calves, ...	13.00
Milk, ...	11.87
Cows, ...	30.00
Cabbage, ...	2.25
Onions, ...	10.25
W. B. Ward, ...	22.50
Apples, ...	19.90
Work on road, ...	5.50

$170.73

The above was received and expended by the Warden by authority of Overseers.   AUDITOR.

EXPENDITURES AT FARM.

Garden seeds, ...	$10.75
Paper, ...	2.00
C. W. Moore, ...	3.00
Winger, ...	2.50
Plow, ...	10.33
Feed bags, ...	1.50
Fertilizer, ...	10.00
Potatoes, ...	2.40
Clothes for Burk and Nealy, ...	15.83
Lumber, ...	8.79
C. Keefe, ...	10.00
Brewers' grains, ...	43.27
L. K. Lovell, ...	4.80
H. F. Lee & Son, ...	7.55
H. Rutter, ...	9.89
Sprouts, ...	22.50
Incidentals, ...	5.62
	$170.73

EXPENDITURES AT FARM BY ORDERS DRAWN ON TREASURER.

Frank Pousland, ...	$84.52
Henry F. Lee & Son, ...	276.80
F. L. Howe, ...	172.00
Robinson & Jones, ...	37.50
L. K. Lovell, ...	65.42
William Stearns, ...	8.90
Frank Haynes, ...	8.13
M. J. Maloney, ...	62.44
S. Russell, ...	137.49
E. P. Butler, ...	100.06
J. H. McAulliff, ...	24.77
O. L. Keefe, ...	81.90
A. H. Parker, ...	40.00
Union Lumber Co., ...	40.51
L. H. McManus, ...	27.63
Irving Brothers, ...	115.00
P. A. Leary, ...	7.25
H. P. Parker, ...	30.00
W. B. Ward, ...	22.50
	$1,342.82

Of the above amount the sum of $420.16 was used for cows, lumber, fertilizer and manure.

ORDERS APPROVED FOR OUTSIDE AID AND BILLS DUE MARCH 1, 1894.

North Brookfield, ...	$213.18
Commonwealth of Massachusetts, . . .	255.36
H. P. Parker & Son, salary, ...	284.47
Dr. C. H. Boodey, ...	26.00
John McAuliff, ...	17.49
E. H. Bemis, ...	37.50
Westboro Insane Hospital, ...	41.79
City of Brockton, ...	27.00
Robinson & Jones, ...	27.86
City of Springfield, ...	2.48
E. A. Atwood, ...	100.38
M. J. Maloney, ...	24.77
T. S. Sherman, ...	2.75
William Stearns, ...	15.00
W. H. Bent, ...	9.00
H. F. Lee & Son, ...	75.18
Taunton Insane Hospital, ...	41.79
Worcester Insane Hospital, ...	41.79
E. P. Butler, ...	17.05
J. B. Charboneau, ...	27.03
C. W. Bemis, ...	108.50
M. A. Carroll, ...	22 50
J. B. Charbonneau, ...	48.00
W. B. Ward, ...	75.71
Robinson & Jones, ...	70.11
W. H. Jameson, ...	5.00
Westboro Insane Hospital, ...	84.97
Taunton " "	84.96
M. J. Maloney, ...	59.03
City of Boston, ...	14.00
City of Lowell, ...	10.10
Worcester Insane Hospital, ...	84.96
C. Randolph, ...	78.00
Carried forward,	$2,033.71

Brought forward.								$2,033.71
E. P. Butler,	.	.	.	.	.	.	.	56.60
C. H. Boodey,	.	.	.	.	.	.	.	52.00
David P. W. Loker,	.	.	.	.	.	.	.	6.00
Frank S. Johnson,	.	.	.	.	.	.	.	31.50
Town of Natick,	.	.	.	.	.	.	.	6.00
Lucy J. Carter,	.	.	.	.	.	.	.	20.00
Thomas Bryant, Jr.,	.	.	.	.	.	.	.	1.00
E. P. P. Loker,	.	.	.	.	.	.	.	36.00
M. A. Bond,	.	.	.	.	.	.	.	3.00
J. M. Moore,	.	.	.	.	.	.	.	71.00
Frank Gerry,	.	.	.	.	.	.	.	15.00
Theo. S. Sherman,	.	.	.	.	.	.	.	2.35
E. Holway,	.	.	.	.	.	.	.	26.00
								$2,360.16

NOTE,—Of the above amount there was paid the sum of $635.62 for insane bills.

OUTSTANDING CLAIMS, MARCH 1, 1895.

Chas. H. Boodey,	.	.	.	.	.	.	.	$62.00
E. A. Atwood,	.	.	.	.	.	.	.	235.94
E. P. Butler,	.	.	.	.	.	.	.	10.00
H. H. Rutter,	.	.	.	.	.	.	.	7.57
Westboro Insane Hospital,	.	.	.	.	.	.	42.72
Taunton " "	.	.	.	.	.	.	.	42.71
Worcester " "	.	.	.	.	.	.	.	42.71
A. D. Loker,	.	.	.	.	.	.	.	10.02
North Brookfield,	.	.	.	.	.	.	.	124.56
H. P. Parker,	.	.	.	.	.	.	.	389.37
S. Russell,	.	.	.	.	.	.	.	55.00
								$1,022.60

DUE THE TOWN FROM OTHER TOWNS.

North Brookfield,	.	.	.	.	.	.	.	$233.14
Town of Lexington,	.	.	.	.	.	.	.	52.00
Town of Wrentham,	.	.	.	.	.	.	.	66.10
Bill due the town farm,	.	.	.	.	.	.	62.35
Total,	.	.	.	.	.	.	.	$413.59

APPRAISED VALUE OF TOWN PROPERTY.

Real estate, ... $5,800.00
Personal property, ... 1,450.00

We would respectfully recommend an appropriation of twenty-five hundred dollars ($2,500.00), to pay outstanding claims and for the support of the poor for the ensuing year.

Respectfully submitted,

DAVID P. W. LOKER,
WILLARD B. WARD,
Overseers of the Poor of the Town of Wayland.

REPORT OF SUPERINTENDENT OF HIGHWAYS.

The total amount of appropriations for highways and bridges for the past year, was two thousand five hundred and seven dollars and twenty one cents ($2,507.21.) Appropriated at the annual town meeting in March, two thousand dollars ($2,000.) At a special meeting in January, five hundred dollars ($500.00.) Unexpended balance of 1893, seven dollars and twenty two cents ($7.22.) Itemized bills for the above amounts are on file in the Selectmen's office. Overdrawn, one hundred and fourteen dollars and sixty five cents ($114.65.)

MARCH.

W. C. Neal, 3 days, 6 hours, . . .		$ 6.00
W. C. Neal, horse, 1 day, 4 hours,	.	2.47
B. Tatro, 7 hours, ...		1.56
Alex Spear, 1 day, 7 hours, . . .		3.52
T. S. Sherman, 5 days, ...		10.00
T. S. Sherman, horse, 1 day, . . .		1.50

$25.05

APRIL.

L. A. Loker, 10 days, 5 hours, . .		$21.11
L. A. Loker, horse, 8 days, 8 hours,	.	15.45
C. A. Roak, 8 days, 3 hours, . . .		16.68
C. A. Roak, horse, 8 days, . . .		14.00
Wilson Porter, 5 days, 5 hours, . .		11.10
Wilson Porter, horses, 5 days, 5 hours, .		19.44
W. C. Neal, 7 days, 8 hours, . . .		15.79
W. C. Neal, horses, 7 days, 2½ hours, .		25.47
T. B. Hawes, 8 days, ...		16.00
T. B. Hawes, horse, 8 days, . . .		14.00
John Hurley, 8 days, 1½ hours, . .		16.34
Rupert Porter, 7 days, 3 hours, . .		14.66
John McElroy, 8 days, ...		16.00
M. T. Damon, 5 days, ...		10.00

B. Tatro, 2 days, ...	$4.00
W. Tatro, 2 days, ...	4.00
L. J. Bemis, 3 days, 3½ hours, . .	6.75
L. J. Bemis, horse, 8 hours, . . .	1.52
1893, W. A. Jessup, 3 days, . . .	6.00
J. W. Hammond, 204 loads gravel, 10, .	20.40

$268.71

MAY.

L. A. Loker, 15 days, 4½ hours, . .	$30.96
L. A. Loker, horse, 15 days, 3 hours, .	26.83
Union Lumber Company, plank for Sherman's Bridge, ...	67.53
Wood, Barker & Co., planks for guard rails, ...	12.72
Rutter & Rideout, 2 cask nails, . .	3.00
Fiske & Co., fuse caps and dynamite, .	8.82
C. H. May, 6 days, 5 hours, . . .	13.00
C. H. May, horses, 7 days, . . .	24.50
T. B. Hawes, 3 days, ...	6.00
T. B. Hawes, horse, 3 days, . . .	5.25
John Hurley, 11 days, 1½ hours, . .	22.33
George E. Sherman, 3 days, . . .	6.00
James Murphey, 4 days, 1½ hours, . .	8.33
Napoleon Lalour, 7 days, 1½ hours, .	15.35
C. A. Roak, horse, 4 days, 1½ hours, .	8.34
C. A. Roak, horse, 4 days, 1½ hours, .	7.29
Rupert Porter, 12 days, 6½ hours, . .	25.34
John McElroy, 7 days, 8½ hours, . .	15.89
Thomas L. Hynes, 6 days, 2 hours, .	12.46
Thomas L. Hynes, horse, 1 day, . .	1.75
T. F. Maynard, 3 days, 1 hour, . .	6.23
M. W. Hynes, 6 days, 7 hours, . .	13.58
M. W. Hynes, horse, 3 days, 4 hours, .	6.03
M. W. Hynes, 83 chestnut posts at 15 cents, ...	12.45

$358.97

JUNE.

L. A. Loker, 12 days, 6½ hours,	$25.43
L. A. Loker, horse, 12 days, 6½ hours,	22.22
John Hurley, 11 days, 2½ hours,	22.53
Rupert Porter, 11 days, 5 hours,	23.11
Wilson Porter, 7 days,	14.00
Wilson Porter, horses 7 days,	24.50
C. A. Roak, 10 days,	20.00
C. A. Roak, horse, 10 days,	17.50
John McElroy, 7 days,	14.00
1893, Stone Brothers, cap stone for Bridge,	4.00
M. W. Hynes, 15 days, 5 hours,	31.10
M. W. Hynes, 33 chestnut posts, at 15 c.	$4.95
M. W. Hynes, horses, 15 days,	52.46
Thomas L. Hynes, 16 days, 4 hours,	32.88
Thomas L. Hynes, 13 days, 2 hours, horse,	23.13
Thomas F. Maynard, 10 days, 5½ hours,	21.21
Thomas F. Maynard, horses, 10 days, 2 hours,	35.76
Thomas Dowey, 16 days, 5 hours,	33.10
P. S. Zimmerman, 3 days, 8 hours,	7.77
Henry P. Sherman, 12 days, 3 hours,	24.66
L. A. Loker, 11 days, 7½ hours,	23.60
L. A. Loker, horse, 11 days, 1¼ hours,	19.54
W. D. Parlin, 1 tree pruned,	1.00
Ames Plow Company, 1 gravel screen,	7.75
Wilson Porter, 7 days,	14.00
Wilson Porter, horses, 7 days,	24.50
C. A. Roak, 7 days,	14.00
C. A. Roak, horse, 7 days,	12.25
W. C. Neal, 5 days,	10.00
W. C. Neal, horses, 5 days,	17.50
C. H. May, 1 day, 5 hrs.,	3.11
C. H. May, horses, 1 day, 5 hrs.,	5.44
James Murphy, 17 days,	34.00
John McElory, 7 days,	14.00
Rupert Porter, 9 days, 7½ hrs.,	19.56
John Hurley, 10 days, 3 hrs.,	20.64
T. B. Hawes, horse, 5 days,	8.75
M. Hurley, 3 days, 4 hrs.,	6.88
1893, C. L. Smith, 2 hrs.,	.44
	$711.29

JULY.

L. A. Loker, 8 days, ...	$16.00
L. A. Loker, horse, 8 days, . . .	14.00
Wilson Porter, 7 days, ...	14.00
Wilson Porter, horses, 7 days, . .	24.50
C. A. Roak, 7 days, ...	14.00
C. A. Roak, horse, 7 days, . . .	12.25
Rupert Porter, 7 days, ...	14.00
John Hurley, 7 days, ...	14.00
James Murphy, 7 days, ...	14.00
John McElroy, 1 day, ...	2.00
Joseph Gladice, 5 days, 8 hrs., . .	11.75
M. Hurley, 3 days, ...	6.00
P. D. Gorman, 4 days, ...	8.00
T. B. Hawes, horse, 7 days, . . .	12.25
Henry F. Lee, Spikes, ...	1.68
W. C. Neal, 7 days, ...	14.00
W. C. Neal, horses, 7 days, . . .	24.50
T. W. Frost, repairing guide boards, .	7.00
1893. J. N. Hammond, 16 loads gravel at 10c., ...	1.60
1893. E. P. Butler, spikes, . . .	.40
" Robinson & Jones, post and plank,	1.47
" E. Butler, nails, ...	1.43

$228.83

AUGUST.

L. A. Loker, 16 days, 3½ hours, . .	$32.75
L. A. Loker, horse, 5 days, 8½ hrs., .	10.39
M. W. Hynes, 6 days, ...	12.00
M. W. Hynes, horse, 5 days, 4 hrs., .	9.53
W. L. Parlin, drain pipe, . . .	4.68
Rupert Porter, 2 days, 8 hrs., . .	5.80
M. Moran, stone for culvert, . . .	3.00

$78.15

SEPTEMBER.

L. A. Loker, 9 days, 1½ hrs., . . .	$18.10
L. A. Loker, horse, 6 days, 5½ hrs., .	11.57
John Hurley, 5 days, ...	10.00
M. W. Hynes, 10 days, 2 hours, . .	20.47

M. W. Hynes, horses, 7 days, 1 hr.,   . $24.74
. L. Hynes, 10 days, 2 hrs., .   .   .   20.47
. L. Hynes, horse, 5 days,   .   .   .   8.75
T. F. Maynard, 2 days, 5 hrs.,   .   .   5.11
T. F. Maynard, 10 days,   .   .   .   17.50
Thomas Dowey, 5 days, ...   10.00
P. S. Zimmerman, 5 days,   .   .   .   10.00
W. C. Neal, 5½ hrs., ...   1.23
W. C. Neal, horses, 5½ hrs., .   .   .   2.14
P. A. Leary, sharpening picks and drill, .   8.55
      ————— $168.63

OCTOBER.

L. A. Loker, 10 days, ... $20.00
L. A. Loker, horse, 8 days, 5 hrs.,   .   14.97
Wilson Porter, 4 days, 5 hrs.,   .   .   9.10
Wilson Porter, horses, 4 days, 5 hrs.,   .   15.95
C. A. Roak, 4 days, ...   8.00
C. A. Roak, horse, 4 days,   .   .   .   7.00
T. B. Hawes, 4 days, ...   8.00
T. B. Hawes, horse, 4 days,   .   .   .   7.00
James Murphy, 4 days, ...   8.00
P. D. Gorman, 4 days, ...   8.00
John McElroy, 4 days, ...   8.00
J. N. Hammond, 65 loads gravel at 10c.,   6.50
L. A. Loker, 2 days, ...   4.00
L. A. Loker, horse, 2 days,   .   .   .   3.50
M. W. Hynes, 3 days, 8 hrs., .   .   .   7.78
M. W. Hynes, 3 days, 7 hrs. for horse, .   6.61
T. L. Hynes, 3 days, ...   6.00
T. L. Hynes, horse, 3 days,   .   .   .   5.25
T. F. Maynard, 2 days, 2 hrs.,   .   .   4.45
T. F. Maynard, horses, 2 days, 1 hr.,   .   7.38
Thomas Dowey, 2 days, 1 hr.,   .   .   4.22
P. S. Zimmerman, 2 days,   .   .   .   4.00
      ————— $173.71

DECEMBER.

L. A. Loker, 2 days, 8½ hours,   .   .   5.77
L. A. Loker, horse 2 days, 8½ hours   .   4.57
L. A. Loker, 2 cedar guide posts,   .   .   1.00

M. W. Hynes, 7 hours, ... $1.56
M. W. Hynes, horses, 7 hours, . . 2.72
M. W. Hynnes, 17 loads gravel at 10c. . 1.70

$17.32

JANUARY.

L. A. Loker, 4 days, 2½ hours, . . $8.46
L. A. Loker, horse 3 days 2½ hours, . 5.55
L. A. Loker, 56 feet plank, ...98
P. D. Gorman, 1 day 3½ hours . . 2.77
C. A. Roak, 1 day, 4 hours, . . . 2.88
C. A. Roak, 1 day, 4 hours, . . . 2.51
Wilson Porter, 2 days, ... 4.00
Wilson Porter, 2 days, horses, . . 7.00
W. C. Neal, 2 days, 3 hours, . . . 4.67
W. C. Neal, horses, 2 days, three hours, . 8.17
L. A. Loker, 1 day, ... 2.00
L. A. Loker, horse, 7 hours, . . . 1.34
M. W. Hynes, 1 day, 1 hour, . . . 2.23
M. W. Hynes, 1 day, 4 hours, . . 2.52
T. L. Hynes, 1 day, 8½ hours, . . 3.90
T. L. Hynes, horse, 1 day, 8½ hours, . 3.39
John Clark, 2½ hours, ...50
J. R. Hawkins, 7 hours, ... 1.50
James Nichols, 7 hours, ... 1.50
Henry Imminck, 7 hours, . . . 1.50

$67.38

FEBRUARY.

L. A. Loker, 12 days, 1½ hours, . . $24.11
L. A. Loker, horse, 7 days 5 hours, . 13.22
Wilson Porter, 1 day, 1½ hours, . . 2.33
Wilson Porter, horses, 2 hours, . . .77
W. C. Neal, 8½ hours, ... 1.88
W. C. Neal, horses, 2 hours, ...78
Alex Spear, 3 days, 3 hours, . . . 6.65
Paul Loker, 4½ hours, ... 1.00
Paul Loker, horses, 1½ hours, . . .57
Len Sarshfield, 1 day, 2½ hours, . . 2.53

Frank Howe, 3 days, 4 hours, . . .	$6.88
Frank Howe, horses, 1½ hours, . .	.57
E. A. Carter, 7 hours, ...	1.55
Henry Tyrrell, 2 days, 3 hours, . .	4.62
Everett Jennison, 2 days, ½ hour, . .	4.10
C. A. Roak, 7 days, 1 hour, . . .	14.23
C. A. Roak, horse, 1 day, 1 hour, . .	1.94
Charles Newton, 4 days, 8½ hours, . .	9.89
Frank Bemis, 1 day, 1½ hours, . .	2.33
Arthur T. Welch, 6½ hours, . . .	1.33
Bert Ward, 8 hours, ...	1.76
Charlie Fullick, 5 hours, . . .	1.11
A. H. Knowlton, 5 hours, . . .	1.11
M. W. Hynes, 9 days, ...	18.00
M. W. Hynes, horses, 8 days, ½ hr., .	28.18
Thomas L. Hynes, 8 days, 7 hrs., . .	17.59
T. L. Hynes, horse, 6 days, . . .	10.50
Thomas F. Maynard, 10 days, 3½ hrs., .	20.82
Thomas F. Maynard, 3 loads gravel at 10c.	.30
Thomas F. Maynard, horse, 8 days, .	13.99
Thomas Maynard, 4 days, 2½ hrs., . .	8.53
Thomas Dowey, 10 days, 4½ hrs., . .	21.00
Timothy Coughlin, 13 days, 5½ hrs., .	27.18
A. E. Wellington, 6 days, 3¾ hrs., . .	12.82
Thomas Lane, 11 days, 8 hrs., . .	23.78
Thomas Bowles, 7 hrs., ...	1.56
C. H. Richardson, 6 days, . . .	12.00
J. W. Smith, 1 day, 8½ hrs., . . .	3.90
J. F. Malloy, 6 days, ...	12.00
H. C. Haynes, 5 days, 5½ hrs., . .	11.20
John J. Rowen, 4 days, 5 hrs., . .	9.15
Chas. F. Dickey, 6 days, . . .	12.00
J S. Dickey, 2 days, 5 hrs., . . .	5.11
H. F. Haynes, 5 days, 8 hrs., . .	11.86
P. S. Zimmerman, 5 days, 4 hrs., . .	10.90
H. G. Hammond, 2 days, 5¼ hrs., . .	3.14
John Hurley, 2 days 5 hrs., . . .	5.11
James Murphy, 5 days, 6½ hrs., . .	11.39
J. B. McElroy, 1 day, 4½ hrs. . . .	3.00
B. S. Hemmenway, 3 days, 4 hrs., . .	6.88

Geo. L. Baker, 2 days, 5 hrs.,	.	.	$5.06
H. P. Parker, 2 days,	. .	.	4.00
H. P. Parker, horses, 4 hrs.,	.	.	1.52
George Hancock, 4 hrs., '	.	.	.88
George W. Videon, 1 day, 1 hr.,	.	.	2.22
J. R. Hawkins, 4 days, 7½ hrs.,	.	.	9.77
James Nichols, 6 days,	. .	.	12.00
John Linehan, 5½ hrs.,	. .	.	1.22
John Dunn, 7 hrs.,	. .	.	1.56
John Clark, 3 days, 3 hrs.,	.	.	6.67
E. W. Kendall, 7 hrs.,	. .	.	1.56
C. L. Smith, 1 day,	. .	.	2.00
B. W. Smith, 1 day, 5 hrs.,	.	.	3.10
P. A. Leary, repairing tools,	.	.	1.05
A. B. Sherman, 8 days, 7 hrs.,	.	.	17.50
A. B. Sherman, horses, 4 days, 4 hrs.,	.	14.80
John H. Coakely, 5 days, 8 hrs.,	.	.	11.77

$523.83

Expended, $2,621.87.

I find the roads and bridges in a bad condition and will continue to be so unless we have more money appropriated. I have repaired two bridges and seven culverts, and there are two bridges that are unsafe and must be repaired immediately. There are no outstanding bills. The snow bill was $607.52.

L. A. LOKER,
Superintendent of Streets.

SUPERINTENDENT OF THE WAYLAND WATER WORKS REPORT.

GENTLEMEN, — My two years as Superintendent of Water Works has convinced me of one thing, and that is, that the town would have been better off in dollars and cents, and their property in better shape if they had employed a Superintendent by the year to look after the works, instead of expecting a man to do it for the sum paid for same.

I venture to say there is not another water works in the country of this size that does not engage a superintendent by the year.

I know from my own experience that it is impossible to give the water takers the best service possible and keep the works in any kind of shape unless a man put all of his time in same.

The reservoir got very low last fall, caused by no rain and a wasteful use by water takers, for just as the water began to get low, a great many went to running their faucets about all the time, and of course got poorer water, and came near taking all the water in the reservoir.

I have not done any very extensive repairs this year. The Maintenance Account is:

1894.
Oct. 2.   Cash paid W. W. Wright for labor,   .   . $7.50
   "   Cash paid Samuel Hobbs & Co., material,   . 13.45
   "   Cash paid James Devine for labor,   .   . 6.45
          Cash paid Walworth Mfg. Co., material,   . 33.83
   "   Cash paid H. G. Dudley as supt. for labor, . 65.86
Nov. 22. Cash paid P. A. Leary as supt. for labor,   . 2.30
Dec.   Cash paid H. G. Dudley, labor and material, . 31.65
1895.
Feb. 27. Cash paid H. G. Dudley, labor and material, . 64.77
                                                        _____
                                                        $225.81

The water is used by the following:

Families, ...	234
Manufactories, ...	8
Public buildings, ...	4
Miscellaneous, ...	12
Horses, ...	81
Cows, ...	74

Respectfully submitted,

HENRY G. DUDLEY,
Superintendent.

WAYLAND WATER COMMISSIONERS' REPORT.

WAYLAND WATER COMMISSIONERS *in account with* HENRY F. LEE,
Town Treasurer.

CR.

1894. Appropriation for hydrants, ...		$384.00
April 25. By water rates of 1893 paid to Town Treasurer,		46.00
July 6. By " 1894 " "		110.00
Oct. 3. By " " " "		393.00
Nov. 2. By " ' '		200.50
1895.		
Jan. 1. By "		489.25
Feb. 28. By "		406.17
Feb. 28. By "		303.75
		$2,332.67

DR.

1894.

April 25. To order No. 0 on Town Treasurer for water rates of 1893 deposited in Natick Five Cents Savings Bank for a water works sinking fund, ...		$46.00
Oct. 2. To order No. 1, W. W. Wight, , .		7.50
Oct. 2. To order No. 2, Samuel Hobbs & Co., .		13.45
Oct. 2. To order No. 3, James Devine, . . .		6.45
Oct. 2. To order No. 4, Walworth Manufacturing Company, . . , . . .		33.83
Oct. 2. To order No. 5, H. G. Dudley, . . .		65.86
Nov. 2. To order No. 6, P. A. Leary, . . .		2.30
Dec. 31. To order No. 7, H. G. Dudley, . . .		31.65
1895.		
Feb. 28. To order No. 8, H. G. Dudley, . . .		64.77
Feb. 28. Interest on water bonds transferred to interest account, ...		1,450.00

Feb. 28. To order No. 9, on Town Treasurer for balance of water funds invested in the Watertown Savings Bank, ... $610.86

$2,332.67

CHARLES H. BOODY,
WILLIAM H. BENT,
HENRY G. DUDLEY,
Wayland Water Commissioners.

WAYLAND, Feb. 28, '95.

WAYLAND WATER WORKS SINKING FUND.

1895.

Feb. 28.   Amount deposited in Natick Five Cents
Savings Bank, ... $3,645.74
Amount deposited in Natick Five Cents Sav-
ings Bank, April 30, 1894, . . . 46.00
Interest on above deposit to Nov. 1, 1894, 1,605.28
Amount deposited in Suffolk Savings Bank,
Boston, ... 1,000.00
Interest on above deposit to Oct. 1, 1894, 284.66
Amount deposited in Home Savings Bank,
Boston, ... 2,292.38
Interest on above deposit to Oct. 1, 1894, 384.98
Amount deposited in Framingham Savings
Bank, ... 1,205.21
Interest on above deposit to Nov. 1, 1894, 125.36
Amount deposited in North End Savings
Bank, Boston, ... 1,459.40
Interest on above deposit to Jan. 1, 1895, 78.42
Amount invested in the Watertown Savings
Bank, ... 610.86

$12,738.29

CHARLES H. BOODY,
WM. H. BENT,
HENRY G. DUDLEY,
Commissioners of the Wayland Water Works Sinking Fund.

REPORT OF FIRE ENGINEERS.

The Department has responded to only two alarms during the year, viz.,

May 2.   False alarm.

June 18.   Fire in shop occupied by Scotland & Campbell and owned by T. D. Bent. The Department after laying fourteen-hundred and fifty feet of hose was unable to reach the fire with water. The building was totally consumed with its contents.

The Engineers were appointed by the Selectmen as a committee to extend the Fire alarm system to Simpson's Corner and make necessary repairs. This has been done in a satisfactory manner at an expense of two hundred dollars, the amount of the appropriation

The department is in an excellent condition, both as regards membership and apparatus. The new fire alarm box located at Simpson's Corner is numbered 27.

RALPH BENT,
H. B. PHALEN,
Engineers.

COCHITUATE, MARCH 8, 1895.

REPORT OF SUPERINTENDENT OF NORTH AND CENTRE CEMETRIES.

FROM MARCH 1, 1894, to MARCH 1, 1895.

Appropriated, ...	$50.00
Unexpended balance of 1893, . ˙ . . .	14.40
	$64.40

EXPENDED.

To labor, at 20 cents per hour, ...	$35.40
L. J. Bemis, to carting gravel, ...	7.20
Unexpended balance, ...	21.80
	$64.40

CASH RECEIVED AND PAID TOWN TREASURER.

Lots, ...	$2.00
Grass, ...	5.00
	$7.00

T. S. SHERMAN,
Superintendent.

REPORT OF LAKEVIEW CEMETERY COMMITTEE.

For the Year Ending Feb. 28, 1895.

Appropriated, ... $50.00
Unexpended balance for 1893, . . . 8.21
                                              ——— $58.21
Order 1, J. C. Butterfield, ... $6.50
  " 2, Wm. Parlin, ... 16.50
June 30, Treasurer's check, ... 35.21
                                              ——— $58.21

Cash received and paid Treasurer for sale of lots, . $45.00

H. B. PHALEN,
WM. W. LOVEJOY,
Town Committee.

REPORT OF THE TREASURER FOR THE YEAR ENDING FEB. 28, 1895.

APPROPRIATIONS.

1894.

March 26. For schools, care of rooms and fuel, . $5,700.00

School supplies, ... 450.00

Highways and bridges, . . . 2,000.00

Incidentals, ... 1,200.00

Firemen's pay, ... 224.00

Support of poor, ... 2,500.00

Salaries, ... 1,200.00

Collection of Taxes, ... 300.00

Abatements, ... 400.00

Hydrants, ... 384.00

Repairs on school buildings, . . 200.00

Lakeview cemetery, ... 50.00

North and Centre cemeteries, . . 50.00

Library, ... 300.00

Electric lights, ... 340.00

Suppression of illegal sale of intoxicating liquors, ... 200.00

Interest, ... 3,000.00

Overdraft on incidentals, . . . 200.00

Overdraft on salaries, . . . 50.00

Extension of fire alarm, . . . 200.00

May 10. Lakeview cemetery, $100, not assessed

New school house, ... 4,000.00

Repairs on Centre school house, . . 300.00

Steam for fire alarm, ... 150.00

1895.

Jan. 16. Highways, ... 500.00

Support of poor, . . . · 500.00

$24,398.00

1894.

March 26.	From contingent fund,	. $4.000.00	
	" "	. 300.00	
	"	. 150.00	
1895.			
Jan. 16.		. 500.00	
	" "	. 500.00	
	Town tax assessed,	. 18,948.00	
			$24,398.00

SCHOOLS, CARE OF ROOMS AND FUEL.

1894.

March 1.	Unexpended balance, ...	762.13
" 26.	Appropriation, ...	5,700.00
1895.		
Jan. 7.	Donation fund, ...	12.00
" 26.	School fund (State), ...	245.08
Feb. 1.	Dog licenses (half), ...	87.43
		$6,806.64
1894-95.	Amount expended, . . . $6,329.94	
1895.		
March 1.	Unexpended balance, . . 476.70	
		$6,806.64

SCHOOL SUPPLIES.

1894.

March 1.	Unexpended balance, ...	$15.78
" 26.	Appropriation, ...	450.00
1894-95.	Overdrawn, ...	31.44
		$497.22
1894-95.	Amount expended, . . . $497.22	

HIGHWAYS AND BRIDGES.

1894.

March 1.	Unexpended balance, ...	$7.22
" 26.	Appropriation, ...	2,000.00
1895.		
Jan. 16.	Appropriation, ...	500.00
		$2,507.22
1894-95.	Overdrawn, ...	114.65
		$2,621.87
1894-95.	Amount expended, . . . $2,621.87	

SUPPORT OF POOR.

1894.

March	1,	Unexpended balance, . .	$39.62
"	26,	Appropriation, . . .	2500.00
May	2,	Overseers of Poor, . .	646.23
		Town of Lexington . .	52.00
		" " Natick, . . .	133.64

$3,371.49

1895.

Jan. 16, Appropriation, . . . $500.00

$3,871.49

1894–95. Amount expended, . $3,702.98
    Unexpended balance, . $168.51

$3,871.49

INCIDENTALS.

1894.

March 1.	Unexpended balance, ...			.15
" 26.	Appropriation, ...		.	1,200.00
. "	" for overdraft, '93–'94,		.	200.00

$1,400.15

1894–95. Amount overdrawn, ...   8.54

$1,408.69

1894–95. Amount expended, . . . $1,408.69

SALARIES.

1894.

March 1.	Unexpended balance, . . .		.	$28.69
" 26.	Appropriation, . . .		.	1,200.00
" "	" for overdraft, '93–'94		.	50.00

	Expended, ...	.	$1,278.69
March 31.	A. G. Bennett, auditor, .	$50.00	
April 2.	Henry G. Dudley, . . .	70.00	
	Joseph Candlin, . .	50.00	
	Edward Carter, . . .	59.50	
	Lizzie E. Mitchell, . . .	50.00	

July 28.	H. G. Hammond,	.	.	.	$47.25
	R. T. Lombard,	.	.	.	57.75
	Nellie Rice Fiske,	.	.	.	52.00
	R. T. Lombard,	.	.	.	89.00
	T. L. Sawin,	.	.	.	20.00

1895.

Feb. 28.	Charles H. Boody,	.	.	.	45.00
	H. G. Hammond,	.	.	.	8.75
	L. E. Mitchell,	.	.	.	46.00
	T. W. Frost,	.	.	.	50.00
	F. W. Frost,	.	.	.	150.00
	E. P. Butler,	.	.	.	75.00
	W. H. Jameson,	.	.	.	25.00
	D. W. Mitchell,	.	.	.	20.00
	Edward Carter,	.	.	.	10.50
	David P. W. Loker,	.	.	75.00
	L. H. Sherman,	.	.	.	20.00
	W. B. Ward,	.	.	.	25.00
	Unexpended balance,	.	.	182.94
					$1,278.69

FIREMEN'S PAY.

1894.

March 1.	Unexpended balance,	.	.	$224.00
" 26.	Appropriation, .	.	.	224.00
				$448.00

March 1.	Amount expended, 1894-95	.	$224.00
1895.			
March 1.	Unexpended balance,	.	224.00
			$448.00

COLLECTION OF TAXES.

1894.

March 1.	Unexpended balance,	.	.	$300.00
" 26.	Appropriation, .	.	.	300.00
				$600.00

	Expended,	.	.	.	$300.00
1895.					
March 1.	Unexpended balance,	.	.	300.00
					$600.00

ABATEMENT OF TAXES.

1894.

March 1. Overdrawn, ...	$870.50		
Nov. 23. Taxes of 1892, . . .	7.00		
" " 1893, . . .	6.35		
" " 1894, . . .	169.90		
Feb. 28, 1895. Taxes of 1894, . .	16.40		
March 26, 1894. Appropriation, . .		$400.00	
Feb. 28, 1895. Overdrawn, . . .		670.15	
	$1,070.15	$1,070.15	

TAXES OF 1891.

Mar. 1, 1894. Balance due, . . . $475.18		
Feb. 28, 1895. Received from collector, .	$15.98	
" " Amount due from collector,	459.20	
$475.18	$475.18	

TAXES OF 1892.

Mar. 1, 1894. Balance due, . . $6,305.62		
" " Received from collector,	$5,450.32	
Feb. 28, 1895. Am't due from collector,	855.30	
$6,305.62	$6,305.62	

TAXES OF 1893.

Mar. 1, 1894. Balance due, . . $8,306.83		
" " Received from collector,	$3,277.71	
Feb. 28, 1895. Am't due from collector,	5,029.12	
$8,306.83	$8,306.83	

TAXES OF 1894.

Amount as assessed due from Collector, ...		$22,059.75
Received from Collector,	$13,336.43	
1895.		
Feb. 28. Amount due from Collector, .	8,723.32	
		$22,059.75

REPAIRS ON SCHOOL BUILDINGS.

1894.

March 1.	Unexpended balance, ...		$46.88
26.	Appropriation, ...		200.00
1894–95.	Amount expended, . .	$242.55	
1895.			
March 1.	Unexpended balance, . .	4.33	
		$246.88	$246.88

REBUILDING STONE BRIDGE.

1894.

March 1.	Unexpended balance, ...	$500.00
June 1.	Transferred to contingent fund, . .	$500.00

HYDRANTS.

1894.

March 26.	Appropriation, ...	$384.00
1895.		
Feb. 28.	Paid Water Commissioners, . .	$384.00

LAKEVIEW CEMETERY.

1894.

March 1.	Unexpended balance, ...	$8.21
26.	Appropriation, ...	50.00
		$58.21
April 28.	Paid W. D. Parlin, . . . 16.50	
May 26.	John C. Butterfield, . . 6.50	
June 30.	Wm. Lovejoy, . . . 35.21	
		$58.21

NORTH AND CENTRE CEMETERIES.

1894.

March 1.	Unexpended balance, . . $14.40	
26.	Appropriation, . . . 50.00	
		$64.00
	Paid T. S. Sherman, . . $42.60	
1895.		
March 1.	Unexpended balance, . . 21.80	
		$64.40

CEMETERY ACCOUNT.

1895.

Feb. 28. Received from T. S. Sherman,
for grass and lots, . . $7.00
Received from Wm. Lovejoy, . 45.00

$52.00

DECORATION DAY.

1894.

March 1. Unexpended balance, . . $68.50

May 26. Paid Natick and Cochituate St.
Railway Co., . . . $13.89
Paid L. D. Draper, . . . 25.00

June 1. To Contingent Fund, . . 29.61

30. Paid C. H. Thing, . . . 29.61
Overdrawn, ... 29.61

$98.11 $98.11

ELECTRIC LIGHTS.

1894.

March 1. Unexpended balance, . . $67.52

26. Appropriated, . . . 340.00
Paid Natick Electric Light Co., $354.18

1895.

March 1. Unexpended balance, . . 53.34

$407.52 $407.52

SUPPRESSION OF ILLEGAL SALE OF INTOXICATING LIQUORS AND SPECIAL POLICE.

1894.

March 1. Unexpended balance, . . $77.90

26. Appropriation, ... 200.00

$277.90

May 26. Paid L. H. Wakefield, . . $5.00
John Lamarine, . . 2.50

June 1. To contingent fund, . . 70.40

30. Paid Clinton E. Hibbard, . 26.00

July 28. M. W. Hynes, . . 6.00

July 28.	Paid P. D. Gorman,	.	.	$6.00
	W. C. Neal,	.	.	6.00
	T. E. Glennon,	.	.	6.00
	J. E. Linnehan,	.	.	6.00
Nov. 24.	C. E. Hibbard,	.	.	21.00
1895.				
Feb. 23.	J. W. Moore, .	.	.	5.30
	A. D. Collins, .	.	.	5.30
	L. H. McManus,	.	.	4.14
March 1.	Unexpended balance,			108.26

$277.90

PUBLIC LIBRARY.

1894.

Mch. 26.   Appropriation,   .   .   . $300.00

1895.

Feb. 1.   Dog Licenses, (half),   .   . 87.43

$387.43

Paid Treasurer of Library Fund, $387.43

STATE TAX.

1894.

July 28.   Levied and assessed,   .   . $1,460.00

Dec. 11.   Paid Treas. of Commonwealth, $1,460.00

COUNTY TAX.

1894.

July 28.   Levied and assessed,   .   . $1,596.67

Nov. 15.   Paid County Treasurer, .   . $1,596.67

INTEREST ON TOWN DEBT.

1893-94.

Tempoary Loans,   .   . $613.15

Town Debt :

Paid coupons on Town Bonds,   2,225.00

"   "   " Water Bonds,   1,410.00

"   interest "   "   "   40.00

"   "   Note of Allen Fund,   60.00

"   "   Donation Fund, .   78.00

"   "   Loker Fund,   . 100.00

$4,526.15

1894.

March 1. Unexpended balance, . . $4.83
    26. Appropriation, . . 3,000.00
June 1. Transferred from Water Rates, 1,450.00
        Overdrawn, ... 71.32
                                  $4,526.15

TEMPORARY LOANS.

1894.

July 30. Paid Natick National Bank, note of
          August 27, 1892, . . . $2,000.00
Oct. 3. Paid Natick National Bank, note of Jan.
          16, 1894, ... 2,000.00
Oct. 18. Paid Natick National Bank, note of
          April 18, 1894, . . . 5,000.00
Nov. 15. Paid Natick National Bank, note of
          April 3, 1892, . . . 4,000.00
1895.
Feb. 13. Paid National Bank, note of Feb. 26, '93, 2,000.00
1894.
March 1. Notes outstanding, . . $15,000.00
April 18. Borrowed in anticipation of
         taxes '94, . . . 5,000.00
July 16. Borrowed in anticipation of
         taxes '94, . . . 5,000.00
1895.
Jan. 18. Borrowed in anticipation of
         taxes '94, . . . 4,000.00
March 1. Outstanding notes, . . 14,000.00
                                  $29,000.00

BOARD OF WATER COMMISSIONERS.

1894.

June 1. Transferred to interest acct., $1,450.00
1893-94. Paid Wm. H. Bent, clerk, . 882.67
                                  $2,332.67

        Received from W. H. Bent,
          clerk, ... $1,948.67
1895.
Feb. 28. Transferred from Hydrants, 384.00
                                  $2,332.67

EXTENSION OF FIRE ALARM.

1894.

Mar. 26.	Appropriations, . . .	$200.00
July 28.	Paid Henry B. Phalen, . .	200.00

REPAIRS ON CENTRE HIGH SCHOOL.

1894.

Mch. 26.	Appropriation, . . .		$300.00
April 28.	Paid Thomas J. Dowey, .	$4.50	
Aug. 25.	Frank Haynes, . .	185.15	
Sept. 29.	T. W. Frost, . .	38.52	
Dec. 29.	B. F. Smith & Bros., .	66.00	
1895.			
March 1.	Unexpended balance, . .	5.83	
			$300.00

STEAM FOR FIRE ALARM.

1894.

March 1.	Unexpended balance, . .	$150.00	
26.	Appropriation, . .	150.00	
			$300.00
April 28.	Paid Wm. H. Bent, . .	$150.00	
1895.			
March 1.	Unexpended balance, . .	150.00	
			$300.00

COMMITTEE ON SCHOOL ALTERATIONS.

1894.

March 1.	Unexpended balance, ...		$1,00.00
June 1.	To contingent fund, . . $	100.00	
Mar. 26.	From the contingent fund, appropriated		
	for new school house, .	4,000.00	
	Repairs on Centre School house,	300.00	
	Appropriated for fire alarm, .	150.00	
Apr. 28.	Samuel Patch, drafting plans,	275.00	
	Treasurer of Commonwealth of Mass.,		
	corporation tax refunded, .	654.00	
1895.			
Jan. 16.	Appropriated for highways, .	500.00	
"	" poor, .	500.00	

'94–'95.

State aid, ...	$864.00	
Military, ...	258.00	
		$6,853.54

1894.

March 1.	Unexpended balance, ...	355.33
April 2.	From Joseph Candlin, rent of hall, .	7.90
" 12.	" James S. Draper, library fund, .	500.00
" 12.	W. B. Ward, collector interest on taxes of 1891, ...	142.21
	Gilbert & Barker Manufacturing Co., oil barrels, ...	2.30
" 30.	Middlesex So. District Court, fines, .	49.13
May 26.	Geo. E. Sherman, auctioneer's license, .	2.00
June 30.	Peter Zimmerman, rent of hall, . .	9.00
" 1.	Balance on school building appropriation,	24.96
" 1.	Stone's bridge, ...	500.00
" 1.	Decoration day, ...	29.61
June 1.	From sup. illegal sale of intox. liquors appro., ...	70.40
	From committee on school alterations, .	100.00
July 2.	From Middlesex So. Dist. Court fines,	10.00
Sept. 29.	Natick & Cochituate St. R. R. Co.,	25.00
Oct. 2.	From Samuel Russell, butchers' license,	1.00
27.	P. S. Zimmerman, rent of hall, .	5.00
Nov. 14.	" " " " .	5.50
Dec. 11.	From corporation tax, ...	1,364.95
	Nat'l Bank tax, ...	781.80
	Military aid, ...	168.00
	State "	755.00

1895.

Jan. 5.	From L. A. Dudley school furniture, .	8.00
7.	P. S. Zimmerman rent of hall, .	10.00
26.	" " " "	10.00
	From T. W. Frost, rent of hall, . .	20.00
Feb. 1.	" " " " . .	85.00
13.	" " " " . .	2.50
	From W. B. Ward, for int. and costs on tax title, ...	4.21

Feb.	13.	From Gilbert & Barker Mfg. Co., oil bbls.	$2.35
	23.	L. K. Lovell, Centre scales, . .	29.00
		L. A. Dudley, apples, . . .	.75
	25.	L. A. Loker, old lumber, . .	3.80
	28.	E. A. Atwood, Cochituate scales, .	10.33
		W. B. Ward, interest on taxes of 1892, ...	200 00
		W. B. Ward, rent of hall for 1894,	15.00
		Overlayings on taxes of 1894, .	31.08
		Additional assessments, . .	5.60
		" " .	8.40
		" " Polls, .	10.00

	$5,365.11
Overdrawn, ...	1,488.43
	$6,853.54

NEW SCHOOL HOUSE, WAYLAND CENTRE.

1894.

March 26.	Appropriation, ...	$4,000.00

1895.

March 1.	Unexpended balance, ...	4,000.00

TAX TITLE.

Nov. 23, 1894, ...	$78.39

OBLIGATIONS OUTSTANDING.

July 29, 1893. Borrowed in anticipation of taxes of 1893, . . .	$5,000.00	
July 16, 1894. Borrowed in anticipation of taxes of 1894, . . .	5,000.00	
Jan. 18, 1895. Borrowed in anticipation of taxes of 1894, . . .	4,000.00	
		$14,000.00
Nov. 3, 1863. Draper Library Fund, on demand, at 6 per cent., . .	$500 00	
Jan. 1, 1875. Allen Fund, on demand, at 6 per cent., ...	1,000.00	
Aug. 1, 1878. Water Bonds, due Aug. 1, 1898, at 5 per cent., . .	25,000.00	

Oct. 1, 1878. Town Bonds, due Oct. 1,
    1898, at 5 per cent., . . . $44,500 00
Jan. 1, 1881. Mrs. Child's Library Fund,
    on demand, at 6 per cent., . .   100.00
Oct. 1, 1882. Water Bonds, due Oct. 1,
    1902, at 4 per cent., . . .   4,000.00
July 27, 1888. Water Bonds, due July
    27, 1898, at 4 per cent., . .   1,000.00
Jan. 1, 1889. Donation Fund, on de-
    mand, at 6 per cent., . . .   1,300.00
April 1, 1891. Loker Fund, on demand,
    at 5 per cent., ...   2,000.00
April 12, 1894. Ella Draper, Library
    Fund, on demand, at 6 per cent.,   500.00
                                      ————— $79,900.00

HENRY F. LEE IN ACCOUNT WITH THE TOWN OF WAYLAND.

Dr.

1894.

March 1.	To cash as per audit	$1,813.03
	Joseph Caudlin, rent, . . .	7.90
	Court fines, ...	49.13
	Ella Draper, library fund, . . .	500.00
	Interest on taxes, '91, . . .	142.21
	Sale, oil barrels, ...	2.30
	Geo. E. Sherman, license. . .	2.00
	Rent of hall, ...	163.00
	Court fines, ...	10.00
	Use of road scraper, ...	25.00
	Samuel Russell, license, . .	1.00
	Costs on tax bills, ...	4.21
	Sale of oil barrels, ...	2.35
	Sale of scales, ...	29.00
	Apples sold L. A. Dudley, . .	75
	Sale of grass and lots N. and C. Cemeteries, ...	7.00
	Sale of grass and lots Lakeview Cemetery, ...	45.00
	Sale of lumber, ...	3.80

1894.

March 1. To Sale of Cochituate scales, . . . $10.33

Interest on tax, '92, ... 200.00

Sale of furniture, ... 8.00

Donation fund, ... 12.00

State school fund, ... 245.08

Dog licenses refunded, . . . 174.86

Overseer of poor, ... 830.87

Water rates, ... 1,948.67

Corporation tax, ... 1,364.95

National Bank tax, ... 781.80

Military and State aid, . . . 923.00

Borrowed in anticipation of taxes, . 14,000.00

Taxes 1891, '92, '93 and '94, . . 21,802.40

$45,109.64

CR.

By Selectmen's orders, ... $18,333.91

State tax, ... 1,460.00

County tax, ... 1,596.67

State and military aid, . . . 1,122.00

Interest, ... 4,526.15

Notes, ... 15,000.00

Water commissioners' orders, . . 882.67

1895.

$42,921,40

March 1. Cash on deposit, ... 2,188.24

$45,109.64

HENRY F. LEE, *Treasurer.*

AUDITOR'S REPORT.

The bonds of various town officers are on file with the Selectmen.

The books of the Treasurer, Water Commissioners, Tax Collector, Overseers of Poor, are correctly kept.

Vouchers are on file for money expended.

I find that the interest on town notes belonging to the library fund, has not been paid for two years, owing to the fact that the notes cannot be found, they never having reached the hands of the present treasurer or his immediate predecessor.

TRIAL BALANCE.

Unexpended balances, ...	$ 5,747.71
Temporary loans, ...	14,000.00
	$19,747.71

Overdrawn, ...	$2,414.14	
Uncollected taxes, ...	15.066.94	
Tax title, ...	78.39	
Cash, ...	2,188.24	
		$19,747.71

DANIEL BRACKETT, *Auditor.*

ANNUAL REPORT

OF THE

SCHOOL COMMITTEE

OF THE

TOWN OF WAYLAND

FOR THE YEAR 1894-95.

The day is past when it is at all necessary for any arguments to be made to have people admit that education is a great necessity. It is clear to every thoughtful person, as a general thing, that a good education is of far greater value than wealth and a richer inheritance than the best fortune that could be put into the hands of any young person.

While the State makes it obligatory upon our towns to provide educational training for our children, it should be looked upon by every intelligent person as the wisest possible outlay of money and care.

One of the most urgent needs at the present time is a greater annual per centage of graduates from our schools. It is very deplorable that so many fail to finish the course of studies in our grammar schools. There is no correspondence between the members of those who enter our schools and those who complete their course.

While there are fifty or sixty enter every year, it is seldom that more than ten graduate. The High School graduates are even smaller. Now, if ever, do young men and women need as broad an education as they can get. With every passing decade competition is growing more and more keen. And with that growth it is becoming more certain that the person who is best equipped mentally and physically will win. To be thoroughly fitted for life's duties in the better openings which now come to our young people, it is necessary that our children at least pass through the grammar school, and if possible, the high. Here comes before us the necessity of parental influence. Until human nature is re-made children will not see the necessity of their attendance at school. And, therefore, parents must be held responsible if it be cut short. So parents we ask the question, why cut it short ? You feel solicitous for the proper physical development of your child. This is as it should be, but you ought to feel equally concerned about the progress in all lines of mental culture.

Look around and you will see that these are days of mental conflict. As muscle used to decide supremacy, so now does mind. The world at the present time is one vast battlefield, on which single individuals are taking captive multitudes who have not been trained to think for themselves. Under these circumstances the permanency of our republic calls for an educated citizenship.

Opportunities were never so good as now, since the legislature has made it compulsitory for towns to furnish text-books as well as teachers ; education is brought within the reach of all families. With these advantages it becomes imperative on the part of parents to demand their childred's careful attendance at school. It is needful that the town provide the very best skilled teachers that can be procured.

If the town furnish advantages for the best education and the parent enforces the attendance and careful work of the child it may naturally be expected that on the part of the child there will be a search after principles, the following of which will give the nation men and women of power.

Days more favorable for the accomplishment of these results were never known. Never was there in our state a better class of thoroughly trained teachers than now. School studies were never made so interesting and attractive to the child. The system of teaching is conducted on the best methods for the rapid mental improvement and if taken advantage of will produce a class of citizens that will be an honor to the nation.

At the commencement of the fall term 1894, we found that we had to commence with several new teachers ; and we can congratulate the town upon our obtaining so good teachers, considering the salaries we have to pay. And here let it be said, that money cannot be better expended than in paying fair salaries for good teachers, and when obtained be able to retain them. It is detrimental to any school to be compelled to change teachers, as each generally has a different system and by the time one is started and fairly under way a new teacher steps in to start a new system thereby delaying the schools in their studies.

From our knowledge of our schools we are able to judge that so far as our teachers are concerned our schools are in a good condition and rank well, we believe, with schools of the same grade in other towns.

The committee has kept the expenses as close as possible, and we recommend for the pay of teachers, fuel, care of buildings, etc., the same as last year, $5,700. For supplies, $500. For repairs, $200.

We recommend that the school buildings at Cochituate be painted and that a sufficient sum be appropriated for the same. For financial statement of the receipts and expenditures of the school fund see treasurer's and auditor's report.

Respectfully submitted,

C. H. BOODY,
L. ANNA DUDLEY,
L. E. MITCHELL,
School Committee.

REPORT OF THE LIBRARY TRUSTEES FOR THE YEAR ENDING FEB. 28, 1895.

After making an inspection of the Library during the first week in January, the Trustees are happy to report the books and other property there in fairly good condition. After the constant use to which the original portion of the Library has been subjected for nearly half a century, age and constant service will assert themselves in the general appearance of the books.

If we could have an appropriation for the maintenance of the Library sufficient to enable us to open the Library rooms two days in the week to the public, we are confident the benefits derived would more than compensate for the additional expense, the circulation of books would be increased, and the advantage of its valuable reference books to the teachers and scholars of the schools better appreciated.

One of the indispensable aids to a community in promoting the circulation and usefulness of a library is a good catalogue of its books. It is not only a guide in the selection of books, but in the record of titles made, an incentive is given to readers to avail themselves of the opportunity to use them.

We have upon our Library shelves the accessions of seven years uncatalogued, and it must be clear to the mind of every one that the greater part of the town's people are deprived of the benefit to be derived from those books.

Carlisle once said: "A library is not worth anything without a catalogue. It is a Polyphemus without an eye in his head, and you must front the difficulties whatever they may be of making proper catalogues."

As a residential town Wayland is being looked upon with increasing favor, and we have strong faith and hope with its present advantages it will continue to be so considered.

Our Library of twelve thousand and more volumes will be an attraction to persons who may be considering a permanent residence, and it should be maintained and cared for now, with its larger number of volumes and more expanded growth, as in former years it was during its infancy. As a necessary adjunct to its enlargement is a greater expense in its support. A larger sum is needed each year in keeping the old books in proper repair and in purchasing new ones of a character to keep the Library at its previous high standard. This expense should be met by a larger appropriation. We have been reminded during the last year of how much we are indebted to our venerable townsman and former librarian, Mr. James S. Draper, by his munificent gift to increase the fund for the benefit of the Library. After his long and faithful service as librarian this generous endowment for the Library is highly appreciated.

We wish to call the attention of the town to the manner in which the librarian has discharged her duties. Having gained by several years experience a thorough familiarity with the Library, she has been able to discharge her duties faithfully and with satisfaction to the Trustees, which is thoroughly appreciated.

Our librarian's report contains the necessary details and statistics for your consideration.

HENRY D. PARMENTER,
JOHN CONNELLY,
L. E. MITCHELL,
RICHARD T. LOMBARD.
ELLEN M. BRAMAN,
E. A. HEARD,

WAYLAND, March 7, 1895.

LIBRARIAN'S REPORT.

The following report pertaining to the Librarian's department for the year 1894 is respectfully submitted to the library trustees:

ACCESSIONS.

	Books.
By purchase	173
By gift	43
Bound and transferred from the pamphlet department	26
Total	242
Whole number of volumes in the Library	12,204
Pamphlets presented	352

CIRCULATION.

In Cochituate village	1,587
In Wayland centre	4,113
Total	5,700

DONORS OF BOOKS AND PAMPHLETS.

	Books.	Pamphlets.
Bacon, Mrs. Eugene		16
Baldwin, Mrs. Wm. H.	1	
Braman, Miss Katharine		39
Campbell, Miss Carrie H.	3	10
Draper, Mr. J. S.	1	
Dudley, Miss Anna		39
Dudley, Mrs. Wm. S.		24
Fowler, Mr. F. F.	2	
Hapgood, Mr. Warren	1	
Heard, Mrs. S. E.	1	26
Hoar, Mr. G. F.		1
Morse, Miss Eunice		34
Nichols, Mr.	1	13
Potter, Mrs. Alfred C.		6

	Books.	Pamphlets.
Reeves, Miss M. E.	3	7
Rice, Mrs. Charles	1	3
Shaw, Mr. Francis	1	
State Government	6	
Tolman, Mr. Adams	1	
Thing, Mr. Charles	1	
Trustees Public Reservation	1	
Voorhees, Mr. D. W.		51
Whitney, Miss L. F.	1	16
United States Government	13	8

CLASSES OF READING.

Art	.07	Juvenile		.15
Biography	.05	Religion and Morals		.05
Fiction	.48	Science		.06
History	.08	Travels		.06

Fifteen "Public Library Reports" have been sent as follows : Brookline, Brooklyn, Boston Public, Cleveland, Concord, Fall River, Harvard College, Hopedale, Lawrence, Newton, Salem, State Library, Taunton ; also University of Pennsylvania and Harvard University reports with one from the Children's Hospital in Boston.

In the issue of books during the year ending Dec. 31st, 1894, will be noted a slight increase in numbers, and the percentage of instructive reading is commendable. The choice of books seems to move in waves, like the weather, attributable, it may be presumed, to criticisms or suggestions which are so plentifully brought to public notice: The young people have therein sustained interest and the books have received more careful use than in previous years. The time may come when a borrowed book will be treated as well as one's own. The selection of books compares favorably with other years, but there have been many much needed publications of which we have been deprived through lack of funds. Among our purchases is a new edition of Scott, one of Balyae of twenty-eight volumes, and a selection of the choicest from the new books. For further particulars see tablets.

The Reading Room has been rendered more attractive by the addition of current magazines, and has been appreciated. We have received numbers of miscellaneous books, magazines, agricultural papers and pamphlets on various subjects, as follows : — one curious Bible, The American Academy, Science, Twentieth Century, and The Land of Sunshine, illustrating Southern California in an attractive form, Harper's Monthly and Century Magazines, have been sent regularly by a friend.

It is almost impossible that the library can render any amount of service, to the schools, in the present condition of its opening, but once in a week. The teachers are too pressed for time in their routine duties to make out extended lists, yet there are many volumes in the library, which would be of great assistance to both teacher and scholars if they could be more readily obtained.

The gift to the library from its venerable past librarian, is another evidence of the deep and lasting interest he has felt in the institution, with which he was so long and so ably connected.

A book wrongly accredited to Mrs. E. A. Atwood, in last year's report, should have read Mr. E. H. Atwood, who gave a History of the 22d Massachusetts Infantry in the Civil War. Appended to to this statement is a list of books, in numerical order, added to the library this year : —

Received for fines, ...	$9.46	
" " cards, ...	1.93	
" " catalogues, ...	1.30	
Paid to treasurer, . . .		$12.69
Received for incidental expenses, . .	$12.00	
In the hands of the librarian, . . .	1.81	
		$13.81
Paid out for incidentals, ...		13.61
In the hands of the librarian, . . .		$ .20

SARAH E. HEARD,
Librarian.

March 4, 1895.

HENRY F. LEE, TREASURER, IN ACCOUNT WITH LIBRARY FUNDS.

Dr.

1894.	To Town of Wayland, unex- pended appropriation of 1893, ...	$105.82	
	Town of Wayland, appro- priation of 1894, . .	300.00	
	Town of Wayland, dog li- censes (half), . .	87.43	
	Wayland library fines, etc.,	12.69	
			$505.94

Cr.

1894.			
Mar. 23.	The New Book Club, . .	$ 7.00	
April 1.	By S. E. Heard, salary, 3 months to date, . .	50.00	
	N. R. Gerald, salary, 3 months to date, . .	40.00	
2.	Wayland Book Club, .	13.00	
28.	S. E. Heard, incidental expenses, . . .	12.00	
May 23.	DeWolfe, Fiske & Co., books, . . .	37.95	
26.	William Jessop, wood, .	6.00	
June 4.	J. D. F. Brooks, binding,	4.35	
30.	S. E. Heard, salary, 3 months to date, . .	30.00	
Sept 29.	DeWolfe, Fiske & Co., books, . . .	24.54	
30.	S. E. Heard, salary, 3 months to date, . .	50.00	
Oct. 6.	DeWolfe, Fiske & Co., books, ...	64.00	
	DeWolfe, Fiske & Co., books, ...	42.85	

Dec. 29.	S. E. Heard, salary, 3 months to Jan. 1, '95, .	$50.00
1895.		
Jan. 14.	J. D. F. Brooks, binding,	3.80
26.	P. S. Zimmerman, labor on wood, etc., . .	6.40
Feb. 23.	American Express Co., carting books between Wayland and Cochituate,	40.50
	Amount expended,	$502.39
	Balance, ...	3.55
		$505.94

ACCESSION OF TITLES IN 1894.

68

OFFICIAL REPORTS

OF THE

TOWN OF WAYLAND,

FOR ITS

One Hundred and Sixteenth Municipal Year,

FROM

MARCH 1, 1895, TO MARCH 1, 1896.

CAMBRIDGE :
LOMBARD & CAUSTIC, PRINTERS,
26a BRATTLE STREET.
1896.

OFFICIAL REPORTS

OF THE

TOWN OF WAYLAND,

FOR ITS

One Hundred and Sixteenth Municipal Year,

FROM

MARCH 1, 1895, TO MARCH 1, 1896.

CAMBRIDGE:
LOMBARD & CAUSTIC, PRINTERS,
26a BRATTLE STREET.
1896.

LIST OF TOWN OFFICERS, 1895-96.

The following is a list of the officers of the Town of Wayland and when their term expires :

Town Clerk.

Term Expires.

RICHARD T. LOMBARD, ... 1896

Treasurer.

HENRY F. LEE, ... 1896

Auditor.

LORENZO K. LOVELL, . : . . . 1896

Collector of Taxes.

WILLARD B. WARD, ... 1896

Treasurer of Library Funds.

HENRY D. PARMENTER, ... 1896

Selectmen.

THOMAS W. FROST, ... 1896
DAVID P. W. LOKER, ... 1896
DANIEL D. GRIFFIN, ... 1896

Overseers of Poor.

DAVID P. W. LOKER, ... 1896
WILLARD B. WARD, ... 1896
GEORGE B. HOWE, ... 1896

School Committee.

LIZZIE E. MITCHELL, ... 1896
———————— 1897
L. ANNA DUDLEY, ... 1898

Assessors.

HORATIO G. HAMMOND, ... 1896
RICHARD T. LOMBARD, ... 1897
EDWARD CARTER, ... 1898

Water Commissioners.

HENRY G. DUDLEY, ... 1896
WILLIAM H. BENT, ... 1897
CHARLES H. BOODEY, ... 1898

Trustees Public Library.

JOHN CONNOLLY, ... 1896
RICHARD T. LOMBARD, ... 1896
EMILY A. HEARD, ... 1897
LIZZIE E. MITCHELL, ... 1897
ELLEN M. BRAMAN, ... 1898
ALFRED A. CARTER, ... 1896

Constables.

A. DAVID COLLINS, ... 1896
FREDERICK E. DEERING, ... 1896
THOMAS E. GLENNAN, ... 1896
CLINTON E. HIBBARD, ... 1896
JOHN E. LINNEHAN, ... 1896
LAWRENCE H. McMANUS, ... 1896
FRANK P. QUACKENBUSH, ... 1896

Trustees Allen Fund.

ISAAC DAMON, ...	1896
DANIEL D. GRIFFIN, ...	1896
LUTHER H. SHERMAN, ...	1896

Fence Viewers.

ALBION F. PARMENTER, ...	1896
ISAAC DAMON, ...	1896
EDWARD CARTER, ...	1896

Field Driver.

IRA D. DICKEY, ...	1896

Sealer of Weights and Measures.

RICHARD T. LOMBARD, ...	1896

Measurers of Wood and Bark.

GEORGE B. HOWE, ...	1896
WILLIAM S. LOVELL, ...	1896
EDWARD CARTER, ...	1896

Surveyor of Lumber.

FRANK HAYNES, ...	1896

Superintendent of North and Centre Cemeteries.

THEO. S. SHERMAN, ...	1896

Superintendent Lakeview Cemetery.

NATHAN S. WALTON, ...	1896

Committee on Finance.

LUTHER H. SHERMAN, ...	1896
RICHARD T. LOMBARD, ...	1896
EDWIN W. MARSTON, ...	1896
THOMAS W. FROST, ...	1896
CHARLES W. DEAN, ...	1896

Committee on Decoration Day.

RICHARD T. LOMBARD, ...	1896
GEORGE E. SHERMAN, ...	1896
DANIEL W. RICKER, ...	1896
CHARLES H. THING, ...	1896
CHARLES H. MAY, ...	1896

Engineers of the Fire Department.

RALPH BENT, Chief, ...	1896
EDWIN W. MARSTON, ...	1896
HENRY B. PHALEN, ...	1896

Inspectors of Cattle and Provisions.

THOMAS W. FROST, ...	1896
THOMAS BRYANT, ...	1896

Superintendent of Streets.

LEONARD A. LOKER, ...	1896

Registrars of Voters.

LUTHER H. SHERMAN, ...	1896
THEO. L. SAWIN, ...	1897
DELOSS W. MITCHELL, ...	1898
RICHARD T. LOMBARD, Town Clerk, *ex-officio*, .	1896

TOWN WARRANT.

To DAVID P. COLLINS *or either of the Constables of the Town of Wayland, in said County,* GREETING :

In the name of the Commonwealth of Massachusetts, you are directed to notify the qualified voters of said Town of Wayland, to meet at the Town Hall, Wayland Centre, Monday, March 23, A. D. 1896, at 8 o'clock A. M., then and there to act on the following articles :

ARTICLE 1.   To choose by ballot a Moderator to preside in said meeting.

ART. 2.   To choose a Town Clerk, Treasurer, Collector of Taxes, Auditor, three Selectmen, three Overseers of the Poor, Treasurer of the Library Funds, and seven Constables, all for one year.   Also one School Committee, one Assessor, one Water Commissioner, two Trustees of the Public Library, all for three years. Also one School Committee for one year, unexpired term of C. H. Boodey resigned.   Also to answer the following question.

Shall licenses for the sale of intoxicating liquors be granted in the town of Wayland for the year ensuing.   For the purposes specified in this Article the poll will be opened immediately after the election of a Moderator, and will remain open continuously till 2 o'clock P. M., when it may be closed unless the meeting shall otherwise determine.   All names must appear upon the official ballot and be voted for in accordance with Chapter 386 of the Acts of the year 1890.

ART. 3.   To choose all other necessary Town Officers, Agents, and Committees, and hear reports of Town Officers, Trustees, Agents and Committees, and act thereon.

Art. 4. To see how much money the town will grant for paying interest and existing liabilities; for roads, bridges and culverts, for sidewalks, for assisting and maintaining the Poor, for schools, school supplies and repairs, for transportation of scholars, for the fire department, for abatement of taxes, for paying Town Officers, for paying military aid, and assisting needy soldiers, sailors and their families, for decorating soldiers' graves, for lighting streets, for repairing and improving town property, for suppressing the illegal sale of intoxicating liquors, for all necessary town use, and order the same to be assessed, or do or act.

Art. 5. To appropriate the license money on dogs, refunded by the County Treasurer, or do or act.

Art. 6. To authorize the Selectmen to consult counsel on important town cases.

Art. 7. To see if the town will authorize its Treasurer with the approval of the Selectmen to borrow money, temporarily, in anticipation of taxes for 1896, and if so, in what manner and how much.

Art. 8. To see if the town will authorize its Tax Collector for 1896 to use all means for collecting taxes which are delegated to Town Treasurers when appointed to collect the taxes of a town.

Art. 9. To see if the town will accept the list of Jurors as revised by the Selectmen.

Art. 10. To see if the town will appropriate the sum of fifty dollars for the purpose of erecting a stone tablet or monument on the Town Hall lot, to designate that in Wayland was established the first free Public Library in Massachusetts, or do or act.

Art. 11. To see if the town will build a school house at Wayland Centre, and appropriate money therefor, or do or act.

Art. 12. To see if the town will authorize its Treasurer to borrow money to build a school house at Wayland Centre and establish a sinking fund, under Chapter 29 of the Public Statutes, to provide for the payment of said loan, or under any act of the General Court, or do or act.

ART. 13. To see if the town will order and direct the sale of the North and Centre High school buildings, Also order and direct the sale of the Centre Primary school building and land, the Rutter school building and land, and the Thomas school building and land. And that the Treasurer of the town be authorized and empowered to sign and execute a deed or deeds of said premises to the purchaser or purchasers for and in behalf of the town, or do or act.

ART. 14. To see if the town will elect a committee to investigate the matter of introducing Water into Wayland Centre for protection against fire and for domestic use, and to ascertain if the present water supply is sufficient, or the water basin needs to be enlarged or improved, and the probable expense of the same and to report to a future Town Meeting, or do or act.

ART. 15. To see if the town will appropriate the sum of fifty dollars to place a marker at the grave of each revolutionary soldier or sailor buried in this town, the expense not to exceed one dollar each; and to elect a committee, or do or act.

ART. 16. To see if the town will instruct its Selectmen to cause the Boston & Maine Railroad Company to remove all the piles in Sudbury river, within the limits of the railroad location, not required to support the railroad bridge, or do or act.

ART. 17. To see if the town will appropriate the money received from Superintendents of Cemeteries for the sale of lots for the purpose of beautifying the cemeteries, or do or act.

ART. 18. To see if the town will authorize the Water Commissioners to replace the two-inch with four-inch pipe leading from the residence of B. S. Hemmenway to Charles H. May on Main street, so that hydrants can be attached for fire purposes, or do or act.

ART. 19. To see if the town will vote to except Chapter 417, Section 269, Public Statutes, relative to electing its Overseers of the Poor, or do or act.

ART. 20. To see if the town will vote to raise the Salaries of the Overseers of the Poor to forty dollars a year, the Clerk to receive ten dollars extra, or do or act.

ART. 21. To see if the town will appropriate the sum of two hundred and seventy-five dollars to paint the buildings at the Town Farm, or do or act.

ART. 22. To see if the town will vote to sell its lot of land adjoining Lake View Cemetery, and appoint a committee to carry said vote into effect, and to execute a deed of said lot to the purchaser for and in behalf of the town, or do or act.

ART. 23. To see what action the town will take relative to paying the tuition of its scholars attending High schools in adjoining towns, or do or act.

ART. 24. To see if the town will vote to add the lot of land recently obtained from E. B. Loker, to the Cochituate Grammar school house lot or do or act.

ART. 25. To see if the town will appropriate a sufficient sum of money to fence the town lot in the rear of the Cochituate Grammar school house, and remove the school out buildings to the western boundary of said lot, or do or act.

ART. 26. To see what action the town will take relative to the claims of Chester B. Williams and Henry B. Phalen for damage.

ART. 27, To see if the town will vote to enlarge the culvert near the residence of C. B. Williams, appropriate money for the same, or do or act.

ART. 28. To see what action the town will take relative to holding its Special Town Meetings in the evening, or do or act.

ART. 29. To see if the town will appropriate the sum of two hundred dollars to gravel the plain road leading from Isaac Damon's to the John Curtain place, or do or act.

ART. 30. To see if the town will appropriate six hundred dollars to fill and grade land in front of the estates of Samuel D. Reeves and Susan A. Pierce.

ART. 31. To instruct the Selectmen to call upon and request the County Commissioners, of Middlesex County, to appoint an early day to report upon the grading of the "Pelham" or Heard's Pond road in this town, upon which a primary hearing was had and a survey made in November, 1891.

ART. 32. To see what action the town will take in reference to the Bill in Equity filed by Samuel D. Reeves, or do or act.

ART. 32. To see if the town will establish a High school, or do or act.

And you are directed to serve this warrant by posting up attested copies thereof at the Town Hall, and at each of Post offices in Wayland Centre and Cochituate Village, seven days, at least, before said March 23, 1896.

Hereof fail not and make return of this warrant, with your doings thereon to the Town Clerk on or before the day appointed for holding said meeting.

Given under our hands this ninth day of March, year of our Lord eighteen hundred and ninety-six.

THOMAS W. FROST,   *Selectmen*
DAVID P. W. LOKER,   *of*
DANIEL D. GRIFFIN,   *Wayland.*

WAYLAND BY-LAWS.

COMMONWEALTH OF MASSACHUSETTS.

MIDDLESEX, ss.

In the Superior Court within and for the County at Middlesex, Anno Domini 1885.

The following By-Laws of the town of Wayland are presented to this Court for approval, to wit:

1.   Notice of every Town Meeting shall be given by posting a copy of the warrant therefor in three or more public places in the town, at least seven days before the time appointed for such meeting.

2.   The Town Clerk shall at the time and place appointed, call the meeting to order and forthwith proceed to read the warrant for the meeting, and the return of the person or persons who served it; he shall then call upon the voters present to bring in their votes for moderator (if one be required at said meeting) and shall preside until a moderator is chosen and assumes the office.

3.   No vote fixing the time for closing a ballot shall be reconsidered after said ballot shall have begun; but an extension of the time may be had by vote without reconsideration.

4.   Every motion or order which is of a complicated nature, or of unusual length shall be reduced to writing, also all other motions at the pleasure of the presiding officer.

5.   The powers and duties of a presiding officer not especially provided for by law, or by these By-Laws, shall be determined by the rules and practice contained in Cushing's Manual so far as they are adapted to the conditions and powers of the town.

6.   The financial year shall begin on the first day of March and end the last day of the February following,

7.   The Annual Town Meeting shall be held on the fourth Monday of March in each year, at such time as the Selectmen may appoint, at the town hall.

8. The Selectmen, Overseers of the Poor, Treasurer, School Committee, Auditor, Water Commissioners, Treasurer of the Water Board, Collector of Taxes, Town Clerk, Treasurer of Library Funds and Treasurer of Allen Fund, shall, and such other town officers, agents or committees of the town as may deem it expedient may, make written annual reports of all matters pertaining to their several departments, relating to the general interest and welfare of the town. All such reports shall be delivered to the Auditor on or before March 7th of each year, and the Selectmen shall deliver to the Auditor on or before March 10 of each year, a copy of the annual Town Warrant. The Auditor shall cause all such reports and the Town Warrant to be printed in pamphlet form and distributed to the voters of the town by leaving a copy thereof at each dwelling house, at least three days before the annual town meeting each year.

9. The Treasurer, Overseers of the Poor, and School Committee, shall report an estimate of the sums of money needed to defray the necessary charges of their several departments, and the Selectmen shall report an estimate of what other sums of money may be needed to defray the necessary town charges and expenditures for the year ensuing.

10. The Selectmen shall hold regular business meetings at least once a month, of which due notice shall be given.

11. All bills against the town shall be made out in detail with the proper date for each item and shall be approved by a majority of the Board contracting said bill and shall be presented to the Board of Selectmen for examination and approval and if found correct, they shall give an order on the Treasurer to pay the same, said order to specify from what appropriation the same is to be drawn.

12. The Selectmen shall notify the Treasurer of the amount of orders drawn at each meeting and the Treasurer shall not be required to pay the same until twenty-four hours after such notice.

13. A list of all taxes shall be committed to the Collector on or before August 1, and the Collector shall pay into the treasury, one-half of said taxes on or before October 1, including the County tax, and the balance of the taxes on or before January 1, and shall settle with the town on or before the first day of the following July. On all taxes remaining unpaid October 1, interest shall be charged at the rate of

six per cent. per annum. In enforcing the payment of taxes, the Collector shall proceed by sale of the property. The Collector shall make weekly payments to the Treasurer, provided the sum in his hands amounts to one hundred dollars or more. The Collector shall have and possess all the authority, powers and privileges delegated to Town Treasurers when they are made Collectors of Taxes.

14. The Collector shall within thirty days after receiving the list of taxes, make out a tax bill to every person, corporation or company of persons named in such tax list, in which bill shall be printed the rate of taxation, the time when all taxes are due and payable, and the time when interest will be charged, and shall deliver, or mail through the Post Office to every person so taxed, his tax bill.

15. All unappropriated money paid into the Treasury shall be carried to an account to be kept by the Treasurer, called the " Contingent Fund," and no money shall be drawn therefrom except by a vote of the town; and all balances of appropriations of the preceding year, remaining unexpended June 1 each year, shall be carried to said account, except the unexpended balances of the poor account, schools, abatement of taxes, and interest which shall remain to the credit of said accounts. All moneys for soldiers' aid shall be drawn from the Contingent Fund, on orders from the Selectmen, as if especially appropriated.

16. The Town Treasurer shall not borrow any money on behalf of the town upon any promissory note or other obligation executed by him, as such Treasurer, unless the same is first countersigned by the Selectmen or by a majority of them.

17. No town officer or board of officers shall contract any debt or obligation on behalf of the town, beyond the appropriation to which said debt or obligation would be chargeable except on the unanimous vote of the Board so contracting said debt and the unanimous approval of the Board of Selectman, and in such case not to exceed the sum of five hundred dollars in any one year; and the Selectman shall in their annual report state what emergency required such action.

18. All Boards of standing town officers shall cause records of their doings and accounts to be kept in suitable books and the persons having charge of the same shall transmit them to their successors in office. Whenever any vote affecting any town officer or officers is

passed, the Clerk shall transmit a copy of the same to such officer (officers), and the said copy shall be kept by said officers and be transmitted to their successors if anything therein contained shall appertain to their duties.

19. The Water Commissioners shall choose a Clerk and Superintendent. The Clerk shall keep a record of said Board under its direction and shall keep a set of books in which shall be entered — all receipts and expenditures of the Water Works, and shall collect all bills for the use of water or ortherwise pertaining to said Water Works, and shall on the last day of each month, pay the same over to the Town Treasurer. The Clerk shall give bond with sufficient sureties in not less than two thousand dollars, for the faithful performance of his duties, said bond to be filed with and kept by the Selectmen. The Superintendent under the direction of the Water Commissioners shall have the general superintendence of the out door work connected with the Water Works.

20. The Treasurer of the Water Works' Sinking Fund shall give a sufficient bond with sureties for the fathful performance of his duties; said bond to be filed with and kept by the Selectmen.

21. The Water Commissioners shall have authority to draw orders on the Town Treasurer for such sums of money as may be required for the proper maintenance of the Water Works; and said orders to be paid by the Treasurer from money received from water rates.

22. At the Annual Town Meeting the town shall choose, by ballot, the Treasurer of the Library Funds.

23. The Auditor and any voter shall, at all reasonable times, have access to the books of the town, and have the right to examine them and take copies thereof.

24. No person shall pasture or tether any animal upon any street in the town, except within the limits of such streets adjoining his own premises, without the consent of the owner or occupant of the land adjoining the street where pasturage is wanted; in either case the animal must be in charge of a keeper.

25. Whoever wilfully, maliciously, or wantonly, without cause, destroys, defaces, mars or injures any school-house or other public building, or any out building, shed, fence, wall, furniture, apparatus

or other property belonging to or connected with such school-houses or other public building, shall be punished by a fine not less than five dollars, nor exceeding fifty dollars. No occupant of any house where there is or has been recently small pox, scarlet fever, diphtheria or other infectious or contagious diseases shall be permitted to attend any public school in the town, until a certificate of a regular physician that there is no longer danger of infection is obtained and presented to the teacher. The School Committee shall post or cause to be posted a copy of this section in every school room in the town.

26. No building shall be moved over any public way without a permit from the Selectmen, and the Selectmen shall not grant such permit, when such removal will cause destruction or serious injury to shade trees standing in said way, or owned by any person and projecting over said way, unless the consent of the person on whose premises such trees may stand shall first be obtained. And any person moving any building through any public way (either with or without a permit) shall, with the owner of said building, be jointly and severally liable to the town for all damages, costs and expenses which the town may be compelled to pay in consequence of such removal or in consequence of any obstruction, incumbrance or injury occasioned thereby.

27. No person shall place or cause to be placed in any public way or square, without the written consent of the Selectmen, any dirt, wood, timber or other material to obstruct or mar the appearance of said way or square.

28. No person shall behave himself or herself in a rude or disorderly manner, or use any indecent, profane or insulting language in any public place in the town or near any dwelling house or other building therein, or be and remain upon any sidewalk, doorstep or other projection from any house or building, so as to annoy or disturb any person or obstruct any passage to the same. No person shall throw any stones, snowballs, base balls or other missiles, or coast or course upon any sled, or play at base ball or foot ball in any public way, or obstruct in any manner the travel upon said way, nor make any alarming noise or outcries to the disturbance of persons in the town.

29. No person shall tie or fasten any horse, cattle or team to any of the trees in public ways of the town, nor drive into the same any nails, spikes, hooks or clasps, nor affix any boards thereto.

30. No person shall post, affix, or in any way attach any poster, handbill notice, advertisement, or placard, or paint, draw or stamp any letter, figure, advertisement or mark upon or into or otherwise deface any wall, fence, post, tree, building or structure not his own, within the town, without the permission of the owner of said wall, fence, post, tree, building or structure.

31. Every violation of the foregoing By-laws, not otherwise provided for shall be punishable by a fine of not less than two dollars, nor more than twenty dollars, and all penalties recovered from such violation shall be paid into the Treasury of the town, to inure to such use as the town shall from time to time direct.

Which said By-laws being seen and understood by the Court, are on this fourth day of February, in the year of our Lord one thousand eight hundred and eighty-six approved.

In testimony with the foregoing is a true copy of the record, I hereto {SEAL.} set my hand and affix the seal of said Superior Court, this sixth day of February, in the year of our Lord one thousand eight hundred and eighty-six.

WILLIAM C. DILLINGHAM,

2d Assist. Clerk.

ADDITIONAL BY–LAWS.

Adopted by the town June 24, 1893, and approved by the Probate Court, July 1893.

1. The town of Wayland hereby avails itself of the several provisions of the Statutes of this Commonwealth, now in force, relating to habitual truants and absentees from school and in pursuance of authority conferred thereby adopts the following By-Laws.

2. All children between the ages of seven and fifteen years, residing in this town, and who may be found wandering about in the streets or public places of said town, having no lawful occupation or business, not attending school, and growing up in ignorance shall be committed to such truant school as shall be designated by the School Committee for confinement, instruction and discipline.

3. Two or more truant officers shall be appointed annually, whose duty it shall be to inquire into all the violations of the truant laws, and of the laws relating to compulsory education, and to do all the acts required of them by the Laws of the Commonwealth.

4. It shall be the duty of every truant officer, previous to making any complaint under these laws, to notify the truant or absentee from school, also his parent or guardian of the offence committed, and of the penalty therefor, and if the truant officer can obtain satisfactory pledges for the restraint and reformation of the child, he may at his discretion forbear to prosecute, so long as such pledges are faithfully kept.

5. It shall be the duty of the School Committee, the teachers of the public schools and the citizens generally to aid the truant officers as far as possible in the discharge of their duties.

6. It shall be the duty of the truant officers to keep a full record of all their official acts, and make an annual report thereof to the School Committee, who shall publish the same with their own report.

7. Nothing in these By-laws shall be so construed as to alter or impair the obligation and duty of teachers to enforce punctuality and regularity of attendance, and to preserve good order and discipline.

A true copy of the By-laws of the town of Wayland.

Attest :

RICHARD T. LOMBARD,

March 1, 1896.   *Town Clerk.*

LIST OF JURORS.

For the Town of Wayland, 1896, as prepared by the Selectmen:

Russell E. Frye,
William T. Dudley,
John J. McCann,
Albion F. Parmenter,
Granville L. Loker,
Sidney Loker,
Theo. L. Sawin,
Peter S. Zimmerman,
John E. Linnehan,
Ernest E. Butler,
E. W. Marston,
Andrew A. Norris,
Isaac C. Damon,
Adoniram J. Puffer,

Frank Lupien,
Luther H. Sherman,
Horatio G. Hammond,
Harry H. Rutter,
Isaac S. Whittemore,
Roscoe C. Dean,
Colin C. Ward,
Allan B. Sherman,
Edward B. Smith,
Elijah H. Atwood,
George E. Sherman,
Clinton E. Hibbard,
Theo. S. Sherman,
Edgar B. Loker.

THOMAS W. FROST, ⎫ *Selectmen*
DAVID P. W. LOKER, ⎬ *of*
DANIEL D. GRIFFIN, ⎭ *Wayland.*

REPORT OF SELECTMEN.

WAYLAND, March 2, 1896.

The Selectmen hereby submit their annual report as required by the By-laws of the town.

We have appointed the following officers as required by Statute:

Engineers of Fire Department.

RALPH BENT.   EDWIN W. MARSTON.   HENRY B. PHALEN.

Undertakers.

ANDREW S. MORSE.   DAVID P. W. LOKER.

Inspectors of Cattle and Provisions

THOMAS W. FROST.   THOMAS BRYANT.

Registrar of Voters.
DELOSS W. MITCHELL.

Superintendent of Streets.
LEONARD A. LOKER.

Auctioneer.
GEORGE E. SHERMAN.

ELECTION OFFICERS.

Precinct 1.

Warden.—ALBION F. PARMENTER.
Clerk.—JAMES A. DRAPER.
Inspectors.—M. W. HYNES.
EDWARD CARTER.
PETER S. ZIMMERMAN.
WILLIAM H. CAMPBELL.

Precinct 2.

Warden.—H. B. PHALEN.
Clerk.—ALFRED H. BRYANT.
Inspectors.—E. B. SMITH.
R. E. FRYE.
RALPH BENT.
ED. A. PARTRIDGE.

We have perambulated the town lines between Wayland and Lincoln, and between Natick and Wayland, and between Sudbury and Wayland, and reset the bounds where needed, and found the others in condition.

In accordance with a vote of the town, the schoolhouse at Cochituate has been repainted.

Upon the request of the Public Record Commissioner we have had the old and important records of the town rebound, and the records of births, deaths and marriages from 1780 to 1842 are being copied and arranged.

The appropriation for lights, at Wayland Centre, being exhausted, we have had the lanterns stored in the basement of the Town Hall.

In accordance with votes of the town, we have purchased gravel land of Mrs. Annie Alward, and also exchanged land for gravel with Mr. Albert L. Adams, which will supply all the gravel needed for a number of years.

We have also made efforts to have a State Road built in Wayland, and have reason to expect that the road from Wayland Centre to the Weston line will be taken by the State for this purpose, as surveys have been made of the same and filed with the State Commissioners of Highways.

We have been compelled to overdraw the accounts for Incidentals to the amount of $534.92, and this was made necessary by drawing upon this account for the expense of surveying the Boston Road and by drawing on it for the relief of needy soldiers.

We would recommend that the Selectmen have authority to draw on the Contingent Fund for relief of soldiers, as they do for State Aid.

We deem it unnecessary to make any estimates for the various needs of the town for the ensuing year as the Finance Committee is to consider all matters relating to the appropriation of money.

Respectfully submitted,

THOMAS W. FROST, } *Selectmen*
DAVID P. W. LOKER, } *of*
DANIEL D. GRIFFIN, } *Wayland.*

REPORT OF THE OVERSEERS OF THE POOR.

To the Selectmen of Wayland.

The annual report of the Overseers of the Poor for the year ending March 1, 1896, is herewith presented. Mr. H. P. Parker, Superintendent of the Almshouse, will sever his relation with the institution on April 1, 1896, after having completed six years of most efficient service.

The following persons have been aided during the year, as follows:

OUT-DOOR POOR.
(PARTIAL SUPPORT.)

Families aided, ...	5	
Persons aided, ...	12	
	—	17

IN-DOOR POOR.
(FULL SUPPORT.)

Almshouse, ...	7	
State Lunatic Hospital, ...	3	
	—	—
Total number of persons aided, . . .		27

FINANCIAL STATEMENT.

Showing actual Receipts and Expenditures for the year.

Appropriation, ...	$2,500 00	
Unexpended balance March 1, 1895, . .	168 51	
Additional appropriation November, 1895, .	600 00	
		$3,268 51

REIMBURSEMENTS.

From Town of Lexington, ...	$52 00	
" North Brookfield, . .	315 20	
" Natick, ...	130 39	
" Southboro, ...	52 50	
		$550 09

ALMSHOUSE RECEIPTS.

Sale of Milk,	$591 08	
" Eggs,	51 19	
" Poultry,	46 35	
" Potatoes,	7 50	
·· Calves,	12 50	
·· Horse,	50 00	
" 5 Cows,	135 00	
Labor,	4 50	
Pasturing,	6 00	$904 12
Total receipts,		$4,722 72

EXPENDITURES.

OUT-DOOR POOR.

Having a settlement in Wayland, residing elsewhere.

A. Normandin,	$41 99	
E. Roberts and others, March 1, 1895,	124 56	
M. L. Hardy,	112 00	
W. H. Mullen,	9 35	
Donavan,	48 55	
Emily Sumpter,	73 25	$409 70

Having a settlement in Wayland and residing there.

J. Chinett,	$27 28	
Anna Burrill,	143 50	
Etta Smith,	10 00	
G. C. Chalmers,	36 00	
Ann Painter,	52 00	
One person,	1 40	
One person,	7 05	$277 23

Having a settlement in other cities and towns.

H. W. Dean, Natick,	$163 97	
J. F. Hawkins, Southboro,	165 20	
Carried forward,		$329 17

Brought forward,	$329 17	
H. Cormier, North Brookfield, . . .	211 88	
E. Hallowell, Lexington, ...	52 00	
		$593 05
Total Out-Door Poor, . . .		$1,279 98

IN-DOOR POOR.
In Insane Hospital.

J. A. Wing, Worcester, ...	$212 17	
Ellen Burke, Taunton, ...	212 81	
Carrie Davis, Westboro, ...	212 19	
Total in Insane Hospital, . . .		$637 17

ALMSHOUSE.

Groceries, ...	$329 18
Provisions, ...	371 97
Grain, ...	475 64
Medical attendance and medicine, . .	16 05
Clothing, ...	15 00
Shoes, ...	3 30
Hay and grass, ...	23 57
Fuel, ...	31 49
Labor, ...	60 75
Bedding, ...	14 25
Hardware, ...	9 30
Tools, ...	48 37
Cows and calf, ...	157 00
Repairs on tools, ...	14 98
Burial of inmate, ...	18 00
Repairs to wagons, etc., 1895, . . .	41 98
Blacksmithing, ...	25 08
Fertilizer, ...	42 50
Seeds, ...	30 60
Cash, C. W. Moore, ...	5 00
Warden's salary, ...	320 83
Miscellaneous, ...	4 90
Warden's salary March 1, 1895, . .	389 37

Total Almshouse expenditures, . .	$2,449 11

Total expenditures In-Door Poor, . . . $3,086 28
Net cost Almshouse, ... $2,017 76
    420 Tramps were lodged and furnished with 656 meals.

MISCELLANEOUS.

Medical service, March 1, 1895, . . . $62 00
Travelling expenses and settlement of cases, . 103 72
Stationery, ... 4 50
                                    ——— $170 22

RECAPITULATION.

Total receipts, ... $4,722 72
Expenditures Out-Door Poor, . . . $1,279 98
Expenditures In-Door Poor, ... 3,086 28
Miscellaneous, ... 170 22
Total expenditures, ... 4,536 48
Expenditure acct. for year ending March 1, '95, 1,225 16

Net cost, ... $3,311 32
Reimbursements due, ... 149 40

    Claims due March 1, 1895 and paid during current year.
Warden's salary, ... $389 37
E. A. Atwood, ... 235 94
C. H. Boody, ... 62 00
E. P. Butler, ... 10 00
H. H. Rutter, ... 7 57
Westboro Insane Asylum, ... 41 72
Taunton Insane Asylum, ... 42 71
Worcester Insane Asylum, ... 42 71
A. D. Loker, ... 10 02
North Brookfield, ... 124 56
Samuel Russell, ... 55 81
City of Boston, ... 60 00
C. L. Keefe, ... 95 00
Repairs to wagons, etc., ... 45 00
Hudson, ... 42 75
                                    ———$1,225 16

REIMBURSEMENTS DUE.

From Town of Natick, ...	$33 58	
" " Southboro, ...	19 10	
For milk from Almshouse, ...	96 72	
		$149 40

INMATES OF ALMSHOUSE DURING THE YEAR.

Sarah Puffer, March 1, 1895.

James Burke, March 1, 1895.

Benjamin Nealey, March 1, 1895.

George F. Bond, March 1, 1895, died February 5, 1896.

James Foley, admitted November 15, 1895.

Dennis Mullen, admitted November 27, 1895.

C. W. Moore, admitted March 1, 1895, discharged April 1, 1895.

INVENTORY OF PROPERTY AT ALMSHOUSE.

Farm implements, ...	$292 00	
9 cows, ...	365 00	
1 bull, ...	15 00	
60 fowls, ...	42 00	
Hay, ...	165 00	
Barley stores, ...	24 00	
40 bushels potatoes, ...	16 00	
Coal and wood, ...	38 00	
Furniture and utensils, ...	290 00	
Provisions, ...	21 46	
Manure, ...	90 00	
		$1,358 46

An appropriation of three thousand dollars is asked for.

Respectfully submitted,

DAVID P. W. LOKER,
GEORGE B. HOWE, } *Overseers*
WILLARD B. WARD, } *of the Poor.*

REPORT OF THE LIBRARY TRUSTEES FOR THE YEAR ENDING FEBRUARY 28, 1896.

The annual inspection of the library was made in January and the books were found to be in good condition generally. Many books, however, are beginning to show their age, and the results of repeated handling. The library having been in operation for nearly forty-five years, many of the older sets are in sad need of being replaced.

The idea is becoming more prevalent that the Public Library is as much a part of the great scheme of free education as the public school only in a different way. More interest in the Public Library idea is being manifested day by day, and with this increased interest there comes a desire to know who was the originator of the idea, and where the first library was established.

It has become a well known fact that Rev. Francis Wayland, D.D., was the first one to put this idea into actual operation in the state of Massachusetts, and the town of Wayland was the birthplace of the first free Public Library. Now it devolves upon the town of Wayland to see that its Library, which is the oldest Free Public Library in Massachusetts, if not in the world, keeps up the standard which belongs to such an institution. In order to do this it is necessary that we should appropriate as much as we possibly can for its maintenance.

It has been customary to have the Library open but one afternoon and evening in the week. We would recommend and ask that a sufficient appropriation be made to enable the Trustees to keep it open at least two afternoons and evenings in each week, thus enabling the scholars in our Public schools to more fully avail themselves of books of reference contained therein; also to allow the townspeople more ready access to the great fund of information which is rightfully theirs, and give the general public greater opportunity to visit it.

The special appropriation for cataloguing was three hundred and seventy-five dollars. After going into the matter carefully the Trustees decided that the sum would be entirely inadequate to prepare and print a finding catalogue as it was necessary that all the books in the Library should be included in such a catalogue. After a thorough investigation it was unanimously voted to adopt what is called the "Card Catalog." We were fortunate in securing the services of Rev. Edgar J. Banks a citizen of the town, who from experience and education was particularly fitted for the work. Under the direction of the Trustees Miss Emily A. Heard was associated with him, and the catalogue, with a duplicate at Cochituate, was completed to the entire satifaction of the Board and with credit to those who prepared it. While it is not expected that perfection has been attained it is so nearly correct that with attention and use it can be so made. It cannot be expected that a change so radical can be made without criticism or that all will be suited yet we believe that in time the wisdom of the change will be fully vindicated. The system is in use in all the leading Libraries throughout the country.

In May the Board was notified that Mr. Henry D. Parmenter, for many years deeply interested in the welfare of the Library and a member of the Board of Trustees had resigned as a member, and at a joint meeting of the Selectmen and Trustees Mr. Alfred A. Carter was elected to fill the vacancy.

Statistical information will be found in the Librarian's Report.

ELLEN M. BRAMAN,
EMILY A. HEARD,
ALFRED A. CARTER,
L. E. MITCHELL,
R. T. LOMBARD,
JOHN CONNELLY.

} *Trustees.*

LIBRARIANS' REPORT.

To the Library Trustees.

Statistical information for the years 1895-6, is submitted as follows:

ACCESSIONS.

	Books
By purchase,	38
By gift,	47
Bound and transferred from the pamphlet department,	25
Total,	110
Whole number of volumes in the Library,	12,314
Pamphlets presented,	203

CIRCULATION.

In Cochituate village,	1,568
In Wayland Centre,	4,138
Total,	5,706

DONORS OF BOOKS AND PAMPHLETS.

	Books.	Pamphlets.
Baldwin, William H,	1	1
Bradley, Rev. C. D.,		1
Brooks, Mr. George M.,	1	
Bush, Mrs.,		3
Davis, Dr. C. E.,	1	
Dudley, Miss Anna,		Christian Registers
Dudley, Mrs. Wm. T.,		12
Earle, Mrs. A. M.,	1	
Fowler, Mrs. F. H.,	1	
Heard, Miss Mary,	2	
Heard, Mrs. S. E.,		20
Leach, Mrs. George,	2	
Loring, Miss A. P.,	1	
Moore, Mr. H. O.,	1	

Oviatt, Dr. George, E. 1
Parsons, Dr. T. W., estate of, ... 12   91
Reeves, Mrs. Jacob, ... 3   21
Rice, Mrs. Charles, ... 1   9
State Government, ... 10   6
Thomas, Mrs. James, ... 1   18
U. S. Government, ... 8   20
Zebaldos, Don E. S., ... 1

CLASSES OF READING.

Art,	.04	Juveniles,	.11
Biography,	.08	Poetry,	.07
Essays,	.09	Religion,	.04
Fiction,	.38	Science,	.04
History,	.08	Travels,	.07

Library Reports have been sent as follows: Brookline, Brooklyn, Boston Public, Bronson, Cleveland, Fall River, Harvard College, Hopedale, Lawrence, Mount Holyoke, Newton, Salem, State Library, Syracuse, Taunton, also from Trustees of Public Reservation, Indian Rights Association, University of Pennsylvania and Harvard University catalogue.

The Reading Room has received regularly Harper's Monthly, Century Magazine, Christian Register, The Land of Sunshine, Traveler's Record, Cochituate Enterprise.

Received from fines, ... $7 26
    "   cards, ... 1 88
    "   catalogues, etc., . . . 2 35
Paid to Treasurer, ... $11 49
Received for incidental expenses, . . . 12 20
Paid out, ...   12 20

S. E. HEARD,

February 28, 1896.   *Librarian.*

HENRY D. PARMENTER, TREASURER, IN ACCOUNT WITH LIBRARY FUNDS.

Dr.

1895.

March	30.	To Town of Wayland, unexpended appropriation for 1894, ...		$3 55
	30.	Interest on Library Funds to Jan. 1, 1895,		129 50
	30.	Town of Wayland appropriation for 1895,		300 00
1896.				
Jan.	1.	Interest on Library Funds to Jan. 1, 1896,		66 00
Feb.	28.	Wayland Library fines collected, . .		11 49
	28.	Town of Wayland, dog licenses, . .		62 87
		Cochituate Branch, fines, .	3 97	
		cards sold, . .	2 17	
		catalogues (2) .	50	
				6 64

$580 05

Cr.

1895.

April	1.	By S. E. Heard, salary 3 mos. to date, .	$50 00
	1.	J. D. F. Brooks, bill for binding, . .	4 05
	10.	N. R. Gerald, salary to April 1, 1896 .	40 00
June	8.	S. E. Heard, incidental expenses, . .	12 00
	27.	American Express, carting books between Wayland and Cochituate to July 1, '95,	10 00
	28.	E. A. Heard, wood bill, . . .	25 50
	28.	S. E. Heard, salary to July 1, . .	50 00
July	20.	E. M. Braman, Book Club magazines, .	7 00
Aug.	5.	A. Storrs & Bement Co., 50 m. blanks, . .	42 00
	12.	Frank Haynes, carpenter bill, . .	25 69
Sept.	2.	J. D. F. Brooks, bill, ...	4 85
	26.	Wayland Book Club, magazines, etc., .	13 00
	28.	DeWolfe Fiske & Co., ...	31 40

Carried forward, $315 49

		Brought forward,					$315	49
	28.	American Express,	.	.	.	.	9	83
	28.	S. E. Heard, salary to Oct. 1, 1895,	.				50	00
Oct.	18.	Patrick Jennings,	.	.	.	.	3	25
Dec.	7.	DeWolfe, Fiske & Co.,		.	.	.	5	34
	7.	J. F. Burke,	.	.	.	.	3	50
	27.	S. E. Heard, salary to January 1, 1896,					50	00
	27.	J. D. F. Brooks, bill,	.	.	·	.	5	15
	20.	American Express Co., bill to Jan. 1, '96					9	08
Feb.	28.	Balance,	.	.	.	.	.	128	51

$580 05

ACCESSIONS IN 1895.

COLLECTOR'S REPORT.

TAXES OF 1891.

Balance due March 1, 1895	$459 20
Interest paid on tax of 1891	$462 25

TAXES OF 1892.

Balance due March 1, 1895	$871 70
Paid Treasurer	341 10
	$530 60
Interest paid on tax of 1892	$404 64

TAXES OF 1893.

Balance due March 1, 1895	$5,029 12
Paid Treasurer	4,098 23
	$930 89
Interest paid on tax of 1893	$499 56

TAXES OF 1894.

Balance due March 1, 1895	$8,723 32
Paid Treasurer	3,087 88
	$5,635 44
Interest paid on tax of 1894	$150 00

Taxes of 1895.

Town tax	$20,637 65
County tax	1,491 95
State tax	945 00
Overlayings tax	1 32
Marsh Land tax	330 51
Overlayings tax	1 51
Additional Assessments	26 00
	$23,433 94
Paid Treasurer	13,924 98
	$9,508 96

WILLARD B. WARD,

Collector.

ASSESSORS' REPORT.

FOR YEAR ENDING FEB. 29, 1896.

Value of real estate, May 1, 1895 . . .	$1,214,990 00
" personal estate, May 1, 1895 . . .	299,735 00
Total valuation, May 1, 1895	$1,514,725 00
" " May 1, 1894	1,496,120 00
Increase	$18,605 00
Taxes assessed for town purposes . . .	$20,637 65
Overlayings	1 32
Additional assessments . . - . .	8 00
State tax	945 00
County tax	1,491 95
Total amount assessed	$23,083 92

Number of polls, May 1, 1895 . . . 557	
Additional polls assessed, 1895 . . . 4	
Number polls assessed May 1, 1894 . . 559	
Total increase of polls 2	

Number persons assessed 854	
" residents assessed on property . . 401	
" non-residents assessed on property . 137	

Total value of land	$482,910 00
" " buildings	732,080 00
" " church property . . . ·	30,240 00
" " town property	105,793 00

Number horses assessed 384	
" cows " 730	
" sheep " 16	

Number swine   "   216
   "   fowls   "   .   .   . 1630
   "   neat cattle other than cows .   . 89
   "   dwelling houses   .   .   . 423
   "   acres of land .   .   .   . $9,144\frac{5}{10}$

Rate of taxation, 1895, per thousand . . .	$14 50
" " 1894 " " . . .	14 00
Abatements of taxes of 1892	$126 84
" " 1893	52 89
" " 1895	7 14
Total abatements	$186 87
Amount of special assessment under Chapter 426 of the Acts of 1894	$332 02
Overlayings	1 51
Total assessment under said act . . .	$333 52

Respectfully submitted,

RICHARD T. LOMBARD,   *Assessors*
EDWARD CARTER,   *of*
HORATIO G. HAMMOND,   *Wayland.*

REPORT OF THE SUPERINTENDENT OF THE WAYLAND WATER WORKS.

GENTLEMEN :

The Water Commissioners of the present year decided that it was best for the interest of the town and also for the water takers to finish laying a four-inch pipe on King street. I have laid the same (about 400 feet), I have also repaired a number of hydrants which are now as good as new. Another source of expense are the small service pipes which are filling up, and of course must be cleaned out. I have cleaned out about twelve hundred feet of same this year. There has been plenty of water in the pond this year and I have had very few complaints of quality of same.

THE MAINTENANCE ACCOUNT IS

1895.

Aug.	21.	To cash P. D. Woods & Co., . .	$172 67
Sept.	11.	Perrin Seamans & Co., . .	53 78
Nov.	14.	Walworth Manufacturing Co., .	87 20
1896.			
Jan.	15.	H. G. Dudley as superintendent,	508 92
			$822 57

The water at present is in use by the following:

Families, ...	229
Manufactories, ...	10
Public buildings, ...	4
Miscellaneous, ...	11
Horses, ...	74
Cows, ...	72

Respectfully submitted,

H. G. DUDLEY,

Superintendent.

Wayland, February 29, 1896.

WAYLAND WATER COMMISSIONERS' REPORT.

WAYLAND WATER COMMISSIONERS IN ACCOUNT WITH HENRY F. LEE, TOWN TREASURER.

CR.

1895.				
		Appropriation for hydrants,	$384	00
April	13.	By water rates paid to Town Treasurer,	264	17
	29.	" " "	119	50
1896.				
Jan.	14.		1,149	32
Feb.	28.		466	00
	29.		168	25
	29.	" '	51	50
		Balance overdrawn	53	50
			$2,656	24

DR.

1895.				
April	29.	To order No. 1,. on Town Treasurer for balance of water funds 1894, invested in Watertown Savings Bank for a water works sinking fund	$383	67
Aug.	21.	To order No. 2, on Town Treasurer, to R. D. Woods & Co.	172	67
Sept..	11.	To order No. 3, on Town Treasurer, to Perrin Seaman & Co.	53	78
Nov.	14.	To order No. 4, on Town Treasurer, to Walworth Manufacturing Co. . .	87	20
1896.				
Jan.	15.	To order No. 5, on Town Treasurer, to H. G. Dudley, Superintendent . . .	508	92
		Carried forward,	$1,206	24

Brought forward, $1,206 24

     To interest on water bonds transferred to
       interest account 1,450 00

                                      $2,656 24

CHAS. H. BOODEY,   *Wayland*
WM. H. BENT,   *Water*
H. G. DUDLEY,   *Commissioners.*

Wayland, February 29, 1896.

REPORT OF COMMISSIONERS OF WAYLAND WATER WORKS SINKING FUND.

1896.

Feb.   29.   Amount deposited in Natick Five Cents
                    Savings Bank, Natick, Mass.,   .   . $3,691 74
                Interest on above deposit to Nov. 1, 1895,   1,819 18
                Amount deposited in Suffolk Savings Bank,
                    Boston, Mass., ... 1,000 00
                Interest on above deposit to Oct. 1, 1895,   329 98
                Amount deposited in Home Savings Bank,
                    Boston, Mass., ... 2,292 38
                Interest on above deposit to Oct. 1, 1895,   493 12
                Amount deposited in Framingham Savings
                    Bank, Framingham, Mass., .   .   . 1,205 21
                Interest on above deposit to Nov. 1, 1895,   179 08
                Amount deposited in North End Savings
                    Bank, Boston, Mass., ... 1,459 40
                Interest on above deposit to Jan. 1, 1896,   140 48
                Amount deposited in Watertown Savings
                    Bank, Watertown, Mass.,   .   .   . 994 53
                Interest on above deposit to Oct. 1, 1895,   16 04

                                                    $13,621 14

CHAS. H. BOODEY, ⎱   *Commissioners of*
WM. H. BENT,   ⎰   *Wayland Water Works*
H. G. DUDLEY,   ⎰   *Sinking Fund.*

Wayland, February 29, 1896.

REPORT OF FIRE ENGINEERS.

The Fire Department responded to the following alarms during the year:

April 16, 1895. 2.30 P. M., out building at C. A. Roak's.

June 8, 1895. 8.45 P. M., out building at Ambrose Bryant's.

October 16, 1895. 10.45 P. M., dwelling of B. F. Adams.

December 13 1895. 7.40 P. M., dwelling of O. W. Harris.

December 22, 1895. 1.07 P. M., assistance to a man who had fallen through the ice at Lake Cochituate.

February 17, 1896. 11.30 P. M., ice house of W. C. Heald.

The department is in excellent condition in every respect.

RALPH BENT, *Chief,*
E. W. MARSTON, } *Engineers.*
H. B. PHALEN, *Clerk,*

COCHITUATE, March 9, 1896.

REPOPT OF SUPERINTENDENT OF HIGHWAYS.

The total amount appropriated for the past year was two thousand three hundred dollars ($2,300.00). Appropriated at the annual March meeting, two thousand dollars (2,000.00). At a special meeting in November, three hundred dollars ($300.00). Itemized bills of all money expended are on file at the Selectmen's office. Overdrawn, ninety-four dollars and forty-nine cents ($94.49).

MARCH.

	DAYS.	HOURS.	
L. A. Loker	10	6 1-2	$21 42
L. A. Loker, horse . . .	7	5 1-2	12 35
M. W. Hynes, . . .	5	3	10 67
M. W. Hynes, horse . .	7	1	12 42
T. L. Hynes	3	2 1-2	6 56
L. H. McMann, sharpening picks			85
Thomas Dowey . . .	1	7 1-2	3 68
Samuel Davidson . . .	1	2	2 45
J. F. Malloy		7	1 56
Wilson Porter . . .	2		4 00
Thomas Lane . . .	3	6	7 34
Paul Loker	3		6 00
G. W. Philbrick . . .	3	8	7 78
J. McDonald . . .	2	5	5 10
J. McDonald, horse . .	2	5	4 45
G. L. Baker		4	88
A. B. Sherman . . .	10	3	20 60
A. B. Sherman, horse . .	3	5	5 80
			$133 71

APRIL.

	DAYS.	HOURS.		
L. A. Loker	12	3	$24	66
L. A. Loker, horse . .	12	3	21	56
Wilson Porter . . .	9		18	00
Wilson Porter, horse . .	18		31	50
W. C. Neal	9		18	00
W. C. Neal, horse . . .	18		31	50
C. A. Roak	2	8	5	78
C. A. Roak, horse . . .	2	8	5	05
E. A. Carter	6	7	13	55
James Murphy . . .	6	7 1-2	13	65
John McLlory . . .	6	8	13	78
B. S. Hemenway . . .	1	4	2	89
M. Guilford		3 1-2	1	00
M. W. Hynes . . .	3		6	00
M. W. Hynes, horse . .	4	7	8	35
T. L. Hynes	2	3	4	68
T. L. Hynes, horse . .	2	3	4	08
T. F. Maynard . . .	2	1-2	4	11
Thomas Dowey . . .	2	4	4	89
George Tyler & Co., road scraper, knives			8	90
Robinson & Jones cement .			1	00
W. D. Parlin, grub hoe, handle and hoe			1	11
John Hurley	6	8	13	76

$257 80

MAY.

	DAYS.	HOURS.		
L. A. Loker	8	4	$16	80
L. A. Loker, horse . .	8	3	14	57
Wilson Porter . . .	7	1	14	22
Wilson Porter, horse . .	14	2	24	89
W. C. Neal	7	1	14	22

Carried forward, $84 70

Brought forward,			$84	70
W. C. Neal, horse .	.	14	2	24 89
E. A. Carter .	.	6		12 00
John Hurley .	.	6		12 00
M. W. Hynes	.	7	2 1-2	14 56
M. W. Hynes, horse	.	14	5	25 44
T. L. Hynes .	.	6	2 1-2	12 53
T. L. Hynes, horse	.	4	7	8 34
T. F. Maynard	.	6	5 1-2	13 23
Thomas Dowey	.	4	1	8 22
P. S. Zimmerman	.	8	2	16 45
L. A. Loker	.	7	4 1-2	15 00
L. A. Loker, horse .	.	6	7	11 85
J. J. Erwin	.	7	4	14 80
J. J. Erwin, horse .	.	3	1	5 45
M. W. Hynes .	.	3	4	6 89
M. W. Hynes, horse	.	3	4	6 02
Thomas L. Hynes	.	3	4	6 89
T. F. Maynard	.	1	6 1-2	3 45
Thomas Dowey	.	1	4	2 89

$305 60

JUNE.

	DAYS.	HOURS.	
L. A. Loker .	7	1	$14 22
L. A. Loker, horse .	3	5	6 22
W. D. Pailin, 100 lbs. nails			1 75
M. W. Hynes .	7	1	14 22
M. W. Hynes, horse	14	2	24 88
T. L. Hynes .	7	1	14 22
T. L. Hynes, horse .	7	1	12 44
M. Guilford .	4	1	8 22
P. S. Zimmerman	7	1	14 22
Edward Eagan	3		6 00
Thomas Dowey .	7	1	14 22

Carried forward, $134 61

Brought forward,			$134	61
T. F. Maynard	7	1	14	22
T. F. Maynard, horse	14	2	24	88
Weston, Rollins	3		6	00
L. A. Loker	12	6 1-2	25	45
L. A. Loker, horse	5	1 1-2	9	05
Wilson Porter	5		10	00
Wilson Porter, horses	5		17	50
T. B. Hawes	11	5	23	11
John McLlory	9	3 1-2	18	78
E. A. Carter	2	5	5	11
Howe's Express Company, 1 bbl. tar				50
Natick Gas Company, 1 bbl. tar			4	00
Union Lumber Company			97	84
M. W. Hynes	8	4 1-2	17	00
M. W. Hynes, horses	8	4 1-2	29	72
T. L. Hynes	7	8 1-2	15	90
T. L. Hynes, horse	8	4 1-2	14	86
T. F. Maynard	8	4 1-2	17	00
T. F. Maynard horses	8	4 1-2	29	72
James Eagon	9	3 1-2	18	79
James Eagon, horse	9	3 1-2	32	82
Edward Eadon	4		8	00
T. J. Dowey	8	4 1-2	17	00
Weston Rollins	8	3 1-2	16	79
P. S. Zimmerman	7	3 1-2	14	79
T. W. Frost, guide boards			6	50
			$625	94

JULY.

	DAYS.	HOURS.		
L. A. Loker	13	5	$27	11
L. A. Loker, horse	11	7	20	60
E. A. Carter	4		8	00
M. W. Hynes, 57 posts at 15 cents			8	55
W. D. Pailin, drain pipe			21	31
			$85	57

AUGUST.

	DAYS.	HOURS.	
L. A. Loker	16	2 1-2	$32 56
L. A. Loker, horse . . .	15	8 1-2	27 90
Wilson Porter . . .	13		26 00
Wilson Porter, horses . .	13		45 50
M. Hurley	12	7	25 55
J. B. McLlory . . .	9	3	18 66
J. R. Hawkins . . .	12	-2	24 44
M. W. Hynes	8	5	17 02
M. W. Hynes, horses . .	7	1-2	24 66
T. L. Hynes	6	7	13 56
T. L. Hynes, horse . . .	6	3	11 08
T. F. Maynard . . .	5	4	10 89
T. F. Maynard, horse . .	2	6 1-2	9 55
T. J. Dowey	3	1 1-2	6 34
J. R. Hawkins . . .	2		4 00
William Randolph . . .	8	6	17 33
M. Guilford, paving . .	8	6	25 97
W. E. Reaves, 55 loads gravel at 10c.			5 50
L. A. Loker	8	1	16 22
L. A. Loker, horse . . .	8	1	14 19
Wilson Porter . . .	6	5	13 10
Wilson Porter, horses . .	6	5	22 94
T. B. Hawes	19	8	39 76
M. G. Hurley	6		12 00
J. B. McLlory . . .	6	5	13 11

$477 83

SEPTEMBER.

	DAYS.	HOURS.	
L. A. Loker	1	6	3 33
L. A. Loker, horse . . .	1	6	2 90
W. C. Neal		6	1 35
W. C. Neal, horses . . .		6	2 34

Carried forward, $9 92

Brought forward,				$9 92
Wilson Porter, . . .	5	6	11 30	
Wilson Porter, horse . .	5	3 1-2	18 85	
T. B. Hawes	2		4 00	
Robert Cummings, 336 loads gravel at 5 cents . . .			16 80	
J. B. McLlory . . .	5	2	10 44	
A. O. Dunham . . .	1	4	2 88	
William Stearns, repairing guide-boards and gravel screen .			5 85	
				$80 04

OCTOBER.

	DAYS.	HOURS.		
L. A. Loker	2	2	4 44	
L. A. Loker, horse . . .	2	2	3 88	
W. D. Pailin, drain pipe . .			26 70	
M. W. Hynes . . .	6	5	13 11	
M. W. Hynes, horses . .	5	6	18 65	
M. W. Hynes, 2 guide posts .			60	
T. L. Hynes	5		10 00	
P. S. Zimmerman . . .	2		4 00	
Michael Guilford, paving . .	1		3 00	
				$84 38

NOVEMBER.

	DAYS.	HOURS.		
L. A. Loker		5	$1 11	
L. A. Loker, horse . . .		5	95	
Wilson Porter . . .	2		4 00	
Wilson Porter, horses . .	1	7	6 20	
J. B. McLlory . . .	1	6	3 33	
M. W. Hynes	1		2 00	
M. W. Hynes, horses . .	1		3 50	
T. L. Hynes	1		2 00	
E. W. Marston, labor and lumber			2 55	
				$25 64

DECEMBER.

	DAYS.	HOURS.		
L. A. Loker	3	3	6	66
L. A. Loker, horse	3		5	25
A. B. Sherman	27	6	55	33
A. B. Sherman, horse	20	8	36	56
A. B. Sherman, 150 loads gravel at 8 cents			12	00
W. D. Pailin, 1120 lbs. iron pipe			19	60
Wilson Porter	5	1	10	20
Wilson Porter, horse	9	5	16	71
W. C. Neal	1	4 1-2	3	00
W. C. Neal, horse	3		5	25
M. G. Hurley	4	5	9	10
C. W. Loker	2	1	4	20
J. B. McLlory	4	3	8	67
Louis Courrier	3	1-2	6	10
George Sumpter		4 1-2	1	00
L. A. Loker	1	2	2	44
L. A. Loker, horse	1	2	2	13
Wilson Porter	4		8	00
Wilson Porter, horses	4		14	00
W. C. Neal	4		8	00
W. C. Neal, horses	4		14	00
Rupert Porter	2		4	00
Louis Courrier	3	3 1-2	6	72
Fred W. Bradshaw		6	1	32
M. W. Hynes	1	2	2	45
M. W. Hynes, horse	1	2	2	13
James Eagon	1		2	00
M. G. Hurley	3		6	00
P. A. Leary			1	40

$274 22

FEBRUARY.

	DAYS.	HOURS.		
L. A. Loker	2	1	4	22
L. A. Loker, horse	2	1	3	68
M. W. Hynes	1	6	3	34
M. W. Hynes, horse	1	6	2	92
Wilson Porter	1	4	2	87
Wilson Porter, horse	1	6	2	85
N. Latour	1		2	00
A. Spear		7 1-2	1	65
A. Spear, horse		6	1	14
A. Spear, 2 loads gravel				20
Union Lumber Co., lumber			11	70
T. B. Hawes	1	1-2	2	10
T. B. Hawes, horse	1	1-2	1	84
A. B. Sherman		6	1	20
A. B. Sherman, 10 lbs. spikes				40
L. H. McManus			1	65

$43 76

L. A. LOKER,
Superintendent of Streets.

REPORT OF SUPERINTENDENT OF NORTH AND CENTRE CEMETERIES.

FROM MARCH 1, 1894, TO MARCH 1, 1895.

Appropriated, ...	$50 00	
Unexpended balance of 1894, . . .	21 80	
		$71 80

EXPENDED.

To labor at 20 cents per hour, . . .	$34 00	
Unexpended balance, ...	37 80	
		$71 80

CASH RECEIVED AND PAID TOWN TREASURER.

For lots and estate, ...	$25 00
Due the Town for lots, ...	$5.00

T. S. SHERMAN,
Superintendent.

REPORT OF LAKEVIEW CEMETERY.

FOR THE YEAR ENDING FEBRUARY 29, 1896.

Appropriated March 25, 1895, . . . $150 00

Orders drawn,
May 30th, W. W. Lovejoy, ... $31 24
July 30th, W. W. Lovejoy, ... 114 16
November 30th, C. A. Ranks, . . . 3 05
Unexpended balance in Treasury, . . . 1 55
————— $150 00

ANN M. LOVEJOY,
FOR WM. W. LOVEJOY.

REPORT OF TOWN CLERK AND REGISTRAR.

WAYLAND, January 1, 1896.

To the Inhabitants of the Town of Wayland:—

I hereby transmit the Annual Report of the Clerk and Registrar for the year ending December 31, 1895.

BIRTHS.

Whole number, registered during the year is thirty, being four less than in 1894, of the number sixteen were males and fourteen were females.

Born of native parents 14
"   of foreign parents 5
"   of native and foreign parents 11

DEATHS.

Whole number registered during the year is thirty, being one more than in 1894.

CONDITION.

Married 13
Widowed 7
Single 10
Native born 24
Foreign born 6

NAMES AND AGES OF PERSONS DECEASED DURING THE YEAR 1895, WHO WERE OVER SEVENTY YEARS OF AGE.

	YEARS.	MONTHS.	DAYS.
Jonas Garfield	87	3	
Harriet Bullard	86	7	8
Rachel T. Damon	82	6	5
Elizabeth A. Farmer	82	1	12
Mary P. Dudley	81	5	
Thomas Bryant	80	3	15
Charles Fairbank	75	2	14
Patrick Dolan	74		
Jacob Corman	70	9	26
Edward Pousland	70	11	

NOSOLOGICAL TABLE.

Disease of the brain	1
Anaemia	1
Disease of prostate gland	1
Cancer	1
Cirrhosis of liver	2
Bronchitis	2
Diphtheria	3
Consumption	2
Old age	2
Meningitis	1
Uraemia	1
Apoplexy	2
Pneumonia	3
Chronic rheumatism	1
Acute gastritis	1
Influenza	2
Scrofula	1
Inanition	1
Cholera Infantum	1
Epilepsy	1

MARRIAGES.

Whole number registered during the year is nineteen, being three more than in 1894.

Native birth of both parties 15
Native and foreign birth 4
First marriage of both parties 16
First of one and second of the other 2
Second marriage of both parties 1

DOGS.

Whole number of persons licensed to keep dogs for the year ending November 30, 1894 is seventy-nine.

78 males at $2.00 . . . . . . $156 00
1 female at $5.00 . . . . . . 5 00

$161 00
79 licenses at 20 cents 15 80

Paid over $145 80

Balance on hand February 29, 1896 . . . $89 40
Number of registered voters, November 1895 . . 428
Number in precinct 1 149
Number in precinct 2 279
Ballots cast in precinct 1 111
Ballots cast in precinct 2 229

340

Number of women registered 56
Precinct 1 29
Precinct 2 27
Number who voted 35

Vote for Governor:

	Precinct 1.	Precinct 2.
Elbridge G. Brown		12
Frederic T. Greenhalge .	60	137
Edward Kendall .	2	3
Moritz E. Ruther .	1	
Geo. Fred Williams	48	74

Vote for Senator, 4th Middlesex District:

	Precinct 1.	Precinct 2.
Lafayette Dudley	7	9
John Heffron		12
John J. McCann .	34	57
Geo. A. Reed	62	134

Vote of Wayland for Representatives, 28th Middlesex District:

	Precinct 1.	Precinct 2.
Walter Adams	42	72
Charles H. Balcom		14
Norman B. Douglass	8	15
Charles H. Dowse	42	64
James F. Leland .	7	15
John M. Merriam	51	98
E. Lewis Moore .	49	99

TOTAL VOTE FOR REPRESENTATIVES IN 28TH MIDDLESEX DISTRICT.

	Walter Adams.	Charles H. Balcom.	Norman B. Douglass.	Charles H. Dowse.	James F. Leland.	John M. Merriam.	E. Lewis Moore.
Framingham..............	850	64	40	740	38	806	813
Holliston................	242	23	48	245	67	186	161
Sherborn................	53	1	58	79	70	19	21
Wayland	114	14	23	106	22	149	148
Total..............	1,259	102	169	1,170	197	1,160	1,143

During the year the Selectmen have directed the Clerk to have such of the old records as required, to be rebound. This has been done, and all the records of the town are now in excellent condition except the records of births, deaths and marriages from the year 1780 to 1842, and these are being copied and put in proper form: when this work is completed our records from 1639 to the present time will compare favorably with any town in the state.

Respectfully submitted,

RICHARD T. LOMBARD,

February 29, 1896.   *Town Clerk.*

REPORT OF THE TREASURER.

For the Year Ending February 29, 1896.

APPROPRIATIONS.

1895.

March 25. For schools, care of rooms and

fuel, ...	$5,700 00
School supplies, . .	450 00
Highways and bridges, .	2,000 00
Overdraft, . . .	114 65
Incidentals, . . .	1,200 00
Firemen's pay, . .	224 00
Support of poor, . .	2,500 00
Salaries, . . .	1,200 00
Collection of taxes, . .	300 00
Abatements, . . .	800 00
Hydrants, . . .	384 00
Repairs on school buildings,	200 00
Lakeview Cemetery, .	150 00
North and Centre Cemeteries, . . .	50 00
Library, . . .	300 00
" catalogue, . .	375 00
Interest, . . .	3,000 00
Suppression of illegal sale of intoxicating liquors,	200 00
Electric lights, . .	340 00
Street lights, . . .	350 00
Pump at High school house	20 00
Repairs on highway, (Mrs. Simpson's corner), .	250 00

Carried forward, $20,107 65

Brought forward,			$20,107 65	
	Fence at Lakeview cemetery	125 00	
	Decoration Day, . .	100 00	
	Moderator . . .	5 00	
	Sidewalks . . .	300 00	
	Superintendent of schools .	250 00	
July	15.	" "	250 00	
	Painting Cochituate and		
	Lokerville school houses	250 00	
	Gravel	150 00	
Nov.	26.	Highways . . .	300 00	
	Poor	600 00	
			————$22,437 65
1895.			
March	25.	From contingent fund . .	250 00	
July	15.	" " " . ..	250 00	
July	15.	" " " . . .	250 00	
July	15.	"	150 00	
Nov.	26.	"	300 00	
Nov.	26.	" " " . .	600 00	
	Town tax assessed . .	20,637 65	
			————$22,437 65

SCHOOLS, CARE OF ROOMS AND FUEL.

1895.				
March	1.	Unexpended balance . .	$476 70	
March	25.	Appropriation . . .	5,700 00	
1896.				
Jan.	1.	Donation fund . . .	12 00	
Jan.	27.	School fund (State) (three-fourths)	201 90	
Jan.	31.	Dog license (half) . .	68 97	
1895–96.	Overdrawn	204 57	
1895–96.	Amount expended . .	————	$6,664 14

SCHOOL SUPPLIES.

1895.				
March	25.	Appropriation . . .	$450 00	
July	15.	Transferred from Incidentals .	42 00	
	School fund (State) (one-fourth)	67 30	
			————	$559 30

1894–95.	Overdrawn	$31 44	
	Amount expended . . .	493 13	
	Unexpended balance . .	34 73	
			$559 30

HIGHWAYS AND BRIDGES.

1895.

March	25.	Appropriation . . .	$2,000 00	
		" for overdraft of 1894	114 65	
Nov.	26.	Appropriation . . .	300 00	
			$2,414 65	
1895–96.		Overdrawn	94 49	
1895–96.		Amount expended . . .		$2,509 14

INCIDENTALS.

1895.

March	25.	Appropriation . .	$1,200 00	
July	15.	Transferred from gravel .	75 00	
1895–96.		Overdrawn	534 92	
				$1,809 92
March	1.	Overdrawn of 1894 . .	8 54	
1895–96.		Amount expended . . .	1,801 38	
				$1,809 92

SUPPORT OF POOR.

1895.

March	1.	Unexpended balance . .	$168 51	
March	25.	Appropriation . . .	2,500 00	
Nov.	26.	" . . .	600 00	
		Town of Lexington . .	52 00	
		" North Brookfield .	315 20	
		" Southboro . .	52 50	
		" Natick . . .	130 39	
		Overseers of Poor . . .	591 08	
				$4,409 68
1895–96.		Amount expended . . .	$4,243 21	
		Unexpended balance . .	166 47	
				$4,409 68

SALARIES.

1895.

March	1.	Unexpended balance	.	.	$182 94
March	25.	Appropriation	.	.	1,200 00

                                                        $1,382 94

March	30.	Daniel Brackett	.	.	$50 00
		H. B. Phalen	.	.	10 00
		Henry F. Lee	.	.	200 00
		William H. Bent	.	.	95 00
		H. B. Phalen	.	.	25 00
		A. F. Parmenter	.	.	4 00
April	27.	Ralph Bent	.	.	10 00
		M. W. Hynes	.	.	4 00
		Delos W. Mitchell	.	.	4 00
		P. S. Zimmerman	.	.	2 00
		Andrew S. Morse	.	.	4 60
		Henry G. Dudley	.	.	70 00
		E. W. Marston	.	.	20 00
July	27.	H. G. Hammond	.	.	45 50
		Edward Carter	.	.	68 25
August	31.	R. T. Lombard	.	.	42 00
Sept.	28.	Nellie Rice Fisk	.	.	52 00
October	26.	Edward Carter	.	.	21 00
Nov.	30.	R. T. Lombard	.	.	28 00
		H. B. Phalen	.	.	5 00
		P. S. Zimmerman	.	.	5 00
		John E. Linehan	.	.	5 00
		M. W. Hynes	.	.	5 00
		R. E. Frye	.	.	5 00
		C. E. Hibbard	.	.	6 50
		A. F. Parmenter	.	.	5 00
		Edward Carter	.	.	5 00
		E. M. Patridge	.	.	5 00
		James A. Draper	.	.	5 00
		E. F. Lawrence	.	.	5 00

Carried forward, $811 25

		Brought forward,				$811	25		
		Frank Bullard	.	.	.	5	00		
		William H. Campbell	.	.		5	00		
Dec.	28.	E. B. Smith .	.	.	.	5	00		
1896.									
Feb.	29.	R. T. Lombard	.	.	.	75	00		
		R. T. Lombard	.	.	.	10	50		
		Edward Carter	.	.	.	7	00		
		Horatio G. Hammond	.	.	10	50			
		L. H. Sherman	.	.	.	25	00		
		L. E. Mitchell	.	.	.	42	00		
		T. L. Sawin	.	.	.	20	00		
		D. W. Mitchell	.	.	.	20	00		
		T. W. Frost	.	.	.	75	00		
		W. B. Ward	.	.	.	25	00		
Feb.	29.	George B. Howe	.	.	.	25	00		
		D. D. Griffin	.	.	.	50	00		
		D. P. W. Loker	.	.	.	75	00		
		Charles H. Boodey	.	.	30	00			
		Unexpended balance	.	.	66	69			
								$1,382	94

FIREMEN'S PAY.

1895.								
March	1.	Unexpended balance	.	.	$224	00		
March	25.	Appropriation	.	.	224	00		
							$448	00
March	1.	Amount expended 1895-96	.	$224	00			
1896.								
March	1.	Unexpended balance	.	.	224	00		
							$448	00
1894.								
March	1.	Unexpended balance	.	.	$300	00		
"	25.	Appropriation	.	.	300	00		
							$600	00
		Amount expended .	.	.			$600	00

ABATEMENT OF TAXES.

1895.

March	1..	Overdrawn .	.	.	.	$670 15	
Oct.	26.	Taxes of 1892	·	.	.	9 80	
Oct.	26.	" 1892	.	.	.	117 04	
Oct.	26.	" 1893	.	.	.	18 51	
Oct.	26.	" 1893	.	.	.	34 88	
Oct.	26.	" 1895	.	.	.	7 14	
							$857 52
March	25.	Appropriation	.	.	.	$800 00	
1896.							
Feb.	29.	Overdrawn .	.	.	.	57 52	
							$857 52

TAXES OF 1891.

1895.

March	1.	Balance due .	.	.	.	$459 20	
1896.							
Feb.	29.	Amount due from Collector		.		459 20	

TAXES OF 1892.

1895.

March	1.	Balance due .	.	.	.	$855 30	$855 30
1896.							
Feb.	29.	Received from Collector		.		$324 70	
Feb.	29.	Amount due from Collector		.		530 60	
							$855 30

TAXES OF 1893.

1895.

March	1.	Balance due .	.	.	.	$5,029 12	$5,029 I2
		Received from Collector .		.		$4,098 23	
		Due from Collector		.		930 89	
							$5,029 12

TAXES OF 1894.

1895.
March   1. Balance due $8,723 32 $8,723 32
1896.
Feb.   29. Received from Collector .   . $3,087 88
Feb.   29. Amount due from Collector   . $5,635 44
                                                   ———— $8,723 32

TAXES OF 1895.

        Amount   assessed   due   from
              Collector   .   .   .$23,433 94 $23,433 94
1896.
Feb.   29. Received from Collector   .$13,924 98
            Amount due from Collector   . 9,508 96
                                                   ———— $23,433 94

REPAIRS ON SCHOOL BUILDINGS.

1895.
March   1. Unexpended balance   .   . $4 33
March   25. Appropriation   .   .   .   200 00 $204 33
1895–96.   Amount expended .   .   . $154 95

1896.
Feb.   29. Unexpended balance   .   .   49 38 $204 33

HYDRANTS.

1895.
March   25. Appropriation   .   .   . $384 00
1896.
Feb.   29. Paid Water Commissioners   . $384 00

LAKEVIEW CEMETERY.

1895.

March	25.	Appropriation . . .	$150 00	$150 00
May	30.	Paid William Lovejoy . .	$31 24	
July	27.	" " " . .	114 16	
Nov.	30.	" " " . .	3 05	
			$148 45	
1896.				
March	1.	Unexpended balance . .	1 55	
				$150 00

NORTH AND CENTRE CEMETERIES.

1895.

March	1.	Unexpended balance . .	$21 80	
March	25.	Appropriation . . .	50 00	
				$71 80
May	25.	Paid T. S. Sherman . .	$21 80	
1896.				
Feb.	29.	Paid T. S. Sherman . .	12 20	
			$34 00	
1896.				
March	1.	Unexpended balance . .	37 80	
				$71 80

CEMETERY ACCOUNT.

1895.

March	1.	Unexpended balance . .	$82 00	
1896.				
Feb.	28.	From T. S. Sherman . .	25 00	
Feb.	29.	From U. S. Walton . .	35 00	
				$112 00

DECORATION DAY.

1895.

March	25.	Appropriation . . .	$100 00	$100 00

1895.

March	1.	Overdrawn	$29 61	
May	25.	Paid R. T. Lombard . .	70 39	
				$100 00

ELECTRIC LIGHTS.

1895.

March	1.	Unexpended balance . .	$53 34	
March	25.	Appropriation . . .	340 00	
				$393 34
July	27.	Paid Natick Light Co., . .	$175 02	
Nov.	30.	" " " " . .	87 51	

1896.

January 25.		" " " " . .	58 34	
			$320 87	
March	1.	Unexpended balance . ·	72 47	
				$393 34

SUPPRESSION OF ILLEGAL SALE OF INTOXICATING LIQUORS AND SPECIAL POLICE.

1895.

March	1.	Unexpended balance, . .	$108 26	
	25.	Appropriation . . .	200 00	$308 26
June	29.	Paid D. W. P. Loker . .	40 00	
July	27.	Wm. E. Daniels . .	3 00	
		Edgar Potter . . .	6 00	
		John E. Linnehan . .	3 50	
		M. W. Hynes . .	7 00	
Aug.	31.	A. D. Collins . .	4 00	
		D. P. W. Loker . .	9 00	
		L. .H Wakefield . .	25 00	
	Carried forward,		$97 50	

		Brought forward,			$97 50
Sept.	28.	D. D. Griffin,	.	.	18 00
Dec.	28.	W. E. Daniels	.	.	4 00
		F. W. Manchester			7 00
		J. H. Harris .	.	.	5 00
1896.					
Jan.	25.	D. P. W. Loker	.	.	10 00
	25.	" "	.	.	7 50
	25.	L. H. Wakefield	.	.	15 00
	25.	John Lamarine	.	.	4 00
	25.	H. G. Dudley	.	.	2 00
Feb.	29.	D. P. W. Loker	.	.	31 50
	29.	D. D. Griffin	.	.	2 50

					204 00	
March	1.	Unexpended balance	.	.	104 26	$308 26

PUBLIC LIBRARY.

1895.						
March	25.	Appropriation	.	.	.	$300 00
1896.						
Jan.	1.	Interest on Draper & Childs'				
		notes	.	.	.	66 00
	31.	Dog licenses (half)	.	.	68 97	$434 97
1895.						
April	27.	Paid Treasurer of Library fund			300 00	
Oct.	2.	T. W. Frost " "			6 10	
1896.						
Jan.	1.	Treasurer of " "			66 00	
Feb.	29.	" " "			62 87	$434 97

LIBRARY CATALOGUE.

1895.						
March	25.	Appropriation	.	.	.	375 00
June	29.	Paid E. A. Heard, agent		.	375 00

TEMPORARY LOANS.

1895.

March	1.	Outstanding notes . . . $14,000 00		
April	1.	Natick National Bank note at 4 per cent. on demand . 4,000 00		
May	8.	Natick National Bank note at 4 per cent. on demand . 2,000 00		
July	1.	Natick National Bank note at 4 per cent. on demand . 2,000 00	$22,000 00	
Oct.	1.	Paid Natick National Bank note of April 18, 1894, . 5,000 00		
1896.		Paid Natick National Bank note of January 18, 1895. 4,000 00	$9,000 00	
March	1.	Outstanding notes . . $13,000 00		

$22,000 00

STATE TAX.

1895.

July	26.	Levied and assessed . .	945 00	
		Marsh land tax . . .	330 51	
				1,275 51
Dec.	11.	Paid Treas. of Commonwealth,		1,275 51

COUNTY TAX.

1895.

July	26.	Levied and assecsed . .	1,491 95
Nov.	16.	Paid County Treasurer . .	1,491 95

REPAIRS ON CENTRE HIGH SCHOOL HOUSE.

1895.

March	1.	Unexpended balance . .	$5 83	
	25.	Appropriation . . .	20 00	
				$25 83
May	25.	Paid B. F. Smith . . .	20 00	
		Unexpended balance . .	5 83	
				$25 83

BOARD OF WATER COMMISSIONERS.

1895.

June	1.	Transferred to interest account	$1,450 00
1895-96.		Paid Wm. H. Bent, clerk, .	1,206 24
1895-06.		Received from Wm. H. Bent,	
		clerk	2,218 74
1896.			
Feb.	29.	Transferred from hydrants .	384 00

STEAM FOR FIRE ALARM.

1895.

March	1.	Unexpended balance . .	$150 00
June	29.	Paid Bent & Stevens . .	150 00

REPAIRS ON HIGHWAY, MRS. SIMPSON'S CORNER.

1895.

March	25.	Appropriation . . .	$250 00
1896.			
March	1.	Unexpended balance . .	250 00

FENCE AT LAKEVIEW CEMETERY.

1895.

March	25.	Appropriation . . .	$125 00
1896.			
March	1.	Unexpended balance . .	125 00

MODERATOR.

1895.

March	25.	Appropriation . . .	$5 00
April	27.	Paid H. G. Dudley . .	5 00

SIDEWALKS.

1895.

March	25.	Appropriation . . .	$300 00
1896.			
March	1.	Unexpended balance . .	300 00

NEW SCHOOL HOUSE WAYLAND CENTER.

1895.
March   1.   Unexpended balance   .   . $4,000 00
1896.
March   1.   Unexpended balance   .   .   4,000 00

TAX TITLE.

Nov. 23, 1894 .   .   .   .   .   . $78 39
Dec. 28, 1895 .   .   .   .   .   .   97 94

                                             $176 33
1896.
Jan.   1.   Paid $78 39
March   1.   Amount due 97 94

                                             $176 33

TRANSPORTATION OF SCHOLARS.

1895.
July   15.   Transferred from schools   . $250 00 $250 00

1895–96.   Paid L. M. Temple   .   . $171 00
March   1.   Unexpended balance   .   .   79 00

                                             $250 00

PAINTING COCHITUATE AND LOKERVILLE SCHOOL HOUSES.

1895.
July   15.   Appropriation   .   .   . $250 00 $250 00

August   31.   Paid H. H. Rutter   .   . $13 75
           31.   Charles Richardson & Co.   61 35
Oct.   2.   T. W. Frost .   .   .   164 05
           2.   Charles Richardson & Co.   10 85

                                             $250 00

SUPERINTENDENT OF SCHOOLS.

1895.
March   25.   Appropriation   .   .   . $250 00
July   15.   "   .   .   .   250 00

                                             $$500 00

1895–96.	Amount expended . . .	$415 38	
March	1. Unexpended balance . .	84 62	
			$500 00

GRAVEL.

1895.

July	15. Appropriation . . .	$150 00	$150 00
1895.			
July	15. Paid Annie Alward . .	$75 00	
1896.			
March	1. Unexpended balance . .	75 00	
			$150 00

STREET LIGHTS.

1895.

March	25.	Appropriation . . .	$350 00	$350 00
April	27.	Paid Globe Gas Light Co., .	$177 65	
	27.	Frank Haynes . .	2 34	
	27.	C. H. Thing . . .	7 35	
	27.	G. L. Baker . . .	8 50	
June	29.	J. R. Hawkins . .	1 50	
	29.	C. H. Thing . . .	3 00	
July	2.	H. H. Rutter . . .	12 80	
	27.	Globe Gas Light Co., .	8 05	
	27.	C. H. Thing . . .	50 00	
	27.	C. H. Thing . . .	75	
	27.	H. H. Rutter . . .	6 20	
Oct.	26.	H. H. Rutter . . .	6 90	
Dec.	28.	C. H. Thing . . .	50 00	
1896.				
Feb.	29.	L. H. McManus . .	25	
			$335 29	
March	1.	Unexpended balance . .	14 71	
				$350 00

INTEREST ON TOWN DEBT.

1895.

March 25. Appropriation . . .	$3,000 00	
Transferred from Water Rates	1,450 00	
		$4,450 00
Overdrawn		386 30
		$4,836 30
March 1. Overdrawn, 1894 . . .	$71 32	
1895-96. Temporary Loans . . .	656 48	
Town Debt:		
Paid coupons on Town Bonds	2,225 00	
Paid coupons on Water Bonds	1,410 00	
Paid interest on Water Bonds .	40 00	
Paid interest Note of Allen Fund	60 00	
Paid interest Donation Fund .	78 00	
Paid interest Loker Fund .	100 00	
Paid interest Library Fund .	195 50	
		$4,836 30

TEMPORARY LOANS.

July 16, 1894. Borrowed in anticipation of taxes of 1894	$5,000 00	
April 1, 1895. Borrowed in anticipation of taxes of 1895	4,000 00	
May 8, 1895. Borrowed in anticipation of taxes of 1895	2,000 00	
July 1, 1895. Borrowed in anticipation of taxes of 1895	2,000 00	
		$13,000 00

OBLIGATIONS OUTSTANDING.

Nov. 3, 1863. Draper Library fund on demand at 6 per cent.	$500 00
Jan. 1, 1875. Allen fund on demand at 6 per cent.	1,000 00
Carried forward,	$1,500 00

Brought forward,	$1,500 00
Aug. 1, 1878. Water bonds due Aug. 1, 1898 at 5 per cent.	25,000 00
Oct. 1, 1878. Town bonds due Oct. 1, 1898 at 5 per cent.	44,500 00
Jan. 1, 1881. Mrs. Child's Library fund on demand at 6 per cent.	100 00
Oct. 1, 1882. Water bonds due Oct. 1, 1902 at 4 per cent.	4,000 00
July 27, 1888. Water bonds due July 27, 1898 at 4 per cent.	1,000 00
Jan. 1, 1889. Donation fund on demand at 6 per cent.	1,300 00
April 1, 1891. Loker fund on demand at 5 per cent.	2,000 00
April 12, 1894. James S. Draper Library fund on demand at 6 per cent. . .	500 00

$79,900 00

CONTINGENT ACCOUNT.

1895.

March	1. Overdrawn	$1,488 43
	25. Appropriation schools . .	250 00
July	15. " " . .	250 00
	" " . .	250 00
	" gravel . .	150 00
Nov.	26. " highways . .	300 00
1895–96.	State aid	916 00
	Military aid	248 00
Nov.	26. Appropriation poor . .	600 00
	Unexpended balance . .	773 49

$5,225 92

Cr.

1895.

March	15. Corporation tax . . .	$2 61
	30. License Bond's pool room .	2 00
	W. B. Ward interest on taxes	166 90
Carried forward,		$171 51

Brought forward,			$171	51
April 27.	License Scott's pool room	.	2	00
	T. W. Frost rent of hall	.	2	50
29.	P. S. Zimmerman " "	.	3	00
May 2.	T. W. Frost " "	.	2	50
June 29.	C. H. Thing " "	.	5	00
July 1.	South Middlesex Dist. Court	.	87	43
	W. B. Ward interest on taxes		366	00
	" " "		300	00
	T. W. Frost rent of hall	.	5	00
August 9.	" " "	.	2	50
Oct. 2.	South Middlesex Dist. Court	.	92	12
24.	C. H. Thing rent of hall	.	7	50
Nov. 11.	T. W. Frost " "		2	50
Dec. 11.	Corporation tax . . .		1,680	70
	National Bank tax . .		765	53
	State aid		971	00
27.	Interest on tax title . .		2	00
28.	T. W. Frost rent of hall	·	3	00
	L. A. Loker sale of lumber	.	1	00
	From Selectmen . . .		10	00
Feb. 28.	C. H. Thing rent of hall	.	125	00
29.	W. B. Ward interest on taxes		150	00
	Clark & Corimer license	.	2	00
	W. B. Ward interest on taxes		104	64
	" " "		102	01
	" " "		230	65
	Overlayings on taxes of 1895	.	1	32
	" marshland	.	1	51
	Additional assessments .	.	26	00
				$5,225 92

HENRY F. LEE IN ACCOUNT WITH THE TOWN OF WAYLAND.

1895.		Dr.		
March	1.	To cash as per audit . .	$2,188	24
	15.	Corporation tax . .	2	61
		T. W. Frost, rent of hall .	186	90
		C. H. Thing, rent of hall .	137	50
		Scott	2	00
		Zimmerman . . .	3	00
		Dist. Court fines . .	87	43
		W. B. Ward, interest .	666	00
		District Court . . .	92	12
		Corporation tax . .	1,680	70
		Bank tax . . .	765	53
		Loker	1	00
		W. B. Ward . . .	666	50
		Clark & Comier . .	2	00
		State aid	971	00
		Donation fund . . .	12	00
		State School fund . .	269	20
		Dog License . . .	137	94
		Town of Lexington . .	52	00
		" North Brookfield .	315	20
		" Southboro . .	52	50
		" Natick . .	130	39
		Overseers of Poor . .	607	93
		Borrowed in anticipation of taxes	8,000	00
		Taxes	21,248	42
		Cemeteries . . .	60	00
		Water Commissioners .	2,218	74
		State aid	971	00
		Interest on tax title . .	2	00
		Selectmen . . .	10	00
			$41,539	85

Cr.

By Selectmen's orders . . $21,374 17
State tax 945 00
Marsh land . . . 330 50
County tax . . . 1,491 95
Interest 4,836 30
Notes paid . . . 9,000 00
Water Commissioners orders 1,206 24
State and Military Aid . 1,164 00
————— $40,348 16
Cash 1,161 69

$41,539 85

HENRY F. LEE,
Treasurer.

AUDITOR'S REPORT.

1 have examined the books of the town officers. Those requiring bonds have given them. The bonds have been approved by the proper officers and are on file.

The School Committee's report is bound in a separate book, which is a desirable change, and may lead to other improvements.

The books of the Water Commissioners and Treasurer of Sinking Fund are neatly and correctly kept, and agree in all particulars with the Savings Bank books.

Most of the books kept by town officers show much care and painstaking. The town Treasurer's books are open to some improvements. Business to the amount of over forty thousand dollars has been done by the Treasurer. Every calendar month the books should be balanced by the Treasurer, examined and approved by the Auditor.

I find in the ledger no cash account between the Treasurer and the town, or between the Treasurer and his bank of deposit, except what may be on the stubs of his check book. Mercantile houses doing a business of forty thousand annually require monthly balance sheets and a careful cash account between the house and bank of deposit.

If these or other improved business methods could be adopted, much of the time spent in looking for errors would be saved.

TRIAL BALANCE.

Unexpended balance		$ 6,739 81
Temporary loans		13,000 00
		$19,739 81
Overdrawn	$ 1,331 71	
Uncollected Taxes . . .	17,118 47	
Tax title	97 94	
Cash called for	1,191 69	
		$19,739 81

CORRECTED.

HENRY F. LEE, TREASURER, IN ACCOUNT WITH THE TOWN OF WAYLAND.

Receipts from all Sources.

Cash as per audit	$2,188 24
Corporation tax	2 61
T. W. Frost	17 50
Selectmen	10 00
W. B. Ward, interest	832 90
Scott, license	2 00
Zimmerman	3 00
C. Thing	130 00
District Court fines	87 43
District Court fines	92 12
C. Thing	7 50
T. W. Frost	2 50
Corporation tax	1,680 70
Bank tax	765 53
State aid	971 00
Interest on tax title	2 00
Loker	1 00
W. B. Ward, interest	666 50
Clark & Comier	2 00
Donation fund	12 00
State School fund	269 20
Dog License	137 94
Town of Lexington	52 00
" North Brookfield	315 20
" Southboro	52 50
" Natick	130 39
Overseers of Poor	610 93
Borrowed in anticipation of taxes	8,000 00
Taxes collected	21,248 40
Cemeteries	60 00
Tax title	78 39
Water Commissioners	2,218 74
	$40,650 22

OFFICIAL REPORTS

OF THE

TOWN OF WAYLAND,

FOR ITS

One, Hundred and Seventeenth Municipal Year,

FROM

MARCH 1, 1896, TO MARCH 1, 1897.

Lakeview Press:

TRIBUNE OFFICE, SOUTH FRAMINGHAM, MASS.

1897.

OFFICIAL REPORTS

OF THE

TOWN OF WAYLAND,

FOR ITS

One Hundred and Seventeenth Municipal Year,

FROM

MARCH 1, 1896, TO MARCH 1, 1897.

Lakeview Press:
TRIBUNE OFFICE, SOUTH FRAMINGHAM, MASS.
1897.

List of Town Officers 1896-97.

The following is a list of the officers of the Town of Wayland and when their terms expire.

TOWN CLERK.

RICHARD T. LOMBARD 1897

TREASURER.

HENRY F. LEE 1897

AUDITOR.

ALFRED H. BRYANT 1897

COLLECTOR.

WILLARD B. WARD 1897

TREASURER OF LIBRARY FUNDS.

HENRY D. PARMENTER 1897

SELECTMEN

DAVID P. W. LOKER 1897
ISAAC DAMON 1897
THOMAS W. FROST 1897

OVERSEERS OF POOR.

GEORGE B. HOWE 1897
DAVID P. W. LOKER 1897
WILLARD B. WARD 1897

4

SCHOOL COMMITTEE.

CHESTER B. WILLIAMS	1897
L. ANNA DUDLEY	1898
ANNA B. BENT	1899

ASSESSORS.

RICHARD T. LOMBARD	1897
EDWARD CARTER	1898
HORATIO G. HAMMOND	1899

WATER COMMISSIONERS.

(VACANCY)	1897
CHARLES H. BOODEY	1898
HENRY G. DUDLEY	1899

TRUSTEES PUBLIC LIBRARY.

THEODORE W. BENNETT	1897
LIZZIE E. MITCHELL	1897
RICHARD T. LOMBARD	1898
ELLEN M. BRAMAN	1898
JAMES A. DRAPER	1899
CYRUS W. HEIZER	1899

CONSTABLES.

JEAN B. CHABENNIEU	1897
HENRY G. DUDLEY	1897
JOHN E. LINNEHAN	1897
LAWRENCE H. McMANUS	1897
WILLIAM C. NEAL	1897
GEORGE E. SHERMAN	1897
(VACANCY)	1897

TRUSTEES ALLEN FUND.

ISAAC DAMON	1897
DANIEL D. GRIFFIN	1897
WILLIAM H. CAMPBELL	1897

FENCE VIEWERS.

ALBION F. PARMENTER	1897
ISAAC DAMON	1897
EDWARD CARTER	1897

FIELD DRIVER.

IRA S. DICKEY 1897

SEALER OF WEIGHTS AND MEASURES.

(VACANCY) 1897

MEASURERS OF WOOD AND BARK.

GEORGE B. HOWE 1897
EDWARD CARTER 1897
WILLIAM S. LOVELL 1897

SURVEYOR OF LUMBER.

FRANK HAYNES 1897

SUPERINTENDENT OF NORTH AND CENTRE CEMETERIES.

THEODORE S. SHERMAN 1897

SUPERINTENDENT OF LAKEVIEW CEMETERY.

HENRY B. PHALEN 1897

FINANCE COMMITTEE.

DAVID P. W. LOKER 1897
RICHARD T. LOMBARD 1897
CHESTER B. WILLIAMS 1897
GEORGE B. HOWE 1897
CHARLES H. BOODEY 1897
HENRY F. LEE 1897
ISAAC DAMON 1897

COMMITTEE ON DECORATION DAY.

CHARLES H. MAY 1897
DANIEL W. RICKER 1897
DAVID P. W. LOKER 1897
EDWARD CARTER 1897
PETER S. ZIMMERMAN 1897

ENGINEERS OF FIRE DEPARTMENT.

RALPH BENT, *Chief* 1897
EDWIN W. MARSTON 1897
HENRY B. PHALEN 1897

SUPERINTENDENT OF STREETS.

ISAAC DAMON 1897

REGISTRARS OF VOTERS.

THEODORE L. SAWIN, Chairman 1897
DELOSS W. MITCHELL 1898
LUTHER L. SHERMAN 1899
RICHARD T. LOMBARD, Town Clerk *ex-officio* 1897

Annual Town Meeting, March 22, 1897.

WARRANT.

COMMONWEALTH OF MASSACHUSETTS.

MIDDLESEX SS :

To John E. Linnehan or either of the Constables of the Town of Wayland, in said County,

Greeting :

In the name of the Commonwealth of Massachusetts, you are directed to notify the qualified voters of said Town of Wayland to meet at the Town Hall, Wayland, on Monday, March 22, 1897, at 8 o'clock in the forenoon, then and there to act on the following articles :

ARTICLE 1. To choose by ballot a Moderator to preside in said meeting.

ART. 2. To choose a Town Clerk, Treasurer, Collector of Taxes, Auditor, three Selectmen, three Overseers of the Poor, Treasurer of the Library funds, and seven Constables, all for one year ; one School Committee, one Assessor, one Water Commissioner, two Trustees of the Public Library, all for three years. Also to answer the following question : "Shall licenses for the sale of intoxicating liquors be granted in the town of Wayland for the year ensuing ? "

All names and the said question must appear upon the official ballot and be voted for in accordance with Chapter 386 of the Acts of the year 1890.

For the purpose specified in this article, the polls will be opened immediately after the election of a Moderator, and will remain open continuously till one o'clock P. M., when it may be closed, unless the meeting shall otherwise determine, but must remain open not less than four hours.

ART. 3. To choose all other necessary Town Officers, Agents, and Committees, and hear reports of Town Officers, Trustees, Agents, and Committees, and act thereon.

ART. 4. To see how much money the town will grant for paying interest and existing debts ; for roads and bridges ; for support of poor ; for support of schools, school supplies and repairs on school buildings, and transportation of scholars ; for the fire department; for abatement of taxes, and for all other necessary town purposes, and order the same to be assessed, or do or act.

ART. 5. To appropriate the license money on dogs, refunded by the County Treasurer, or do or act.

ART. 6. To authorize the Selectmen to consult counsel on important town cases.

ART. 7. To see if the town will authorize its Treasurer, with the approval of the Selectmen, to borrow money in anticipation of taxes for the year 1897, and if so, how much, or do or act.

ART. 8. To see if the town will accept the list of Jurors as prepared by the Selectmen.

ART. 9. To see if the town will appropriate the money received for sale of lots in the cemeteries for improving the cemeteries, or do or act.

ART. 10. To see if the town will appropriate the sum of one hundred and fifty dollars to cut down and grade the hill on road leading from the Plain road to house of Dennis McDonnell, or do or act.

ART. 11. To see if the town will appropriate the sum of seventy-five dollars to repair the road leading from the house of J. M. Curtin to Fiske's corner, or do or act.

ART. 12. To see if the town will appropriate fifty dollars to re-lay and widen the culvert on Harrison Avenue, or do or act.

ART. 13. To see if the town will vote to purchase a suitable clock to be placed in the new tower of the Methodist Episcopal church in Cochituate, and to appropriate for said purchase the sum of five hundred dollars, also to provide for the proper care of said clock.

ART. 14. To see if the town will refund to Robert N. Jennison the sum of fifteen dollars and sixty-one cents for taxes paid from 1886 to 1896 on meadow land.

ART. 15. To see if the town will appropriate eighty-five dollars to purchase a snow-plough, or do or act.

ART. 16. To see if the town will instruct its Selectmen, if they deem it advisable, to petition the County Commissioners to relocate, widen, and straighten the road leading from Wayland Centre to Cochituate, from "Johnson's Lane" to the Central Massachusetts Railroad location at Wayland Centre, or do or act.

ART. 17. To see if the town will increase the number of its School Committee to six members, or do or act.

ART. 18. To see if the town will elect a Tree Warden, or do or act.

ART. 19. To see if the town will appropriate fifty dollars for the celebration of the Fourth of July, or do or act.

ART. 20. To see if the town will vote to abate the personal tax of Charles W. Dean for the year 1895, $72.50, and the year 1896, $78.00, or do or act.

ART. 21. To see if the town will appoint a committee to investigate the matter of better school facilities at Cochituate, or do or act.

ART. 22. To see if the town will reduce the water rates in Cochituate, or do or act.

ART. 23. To see if the town will vote to buy the K. of L. building for school or other purposes, or do or act.

Art. 24. To see if the town will vote "That no citizen shall be eligible to but one elective office in any one year," or do or act.

Art. 25. That any citizen holding an elective office shall be ineligible to hold an appointive office under the board of which he is a member, or do or act.

Art. 26. That no member of any board shall be given any contract by the board of which he is a member, or do or act.

And you are directed to serve this Warrant by posting up attested copies thereof at the Town House and each of the post-offices in the town, seven days at least, before the day for holding said meeting.

Hereof fail not, and make due return of this Warrant, with your doings thereon, to the Town Clerk of said town on or before the time appointed for holding said meeting.

Given under our hands this third day of March in the year eighteen hundred and ninety-seven.

DAVID P. W. LOKER,
ISAAC DAMON,
THOMAS W. FROST,
Selectmen of Wayland.

Jury List.

List of Jurors as prepared by the Selectmen for the year 1897.

Russell E. Frye.
Albion F. Parmenter.
Theodore L. Sawin.
John E. Linnehan.
Isaac C. Damon.
Frank Lupien.
Isaac S. Whittemore.
Colin C. Ward.
Edward B. Smith.
Geo. E. Sherman.
Edgar B. Loker.
Andrew S. Morse.
Alfred H. Bryant.

John J. McCann.
Sidney Loker.
Peter S. Zimmerman.
Ernest E. Butler.
Andrew S. Norris.
Adoniren J. Puffer.
Roscoe C. Dean.
Harry H. Rutter.
Allan B. Sherman.
Elijah H. Atwood.
Theodore S. Sherman
James A. Bent.
Edward M. Partridge.

DAVID P. W. LOKER,
ISAAC DAMON,
THOMAS W. FROST,
Selectmen of Wayland.

March 3, 1897.

Report of the Selectmen.

WAYLAND, March 1, 1897.

The Selectmen hereby submit their annual report as re-quired by the By-laws of the town.

We have appointed the following officers as required by Statute.

Engineers of the Fire Department: Ralph Bent, Edwin W. Marston, Henry B. Phalen.

Undertakers: Andrew S. Morse, David P. W. Loker.

Inspectors of Cattle and Provisions: Thomas W. Frost, Thomas Bryant.

Registrar of Voters: Luther H. Sherman.

Superintendent of Streets: Isaac Damon.

Election Officers, Precinct I: Warden, Albion F. Parmenter; Clerk, James A. Draper; Inspectors, M. W. Hynes, Edward Carter, William Stearns, William H. Campbell. *Precinct II:* Warden, H. B. Phalen; Clerk, Thomas Bryant; Inspectors, E. B. Smith, R. E. Frye, Ralph Bent, Ed. A. Partridge.

Special Police: M. W. Hynes.

According to the vote of the town, the culvert near the house of C. B. Williams has been enlarged, and the money appropriated by the town, used; also the road near the Simpson estate has been widened, and the money appropriated for said purpose, used.

According to the directions as laid out by the county commissioners in regard to Sand Hill road, an appropriation of one thousand dollars will be required for grading said road.

An appropriation is necessary for the purchase of gravel, near Cochituate village.

We have purchased of Michael Ronen a small gravel bank.

The Boston & Maine Railroad Co. has removed all piles from the river bed, not required to support the railroad bridge, as ordered by the Selectmen.

We recommend that a sufficient sum of money be appropriated for a special night police in Cochituate village, as it has been necessary since July 1, for our regular officer to serve two nights in a week.

The case, Commonwealth vs. Wayland, has been tried in court, and the decision was in favor of Wayland.

Sheedy vs. Wayland has been settled.

The damage claimed by Henry B. Phalen, caused by water, has been satisfactorily settled.

We have been compelled to overdraw the appropriation for incidentals to the amount of $462.89, being caused in part by defending and settling cases against the town of Wayland.

The town scales at Cochituate have been repaired at the expense of about one hundred dollars ($100.)

The Towns of Framingham and of Weston having petitioned for the State Highway, this town being between the two said towns, we deemed it advisable to petition for the same, which has been done, and a survey is being made.

We deem it unneccessary to make any estimates for the various needs of the town for the ensuing year as the Finance Committee is to consider all matters relating to the appropriation of money.

It gives us pleasure to announce that one of Wayland's public-spirited citizens, Dr. Frank W. Draper, has placed a bronze Tablet in the North cemetery, marking the site of the First Meeting House erected in the town. The inscription is as follows:

ON THIS SITE

IN 1643

The Sudbury colonists built their first meeting house

REV. EDMOND BROWN,

MINISTER.

Ay, call it holy ground,
The soil where first they trod;
They left unstained
What there they found,—
Freedom to worship God.

Respectfully submitted,

DAVID P. W. LOKER,
ISAAC DAMON,
THOMAS W. FROST,
Selectmen of Wayland.

Assessors' Report.

FOR THE YEAR ENDING FEBRUARY 28, 1897.

Value of real estate May 1, 1896	$1,226,580 00
Value of personal estate May 1, 1896 . .	265,375 00
Total valuation May 1, 1896	$1,491,955 00
Total valuation May 1, 1895	1,514,725 00
Decrease	$22,770 00
Taxes assessed for town purposes . . .	$21,459 75
Overlayings	225 75
Additional assessments	312 00
State tax	1,102 50
County tax	1,581 48
Total amount assessed	$24,681 48

Number of polls assessed May 1, 1896 .	548
Number additional polls assessed . .	18
Total polls assessed	566
Number polls assessed May 1, 1895 . .	557
Increase	9
Number persons assessed . . .	847
Number residents assessed on property .	423
Number non-residents assessed on property .	144

Total value of land $486,479 00
"   "   buildings 740,110 00
"   "   church property 30,240 00
"   " - town property 99,271 00
Number of horses 369
  "   cows 776
  "   sheep 41
  "   swine 262
  "   fowl 1,615
  "   neat cattle other than cows . 94
  "   dwelling houses . . 415
  "   acres of land . . . 9,210$\frac{62}{100}$
Rate of taxation for 1896, $15.60 per thousand.
  "   "   " 1895, $14.50 "

Abatements granted for 1893 . . . . $122 36
  "   "   1894 . . . . 34 55
  "   "   1896 . . . . 22 62
  "   of special tax for years 1895 & 1896 3 08
                                                    ————
Total abatements $182 61

Amount of special assessment under Chapter 426
  of the Acts of 1894 . . . . . 330 51
Overlaying 88
                                                    ————
Total assessment under said act . . . $331 39

Respectfully submitted,

RICHARD T. LOMBARD,
EDWARD CARTER,
HORATIO G. HAMMOND.
                              Assessors of Wayland.

Collector's Report.

Taxes of 1891.

Balance due March 1, 1896	.	.	.	$459 20
Abatement	.	.	. $17 05	
Cash	.	. . .	75 ·35	
			———	$92 40
				——— $366 60

Taxes of 1892.

Balance due March 1, 1896	.	. .	$530 60

Taxes of 1893.

Balance due March 1, 1896	.	.	.	$930 89
Paid Treasurer	.	. . .	.	575 77
				——— $ 355 12

Taxes of 1894.

Balance due March 1, 1896 .	.	.	.	$5,635 44
Paid Treasurer	.	. .	.	4,306 58
				——— $1,328 86

Interest paid on tax of 1894, $250.00.

Taxes of 1895.

Balance due March 1, 1896	.	.	.	$9,508 96
Paid Treasurer	.	. .	. .	3,717 72
				——— $5,791 24

Interest paid on tax of 1895, $150.00.

Taxes of 1896	.	. .	.	$25,048 87
Paid Treasurer	.	. .	.	15,332 69
				——— $9,716 18

WILLARD B. WARD, *Collector.*

Report of Town Clerk and Registrar.

WAYLAND, JANUARY 1, 1897.

I hereby transmit the Annual Report of the Clerk and Registrar for the year ending December 31, 1896.

BIRTHS.

The whole number registered during the year is twenty-eight, being two less than in 1895 : of the number, 15 were males, and 13 were females.

Born of native parents	8
" foreign parents	5
" native and foreign parents	15

MARRIAGES.

Whole number registered during the year is twenty-three, being four more than in 1895.

Native birth of both parties	17
Native and foreign birth	3
Foreign birth of both parties	3
First marriage of both parties	21
Second marriage of both parties	1
First of one and second of the other	1

DEATHS.

Whole number registered during the year is twenty-nine, being one less than in 1895.

Married	4
Widowed	8
Single	17
Native born	23
Foreign born	6
Males	16
Females	13

Names of persons deceased during the year who were over seventy years of age :

	Years.	Months.	Days.
Elizabeth Sherman . .	82	10	
George F. Bond . . .	73		
James Sumner Draper . .	84	10	
Eunice H. Bemis . . .	70	3	
Hannah J. Loker . . .	84	1	12
Eliza Whitney . . .	70	2	17
Jeremiah Mullen . . .	75		

NOSOLOGICAL TABLE.

Diphtheria	2
Fractured leg	1
Old age	3
Still-born	2
Suicide	1
Paralysis	3
Disease of brain	1
Blood poison	2
Phthisis	4
Heart disease	1
Malaria	1
Cholera infantum	1
Meningitis	2
Pneumonia	1
Cancer	1
Accident	2
Marasmus	1

DOGS.

Whole number of persons licensed to keep dogs to November 30, 1896, one hundred and fifty-eight.

145 male dogs, at $2 00	$290 00
13 female dogs, at $5.00	65 00
	$355 00
158 licenses, at 20c	31 60
Paid over to County Treasurer . .	$323 40

Number of registered voters, November, 1896 .	445
Number precinct 1	164
" 2	281
Ballots cast precinct 1	143
" 2	256
Number of women registered . : . .	56
" voted	30
Republican electors	257
Democratic electors	96

VOTE FOR GOVERNOR.

Thomas C. Brophy	7
Allen Coffin	3
Frederick O. Prince	11
Geo. Fred Williams	93
Roger Wolcott	243

FOR SENATOR, 5TH MIDDLESEX DISTRICT.

Henry Parsons	246
Chas. H. Boodey . . :	2
Peter S. Zimmerman	1

FOR REPRESENTATIVES, 21ST MIDDLESEX DISTRICT.

Geo. Balcom	94
Wm. H. Laughlin	114
Wm. L. Morse	195
Atherton W. Rogers	218

TOTAL VOTE FOR REPRÉSENTATIVES, 21ST MIDDLESEX
DISTRICT.

	Balcom	Laughlin	Morse	Rogers	Blanks
Marlborough	1274	1156	1318	1023	815
Sudbury,	31	32	119	169	71
Wayland	94	114	195	218	177
	1399	1302	1632	1410	1063

Respectfully submitted,

RICHARD T. LOMBARD,
Town Clerk.

Report of the Committee

The committee submit the following table, giving the names, and such other data as they have been able to obtain, of the men whose graves they have marked. It was found that the graves of Revolutionary soldiers are all in the old North burying ground, this being the original burying ground of the town of Sudbury, of which Wayland was a part until 1780.

Of fifty-three grave-stones examined there, bearing dates covering the proper period, forty-six are in memory of men whose names appear on the town records as having served as soldiers in the Revolution.

Names marked with an asterisk (*) denote men who were at Lexington and Concord, April 19, 1775, as per attested reports of commanding officers on file.

Names marked with a dagger (†) denote men who were at Bunker Hill, June 17, 1775.

The allotments as given are shown on the town records under date of October 26, 1778.

The usual markers of the Society of the Sons of the American Revolution were used, at a cost of $1.00 each.

Appropriation	$50 00
Forty-six markers @ $1.00	46 00
Unexpended balance	$4 00

RICHARD T. LOMBARD,
JAMES A. DRAPER,
ALFRED W. CUTTING.

Committee.

NAME.	Title.	Date of Birth and Death.		Age in 1775.	Allotment in 1778.
Abbott, Ephraim	. .	1745	1815	30	£ 30
*Adams, Benjamin	. .	1751	1843	24	23
*Allen, Josiah	. .	1743	1795	32	50
Baldwin, William	. .	1727	1794	48	50
Curtis, Joseph	Major	1722	1791	53	5
Cutting, Isaac	Captain	1721	1795	54	32
*Cutting, Robert	Captain	1743	1820	32	55
*Cutting, John	. .	1750	1828	25	50
*Damon, Isaac	. .	1739	1829	36	12
Damon, Thomas	Captain	1704	1796	71	20
Damon, Thomas, Jr.	. .	1731	1813	44	57
†*Damon, David	. Corporal	1753	1786	22	. .
Damon, William	. .	1734	1818	41	25
Eames, Aaron	Colonel	1751	1819	24	21
Heard, Thomas	. .	1750	1819	25	53
*Heard, Zachariah	. .	1752	1823	23	. .
†*Heard, Richard	Captain	1720	1792	55	132
*Heard, Richard, Jr.	. .	1754	1840	21	20
*Johnson, Ebenezer	. .	1741	1823	34	50
*Loker, Isaac	Captain	1738	1824	37	76
*Maynard, Daniel	. .	1741	1783	34	50
Maynard, Moses	Captain	1697	1782	78	25
*Maynard, Micah	Captain	1735	1778	40	50
*Maynard, Nathaniel	Captain	1744	1779	31	68
Moulton, Caleb	. . .	1709	1800	66	. .
*Moulton, Caleb	Captain	1745	1821	30	34
Moore, Luther	. .	1754	1826	21	29
*Noyes, James	. .	1749	1791	26	52
*Noyes, John	. .	1746	1814	29	50
Noyes, John	Lieut.	1714	1785	61	73
Reeves, Jacob	. .	1719	1794	56	46
*Reeves, Nathaniel B.	Sergeant	1749	1821	26	20
*Rice, Edmund	. .	1755	1841	20	42
Rice, Nathaniel	. .	1749	1836	26	50
Roby, Ebenezer	. .	1732	1786	43	50
†*Russell, Thaddeus	Captain	1739	1813	36	20
*Rutter, Joseph	. .	1703	1781	72	. .
*Rutter, Joseph, Jr.	. .	1753	1821	22	50
†*Rutter, Thomas	Sergeant	1748	1815	27	20
Staples, Ebenezer	. .	1734	1806	41	18
† Sherman, Ephraim	. .	1757	1837	18	. .
*Sherman Timothy	. .	1748	1819	27	12
† Smith, David	Fifer	1759	1817	16	. .
*Smith, Ephraim	Lieut.	1727	1809	48	22
*Smith, Joseph	Captain	1716	1803	59	95
*Wyman, William	. .	1755	1829	20	30

Report of the Overseers of the Poor for year ending February 27th, 1897.

Mr. M. Temple, the superintendent of the almshouse for the past year, has given very satisfactory service, and has been engaged for the ensuing year.

OUT DOOR POOR, PARTIAL SUPPORT.

Families aided 4
Persons aided 15
—— 19

IN DOOR POOR, FULL SUPPORT.

Almshouse 5
State Lunatic Hospital 3
—— 8

Total number persons aided . . 27

FINANCIAL STATEMENT SHOWING ACTUAL RECEIPTS AND EXPENDITURES FOR THE YEAR.

March 1, 1896.
Unexpended balance $186 32
Appropriation 2,200 00
—— $2,386 32

Reimbursements.

From Town of Lexington	$52	00
Town of Southboro	168	60
Town of Natick	207	40
Aid refunded from John Chinette .	23	00
		$451 00

Almshouse Receipts.

Sale of Milk	$695	09
Eggs	26	20
Poultry	9	75
Produce	164	02
Wood	6	00
Hay	30	00
Cows and calves	126	25
Board of horse	64	00
Sale of hogs	21	83
Labor	48	65
Pasturing	6	00
Balance in exchange of horse . . .	22	00
		$1,219 79
Total receipts		$4,057 11
Overdrawn		199 11
		$4,256 22

Out Door Poor Expenditures.

Having a settlement in Wayland, residing elsewhere.

Artemas Bond	$170	00
N. Normandin and family	121	36
		$291 36

Having a settlement in Wayland, and residing there.

John Chinette	$150	59
Anna Burrill	153	50
G. Chalmers	36	00
Ann Painter	52	00
Jos. Sawyer and family	82	00

Themie Davis	$14 50	
F. X. Davieaux Jr.	99 96	
Mrs. Cheltra	35 00	
		$623 55

Having a settlement in other cities and towns and residing here.

H. W. Dean, Natick	$168 88	
J. F. Hawkins, Southboro	168 00	
Frederick Ellis, Natick	37 44	
E. Hollowell, Lexington	52 00	
F. A. L. Towne and family, Natick . .	2 25	
		$428 57

Total out door poor	$1,343 48

IN DOOR POOR, IN INSANE HOSPITAL.

Clara Davis, Westboro	$169 92	
J. A. Wing, Worcester	169 92	
Ellen Burke, Taunton	169 92	
One person, Westboro	9 29	
		$519 05

ALMSHOUSE EXPENDITURES.

Paid warden's salary	$349 87
Groceries	321 28
Provisions	200 50
Grain	311 37
Seeds	20 96
Hay	52 73
Fertilizer	60 65
Fuel	62 00
Clothing for inmates	13 95
Shoes for inmates	5 35
Medical attendance	18 95
Furniture	48 00
One horse	112 50
Cows	222 50

Paid Fowl	$14 60	
Shoats	14 00	
Blacksmithing and other repairs . .	29 23	
Harnesses	50 50	
Sleigh	35 00	
Hardware and tools	5 25	
Labor	224 53	
Lumber	21 96	
Miscellaneous	132 21	
		$2,327 89

671 tramps were lodged and furnished with 656 meals.

Miscellaneous.

Travelling expenses and settlement of cases	$58 62	
Order books and stationery . . .	7 18	
		$65 80

Total expenditures	$4,256 22

Outstanding Claims.

North Brookfield, bill not received.

Reimbursements Due.

From Town of Natick	$84 88	
Town of Southboro	95 00	
Town of Lexington	52 00	
For milk from Almshouse	149 50	
		$381 38

Inmates of Almshouse During the Year.

Sarah Puffer, March 1st, 1896.
James Burke, " " "
Benjamin Nealey " " "
James Foley, " " "
Dennis Mullen, one month to April 1st, 1896.

INVENTORY OF PROPERTY AT ALMSHOUSE.

Farming implements	$329 45
8 cows	360 00
Hens	30 00
1 horse	100 00
Shoats	6 00
Hay	175 00
Oat fodder	40 00
Corn fodder	6 00
30 bu. potatoes	18 00
Fuel	50 00
Manure	90 00
Furniture and utensils	295 08
Real estate	5,800 00

$7,299 53

APPROPRIATION FOR PAINTING FARM BUILDINGS.

Appropriation		$275 00
Expended	$271 35	
Unexpended balance	3 65	

$275 00

An appropriation of twenty-five hundred dollars is asked for.

Respectfully submitted,

GEORGE B. HOWE,
DAVID P. W. LOKER,
W. B. WARD.

Overseers of the Poor.

Report of the Library Trustees for the Year 1896-7.

The usual inspection was made by the Trustees in January, and everything found to be in a satisfactory condition.

The appropriation for the library having been increased at the last town meeting, it was deemed wise by the Trustees to open the library to the public Wednesday afternoons from three to five-thirty.

The experiment thus far has demonstrated that, while the general public do not require more frequent access to the library, the teachers in the schools and some of the pupils are greatly convenienced in their work by it.

During the year, we have had to record the sad and unexpected death of Miss E. A. Hurd, who has served with efficiency on the board for several years. By the joint action of the Selectmen and the Trustees of the Library, Mr. Theodore Bennett was elected to serve out her unexpired term.

In November, the Trustees received from the sons of Mr. James Sumner Draper, a portrait of their father, which we have placed upon the walls of the library. His life-long and unselfish service for the library will make this one of our most valued possessions.

The accession of new books this year has been quite large; 270 by purchase and 46 by gift. These, we trust, do not fall below the high standard which the library has always endeavored to maintain.

At the last annual town meeting, the Trustees of the Library were commissioned " to erect a stone tablet or monument on the Town Hall lot, to designate that in Wayland was established the first free public library in Massachusetts." This duty has been discharged to the best of our ability with the money appropriated.

For the Trustees,

C. W. HEIZER.

Librarian's Report.

To the Library Trustees:

Statistical information for the year 1895-6 is respectfully submitted as follows :

ACCESSIONS.

By purchase	270
By gift	46
Bound and transferred from the pamphlet department	29
Total	345
Whole number of volumes in the library . . .	12,659
Pamphlets presented	294

CIRCULATION.

In Cochituate village	1,433
In Wayland Centre	3,851
Total	5,284

DONORS OF BOOKS AND PAMPHLETS.

	Books.	Pamphlets.
American Humane Association.		4
American Library Commission		1
Atkinson, Mr. Edward, L. L. D. Ph. D. . .	1	
Baldwin, Mr. Wm. H.	1	

	Books.	Pamphlets
Benton, Mr. J. H.	1	
Bolton, Mr. Chas. K.		9
Bullard, Mr. Willard H.	1	
Cleveland (Ohio) Pub. Library		7
Dudley, Mrs. Wm. T.	3	24
Forbush, Mr. E. H.	1	
Fowler, Mr. E. H.	1	
Heard, Mrs. S. E.		17
Ladies' Commission on S. S. Books		2
Loring, The Misses	4	33
MacNamee, Mr. J. H. H.		1
Oviatt, Dr. George	2	
Rice, Mrs. Chas.		12
Salem Pub. Library		12
State Government	10	9
Sent to the Reading Room		141
United States Government	20	13
Weston Town Library	1	
Wight, Mrs. Henry		9

CLASSES OF READING.

Art	.03	Literature	.09
Biography	.06	Philosophy	.02
Fiction	.44	Religion	.04
History	.09	Science	.05
Juvenile	.12	Travels	.06

Library reports have been received as follows : Aberdeen (Scotland) Public Library, Beverly, Bradford, Brookline, Brooklyn, Cobden Club (London), Concord, Fall River, Forbes Library Northampton, Harvard College, Institute of Technology, Lawrence, Malden, Newton, Salem, St. Louis Merchantile Library Association.

The reading room has received regularly The Century Magazine, Christian Science Journal, Harper's Monthly, Munsey's, The Land of Sunshine, The Pacific North West,

Traveler's Record and Cochituate Enterprise, making the room more attractive and increasing its number of visitors.

Received from fines	. . . .	$10 00
" " cards	. . . .	2 47
" " Catalogues	. . . . . .	1 00
Paid to Treasurer	. . . .	$13 47
Received for incidentals	. . . . . .	12 00
Paid out	. . . .	$12 83

S. E. HEARD.

March 8, 1897.

9546   About Paris.   Richard Harding Davis.
9563   Adam Johnstone's Son.   F. M. Crawford.
9552   Adventures of Capt. Horn.   F. R. Stockton.
9826   Aftermath.   James Lane Allen.
9644   Amazing Marriage, The.   George Meredith.
9595   Amos Judd.   J. A. Mitchell.
9564   Art of Living, The.   Robert Grant.
9571   Art Out of Doors.   Mrs. Van Rensselaer.
9538   As a Matter of Course.   Anna Payson Call.
9572   Autobiography of a New England Farm.   N. H. Chamberlain.
9685   Bachelors Christmas, The.   Robert Grant.
9768   Bay Colony, The.   Wm. D. Northend.
9720   Bell Ringers of Angels.   Bret Harte.
9681   Bernecia.   Amelia E. Barr.
9757   Bicycling For Ladies.   M. E. Ward.
9650   Black Arrow, The.   R. L. Stevenson.
9576   Boyhood in Norway.   H. H. Boyesen.
9652   Briseis.   Wm. Black.
9731   Broken Links.   Mrs. Alexander.
9615   Brother and Sister.   Memoir and Letters of Ernest and Henrietta Renan.
9829   Brownings For the Young.   F. C. Kenyon.
9614   Browning's Poetical Works.
9637   Capt. January.   Laura E. Richards.

9495 Carved Lions, The. Mrs. Molesworth.

9553 Casting Away of Mrs. Lecks and Mrs. Aleshine.

9449 Celia Thaxter's Poems.

9618 Chapters from Some Unwritten Memoirs. Anna Thackeray Ritchie.

9630 Charlotte Bronte and Her Circle. Clement K Shorter.

9455 Chocorua's Tenants. Frank Bolles.

9566 Chronicles of Count Antonio. Anthony Hope.

9544 Cinderella, and other stories. Richard Harding Davis.

9581 Clarence. Bret Harte.

9648 Cliff Dwellers, The. Henry B. Fuller.

9583 Coming of Theodora, The. E. Orne White.

9534 Considerations on Painting. J. La Farge.

9779 Costly Freak, A. Maxwell Grey.

9778 Country of the Pointed Firs. Sarah O. Jewett.

9769 Critical Period of American History. John Fiske.

9558 Days of Auld Lang Syne. Ian Maclaren.

9601 Day of their Wedding. Wm. D. Howells.

9623 Degeneration. Max Nordau.

9795 Dream Life and Real Life. Olive Schreiner.

9450 Drift Weed. Celia Thaxter.

9434 Dr. Izard. A. K Greene.

9551 Dr. Warrick's Daughters. Rebecca H. Davis.

9485 Dukesborough Tales. Philemon Perch.

9626 Echoes from the Sabine Farm. Eugene and Roswell M. Field.

9542 Eliza Pinckney. H. H. Ravenel.

9617 English Seamen in the Sixteenth Century. J. A. Froude.

9586 Experiment in Altruism. Margaret Sherwood.

9435 Exploits of Brigadier Gerard. A. Conan Doyle.

9689 Errant Wooing, An. Mrs. Burton Harrison.

9831 Etiquette of Washington. K. Elwes Thomas.

9661 Eye in its Relation to Health, The. Chas. Prencell.

9649 Familiar Studies of Men and Books. R. L. Stevenson.

9484 Famous American Authors. Sarah K. Bolton.

9600 Fanciful Tales. F. R. Stockton.

9619 Fannie Burney and Her Friends. L. B. Seeley.

9589 Father Stafford. Anthony Hope.

9582 Fidelis. Ada Cambridge.

9549 Lady of Quality. Mrs. F. H. Burnett.
9536 Land of Pluck. Mary Mapes Dodge.
9639 Lesson of the Master, The. Henry James.
9451 Letters of Celia Thaxter.
9616 Letters of Erasmus. J. A. Froude.
9622 Life and Letters of Chas. Bulfinch. Ellen S. Bulfinch.
9584 Life of Nancy. Sarah Orne Jewett.
9548 Lilac Sunbonnet, The. S. R. Crockett.
9665 Lilith. George Macdonald.
9632 Literary Study of the Bible, A. Richard D. Moulton.
9750 Little Mr. Thimblefinger. Joel C. Harris.
9587 Little Wizard, A. Stanley Weyman.
9608 Love Affairs of a Bibliomaniac. Eugene Field.
9453 Lover Saint Ruth. L. Imogen Guiney.
9592 Madame Delphine. George W. Cable.
9602 Madelon. Mary E. Wilkins.
9594 Mad Sir Uchtred. S. R. Crockett.
9773 Makers of Florence. Mrs. Oliphant.
9772 Makers of Venice. Mrs. Oliphant.
9788 March Hares. Harold Frederic.
9531 Margaret Winthrop. A. M. Earle.
9742 Marm Lisa. Kate Douglas Wiggin.
9316 Mary Ronald's Century Cook Book.
9555 Maureen's Fairing. Jane Barlow.
9597 Meadow Grass. Alice Brown.
9807 Memoirs of an Artist. Chas. Francis Gounod.
9547 Men of the Moss Hags. S. R. Crockett.
9784 Mercy Warren. Alice Brown.
9432 Micah Clarke. A. Conan Doyle.
9674 Monk of Fife, A. Andrew Lang.
9770 Mound Builders, The. J. P. MacLean.
9296 Mountains of California. John Muir.
9753 Mr. Rabbit at Home. Joel Chandler Harris.
9693 Mrs. Cliff's Yacht. F. R. Stockton.
9609 My Lady Nobody. Maarten Maartens.
9496 My New Home. Mrs. Molesworth.
9461 My Own Fairy Book. Andrew Lang.
9424 Mystery of Cloomber, The. A. Conan Doyle.
9810 My Village. E. Boyd Smith.

9457 New Alice in Old Wonderland. A. M. Richards.

9488 New England Fields and Woods. Rowland Robinson.

9726 No Gentlemen. Clara Louise Burnham.

9575 Norseland Tales. H. H. Boyesen.

9569 Notes of the Night. C. C. Abbott.

9620 Old Chester. H. Crickmore.

9454 Old English Songs. Illustrated by H. Thompson.

9612 Our Edible Toadstools and Mushrooms. W. H. Gibson.

9625 Parisian Art and Artists. Henry Bacon.

9593 Play Actress, The. S. R. Crockett.

9635 Poems of Johanna Ambrosius.

9452 Poetry for Home and School. Anna Brackett and Ida Eliot.

9821 Power Through Repose. Anna Payson Call.

9456 Prince and the Pauper, The. Mark Twain.

9633-4 Principles of Psychology. William James.

9590 Prisoner of Zenda. Anthony Hope.

9647 Prodigious Adventures of Tartarin of Tarascon.

9799 Puritan Bohemia, A. Margaret Sherwood.

9693 Quaint Nantucket. Wm. R. Bliss.

9606 Red Badge of Courage, The. Stephen Crane.

9410 Red Cockade, The. Stanley Weyman.

9640 Real Thing, The. Henry James.

9677 Release, The. Charlotte M. Yonge.

9670 Rodney Stone. A. Conan Doyle.

9423 Round the Red Lamp. Conan Doyle.

9574 Russian Rambles. Isabel F. Hapgood.

9573 Sainte Beuve. Selected Essays in French.

9686 Scallywag, The. Grant Allen.

9621 Science of Nutrition, The. Edward Atkinson.

9656 Seats of the Mighty, The. Gilbert Parker.

9565 Second Jungle Book, The. Rudyard Kipling.

9662 Sentimental Tommy. J. M. Barrie.

9397 Shadow of a Crime, The. Hall Caine.

9613 Shelf of Old Books. Mrs. James T. Fields.

9585 Singular Life, A. Elizabeth Stuart Phelps.

9700 Sir George Tressady. Mrs. Humphrey Ward.

9774 Sir Robert's Fortune. Mrs. Oliphant.

9596 Sister of a Saint. Grace Ellery Channing.

9580   Slain by the Doons. R. D. Blackmore.
9532   Soil, The. F. H. King.
9694   Sowers, The. Henry Seton Merriman.
9809   Sport Royal. Anthony Hope.
9812   Stories by English Authors ; England.
9811   Stories by English Authors ; France.
9813   Stories by English Authors ; Ireland.
9794   Story of an African Farm. Olive Schreiner.
9556   Strangers at Lisconnel. Jane Barlow.
9605   Successors to the Title. L. B. Walford.
9824   Summer in Arcady. James Lane Allen.
9433   Sweet Clover. C. L. Burnham.
9577   Synnove Solbakken. Bjornsterne Byornson.
9708-9   Targuesara. F. Marion Crawford.
9610   Taxidermy and Zoological Collecting.
9568   This Goodly Frame, The Earth. Francis Tiffany.
9713-14   Three Musketeers, The. Alexander Dumas.
9477   Through Russian Snows. G. A. Henty.
9459   Toinette's Philip. Mrs. C. V. Jamison.
9641   Tom Grogan. F. Hopkinson Smith.
9754   Tommy, Anne, and the Three Hearts. M. O. Wright.
9462   Two Little Pilgrims' Progress. F. H. Burnett.
9646   Under Fire. Capt. Chas. King.
9783   Under the Water Oaks. Marian Brewster.
9559   Upper Room, The. Ian Maclaren.
9541   Use of Life, The. Sir John Lubbock.
9326-7   Vailima Letters, The. R. L. Stevenson.
9631   Victorian Anthology, A. Edward C. Stedman.
9599   Village Watch Tower. Kate Douglas Wiggin.
9775   Violet, The. Julia Magruder.
9642   Waring's Peril. Capt. Chas. King.
9288   Way-marks for Teachers. S. L. Arnold.
9776   Week Away from Time, A.
9777   Week on the Concord and Merrimac River. H. D. Thoreau.
9543   Weir of Hermiston. R. L. Stevenson.
9657   When Valmond Came to Pontiac. Gilbert Parker.
9830   Whist or Bumblepuppy. Pembridge.
9578   White Company, The. A. Conan Doyle.

9832 Winning Whist. Emery Boardman.
9723 Wise Woman, The. C. L. Burnham.
9482 With Clive in India. G. A. Henty.
9540 Wrecker, The. R. L. Stevenson.
9636 Year in the Fields, A. John Burroughs.
9481 Young Carthaginian. G. A. Henty.
9771 Young Folks' History of the Netherlands. A. Young.
9598 Zeit Geist. L. Dougall.

HENRY D. PARMENTER, *Treasurer*,
In account with Library Funds.

DR.

1896.

Mar.	1.	To town of Wayland unexpended appropriation for 1895	$128	51
May		Appropriation in part for 1896	200	00
Sept.	9.	" " full	300	00

1897.

Jan.	4.	Interest on Library funds to Jan. 1	66	00
Feb.	27.	Town of Wayland one-half dog licenses	153	61
Mar.		Wayland Library fines, catalogues and cards	13	47
			$861	59

CR.

1896.

Mar.	28.	By S. E. Heard, salary to Apr. 1, 1896	$50	00
April	1.	American Express Co.	8	93
	22.	N. R. Gerald, salary to Apr. 1	40	00
May	10.	S. E. Heard, incidental expenses	12	00
June		J. Small		75
	24.	New Book Club, magazines	7	00
	27.	S. E. Heard, salary to July 1	50	00
July	1.	American Express Co.	8	93
	1.	F. J. Barnard & Co.	11	77
	18.	DeWolfe, Fiske & Co., amount 3 bills	126	54

Sept.	9.	**By** S. E. Heard, salary in part	.	. .	$25 00
	24.	American Express Co. .	.	. .	8 93
	25.	S. E. Heard, salary to Oct. 1		. .	75 00
Dec.	22.	F. J. Barnard & Co. .	.	. .	12 29
	23.	S. E. Heard, salary to Jan. 1, 1897		.	75 00
	31.	American Express Co.	.	. .	8 93

1897.

Jan.	10.	J. E. Linnehan, wood bill	.	. .	26 00
	10.	Wayland Book Club, magazines	.	.	7 00
Feb.	6.	W. Lovell, lighting street lamp	.	.	1 50
		DeWolfe, Fiske & Co. .	.	. .	98 22

$653 79

Balance March 1, 1897 . . . . . . 207 80

$861 59

Report of the Superintendent of the Wayland Water Works.

GENTLEMEN :—

We have made some changes this year which were needed very much. The hydrant near the Damon place has been moved and is now where it can do some good if needed. We have placed a new hydrant on Plain street, which the property holders have been wanting for a long time. We have also placed a hydrant on land of the town, back of the Grammar School House, laying about one hundred and fifty feet of four inch pipe to same, which will give good hydrant service to the Shoe Shops, in that locality. The water has been extra good this year and plenty of it.

We were obliged to shut off eleven water takers for non-payment of water rates.

The maintenance account is

1896.

June 14.	To cash Walworth Mfg. Co. . . .	$48 83
Aug. 24.	" " " " " . . .	150 06
1897.		
Jan. 21.	" " H. G. Dudley as Superintendent	278 00

$476 89

The water at present is in use by the following :

Families	253
Manufactories	10
Public Buildings	4
Miscellaneous	12
Horses	62
Cows	68

Respectfully submitted,

H. G. DUDLEY,
Superintendent.

WAYLAND, February 27, 1897.

Water Commissioners

DR.

1896.
Feb. 29. Overdrawn $53 50
1897.
Jan. 30. H. G. Dudley 476 89
Feb. 2. Transfer to interest . . . 1,450 00
        Unexpended balance . . . 1 00
                                         $1,981 39

CR.

1396.
Mar. 23. Appropriated for overdraft . . $53 50
Aug. 14. Water rates 230 75
Sept. 18.   " 200 00
Oct. 15.   " 275 00
Dec. 10.   . . . . . 250 00
1897.
Jan. 7.   . . . . . 111 25
Jan. 30.   " 476 89
Feb. 2. Transfer from hydrants . . 384 00
                                           $1,981 39

Note—$675.86 placed to the credit of the sinking fund does not appear in the treasurer's account, the orders reaching him too late to credit to the account this year. This amount would show the receipts for the year to be $2,603.75.

C. H. BOODEY,
H. G. DUDLEY,
Water Commissioners.

Report of Commissioners of Wayland Water Works Sinking Fund.

1897.

Feb. 27. Amount deposited in Natick Five Cent Savings Bank, Natick, Mass.   .   .   . $3,691 74

Interest on above deposit to Nov. 1, 1896 . 2,041 72

Amount deposited in Suffolk Savings Bank, Boston, Mass. 1,000 00

Interest on above deposit to Oct. 1, 1896 . 380 30

Amount deposited in Home Savings Bank, Boston, Mass. · 2,292 38

Interest on above deposit to Oct. 1, 1896 . 605 64

Amount deposited in Framingham Savings Bank, Framingham, Mass.   .   .   . 1,205 21

Interest on above deposit to Nov. 1, 1896 . 220 87

Amount deposited in North End Savings Bank, Boston, Mass. 1,459 40

Interest on above deposit to Jan. 1, 1897 . 205 08

Amount deposited in Watertown Savings Bank, Watertown, Mass.   .   .   . 994 53

Interest on above deposit to Oct. 1, 1896. . 56 84

Amount deposited in Farmers and Mechanics Savings Bank, South Framingham, Mass. 675 86

$14,829 57

C. H. BOODEY,

H. G. DUDLEY,

Commissioners of Water Works Sinking Fund.

WAYLAND, Feb. 27, 1897.

Report of Superintendent of Streets.

WAYLAND, MARCH 1, 1897.

Appropriated for highways and bridges, $2,400. Of this sum, $192.92 was used for the removal of snow, after the close of the financial year, and prior to the annual Town Meeting, leaving a balance of $2,307.08 : of this amount, $2,296.02 have been expended the present year, leaving a balance of $11.06. There are outstanding bills for the removing of snow in January and February of $165.66. I would recommend that the town make provision for the removal of snow, as it is almost impossible to reserve a sufficient sum out of the regular appropriation.

The culvert near the house of L. H. Sherman has been rebuilt, and the bridge near the house of Samuel Russell replanked.

It will be necessary for the town to procure some gravel near Cochituate village the coming year, as the present supply is getting somewhat limited and of poor quality.

Respectfully submitted,

ISAAC DAMON, *Superintendent.*

Report of Supt. of North and Centre Cemeteries

FROM MARCH 1, 1896 TO MARCH 1, 1897.

Appropriated March 23, 1896 . . . $100 00
Unexpended balance of 1895 . . . 37 80
                                    ———— $137 80

EXPENDED.

To labor for men @ 20c. per hour . . $62 00
   "   " horse @ 17c. per hour . . 9 69
Unexpended balance of 1896 . . . 66 11
                                    ———— $137 80

Cash paid Town Treasurer for sale of lots and grass . $17 00

T. S. SHERMAN, *Supt.*

Report of Superintendent Lakeview Cemetery.

1896.			
Feb. 29.	Unexpended balance		$1 55
Mar. 23.	Appropriation		100 00
	Overdrawn		3 12
Apr. 25.	H. B. Phalen	$9 50	
	Robinson & Jones . . .	3 23	
May 28.	H. B. Phalen	53 00	
Oct. 31.	"	29 86	
1897.			
Feb. 27.	H. B. Phalen . . .	9 08	
		$104 67	$104 67

FENCE AT LAKEVIEW CEMETERY.

1896.

Feb. 29. Unexpended balance $125 00

Received from H. F. Lee, treas. $125 00

SALE OF LOTS.

Cash received $50 00

Note—The amount for the sale of lots, $50 ; amount unexpended appropriation for fence, $19.46 ; amount overdrawn, cemetery account, $3.12 : paid to treasurer March 9, 1897, $72.58.

School Building at Wayland Centre.

Appropriation $17,000 00

J. E. Warren & Co., on account as per con-
    tract $10,800 00
A. Drennan, heating and ventilation, on
    account as per contract . . . 2,150 00
Fuller Warren Co., on account as per contract 356 00
E. B. Badger & Sons, copper work . . 175 00
                      ————— $13,481 00

Balance unexpended $3,519 00

FRANCIS SHAW,
HENRY D. PARMENTER,
LLEWELLYN FLANDERS.

Treasurer's Report.

SCHOOLS.

1896.

Mar. 23.
Appropriation . . . , . .	$6,200 00
" for overdraft . . .	204 58
State treasurer	326 92
" state school fund . .	230 06.
Dog license (half)	153 61
Donation fund	12 00
Town of Natick	52 50-
Overdrawn	276 14

Expended $7,455 81		
	$7,455 81	$7,455 81

SUPPORT OF POOR.

Unexpended balance	$186 32
Appropriation	2,200 00
Overseers	1,315 97
Overdrawn	199 11

Expended $3,901 40		
	$3,901 40	$3,901 40

INCIDENTALS.

Appropriation	$1,500 00
" for overdraft	459 92
Overdrawn	462 89

Overdrawn	$459 92
W. F. Garfield	7 00
W. A. Chessman	16 00
C. H. Thing	11 00
A. D. Collins	37 80
G. M. Stevens	17 73
W. C. Neal	16 55
A. H. Bryant	· 2 00
H. F. Lee	22 25
R. T. Lombard	41 19
H. G. Dudley	277 24
Lombard & Caustic	123 22
H. H. Rutter	85 00
J. E. Linnehan	154 95
American Express Company . . .	4 65 ·
C. E. Hibbard	6 00
F. C. Yeager	1 50
J. F. Burke	15 00
W. B. Ward	41 00
W. F. Smith	3 93
P. B. Murphy	4 95
Ralph Bent	7 50
Daniel Brackett	85 00
Thos. Groom & Co.	88 15
P. H. Cooney	175 00
E. P. Butler	6 62
W. W. Wight	5 00
A. W. Mitchell	6 25
F. F. Gerry	171 86
M. W. Hynes	6 00
P. D. Gorman	12 00
T. E. Glennon	6 00
C. E. Reed	2 00
H. B. Phalen	101 00
L. H. McManus	38 00
H. Wellner	24 00
D. W. Ricker	14 74
D. B. Heard	25 22
Hannah Mullen	15 02

T. W. Frost	$8 15
Pratt Bros.	1 25
T. S. Sherman	9 00
Gilbert & Barker Mfg. Co.	2 62
W. D. Parlin	4 78
Edward Carter	6 25
H. G. Hammond	5 00
J. Charbonneau	6 00
Wilson Porter	17 00
Robinson & Jones	18 11
Fairbank Scales Co.	40 97
Geo. McQuesten	31 90
E. W. Marston	8 71
John M. Brown	6 00
Wm. Stearns	25 65
Howe & Co. Express	2 75
Frank Haynes	5 22
E. L. Barry	5 00
D. O. Frost	2 41
W. I. Hussey	1 70
H. B. Braman	15 00
Thos. Bryant	1 00
Isaac Damon	9 50
D. W. P. Loker	13 50
L. H. Sherman	6 00
C. H. Boodey	7 95
B. & M. R. R.	90
L. K. Lovell	5 61
Fiske & Co.	1 74
Wm. M. Fullick	11 90
M. E. Farnsworth	3 00

$2,422 81	$2,422 81

HIGHWAYS AND BRIDGES.

Appropriation		$2,500 00
" for overdraft		94 49
Expended	$2,583 43	
Unexpended balance	11 06	

$2,594 49	$2,594 49

SALARIES.

Unexpended balance		$66 69
Appropriation		1,200 00
H. B. Phalen	$35 00	
A. H. Bryant	5 00	
A. F. Parmenter	5 00	
M. W. Hynes	5 00	
R. E. Frye	5 00	
H. P. Sherman	7 00	
Geo. A. Leach	5 00	
H. G. Dudley	170 00	
H. F. Lee	200 00	
L. K. Lovell	50 00	
Thomas Bryant	200 00	
T. W. Frost	200 00	
Ralph Bent	10 00	
William H. Bent	57 50	
Edward Carter	66 50	
R. T. Lombard	35 00	
H. G. Hammond	42 00	
D. F. Fiske	52 00	
D. W. P. Loker	57 50	
M. W. Hynes	5 00	
Geo. E. Duprey	2 50	
E. B. Smith	5 00	
A. F. Parmenter	5 00	
H. G. Dudley	5 00	
L. A. Loker	5 00	
E. M. Partridge	5 00	
A. C. Bryant	2 50	
R. E. Frye	5 00	
Thomas Bryant	5 00	
J. E. Linnehan	5 00	
E. E. Butler	7 00	
P. A. Leary	2 50	
Isaac Damon	50 00	
J. A. Draper	5 00	
Overdrawn		55 31
	$1,322 00	$1,322 00

SCHOOL SUPPLIES.

Unexpended balance		$34 66
Appropriation		550 00
Expended	$541 01	
Unexpended balance	43 65	
	$584 66	$584 66

INTEREST ACCOUNT.

Appropriation		$3,000 00
" for overdraft		386 30
Water rates		1,450 00
Overdraft		451 73
Overdraft for 1895	$386 30	
Boston Safe Deposit and Trust Company	2,385 00	
" " " "	1,250 00	
Water bond	20 00	
Allen fund	60 00	
Donation fund	78 00	
Loker fund	100 00	
School-house loan	220 00	
J. S. Draper fund	60 00	
Childs fund	6 00	
Temporary loans	722 73	
	$5,288 03	$5,288 03

WATER COMMISSIONERS.

Appropriation for overdraft		$53 50
Water rates		1,543 89
Hydrants		384 00
Overdraft, 1895	$53 50	
Transferred to interest account	1,450 00	
H. G. Dudley	476 89	
Unexpended balance	1 00	
	$1,981 39	$1,981 39

LIBRARY.

Appropriation		$500 00
Dog license (half)		153 62
H. D. Parmenter, treas.	$653 62	
	$653 62	$653 62

MODERATOR·

Appropriation		$5 00
H. G. Dudley	$5 00	
	$5 00	$5 00

HYDRANTS.

Appropriation		$384 00
Transferred to water commissioners . .	$384 00	
	$384 00	$384 00

SIDEWALKS.

Unexpended balance		$300 00
Expended	$281 20	
Unexpended balance	18 80	
	$300 00	$300 00

·FENCE AT LAKEVIEW CEMETERY.

Unexpended balance		$125 00
H. B. Phalen	$125 00	
	$125 00	$125 00

NORTH AND CENTRE CEMETERIES.

Unexpended balance		$137 80
T. S. Sherman	$71 69	
Unexpended balance	66 11	
	$137 80	$137 80

CEMETERY ACCOUNT.

Unexpended balance		$112 00
T. S. Sherman		17 00
Unexpended balance	$129 00	
	$129 00	$129 00

SUPERINTENDENT OF SCHOOLS.

Unexpended balance		$84 62
Transferred from contingencies		500 00
Overdrawn		52 30
Expended, J. A. Pitman	$636 92	
	$636 92	$636 92

FIRE DEPARTMENT.

Unexpended balance		$224 00
Appropriation		224 00
Ralph Bent	$224 00	
Unexpended balance	224 00	
	$448 00	$448 00

ELECTRIC LIGHTS.

Unexpended balance		$72 47
Appropriation		340 00
Natick Electric Light Co.	$350 04	
Unexpended balance	62 43	
	$412 47	$412 47

REPAIRS ON CENTRE SCHOOL HOUSE.

Unexpended balance		$5 83
Transferred to contingencies account . .	$5 83	
	$5 83	$5 83

.COLLECTION OF TAXES.

Appropriation		$300 00
W. B. Ward	$300 00	
	$300 00	$300 00

REPAIRS ON SCHOOL BUILDINGS.

Unexpended balance		$49 38
Appropriation		100 00
C. B. Williams		15 60
Overdrawn		51 59
Expended	$216 57	
	$216 57	$216 57

HIGH SCHOOL HOUSE, WAYLAND.

Unexpended balance		$4,000 00
Appropriation		11,000 00
Transferred from contingent fund . .		2,000 00
Expended	$13,481 00	
Unexpended balance	3,519 00	
	$17,000 00	$17,000 00

ILLEGAL SALE INTOXICATING LIQUORS.

Unexpended balance		$104 26
Appropriation		200 00
Expended	$68 46	
Unexpended balance	235 80	
	$304 26	$304 26

TEMPORARY LOANS.

Notes outstanding		$13,000 00
Natick National Bank		3,000 00

Natick National Bank	.	.	.	.	.	.	$2,000 00
" " "	.	.	.	.	.	.	3,000 00
" " "	.	.	.	.	.	.	2,000 00
Paid Natick National Bank	.	.	.$7,000 00				
Notes outstanding	.	.	.	.16,000 00			

| | $23,000 00 | $23,000 00 |

TRANSPORTATION OF SCHOLARS.

Unexpended balance .	.	.	.	.	.	.	$79 00
Appropriation	.	.	.	.	.	.	500 00
Overdrawn .	.	.	.	.	.	.	20 50
Expended .	.	.	.	.	.	$599 50	

| | $599 50 | $599 50 |

LAKEVIEW CEMETERY.

Unexpended balance .	.	.	.	.	.	.	$1 55
Appropriation	.	.	.	.	.	.	100 00
Overdrawn .	.	.	.	.	.	.	3 12
Expended .	.	.	.	.	.	$104 67	

| | $104 67 | $104 67 |

STREET LIGHTS.

Unexpended balance .	.	.	.	.	.	.	$14 71
Appropriation	.	.	.	.	.	.	50 00
Unexpended balance .	.	.	.	.	.	$64 71	

| | $64 71 | $64 71 |

HIGHWAY NEAR MRS. SIMPSON'S CORNER.

| Unexpended balance . | . | . | . | . | . | . | $250 00 |
| Isaac Damon | . | . | . | . | . | $250 00 | |

| | $250 00 | $250 00 |

DECORATION DAY.

Appropriation		$100 00
Expended	$100 00	
	$100 00	$100 00

CONTINGENT FUND.

1896.

Feb. 29.

Unexpended balance	$852 69
State treasurer, corporation tax . . .	198 76
Centre scales	16 67
District court fines	134 98
J. E. Linnehan, rent of hall . . .	42 50
C. A. Cutting, No. school-house . .	25 00
J. M. Parmenter, Centre school-house and lot	470 00
R. L. Perry, Rutter school-house and lot .	200 00
Patrick Nolan, Thomas " " .	125 00
Pequot Lodge, I. O. O. F., high school building	200 00
N. C. Griffin, land, part of Lakeview cemetery	200 00
Oil barrels	2 05
State treasurer, cattle inspection . .	204 86
Premium on School-house loan . . .	96 25
Interest " " . . .	86 80
S. Russell	1 00
Corporation tax	2,096 20
National bank tax	778 36
Military aid	132 00
State aid	910 00
Cochituate scales	12 85
Interest on tax, 1891	17 05
Overlayings	225 75
"	88
State treasurer, superintendent of schools .	250 00
Additional assessments	312 00
Transferred from repairs on Centre school-house	5 83

Feb. 29. Additional assessments $36 00
Interest on tax, 1894 . . . . . 250 00 .
" " 1895 . . . . . 150 00.

Transferred to superintendent of
schools $500 00
Transferred to interest account 2,500 00
" tablet on monu-
ment 50 00
Transferred to markers soldiers'
graves 50 00
Transferred to high school house 2,000 00
" needy soldiers . 410 17
State and military aid . . 1,182 00
Geo. E. Sherman, auctioneer's
fees 12 00
Unexpended balance . . 1,329 31

$8,033 48 $8,033 48

PAINTING BUILDINGS AT TOWN FARM.

Appropriation $275 00

Expended $271 35
Unexpended balance 3 65

$275 00 $275 00

FENCE COCHITUATE SCHOOL HOUSE.

Appropriation $100 00

Unexpended balance $100 00

$100 00 $100 00

HIGH SCHOOL TUITION.

Appropriation $500 00

Expended $50 00
Unexpended balance 450 00

$500 00 $500 00

CULVERT AND WALL. (NEAR C. B. WILLIAMS' HOUSE.)

Appropriation		$400 00
Expended	$397 01	
Unexpended balance	2 99	
	$400 00	$400 00

GRAVEL ACCOUNT.

Expended	$90 80	
Overdrawn		$90 80
	$90 80	$90 80

OVERDRAFTS 1895-96.

Appropriation		$1,331 75
Schools	$204 58	
Incidentals	459 92	
Highways	94 49	
Abatement Taxes	74 57	
Interest Acct.	386 30	
Water Commissioners	53 50	
Balance	58 39	
	$1,331 75	$1,331 75

SCHOOL HOUSE LOAN.

Puritan Trust Co.		$11,000 00
" " " note No. 1	$1,100 00	
Notes outstanding	9,900 00	
	$11,000 00	$11,000 00

LIBRARY TABLET ON MONUMENT.

Transferred from contingent fund		$50 00
Unexpended	$50 00	
	$50 00	$50 00

MARKERS FOR REVOLUTIONARY SOLDIERS' GRAVES.

Transferred from contingent fund $50 00

Expended. $46 00
Unexpended balance 4 00

$50 00 $50 00

W. B. WARD.
TAX 1891.

1896.
March 1. Amount due $442 15

W. B. Ward $75 35
Balance due Mar. 1, 1897 . . . . 366 80

$442 15 $442 15

TAX 1892.

Due from Collector . . . $530 60

Bal. due from collector Mar. 1, 1897 . . $530 60

$530 60 $530 60

TAX 1893.

Due from Collector . . . $930 89

W. B. Ward $575 77
Balance due March 1, 1897 . . . 355 12

$930 89 $930 89

TAX 1894.

Due from Collector . . . $5,635 50

W. B. Ward $4,306 58
Balance due March 1, 1897 . . . 1,328 92

$5,635 50 $5,635 50

TAX 1895.

Due from Collector . . . $9,508 96

W. B. Ward $3,717 62
Balance due March 1, 1897 . . . 5,791 34

$9,508 96 $9,508 96

TAX 1896.

Amount assessed	$21,459 75	
Overlayings	225 75	
Additional assessments	312 00	
State tax	1,102 50	
County tax	1,581 48	
Special tax	330 51	
Overlayings	88	
Additional assessment	36 00	
W. B. Ward		$15,332 69
Balance due		9,716 18
	$25,048 87	$25,048 87

STATE TAX.

State tax		$1,102 50
State treasurer	$1,102 50	
	$1,102 50	$1,102 50

COUNTY TAX.

Tax		$1,581 48
J. O. Hayden, treasurer	$1,581 48	
	$1,581 48	$1,581 48

SPECIAL TAX.

Tax		$330 51
State treasurer	$330 51	
	$330 51	$330 51

ABATEMENT TAXES.

Appropriation		$200 00
" for overdraft		74 57
Overdraft	$74 57	
Abatements	182 61	
Unexpended balance	17 39	
	$274 57	$274 57

TAX TITLE.

Title		$97 94
Title unpaid	$97 94	
	$97 94	$97 94

OUTSTANDING OBLIGATIONS.

TOWN DEBT.

Nov. 3, 1863.	Draper library fund, demand, 6 % .	$500 00
Jan. 1, 1875.	Allen fund, demand, 6 % . . .	1,000 00
Aug. 1, 1878.	Water bonds, due Aug. 1, 1898, 5 %	25,000 00
Oct. 1, 1878.	Town bonds, due Oct. 1, 1898, 5 %	44,500 00
Jan. 1, 1881.	Mrs. Childs fund, demand, 6 % .	100 00
Oct. 1, 1882.	Water bonds, due Oct. 1, 1902, 4 % .	4,000 00
July 1, 1888.	" " July 1, 1898, 4 % .	1,000 00
Jan. 1, 1889.	Donation fund, demand, 6 % . .	1,300 00
Apr. 1, 1891.	Loker fund, demand, 5 % . .	2,000 00
Apr. 12, 1894.	James S. Draper fund, demand, 6 %	500 00
		$79,900 00

H. F. LEE, *Treasurer*,

In account with TOWN OF WAYLAND.

RECEIPTS FROM ALL SOURCES.			TOTAL EXPENDITURES.		
Mar. 1, 1896.					
Cash balance . .	$1,181 58		Selectmen's orders .	$41,114 20	
Donation fund .	12 00		State tax . .	1,102 50	
State Treas. . .	230 06		County tax . .	1,581 48	
Dog license . .	307 23		Special tax . .	330 51	
Natick (tuition) .	52 50		Water Com. orders .	476 89	
State Treas. . .	326 92		Temporary loans .	7,000 00	
Overseers of Poor .	1,315 97		State & Military aid	1,182 00	

Water rates	.	.	$1,543 89	School house loan	. $1,100 00
T. S. Sherman	.		17 00	Cash balance .	. 2,540 90
Natick bank	.	.	10,000 00		
Puritan Loan & Trust					
Co:	.	.	11,000 00		
Corporation tax	.		198 76		
Centre scales	.	.	16 67		
Dist. court fines	.	-	60 05		
Rent of hall	.	.	2 50		
School buildings	.		1,020 00		
N. C. Griffin, land	.		200 00		
Oil barrels	.	.	2 05		
Cattle commission	.		204 96		
Rent of hall	.	.	5 00		
Dist. court fines	.		12 50		
Premium on loan	.		96 25		
Interest on loan	.		86 80		
State Treas.	.	.	250 00		
Dist. court fines	.		21 95		
Rent of hall	.	.	5 00		
" "	.		4 00		
Samuel Russell	.		1 00		
Corporation tax	.		2,096 20		
National bank tax	.		778 36		
Military aid	.	.	132 00		
State aid	.	.	910 00		
Dist. court fines	.	.	40 48		
J. E. Linnehan	.		20 00		
E. A. Atwood, scales			12 85		
Interest on tax 1891			17 05		
C. B. W., school rep			15 60		
J. E. Linnehan	.		6 00		
Interest on taxes	.		400 00		
W. B. Ward, tax 1891			75 35		
" " " 1893			453 41		
" " " 1894			4,272 03		
" " " 1895			3,716 40		
" " " 1896			15,308 21		
			$56,428 48		$56,428 48

TRIAL BALANCE.

Overdraft schools	.	$276 14	Unex. bal. highways		$11 06
Support of poor	.	199 11	School supplies	.	43 65
Incidentals	. .	462 89	Abatements	.	17 39
Salaries	. .	55 31	Water Com.	.	1 00
Int. on town debt		451 73	Sidewalks	. .	18 80
Supt. of schools	.	52 30	No. & Centre cem.		66 11
Rep. school bldgs		51 59	Fire department	.	224 00
Trans. scholars	.	20 50	Cemetery account		129 00
Lakeview cem.	.	3 12	Electric lights	.	62 43
Gravel	. .	90 80	High school house		3,519 00
Due Coll. tax 1891		366 80	Illegal sale liquor		235 80
" " 1892		530 60	Street lights	.	64 71
" " 1893		355 12	Contingent	. .	1,329 31
" " 1894		1,328 92	Paint farm bldgs.		3 65
" " 1895		5,791 34	Fence C. S. House		100 00
" " 1896		9,716 18	High school tuition		450 00
Tax title	. .	97 94	Culvert and wall	.	2 99
Cash	. . .	2,540 90	Overdrafts	. .	58 39
			Library tablet	.	50 00
			Markers R. S. graves		4 00
			Temporary loans	.	16,000 00
		$22,391 29			$22,391 29

A. H. BRYANT, *Auditor.*

Auditor's Report.

March 23, 1896.

Schools, care of rooms and fuel	$6,200 00
School supplies	550 00
School repairs	100 00
Transportation of Scholars	500 00
Highways and bridges	2,500 00
Incidentals	1,500 00
Fireman's pay	224 00
Support of poor	2,200 00
Collection of taxes	300 00
Abatement of taxes	200 00
Hydrants	384 00
Lakeview Cemetery	100 00
North & Centre Cemeteries	100 00
Public Library	500 00
Interest on town debt	3,000 00
Salaries	1,200 00
Suppression of illegal sale of liquor	200 00
Electric lights	340 00
Lights at Wayland Centre	50 00
Overdraft for 1895	1,331 75
Decoration Day	100 00
Moderator	5 00
Painting town farm Buildings	275 00
High school tuition	500 00

Fence at Cochituate school house $100 00
Culvert and wall near C. B. Williams . . . 400 00
Superintendent of schools 500 00
Library monument 50 00
Markers for revolutionary soldier's graves . . . 50 00
New school house 17,000 00

$40,459 75

March 23, 1896.

From contingent fund $2,500 00
"   " 500 00
"   " 50 00
                 . . . . . . 50 00
                 . . . . . . 2,000 00
"   " 4,000 00
School house loan 11,000 00
Town tax assessed 20,359 75

$40,459 75 $40,459 75

Index.

One Hundred and Eighteenth Municipal Year,

FROM

MARCH 1, 1897, TO MARCH 1, 1898.

Lakeview Press:
TRIBUNE BUILDING, SOUTH FRAMINGHAM, MASS.
1898.

OFFICIAL REPORTS

OF THE

TOWN OF WAYLAND,

FOR ITS

One Hundred and Eighteenth Municipal Year,

FROM

MARCH 1, 1897, TO MARCH 1, 1898.

--- ---

Lakeview Press:

TRIBUNE BUILDING, SOUTH FRAMINGHAM, MASS.

1898.

List of Town Officers of Wayland

FOR 1897-98 AND WHEN THEIR TERMS EXPIRE.

Term Expires

TOWN CLERK.

RICHARD T. LOMBARD 1898

TREASURER.

HENRY F. LEE 1898

AUDITOR.

ALFRED H. BRYANT 1898

COLLECTOR.

WILLARD B. WARD 1898

TREASURER OF LIBRARY FUNDS.

HENRY D. PARMENTER 1898

SELECTMEN.

ISAAC DAMON 1898
PATRICK A. LEARY 1898
ALBION F. PARMENTER 1898

OVERSEERS OF POOR.

GEORGE B. HOWE 1898
DAVID P. W. LOKER 1898
WILLARD B. WARD 1898

SCHOOL COMMITTEE.

L. ANNA DUDLEY 1898
LLEWELLYN FLANDERS (elected to fill vacancy) . 1898
DELOSS W. MITCHELL 1900

ASSESSORS.

EDWARD CARTER 1898
HORATIO G. HAMMOND 1899
RICHARD T. LOMBARD 1900

WATER COMMISSIONERS.

CHARLES 'H. BOODEY 1898
HENRY G. DUDLEY 1899
WM. M. FULLICK 1900

TRUSTEES PUBLIC LIBRARY.

ARTHUR G. BENNETT 1898
RICHARD T. LOMBARD 1898
JAMES A. DRAPER 1899
CYRUS W. HEIZER 1899
JOHN CONNELLY 1900
CHAS. F. RICHARDSON 1900

CONSTABLES.

THOMAS E. GLENNON 1898
JESSE W. JENNISON 1898
JOHN E. LINNEHAN 1898
LAWRENCE H. McMANUS 1898
WILLIAM C. NEAL 1898
PETER S. ZIMMERMAN 1898
  (ONE VACANCY)

TRUSTEES ALLEN FUND.

ISAAC DAMON 1898
DANIEL D. GRIFFIN 1898
WILLIAM H. CAMPBELL 1898

FENCE VIEWERS.

ALBION F. PARMENTER 1898
ISAAC DAMON 1898
EDWARD CARTER 1898

FIELD DRIVERS.

IRA S. DICKEY 1898
GEORGE B. HOWE 1898

SEALER OF WEIGHTS AND MEASURES.
VACANCY.

MEASURERS OF WOOD AND BARK.

EDWARD CARTER 1898
WM. S. LOVELL 1898

SURVEYOR OF LUMBER.
VACANCY.

SUPERINTENDENTS OF CEMETERIES.

HENRY B. PHALEN (Lakeview) 1898
THEO. S. SHERMAN (North and Centre) . . 1898

FINANCE COMMITTEE.

ISAAC DAMON 1898
RICHARD T. LOMBARD 1898
GEORGE B. HOWE 1898
DELOSS W. MITCHELL 1898
CHAS. H. BOODEY 1898
HENRY F. LEE 1898
MICHAEL W. HYNES 1898

COMMITTEE ON DECORATION DAY.

CHAS. H. MAY 1898
L. K. LOVELL 1898
C. A. ROAK 1898
E. C. DAVIS 1898
EDWARD CARTER 1898

ENGINEERS OF FIRE DEPARTMENT.

EDWIN W. MARSTON, *Chief* 1898
ARTHUR J. RICKER 1898
FRANK E. YEAGER 1898

SUPERINTENDENT OF STREETS.

MICHAEL W. HYNES 1898

REGISTRARS OF VOTERS.

JAMES H. CARROLL, *Chairman* 1898
CHARLES F. WHITTIER 1899
THEO. L. SAWIN 1900
RICHARD T. LOMBARD *Town Clerk, ex-officio* . . 1898

Annual Town Meeting, March 28, 1898.

WARRANT·

COMMONWEALTH OF MASSACHUSETTS.

MIDDLESEX SS :

To Jesse W. Jennison, or either of the Constables of the Town of Wayland in said County,

Greeting:

In the name of the Commonwealth of Massachusetts, you are directed to notify the qualified voters of said Town of Wayland to meet at the Town Hall, Wayland, on·Monday, March 28, 1898, at 7.30 o'clock in the forenoon, then and there to act on the following articles, viz.

ARTICLE 1. To choose by ballot a moderator to preside in said meeting.

ART. 2. To choose a Town Clerk, Treasurer, Collector of Taxes, Auditor, three Selectmen, three Overseers of the Poor, Treasurer of the Library Funds, and Seven Constables all for one year, one School Committee, one Assessor, one Water Commissioner, two Trustees of the Public Library, all for three years, one School Committee for one year, one Assessor for one year. Also to answer the following questions : "Shall licenses for the sale of intoxicating liquors be granted in the town of Wayland for the year ensuing ? "

All names of candidates for the offices aforesaid, and the said question must appear upon the official ballot, and be voted for in accordance with Chapter 386 of the Acts of the year 1890.

For the purposes specified in this article the polls will be opened immediately after the election of a Moderator, and will remain open continuously till one o'clock p. m., when it may be closed unless the meeting shall otherwise determine, but must remain open not less than four hours.

ART. 3. To choose all other necessary Town Officers, Agents and Committees, and hear reports of Town Officers, Trustees, Agents and Committees and act thereon.

ART. 4. To see how much money the town will grant for paying interest, and existing debts, for roads and bridges, for support of poor, for support of schools, school snpplies and repairs on school buildings, and transportation of scholars; for the fire department, for abatement of taxes and for all other necessary town purposes and order the same to be assessed, or do or act.

ART. 5 To authorize the Selectmen to consult counsel on important town cases.

ART. 6. To see if the town will authorize its Treasurer, with the approval of the Selectmen, to borrow money in anticipation of taxes for the year 1898, and if so, how much, or do or act.

ART. 7. To see if the town will accept the list of Jurors as prepared by the Selectmen.

ART. 8. To appropriate the license money on dogs, refunded by the County Treasurer, or do or act.

ART. 9. To see if the town will instruct its Representatives in in the General Court to oppose the scheme known as a "Greater Boston" County or any other legislation, which shall tend to dismember Middlesex County, or disrupt its time-honored institutions.

ART. 10. To see if the town will appropriate the sum of one hundred and fifty dollars for repairing Mitchell street, or do or act.

ART. 11. To see if the town will appropriate the sum of five hundred dollars for the purchase of hose and overcoats for the Fire Department, or do or act.

ART. 12. To see if the town will instruct the Selectmen to appoint a Special Police, or do or act.

ART. 13 To see if the town will adopt Chapter 331 of the Acts of the General Court for the year 1888 relating to taking pickerel in any river, stream or pond, in the town, or do or act.

ART. 14. To see if the town will appropriate the sum of two hundred dollars to erect a shed at the Town Farm for the protection of wagons and implements, and appoint a committee to expend the same, or do or act.

ART. 15. To see if the town will direct that the position of janitor of all public buildings shall be let to the lowest bidder, if qualified, or do or act.

ART. 16. To see if the town will appropriate the sum of five hundred dollars for sidewalks, or do or act.

ART. 17. To see if the town will appropriate the money received for sale of lots in the cemeteries for improving the cemeteries, or do or act.

ART. 18. To see if the town will vote to abate the personal tax of Charles W. Dean for the year of 1895 for $72.50, 1896 for $78 00, and 1897 for $80.00, or do or act.

ART. 19. To see if the town will re-open for public travel the road leading from the Framingham to the Natick road, starting near the late residence of the late Joseph Bullard, and from thence to near the residence of Walter E. Reeves, or do or act.

ART. 20. To see what sum the town will appropriate to settle the claim of Susan A. Pierce against the town, or do or act.

ART. 21. To see if the town will refund to Elizabeth Poole the sum of eighteen dollars paid for transporting children to school, or do or act.

ART. 22. To see if the Town will authorize its Treasurer to borrow a sum of money not exceeding fifteen thousand dollars and issue bonds or notes therefor, for the purpose of refunding an equal amount of its Water Fund Bonds falling due July 1st and August 1st, 1898, the same to be borrowed under the terms and conditions and by authority of Chapter 177 of the Acts of the General Court for the year 1896, or do or act.

ART. 23 To see if the town will authorize its Treasurer to borrow the sum of forty-four thousand and five hundred dollars and issue bonds or notes therefor, for the purpose of refunding an equal amount of the bonded debt of the town, which becomes due October 1, 1898, and on what terms and conditions, or do or act·

Art. 24. To see what action the town will take in reference to the actions at law brought against the town by Edmond A. Lupien and by Ambroise A. Lupien, or do or act.

Art. 25. To see if the town will accept the bequest, under the will of the late Warren Gould Roby, of money to build a Public Library building and a lot of land upon which the same is to be erected, or do or act.

Art. 26. To see if the town will vote to increase the appropriation for the Fire Department from $224.00 to $424 00, thereby increasing the pay of each man from $5.00 to $10.00, or do or act.

And you are directed to serve this Warrant by posting up attested copies thereof at the Town House and each of the Post Offices in the town, seven days at least before the day for holding said meeting.

Hereof fail not, and make due return of this warrant, with your doings thereon, to the Town Clerk of said Town on or before the time appointed for holding said meeting.

Given under our hands this seventh day of March in the year eighteen hundred and ninety-eight.

ISAAC DAMON,
ALBION F. PARMENTER,
PATRICK A. LEARY,
Selectmen of Wayland.

A true copy.   Attest,

JESSE W. JENNISON,
Constable.

Jury List·

List of Jurors as prepared by the Selectmen for the Year 1898·

Albion F. Parmenter.
Jeremiah Lyons.
Theodore L. Sawin.
John E. Linnehan.
Frank Haynes.
Frank Lupien.
Isaac S. Whittemore.
Warren B Langmaid.
Edward B. Smith.
George E. Sherman.
Edgar B. Loker.
Andrew S. Morse.
Alfred H. Bryant.

John J. McCann.
Sidney Loker.
William H. Campbell.
Ernest E. Butler.
Andrew S. Norris.
Adoniren J. Puffer.
Wm. F. Garfield.
Wm. S. Lovell.
Allen B. Sherman.
Paul Paradeau.
Edward F. Lee. '
Edward M. Partridge.
Randall W. Porter.

ISAAC DAMON,
ALBION F. PARMENTER,
PATRICK A. LEARY,
Selectmen of Wayland.

March 7, 1898.

Report of the Selectmen.

WAYLAND, March 1, 1898

The Selectmen hereby submit their annual report as required by the By-laws of the town.

The following officers were appointed as required by statute:

Engineers of the Fire Department. Edwin W. Marston, Ralph Bent, Henry B. Phalen. Mr. Bent resigned and Arthur J. Ricker was appointed to fill the vacancy. Later Mr. Phalen resigned and Frank E. Yeager was appointed to succeed him.

Undertakers. Andrew S. Morse, David P. W. Loker.

Inspector of Cattle and Provisions. Thomas Bryant.

Superintendent of Streets. M. W. Hynes.

Special Police. Geo. E Sherman, Henry B. Phalen, John Woodworth.

Truant Officers. T. S. Sherman, Albert F. King.

Registrar of Voters. Theo. L Sawin. There being a vacancy caused by the resignation of Mr. Mitchell, James Carroll was appointed to fill the vacancy. Another vacancy occurring by the death of Mr. L. H. Sherman, Mr. Chas. F. Whittier was appointed to fill the same.

School Committee. A vacancy being caused by the resignation of Mrs. Bent, Mr. L. Flanders was appointed to fill her unexpired term.

Trustee of the Library. Arthur G. Bennett was appointed to fill the vacancy caused by the resignation of Mrs. Braman.

Public Weighers. L. K. Lovell, George B. Howe.

Janitor of Town Hall. John E. Linnehan.

Burial Agent for Indigent Soldiers and Sailors. Edson C. Davis.

Election Officers, Precinct No. 1. Warden, H. P. Sherman; Clerk, J. A. Draper; Inspectors, E. F. Lee, M. W. Hynes, Wm. Stearns, Wm. Campbell. *Precinct No. 2.* Warden, E. E. Butler; Clerk, Thomas Bryant; Inspectors, E. M. Partridge, Chas. H. Seriach, E. B. Smith, A. J. Lamerine.

As per vote of the town the culvert on Harrison avenue was enlarged.

According to the vote of the town, the hill near the house of Dennis McDonald has been cut down and the money appropriated for the same expended.

We have purchased of Michael Rowen a small hill of gravel to be used on the Plain road ; also a hill of gravel from Edgar Loker for use in the south part of the town.

A concrete sidewalk has been built adjoining the estates of Mr. C. B. Williams and Mr. N. R. Gerald costing $350 66, the abutters paying one-half of the cost.

The case of Samuel Reeves vs. the town of Wayland was decided in favor of the plaintiff, judgment being rendered $447.58 which sum was drawn from the contingent fund.

The Sand Hill road was completed by the County Commissioners and the town proportional share paid as per vote.

The State Highway Commissioners awarded the town the sum of $5,000 with which to build a section of macadamized road, commencing at Weston line. At a special town meeting, it was voted that the Selectmen, Superintendent of Streets and W. A. Bullard be a committee to make a contract with the Highway Commissioners which was carried into effect.

The Selectmen deeming it unadvisable for the town to do the work, sublet the contract to Mr. A. J. Wellington of Boston with the proviso that local help be employed, he giving bonds for the completion of the same, which are on file. It being impossible to complete the road last fall, the commission granted an extension of time.

The work was greatly delayed by the unwillingness of the abutters to sign the releases.

We recommend that a committee be chosen to investigate and devise some means of drainage for Main street, Cochituate village. We would also suggest that a small appropriation be made for lighting the principal streets in Wayland Centre.

ISAAC DAMON,
ALBION F. PARMENTER,
PATRICK A. LEARY,
                    Selectmen of Wayland.

Report of Town Clerk and Registrar.

WAYLAND, January 1, 1898.

I hereby transmit the Annual Report of the Clerk and Registrar for the year ending December 31, 1897.

BIRTHS.

The whole number registered during the year is forty-two, being fourteen more than in 1896: Of the number twenty-three were males and nineteen were females.

Born of native parents 27
" foreign parents 10
" native and foreign parents . . . 5

MARRIAGES.

The whole number registered during the year is twenty-four, being one more than in 1896.

Native birth of both parties 17
Native and foreign birth 5
Foreign birth of both parties 2
First marriage of both parties 21
Second marriage of both parties 1
First of one and second of the other . . 2

DEATHS.

Whole number registered during the year is twenty-nine, being the same number registered in 1896.

CONDITION.

Married	9
Widowed	5
Single	15
Native born	26
Foreign born	3
Males	15
Females	14

Names of persons deceased during the year who were over seventy years of age:

	Years.	Months.	Days.
Alpheus D. Loker . . .	73	5	
Hannah Cutting . . .	70		
Charlotte A Coaldwell . .	85	8	8
Ann McClellan	80		
Francis Moore	70	7	
Mary McCann	75		
Persis Allen	83		26
Evinson Stone	73	11	1
Samuel M. Thomas . . .	83	1	11

NOSOLOGICAL TABLE.

Diptheria	1
Pneumonia	1
Malignant Pancreas	1
Scarlet Fever	1
Pernicious Aneumia	2
Paralysis	2
Convulsions	1
Consumption	1
Meningitis	1

Tuberculosis 1
Inflammation of brain . . , . . . 2
Heart disease 2
Old age 1
Brain clot 1
Cerebral hemorrhage 1
Cystitis 2
Apoplexy 1
Still-born 1
Cancer 1
Suicide . . . - 1
Carcinoma of Stomach 1
Pyrosis 1
Appendicitis 1
Nephritis 1

DOGS.

Number of dogs licensed
    99 males, at $2.00 . . . . . $198 00
    18 females at $5.00 . . . . . 90 00

                                                       $288 00
117 licenses at 20 cents 23 40

Amount received $264 60
Number of registered voters, November 1, 1897 . 459
Number precinct 1 159
      "   2 300
Ballots cast precinct 1 135
      "   2 212
Number of women voters 63

VOTE FOR GOVERNOR.

Thomas C. Brophy . . . . . . 6 votes.
William Everett . . . . . . 19 "
Geo. Fred Williams . . . . . . 89 "
Roger Wolcott . . . . . . 217 '

TOTAL VOTE FOR REPRESENTATIVES, 21ST MIDDLESEX DISTRICT.

	Balcom	Brackett	Lombard	Morse	Blanks
Marlborough	1225	824	745	1150	620
Sudbury	21	80	36	74	37
Wayland	88	191	138	130	147
	1334	1095	919	1354	804

At the last annual town election no women voted, although there were sixty-three duly registered.

Since the last annual meeting I have been able to identify the graves of two additional revolutionary soldiers, that of Aaron Damon and William Rice, and it is hoped provision will be made for marking the same.

Respectfully submitted,

RICHARD T. LOMBARD,

Town Clerk.

Assessors' Report.

WAYLAND, March 1, 1898.

To the Inhabitants of the Town of Wayland:

At the last annual Town Meeting it was voted that the assessors' report in print in the annual Town Report "a list of the persons or corporations whose taxes are abated, and the amounts so abated." We question the policy of such a vote, as the assessors' records are open to all, and our experience has convinced us that matters of this kind are better left to those whose duties have made them familiar with the effect of such a proceeding, yet being bound to comply with the vote, the abatements are inserted in this report.

It is desirable that our tax payers and voters should know that while for the last few years our valuation has increased only about nine-tenths of one per cent. our expenditures have increased about ten per cent. Such a condition should be remembered when appropriations are made, as an increasing tax rate cannot be beneficial to the town.

STATISTICS.

Value of Real estate May 1, 1897 . . .	$1,260,090 00
Value of Personal Estate May 1, 1897 . . .	267,115 00
Total Valuation	1,527,205 00
Value May 1, 1896	1,491,955 00
Increase	35,250 00

Taxes assessed for town purposes . . .	$23,036 49
Overlayings	2 34
State Tax	1,102 50
County tax	1,491 95
Additional assessments	112 08
Total assessments	$25,745 36
Special tax on meadow	330 51
Overlayings on same	1 21
Total special tax	$331 72
Number of polls assessed May 1, . . .	599
Additional polls asssessed	12
Total number of polls assessed	611
Number of polls assessed in 1896 . . .	566
Increase of polls	45
Number of persons assessed	899
Number of residents assessed on property . .	409
Number of non-residents assessed on property .	145
Total value of land	$483,385 00
Total value of buildings	776,705 00
Value of church property	30,240 00
Value of town property	120,637 00
Number of horses	393
" cows	719
" sheep	36
" swine	300
" fowls assessed	1680
" dwelling houses	423
" acres of land assessed . . .	9,189½

Rate of taxation for 1897, $16.00 per thousand.
"   "   " 1896, $15.60   "

LIST OF ABATEMENTS.

Taxes assessed in 1891.

Henry B. Fisher, poll	$2 00
Mathew Coakley, poll	2 00
Wm. & J. M. Bent, personal	366 80
Total	$370 80

Taxes assessed in 1892

Charles E. Brummett, poll	$2 00
Mathew Coakley "	2 00
Michael M. Riley "	2 00
Clarence W. Frost "	2 00
Bent Bros. & Co., personal	337 60
Total	$345 60

TAXES ASSESSED IN 1893.

Charles E. Brummett, poll	$2 00
William W. Clark "	2 00
Mathew C. Coakley "	2 00
Geo. Clough	2 00
Joseph Cormier	2 00
Clarence W. Frost "	2 00
Albert S. Lyon	2 00
Henry Mathieu	2 00
Louis Lovely	2 00
Maynard T. Damon "	2 00
Total	$20 00

TAXES ASSESSED IN 1894.

Jessee Amroy poll	$2 00
John Banks "	2 00
Joseph Beauregard "	2 00
Wm. Brown '	2 00

Timothy Buckley	poll	$2 00
Henry Bettis	"	2 00
Jas. A Baldwin	"	2 00
Freeman Bolieau	"	2 00
Michael Collins,	"	2 00
Joseph Conner,	"	2 00
George Clough	"	2 00
John Chenette	"	2 00
William Campbell	"	2 00
Charles Dunham	"	2 00
Owen Dunham	"	2 00
Napoleon Demers	"	2 00
Henry B. Fisher	"	2 00
Clarence W. Frost	"	2 00
Edward Floyd -	"	2 00
William Fergerson	"	2 00
George Gazette	"	2 00
Edward L. Graves	"	2 00
Warren A. Hersey	"	2 00
James Huzzy		2 00
Nathaniel Hill	"	2 00
Clarence Leary	"	2 00
George Leach	"	2 00
Chas. O. McCarthy	"	2 00
James Morey	"	2 00
John E. McLean	"	2 00
Arthur C. Mann	"	2 00
Thomas McGrath	".	2 00
James Nichols	"	2 00
Nelse Olson		2 00
Erwing Perry	"	2 00
Wm. J. Randolph	"	2 00
Eustache Rassicott	"	2 00
Chas V. Rand	"	2 00
Harris Ricker		2 00
Felix Sawyer		2 00
Andrew Scotland	"	2 00
James Scotland	" & personal	2 35

Pierson Shattuck poll	. . . . . .	$2 00
Wm. H. Stearns "	. . . . . .	2 00
Fred A. L. Towne "	. . . . . .	2 00
Harry Turner	. . . . . .	2 00
George Ward	. . . . . .	2 00
Wm. G. Webster "	. . . . . .	2 00
Leroy W.Whittemore " & personal	. . . .	2 42
Felix White "	. . . . . .	2 00
William B. Wyatt "	. . . . . .	2 00
John Yarwood	. . . . . .	2 00
John W. Coakley "	. . . . . .	2 00
Joseph F. Sawyer "	. . . . .	2 00

Total for 1894 .	. . . . . .	$108 77

TAXES ASSESSED IN 1895.

Wm. H. Butterfield, Heirs of, Real Estate .	. .	$18 85
Angelina Tatrault " " .		7 25
Lucy J. Carter " " .	. .	4 35
Adelaide Corless " ..	. .	3 26
Harry H. Rutter		7 25

Total	. . . . .	$40 96

TAXES ASSESSED IN 1896.

Joseph Mathieu, Real Estate	. . . . .	$4 68

TAXES ASSESSED, 1897.

Elizabeth Kelly, real estate	.. . . . .	$7 20
Hazen C. Clement, real estate	. . . . .	8 00
Benj. S. Hemenway, real estate .	. . . .	16 00
Thomas Evans, real estate .	. . . .	1 60
Joseph Mathieu, real estate	. . . .	4 80
James Murphy, real estate .	. . . . .	16 00
Evinson Stone, real estate .	. . . . .	27 20
Arnold Farr, Heirs of, special tax	. . . .	4 60

Total	. . . .	$85 40

Total abatements $976 21

The abatements made to Evinson Stone and James Murphy were made under a statute favoring disabled soldiers.

Respectfully submitted,

RICHARD T. LOMBARD,
EDWARD CARTER,
HORATIO G. HAMMOND,
Assessors of Wayland.

Collector's Report.

Taxes of 1891.

Balance due March 1, 1897	$366	80
Paid Treasurer by abatement	366	80
Interest, $10.48.		

Taxes of 1892.

Balance due March 1, 1897	$530	60
Paid Treasurer	530	60
Interest, $48.38.		

Taxes of 1893.

Balance due March 1, 1897 . . . ., .	$355	12
Paid Treasurer	355	12
Interest, $117.80.		

Taxes of 1894.

Balance due March 1, 1897	$1,328	92
Paid Treasurer	963	96
Balance due	$364	96

Taxes of 1895.

Balance due March 1, 1897	$5,791	34
Paid Treasurer	4,329	75
Balance due	$1,461	59
Interest, $100.00.		

Taxes of 1896.

Balance due March 1, 1897	$9,716 18
Paid Treasurer	3,311 68
	$6,404 50

Interest, $168.00.

Taxes of 1897.

Balance due March 1, 1898	$26,077 08
Paid Treasurer	13,650 02
Balance due	$12,427 06

WILLARD B. WARD,

Collector.

Report of the Overseers of the Poor.

FOR YEAR ENDING FEBRUARY 28, 1898.

Mr. M. Temple, the superintendent of the almshouse for the past two years, has been engaged for the ensuing year.

The general condition of the farm has been considerably improved under his management.

OUT DOOR POOR, PARTIAL SUPPORT.

Families aided	21	
Persons aided	81	
	——	102

IN DOOR POOR, FULL SUPPORT.

Almshouse	3	
State Lunatic Hospitals	3	
	——	6
Total number persons aided . .		108

FINANCIAL STATEMENT SHOWING ACTUAL RECEIPTS AND EXPENDITURES FOR THE YEAR.

Appropriation	$2,500 00

REIMBURSEMENTS.

From Town of Lexington	$52 00	
Town of Spencer	39 00	
Town of Natick .	88 63	
Town of Southboro	127 75	
		$307 38

ALMSHOUSE RECEIPTS.

Sale of milk	$979 89	
Eggs and poultry	27 27	
Produce	85 07	
Cows and calves	58 20	
Board of horse	74 00	
Sale of wood	13 00	
Labor	49 88	
Sale of hay	2 00	
		$1,289 31
Total receipts		$4,096 69

EXPENDITURES OUT DOOR POOR.

Having a settlement in Wayland and residing elsewhere.

Artemas Bond, Boston	$52 00	
Nelson Normandin and family, No. Brookfield	85 37	
Elijah Roberts and family, No. Brookfield .	37 11	
		$174 48

Having a settlement in Wayland and residing there.

John Chinette	$102 83
Anna Burrill	154 75
Joseph Sawyer	10 00
Frank X. Davieaux, Jr. and family	102 58
Ann Painter	52 00
G. C. Chalmers .	27 00
Joseph Cormier and family .	121 68
James Foley	32 93

Bernard Tatro and family $24 00
Louis Cormier and family 4 00
Nelson Latour and family 2 63
Nelson Belmore, Jr. 8 98
                                        ————— $643 38

Having a settlement in other cities and towns and
residing in Wayland.

J. F. Hawkins and family, Southboro . . $171 50
H. W. Dean, Natick 183 82
E. Haldwell, Lexington 52 00
Edward Curran, Spencer . . . , . 4 00
Chas. Dufault and family, Framingham . 23 50
Patrick Fay, State pauper 8 00
                                        ————— $442 82

IN DOOR POOR, IN INSANE HOSPITALS.

Clara Davis, Westboro $169 48
J. A. Wing, Worcester 169 46
Ellen Stanton, Taunton . . . 169 46
                                        ————— $508 40

ALMSHOUSE EXPENDITURES.

Paid warden's salary $395 91
    Groceries 255 63
    Provisions 122 16
    Grain 355 56
    Cows 231 00
    Furniture 16 26
    Medical services 16 60
    Fuel 56 14
    Clothes for inmates 17 56
    Repairs and lumber 65 85
    Hay 56 00
    Fertilizer 54 60
    Blacksmithing 38 33
    Labor 282 22
    Tools 57 69
    Miscellaneous 71 48
                                        ————— $2,092 99

MISCELLANEOUS.

Travelling expenses, settlement of cases,
stationery, order books, etc. . . . $48 28

Total expenditures	$3,910 35
Unexpended balance	186 34
	$4,096 69

OUTSTANDING CLAIMS.

Town of North Brookfield, bill not received.
" Natick, bill not received.
City of Boston, bill not received.
" Haverhill, bill not received.

REIMBURSEMENTS DUE.

From Town of Natick	$151 94	
" " Southboro	43 75	
" " Lexington	52 00	
' " Framingham . . .	23 50	
" Commonwealth of Massachusetts .	8 00	
" Samuel Russell, produce . . .	34 10	
For milk for month of February . . .	92 88	
		$406 17

INMATES AT ALMSHOUSE DURING THE YEAR

Sarah Puffer, March 1, 1897.
James Burke, " "
Benjamin Nealey, " "
James Foley, four months to July 1, 1897.

INVENTORY OF PROPERTY AT ALMSHOUSE.

Farming implements	$389 45
Ten cows	500 00
One horse	90 00
Sixty hens	45 00
Furniture	238 60
Two shoats	8 00

Thirteen tons hay	$166 00	
Twenty cords manuré	100 00	
Fuel	60 00	
Potatoes	15 00	
Provisions	15 00	
	—— ——	$1,627 05
Real estate		5,800 00
		$7,427 05

REMARKS.

The tramp nuisance became so that we were obliged to take advantage of the Tramp Law. The result was very satisfactory.

Below is the abstract of Report upon the almshouse at Wayland May 18, 1897.

EXTERIOR.

Almshouse building in good condition; fire escapes, none; water supply, good but not well distributed; drainage, satisfactory; barns and outbuildings, location distant enough, condition good.

INTERIOR.

Provides no separation of the sexes, nor of sane and insane; rooms found clean and orderly; tolerably furnished; bath rooms, one, but not supplied with hot and cold water; water-closets, two, location attached, condition, good; heating, by stoves only, local and inadequate; ventilation, good.

CARE OF INMATES.

Food is sufficient, of good quality; clothing is suitable and clean; beds and bedding, mattresses and feather beds, bedding enough, clean and free from vermin; bathing supposed to be regular; actual separation of sexes sufficient by day and night, and at meals; hired help, in-door, none, out-door, one; discipline, good.

32

Remarks.

Without structural provision for separation of the sexes there is practical separation at present, the only female inmate being confined to her room. There has been no improvement in the house the past year. The most evident defect is the want of a general and ample supply of heat, stoves being insufficient and dangerous. The efficiency of the bath-room is impaired by the want of hot and cold water which is got only by bringing it in pails. A better arrangement ought to be devised.

CHAS. E. WOODBURY,
Inspector of Institutions.

January 5, 1897.

An appropriation of twenty-five hundred dollars is asked for.

Respectfully submitted,

DAVID P. W. LOKER,
GEORGE B. HOWE,
W. B. WARD.
Overseers of the Poor.

Report of Library Trustees.

We find at the annual examination, the books belonging to the library are all in their places, and save the expected wear-from much handling, in fair condition. We *expect* that books that have been in circulation a long time will show marks of old age, and our bills for rebinding grow larger each year.

We are happy to say that the circulation of our books is increasing each year, showing more and more interest in our library ; but we have had to compel our librarian to say to very many inquirers for *more new books* that we haven't them for lack of funds to buy with.

Last spring there was a spasm of economy that struck some of our people that *only* affected our library, and we were granted but three-fifths of what we asked for, and needed, for we had decided that the library should be opened twice a week, deeming a six months' trial warranted it, causing some more expense, yet we were *cut down* $200 in appropriation, so our new list of additions is much shorter than we wish.

Does it pay, for a few dollars, to cramp our great educator and source of entertainment to so many families? We say not.

During the past season our friend, Mrs. Sidney Hayward, kindly gave one of her celebrated readings for the benefit of the library, the receipts from which ($65) she gave us, relieving us somewhat.

In the near future, we may expect the munificent bequest of our townsman, the late Warren Gould Roby, of $28,000 for the purpose of building a home for our books, will be available ; and let us show to the world that we fully appreciate this gift, not by going . backward, but by taking long steps forward in our efforts to fill its shelves with good books.

It is known throughout the whole country that Wayland has the first free public library in New England.

Do not let it be published to the world that Wayland fails to keep in a flourishing condition that institution which will ever be her greatest monument.

We ask the town to grant us for the coming year the sum of five hundred dollars.

CYRUS W. HEIZER,
R. T. LOMBARD,
C. F. RICHARDSON,
A. G. BENNETT,
JOHN CONNELLY,
J. A. DRAPER,
Trustees.

Librarian's Report.

Statistical information for the year 1897-98 is respectfully submitted.

ACCESSIONS.

	Books.
By purchase.	110
By gift	54
Bound and transferred from pamphlet department .	39
Total	203
Whole number of volumes in the library . . .	12,862
Pamphlets presented	869

CIRCULATION.

In Cochituate village	1,552
In Wayland Centre	4,922
Total	6,474

DONORS OF BOOKS AND PAMPHLETS.

	Books.	Pamphlets.
American Library Commission		1
Bennett, Mrs. Arthur G.	1	
Coolidge, Miss Catherine	1	

Dudley, Miss M. A.		590
Heard, Misses M. & E.		59
Heard, Miss B. E.	2	
Heard, Miss S. E.	7	
King, Mr. Henry F.		1
Leach, Mr. Geo. A.	4	
Loring, The Misses	3	59
Pratt, Messrs. Chas. & F. S	1	
Rice, Mrs. Chas		8
Robinson, Mr. Geo. A.	1	
Salem Public Library		12
Smith, Mr. Elbridge	4	
Sent to the Reading Room	1	145
State Government	8	4
United States Government	20	18
Wayland Social Library of 1796	2	

Library reports have been received as follows: Brookline, Brooklyn, Concord, Forbes Library (Northampton), Lawrence, Salem, Newton, Syracuse, Central, also Cobden Club, Harvard College, Institute of Technology, Indian Rights' Association, Trustees of Public Reservation Reports.

CLASSES OF READING.

Biography	.07	Philosophy	. . .	.03
Fiction .	.44	Religion	. . .	.02
History .	.10	Science.	. . .	.03
Juvenile	.11	Travels	. . .	.07
Literature	.10	Political Economy .	.	.03

The Reading Room has received regularly The Century Magazine, Christian Science, Good Roads, Harper's Monthly, Munsey's, The Land of Sunshine, Woman's Journal, Traveller's Record and Cochituate Enterprise.

SARAH E. HEARD.

February 22, 1898.

9845-6   Alfred, Lord Tennyson, by his Son.   A Memoir.
9866   American Lands and Letters.   Donald G. Mitchell.
9761   At Agincourt.   G. A. Henty.
8225 M   Australasia.   Greville Tregarthen.
9702   Authors and Friends.   Annie Fields.
9805   Ballads.   R. L. Stevenson.
9834-5   Barbara Blomberg.   George Ebers.
9738   Barbara, Lady's Maid and Peeress.   Mrs. Alexander.
9762   Beside Old Hearthstones.   A. E. Brown.
9839   Bohemia with Du Maurier in F. Mocheles.
9666   Book and Heart.   T. W. Higginson.
8225 O   Canada.   J. G. Bourdinot.
9758   Captain Chap.   F. R. Stockton.
9663   Captains Courageous.   Rudyard Kipling.
9823   Choir Invisible, The.   J. Lane Allen.
9688   Christian, The.   Hall Caine.
9747   Citizen Bird.   M. Wright and Elliott Cones.
9786   Colonial Dames and Goodwives.   A. Morse Earle.
9785   Colonial Days in Old New York.   A. Morse Earle.
9828   Complete Bachelor, The.
9710-11 Corleone.   F. M. Crawford.
9696   Correspondence between John Stirling and Emerson.
           Edward Emerson.
8225 N   Crusades.   T. S. Archer.
9668   Cuba in War Time.   Richard F. Davis.
9683   Cup of Trembling.   M. H. Foote.
9722   Dead Selves.   Julia Magruder.
9865   English Lands and Letters.   Donald G. Mitchell.
9673   Epistle to Posterity, An.   M. E. W. Sherwood.
9678   Equality.   Edward Bellamy.
9780   Expert Waitress, The.   A H Springsteed.
9748   Eye Spy.   Wm. H. Gibson.
9858-9   Familiar Letters of Walter Scott.
9860-1   Farthest North.   Fridtjof Nansen.
9756   Frail Children of the Air.   S. H. Scudder.
9741   Francois, The Waif.   George Sand.
9840   Generals' Double, The.   Capt. Chas. King.
9703   Green Book, The, or Freedom Under the Snow.
           Maurus Jokai.

9692	Grey Lady, The. H. S. Merriman.
9868	Growth of the French Nation. G. B. Adams.
9867	Guide to the Study of American History. Ed. by Channing and A. B. Hart.
9764–5	Half Century of Conflict. Francis Parkman.
9797	Hania. Henry Sienkiewicz.
9856	Henry David Thoreau. H. S. Salt.
9687	His Grace of Osmand. F. H. Burnett.
9791	How to Listen to Music. H. E. Krehbiel.
9818–19	Hugh Wynne Free Quaker. S. Weir Mitchell.
9723	Hypocritical Romance, A. Caroline Ticknor.
8880	In the Midst of Alarms. Robert Barr.
8225 K	Japan. David Murray.
9841	Jerome. Mary E. Wilkins.
9895	Journal of the Right Hon. Sir Joseph Banks. Ed. by Sir Joseph D. Hooker.
9800	King Noanette. F. J. Stimson.
9675	Landlord at Lion's Head. Wm. D. Howells.
9843–4	Letters of Elizabeth Barrett Browning. F. Kenyon.
9855	Life of Benvenuto Cellini. J. A. Symonds.
9847–8	Life of Nelson. Capt. A. T. Mahan.
9853	Maria Mitchell, Life Letters, Journal. P. M. Kendall.
9838	Martian, The. G. DuMaurier.
9851	Memories of Hawthorn. Rose Hawthorn Lathrop.
9849	Men of Achievement. Philip G. Hughbett.
9850	Miscellaneous Writings. Mary B. G. Eddy.
9781	Miss Parloa's Young Housekeeper. M. Parloa.
9735	Mistress of Sherburn, The. Amanda Douglas.
9789	My Father as I recall him. Mamie Dickens.
9749	New England Country. Clifton Johnson.
9676	On the Face of the Waters. Flora A. Steel.
9667	Our English Cousins. Richard H. Davis.
9680	Philip and his Wife. Margaret Deland.
9740	Philippa. Mrs. Molesworth.
9162	Phronsie Pepper. Margaret Sidney.
9698	People for Whom Shakespeare Wrote. Charles Dudley Warner.
9659	Pierre and His People. Gilbert Parker.

9653	Poems and Ballads. R. L. Stevenson.
9806	Poems Here at Home. James Whitcomb Riley.
8225 H	Poland. W. R. Morfill.
9743	Polly Oliver's Problem. Kate D. Wiggin.
9669	Princess Aline. Richard H. Davis.
9798	Quo Vadis. Henry Sienkiewicz.
9691	Relation of Literature to Life, The. Chas. D. Warner.
9857	Rocks and Rock Weathering. G. P. Merrill.
9664	Seven Seas, The. Rudyard Kipling.
9752	Sharp Eyes. Rambler's Calendar. Wm. H. Gibson.
9767	Short History of Italy. E. S. Kirkland.
8225 P	Sicily. Edward A. Freeman.
9671	Soldiers of Fortune. Richard H. Davis.
9465	Songs of Childhood. Eugene Field and R. De Koven.
9837	Spoils of Poynton, The. Henry James.
9804	St. Ives. R. L. Stevenson.
9746	Story of the Birds, The. J. N. Baskett.
9854	Story of Jane Austen's Life. Oscar F. Adams.
9842	Story of Jesus Christ. E. Stuart Phelps.
9852	Stories and Legends from Irving.
8225 L	South Africa. George M. Theal.
9660	Sweetheart Travellers. S. R. Crockett.
9658	Trail of the Sword, The. Gilbert Parker.
9894	Travels in West Africa. Mary H. Kingsley.
9796	Trooper Peter Halket of Mashonaland. Olive Schreiner.
8225 I	Tuscan Republic. Bella Duffy.
9862-3	United States of America. N. S. Shaler.
9755	Upon the Tree Tops. Olive Thorn Miller.
8225 J	Venice. Alethia Weil.
9766	Wanderings in Spain. A. J. C. Hare.
9763	War of Independence. John Fiske.
9679	What Necessity Knows. L. Dougall.
9802	Wheels of Chance. H. G. Welles.
9724	White Aprons. Maud W. Goodwin.

HENRY D. PARMENTER, *Treasurer*

In account with Library Funds.

1897.		Dr.		
Mar.	30.	To unexpended appropriation of 1896 .	$207	80
Mar.	30.	Cochituate Branch fines and cards sold .	3	98
June.	18.	Town appropriation for 1897 . .	300 00	
Nov.	8.	Mrs. Beatrice Hayward's entertainment given in aid of the Wayland Library	65	75
1898.				
Jan.	1.	To Interest on Library funds to Jan. 1 .	66	00
Feb.	20.	One-half of Wayland dog license money	98	21
			$741	74

1897.		Cr.		
Mar.		By Frank Haynes carpenters' bill . .	$7	95
	23.	Mrs. S. E. Heard, salary to April 1 .	75	00
	26.	American Express Co.	8	93
May	31.	DeWolfe, Fiske & Co.	71	98
June	11.	A. E. Adams, wood bill . . .	5	50
	19.	Mrs. S. E. Heard, salary to July 1 .	75	00
	28.	American Express Co.	8	93
July	31.	N. R. Gerald, salary to April 1 . .	40	00
Sept.	9.	D. Appleton & Co.	8	00
	22.	Wayland Book Club	7	00
		Library Bureau	2	00
	24.	Mrs. S. E. Heard, salary to Oct. 1 .	75	00
	30.	American Express Co.	8	93
Dec.	6.	Mrs. S. E. Heard, salary to Jan. 1 .	75	00
	7.	F. J. Barnard	13	69
	17.	Patrick Jennings		75
	23.	New Book Club, Mrs. M. L. Rice . .	7	00
	28.	American Express Co.	8	93
1898.				
Jan.	6.	A. H. H. Warren & Co. . . .	7	66
Feb.	15.	DeWolfe, Fiske & Co.	65	86
		James A. Draper	11	62
Mar.	1.	Balance on hand	157	01
			$741	74

Report of the Superintendent of the Wayland Water Works.

GENTLEMEN :—

We have not made any extensions to the works this year, but have had a good deal of trouble with pipes filling up. We have purchased one new hydrant and set the same.

The maintenance account is,

1897.

Feb. 28.	To Labor for February		$6	00
Mar. 10.	Expenses to Boston, Framingham and Watertown		1	20
Mar. 30.	Labor for March		3	50
April 5.	Expenses to Boston			90
7.	Howe & Co.			90
21.	Wm. Jewett		3	25
27.	Walworth Mfg. Co.		27	69
30.	Labor for April		23	00
May 7.	J. B. McIlroy		12	55
30.	Labor for May		19	50
	J. T. Jones		1	55
June 1.	Howe & Co.			65
24.	Boston & Maine R. R.		1	66
30.	Labor for June.		14	50
July 20.	Barrett Mfg. Co.		1	20
30.	Labor for July		13	50
Aug. 12.	James Devine		6	00

42

Aug.	20.	R. D. Wood & Co.	$30 00
	31.	Labor for August	13 50
Sept.	30.	" " September	8 00
Oct.	31.	" " October	6 50
Nov.	15.	Howe & Co.	90
	30.	Labor for November	13 00
Dec.	21.	Walworth Mfg. Co.	17 28
	31.	Labor for December	2 50
1898.			
Jan.	3.	To E. P. Butters	5 52
	6.	W. Porter	1 00
	12.	Fisk & Co.	1 50
Feb.	1.	J. B. McIlroy	6 55
	28.	W. F. Garfield	1 00

$224 80

The water at present is in use by the following :

Families	268
Manufactories	9
Public buildings.	4
Miscellaneous	11
Horses	58
Cows	52

Respectfully submitted,

H. G. DUDLEY,
Superintendent.

WAYLAND, Feb. 28, 1898.

Water Commissioners' Report.

WAYLAND WATER COMMISSIONERS,
In account with HENRY F. LEE, *Town Treasurer.*

1897.

	Balance of account	$1 00
Sept. 14.	By water rates paid Town Treasurer . .	440 00
1898.		
Jan. 6.	By water rates paid Town Treasurer . .	516 00
Feb. 25.	" " " " " . .	565 74
	" " for hydrants . . .	384 00
28.	-	450 96
	. . . . . .	244 80
		$2,602 50

1898.

Feb. 28.	Interest on water bonds transferred to interest account	$1,450 00
	Order No. 1 Maintenance	244 80
	Balance not drawn from Town Treasurer .	907 70
		$2,602 50

C. H. BOODY,
W. M. FULLICK,
H. G. DUDLEY,
Commissioners of Water Works.

Report of Commissioners of Wayland Water Works Sinking Fund.

1898.

Feb. 28. Amount deposited in Natick Five Cent Savings Bank, Natick, Mass. . . . $3,691 74

Interest on above deposit to Nov. 1, 1897 . 2,272 33

Amount deposited in Suffolk Savings Bank, Boston, Mass.. . . . . . 1,000 00

Interest on above deposit to Oct. 1, 1897 . 429 02

Amount deposited in Home Savings Bank, Boston, Mass.. . . . . . 2,292 38

Interest on above deposit to Oct 1, 1897 . 722 78

Amount deposited in North End Savings Bank, Boston, Mass. 1,459 40

Interest on above deposit to Jan. 1, 1898 . 272 98

Amount deposited in Watertown Savings Bank, Watertown, Mass.. . . . 994 53

Interest on above deposit to Oct. 1, 1897 . 99 30

Amount deposited in Framingham Savings Bank, Framingham, Mass., . . . 1,205 21

Interest on above deposit to Nov. 1, 1897 . 263 94

Amount deposited in Farmers' and Mechanics' Savings Bank, South Framingham, Mass. 675 86

Interest on above deposit to Oct. 5, 1897 . 13 50

$15,392 97

C. H. BOODY,
W. M. FULLICK,
H. G. DUDLEY.

Commissioners of Water Works Sinking Fund.

Report of Superintendent of Streets.

WAYLAND, FEB. 28, 1898

GENTLEMEN :

The amount of appropriations for highways for the past year was three thousand dollars ($3,000).

There was also an unexpended balance of eleven dollars and six cents ($11.06), making a total of three thousand eleven dollars and six cents ($3011 06).

Expended for out standing snow bills of previous year, one hundred seventy-four dollars and eleven cents ($174 11).

The total amount expended was three thousand five hundred and sixty three dollars and eight cents ($3,563 08) leaving the account overdrawn five hundred fifty-two dollars and two cents ($552.02).

Owing to the severe storm of Feb. 1 the snow bills were unusually large, amounting to seven hundred eleven dollars and seventy-four cents ($711.74). Itemized bills for above amounts are on file in the selectmen's office.

There should be some means provided to pay snow bills otherwise than drawing from the highway account. I recommend that the town pay the snow bills from the contingent fund.

There was also a special appropriation of one hundred fifty dollars ($150) for the cutting down and grading of McDonell hill. Amount was expended and itemized bills are on file in the selectmen's office.

MICHAEL W. HYNES,
Superintendent of Streets.

SNOW BILLS OF TOWN OF WAYLAND·

HIGHWAY PAY ROLL FOR THE MONTH OF MARCH, 1897.

	Per Day.	Days.	Hours.	Amount
T. L. Hynes, horse	$1 75	1	6½	$3 00
" "	2 00	10	6	21 34
J. W. Hussey	2 00	2	1	4 20
P. Nolan	2 00		8	1 78
J. Lemoine	2 00		4½	1 00
C. Morse	2 00	1		2 00
H. Byron	2 00	1	6	3 32
A. Spear	2 00	1	3	2 64
W. Porter	2 00	2	5½	4 90
W. Porter, horse	1 75	1	8	3 31
I. Damon	2 00	2	3	4 69
I. Damon, horse	1 75	5	1	8 96
W. C. Neal	2 00	1	7	3 56
R. Hawkins	2 00	1	8	3 79
W. Randolph	2 00	2	3	4 69
L. J. Bemis	2 00		4	89
L. J. Bemis, horse	1 75	3	3	5 87
Wm. Randolph	2 00	1	8	3 79
M. Guilfoile	2 00		8	1 78
A. B. Sherman	2 00	11	3	22 66
A. B. Sherman, horse	1 75	5	3	9 20
F. Moore	2 00	2	4½	5 00
M. W. Hynes	2 00·	11	3	22 67
M. W. Hynes, horse	1 75	11	6	20 42
I. S. Dickey	2 00	3	4	6 85
J. Woodworth	2 00	7	½	1 60
L. H. McManus, sharpening picks,				20

$174 11

FOR THE MONTH OF APRIL, 1897.

	Per Day.	Days.	Hours.	Amount
S. S. Davidson	$2 00		5	$1 10
Charles Dickey	2 00		4½	1 00
M. W. Hynes	2 00·	13	1½	26 33

	Per Day.	Days.	Hours.	Amount.
M. W. Hynes, horse	$1 75	28	7½	$50 45
T. L. Hynes	2 00	9	½	18 11
T. L. Hynes, horse	1 75	4		7 00
Frank Quinn	2 00	10	1½	20 33
J. W. Zimmerman	2 00	10	7	21 56
P. S. Zimmerman	2 00	2	7½	5 67
Edward Eagan	2 00	7		14 00
John Murray	2 00	8	2½	16 56
T. J. Dowey	2 00	7	3½	14 78
T. F. Maynard, horse	1 75	13	6	23 90
James Linnehan	2 00	2		4 00
Isaac Damon	2 00	4	3	8 66
Isaac Damon, horse	1 75	6	6	11 65
Napoleon Latour	2 00	7	8	15 78
John Cheneth	2 00	1		2 00
Wilson Porter	2 00	8	2	16 45
Wilson Porter, horse	1 75	13	5	23 72
Charles Morse	2 00	8	4	16 89
H. Allaire	2 00	6		12 00
Ames Plow Co., ½ dozen shovels				3 75
J. D. Macewin, 93 feet of 8-in. pipe				16 74
				$352 43

For the Month of May, 1897.

	Per Day.	Days.	Hours.	Amount
Frank Quinn	$2 00	1	2	$2 00
M. W. Hynes	2 00	16	2	32 45
M. W. Hynes, horse	1 75	46	2	80 88
T. L. Hynes	2 00	19		38 00
T. L. Hynes, horse	1 75	16		28 00
L. J. Bemis	2 00	11		22 00
L. J. Bemis, horse	1 75	22		38 50
John Linnehan	2 00	15		30 00
John Murray	2 00	15		30 00
P. S. Zimmerman	2 00	12		24 00
J. W. Zimmerman	2 00	15		30 00

	Per Day.	Days.	Hours.	Amount.
James Linnehan . .	$2 00	5	4	$10 89
William Randolph . .	2 00	9		18 00
J. F. Malloy . . .	2 00	5	5	11 11
J. F. Malloy, horse . .	1 75	11	1	19 44
Edward Eagan . .	2 00	4		8 00
Thomas Jennings . .	2 00	4		8 00
A. B. Sherman . .	2 00	67		134 00
A. B. Sherman, horse .	1 75	45		78 75
J. J. Erwin . . .	2 00	4	8	9 80
J. J. Erwin, horse . .	1 75	2	6	4 64
John Chenette . .	2 00	17	4½	35 00
Hillair Paradeau . .	2 00	2		4 00
Isaac Damon . . .	2 00	13		26 00
Isaac Damon, horse .	1 75	26		45 50
Isaac Damon, four perch stone				2 00
Turpe Haws . . .	2 00	4	4½	9 00
John Hurley . . .	2 00	5		10 00
John Hurley . . .	2 50	1		2 50
Charles Morse . .	2 00	13		26 00
F. Busby . . .	2 00	4		8 00
Rupert Porter . . .	2 00	4		8 00
N. Latour . . .	2 00	13		26 00
L. Cormier . . .	2 00	12		24 00
L. Cormier, horse . .	1 75	8		14 00
W. C. Neal, horse . .	1 75	4		7 00
J. H. Lee, 6 shovels scythe snath				5 35
Wilson Porter . .	2 00	17	8½	35 87
Wilson Porter, horse .	1 75	34	8½	62 78
		.		$1,009 46

FOR THE MONTH OF JUNE, 1897.

	Per Day.	Days.	Hours.	Amount
Isaac Damon . .	$2 00	27	8	$55 78
Isaac Damon, horse .	1 75	31	6	55 42
Lewis Cormier . .	2 00	10	4	20 89
Wilson, Porter . .	2 00	13	5	27 10
Wilson Porter, horse .	1 75	27	1	47 45

	Per Day.	Days.	Hours.	Amount
N. Latour . . .	$2 00	4		$8 00
T. Hawes . . .	2 00	13	5	27 11
John Chenette . .	2 00	13	5	27 11
Chas. H. Morse . .	2 00	4		8 00
Chas. H. Morse . .	2 00	9	5	19 11
M. W. Hynes . . .	2 00	7	4	14 89
M. W. Hynes, horse .	1 75	19	3	33 82
John Murray . . .	2 00	8	8	17 78
T. L Hynes . . .	2 00	8	8	17 78
T. L. Hynes, horse . .	1 75	12	8	22 55
T. F. Jennings . .	2 00	8	8	17 78
J. W. Zimmerman . .	2 00	8	8	17 78
P. S. Zimmerman . .	2 00	6	8	13 78

$150.00 SPECIAL APPROPRIATION, McDONNELL HILL.

	Per Day.	Days.	Hours.	Amount
L. H. McManus, blacksmithing				5 45
P. S. Zimmerman . .	2 00	3		6 00
M. W. Hynes . . .	2 00	7		14 00
M. W. Hynes, horse .	1 75	15	6	27 43
T. L. Hynes . . .	2 00	7		14 00
T. L. Hynes, horse . .	1 75	14		24 50
J. W. Zimmerman . .	2 00	7		14 00
John Murray . . .	2 00	7		14 00
T. E. Jennings . .	2 00	7		14 00
M. Guilfoyle . . .	2 00	7		14 00
M. Guilfoyle, blasting material				2 62

$602 13

FOR THE MONTH OF JULY, 1897.

	Per Day.	Days.	Hours.	Amount
M. W. Hynes . .	$2 00	3	$\frac{1}{2}$	$6 11
M. W. Hynes, horse .	1 75	5	5	9 72
T. L. Hynes . . .	2 00	2	$4\frac{1}{2}$	5 00
T. L. Hynes, horse .	1 75	5		8 75
John Murray . . .	2 00	3	$\frac{1}{2}$	6 11
J. W. Zimmerman . .	2 00	2	$4\frac{1}{2}$	5 00

	Per Day.	Days.	Hours.	Amount
P. S. Zimmerman . .	2 00	2	4½	5 00
J. F. Malloy . . .	2 00	1		2 00
A. B. Sherman, 222 loads gravel @ 10c.				22 20
P. A. Leary, sharpening picks				4 55
				$74 44

FOR THE MONTH OF AUGUST, 1897.

	Per Day.	Days.	Hours.	Amount
H. Hilliar . . .	2 00	7		14 00
Gilbert Bent, 19 loads gravel @ 10 cts.				1 90
M. W. Hynes . . .	2 00	5	7	11 56
M. W. Hynes, horse .	1 75	7	1	12 43
P. McGloughlin . .	2 00	3	5	7 12
T. L. Hynes . . .	2 00	3	8	7 78
T. L. Hynes, horse . .	1 75	2		3 50
T. J. Dowey . . .	2 00	2	3	4 67
W. D. Parlin, 100 lbs. wire nails				1 90
H. H. Rutter, 52 lbs. wire nails				1 17
				$66 03

FOR THE MONTH OF SEPTEMBER, 1897.

	Per Day.	Days.	Hours.	Amount
M. W. Hynes . .	$2 00	5		$10 00
M. W. Hynes, horse .	1 75	10		17 50
P. McGloughlin . .	2 00	4		8 00
T. L. Hynes . .	2 00	4		8 00
T. L. Hynes, horse .	1 75	8		14 00
J. F. Malloy . .	2 00	3		6 00
J. F. Malloy, horse .	1 75	6		10 50
P. S. Zimmerman	2 00	4		8 00
J. W. Zimmerman .	2 00	4		8 00
Union Lumber Co.				61 71
				$151 71

For the Month of October, 1897.

	Per Day.	Days.	Hours.	Amount
Isaac Damon . . .	2 00	11	5	23 11
Isaac Damon, horse .	1 75	24		42 00
Jacob Stearns. . .	2 00	5	4	10 89
T. B. Hawes . . .	2 00	6		12 00
James Morrissey . .	2 00	5	4	10 89
Chas. Morse . . .	2 00	6		12 00
W. C. Neal . . .	2 00	4	4	8 89
W. C. Neal, horse . .	1 75	8	8	15 55
Noble Webster . .	2 00	6		12 00
Wilson Porter. . .	2 00	6		12 00
Wilson Porter, horse .	1 75	12		21 00
James Murphy . .	2 00	5	4	10 89
M. W. Hynes. . .	2 00	4	6	9 33
M. W. Hynes, horse .	1 75	9	6	16 91
M. W. Hynes, 10 chestnut posts				1 50
P. McGloughlin . .	2 00	5	5	11 11
T. L. Hynes . . .	2 00	17	5	35 11
T. L. Hynes, horse. .	1 75	17	1	29 94
J. F. Malloy . . .	2 00	5	5	11 11
J. F. Malloy, horse. .	1 75	11	1	19 44
P. S Zimmerman . .	2 00	5	5	11 11
J. W. Zimmerman . .	2 00	5	5	11 11
				$347 89

For the Month of November, 1897.

	Per Day.	Days.	Hours.	Amount
M. W. Hynes . .	$2 00	2	6	$5 34
M. W. Hynes, horse .	1 75	5	3	9 30
P. J. McGloughlin .	2 00	1	7	3 56
T. E. Jennings . .	2 00		4½	1 00
Wilson Porter . .	2 00	5		10 00
Wilson Porter . .	1 75	12		21 00
Noble Webster . .	2 00	6		12 00
James Murphy . .	2 00	6		12 00
T. B. Hawes . . .	2 00	6		12 00
W. C. Neal . . .	2 00	6		12 00

	Per Day.	Days.	Hours.	Amount
W. C. Neal, horse . .	$1 75	12		$21 00
James Morrissey . .	2 00	6		12 00
Jacob Stevens . .	2 00	6		12 00
Nelson Mathews . .	2 00	6	5	13 10
Chas. Morse . . .	2 00	6		12 00
Alex Speare . . .	2 00	1	5	2 64
Alex Speare, gravel				25
Isaac Damon . .	2 00	11		22 00
Isaac Damon, horse .	1 75	17	1	29 95

$223 14

For the Month of February, 1898.

	Per Day.	Days.	Hours.	Amount
Chas. Fisk . . .	2 00	1	6½	$3 40
C. W. Bemis . . .	2 00	5	7	11 54
C. L. Fullick . . .	2 00	1	2½	2 55
C. R Maude . .	2 00	3	5	7 10
D. L. Webster . .	2 00	2	4½	5 00
C. I. Flint . . .	2 00		6	1 20
C. A. Roak . . .	2 00		4½	1 05
E. W. Schleicher . .	2 00	1		2 00
C. E. Gerald . . .	2 00	1	7½	3 65
P. D. Gorman . .	2 00	4		8 00
Joseph LaFrance . .	2 00	3	5	7 10
C. H. Carter . . .	2 00	3		6 00
John Woodworth . .	2 00	2	8	5 20
B. F. Adams . .	2 00	2		4 00
J. Morrissey . . .	2 00	3	6	7 22
Wm. C. Neal . .	2 00		6	1 32
Noble Webster . .	2 00	4	6½	9 41
Wilson Porter . .	2 00	6		12 00
Wilson Porter, horse .	1 75	8	4	14 77
James Hawkins . .	2 00	1	2½	2 56
T. W. Hawes . . .	2 00	3	6½	7 43
E. B. Hawes . . .	2 00	1	6½	3 43
E. F. Lawrence . .	2 00	1	3	2 70
W. J. Hussey . . .	2 00	3	2	6 40

	Per Day.	Days.	Hours.	Amount.
A. Speare . . .	$2 00	5	8½	$11 88
G. W. Videon . .	2 00	1	6	3 32
Henry Mathews . .	2 00		4½	1 00
Chas. Magorty . .	2 00		6½	1 43
Isaac Damon . .	2 00	5	6	11 36
Isaac Damon, horse .	1 75	8	4	14 80
A. B. Sherman . .	2 00	33	4	66 88
A. B. Sherman, horse	1 75	8	8	15 55
S S. Davidson . .	2 00	8	4½	17 00
Edward Harrington .	2 00	3		6 00
Bert Harrington . .	2 00	3		6 00
Geo. B. Folsom . .	2 00	6		12 00
John F. Malloy . .	2 00	7	3	14 67
John F. Malloy, horse	1 75	7	3	12 83
P. J. McGloughlin, .	2 00	8	6	17 34
M. W. Hynes, . .	2 00	8	1	16 22
M. W. Hynes, horse .	1 75	19	1	33 43
L. A. Loker, . .	2 00	1		2 00
G. W. Philbrick, . .	2 00	3	5	7 11
G. W. Philbrick, horse,	1 75	1	3	2 33
John Linnehan, . .	2 00	3	3	7 67
P. S. Zimmerman, .	2 00	3	4½	7 00
J. W. Zimmerman, .	2 00	3		6 00
A. E. Wellington, . .	2 00	3	1	6 23
Chas. Jacobs, . .	2 00	2	5	5 25
A. W. Lombard, . .	2 00	3	6½	7 45
Henry F. Lee, . .	2 00	3	5	7 11
Geo. L. Baker, . .	2 00	1	2	2 42
M. Temple, . . .	2 00	1	2	2 22
J. I. Bryden, . .	2 00	3	3	6 67
Patrick Jennings, . .	2 00	3		6 00
L. H. McManus, sharpening bar,				10
John W. Coakley, .	2 00	3	6	7 33
Wm. Flockhart, . .	2 00	3	6	7 33
T. Coughlin, . .	2 00	10	6	21 33
J. McDonald, . .	2 00	6		12 00
J. McDonald, horse, .	1 75	1		1 75

	Per Day.	Days.	Hours.	Amount
James Linnehan, . .	2 00	3		6 00
J. J. McCann, . .	2 00	2	8½	5 89
J. J. McCann, horse, .	1 75	1	4	2 33
Chas. E. Quinn, . .	2 00	3	3	6 67
Frank Quinn, . .	2 00	4		6 00
J J. Rowan, . .	2 00	6	1¾	12 42
J. J. Rowan, . .	1 75	1	1	1 94
Thos. F. Linnehan, .	2 00	4	8	9 78
Thos. F. Linnehan, horse,	1 75	4	4	7 77
Wm. J. Randolph, .	2 00	2	4½	5 00
Thos. L. Hynes, . .	2 00	8	½	16 12
Thos. L. Hynes, horse,	1 75	10	4	18 26
T. F. Maynard, . .	2 00	7	2½	14 56
Thomas J. Dowey, .	2 00	5	5½	11 23
Thomas J. Dowey, horse,	1 75	9	6	16 82
J. R. Hawkins, . .	2 00	2		4 00
J. J. Erwin, . . .	2 00	5		10 00
J. J. Erwin, . . .	1 75	3		5 25
Wm. T. Guilfoile, . .	2 00	1	7½	3 63
Michael Guilfoile, .	2 00	1	6½	3 41
John M. Curtin, . .	2 00	3		6 00
I. S. Dickey, . .	2 00	1	2	2 40
C. H. Richardson, .	2 00		·7	1 55
Thomas F. Linnehan .	2 00	3	3	6 67
Everett W. Small, .	2 00	3		6 00

$550 92

Report of Supt. of North and Centre Cemeteries.

Appropriation for 1897 . . . . $50 00
Unexpended balance, 1896 . . . 66 11
——————— $116 11

EXPENDED.

To labor for men @ 20c. per hour . . $76 11
Labor for horse @ 17c. per hour . . 12 41
Unexpended balance, 1897 . . . 27 59
——————— $116 11

Cash paid Town Treasurer for sale of grass . . $5 00

T. S. SHERMAN,
Superintendent.

Report of Superintendent of Lakeview Cemetery.

		Appropriation		$50 00
		Paid H. F. Lee		3 12
May	29.	Order on Town Treasurer . .	$36 00	
July	31.	" " " . .	14 00	
		Unexpended	3 12	
			$53 12	$53 12
Paid to H. F. Lee, sale of lots				$25 00

H. B. PHALEN,
Superintendent.

School Building at Wayland Centre.

Appropriation	$17,000	00
Francis Shaw	4,569	35
	$21,569	**35**

J. E. Warren & Co.	$14,774	71
C. M. Drennan, heating & ventilation .	. 2,368	21
Fuller, Warren Co.	. 445	00
E. B. Badger & Sons, copper work .	. 175	00
Dwight & Chandler, Architects . .	. 1,097	97
S. H. Woodbridge, heating & ventilation	. 138	55
W. D. Parlin, plumbing	. 259	62
Chandler Desk Co., desks & blackboards	. 923	65
Shepard Norwell & Co., shades . .	. 57	11
B. F. Quimby, school drain, etc. . .	. 929	53
Hinckley & Woods, insurance Aug. 1, 1896		
to Aug. 1, 1898	. 400	00
	$21,569	**35**

FRANCIS SHAW,
HENRY D. PARMENTER,
LLEWELLYN FLANDERS.

Report of Engineers of Fire Department.

The following fires have occurred in the town of Wayland during the past year :

1897.

April 13. Alarm 4.15 p.m. Wood fire rear of Chas. W. Wright's house, German Hill street, Cochituate.

22. Alarm 10.40 a.m. Wood fire rear Moses Mathew's house, Cochituate.

May 19. Alarm 1 a.m. Building of estate of J. M. Bent, occupied by J. O. Dean as shoe factory. Loss, total. No insurance on building ; contents insured.

June 6. Lightning struck residence of Francis Shaw at Wayland, damaging chimney.

24. Building owned by A. M. Lovejoy on Maple street, Cochituate, occupied by C. E. Coakeley. Insured ; cause oil stove.

26. Alarm 3.10 a.m. Burning out of chimney of C. W. Dean & Co.'s factory, Cochituate. No damage.

July 15. House of Frank Ammott, Wayland. Damage slight.

Aug. 4. Dwelling, barn and outbuildings of J: W. Parmenter at Wayland. Lightning struck barn at 4.15 p.m. Insured ; loss, total.

Sept. 7. Ice house of A. L. Adams at Wayland. Insured ; loss, total.

Oct. 18. Alarm 2 p.m. Woods of H. G. Hammond, Cochituate.

25. Alarm 4 p.m. Woods of Isaac Damon, Cochituate.

We report the Fire Department in excellent condition, the membership of both companies being complete, and the engine house, apparatus, etc. well cared for.

We would call to your attention the items wherein our apparatus is deficient : Shortage of hose.   Some of our hose is old and liable to burst if used under pressure.   The overcoats of the firemen also, are old and unfit for service, all of them having been purchased nineteen years ago.   We would, therefore, recommend an appropriation of $500 for the purchase of additional hose, new overcoats, etc.

Great credit is due to the new superintendent of fire alarm for the present efficiency of the system, several changes having been made in the arrangements of batteries, connections, etc., that have added greatly to the strength and certainty of the current.

An automatic circuit breaker has been attached to the town clock, under the direction of the chief engineer. This renders absolutely certain and accurate the daily tests, so long as the clock is running and electric circuit in order.

Respectfully submitted,

E. W. MARSTON, *Chief.*
A. J. RICKER, *1st Asst.*
F. E. YEAGER, *Clerk.*

Finance Committee.

To the Town of Wayland:

The Finance Committee of the town respectfully submit the following report and recommend as follows : —

For schools, fuel and care of building	$7,000 00
School supplies	600 00
Transportation of scholars	1,500 00
Repair of school buildings	150 00
Superintendent of schools	600 00
Fitting High school	200 00
Overdrafts	2,598 20
Highways and bridges	2,000 00
Incidentals	1,500 00
Firemen's pay	224 00
Support of poor	2,500 00
Collection of taxes	350 00
Abatement of taxes . . . . . — . .	1,800 00
Hydrants	384 00
Lakeview cemetery	50 00
North and Centre cemeteries	50 00
Library	300 00
Interest on town debt	3,500 00
Electric lights	357 00
Salaries	1,300 00
School house loan	1,100 00
Notes outstanding April, 1898	2,000 00
Decoration day	100 00
New hose for Fire Department	380 00
	$30,533 20

We recommend that fourteen hundred and fifty dollars be transferred from water rates to pay interest on water bonds

That the selectmen be authorized to draw from the contingent fund such sums of money as may be necessary, not exceeding five hundred dollars, for assisting needy soldiers and their families.

That the overseers of the poor be authorized to build a wagon and tool shed at the poor farm from the money appropriated for support of poor, if in their judgment, there is sufficient money for that purpose.

That the sum of thirty-five hundred dollars, appropriated for interest, be taken from the contingent fund.

That the money for removing snow be drawn from the contingent fund.

The committee have carefully examined the condition of our finances and are fully satisfied that no appropriations should be made except those recommended.

> ISAAC DAMON,
> MICHAEL W. HYNES,
> CHAS. H. BOODY,
> D. W. MITCHELL,
> DAVID P. W. LOKER,
> HENRY F. LEE,
> RICHARD T. LOMBARD,
> *Finance Committee.*

Wayland, March 11, 1898.

Treasurer's Report.

1897.

Mar. 22.

Schools, care of rooms and fuel .	$6,200 00
School supplies	600 00
Transportation of scholars .	1,500 00
Superintendent of schools .	600 00
School repairs	100 00
Support of poor . . .	2,500 00
Incidentals	1,500 00
Highways and bridges . .	3,000 00
Salaries	1,300 00
Interest	3,500 00
Library	300 00
Hydrants	384 00
Fire department . . .	224 00
Lakeview cemetery . . .	50 00
North and Centre cemeteries .	50 00
Electric lights	340 00
Decoration day	150 00
Overdrafts, 1896-7 . . .	1,663 49
Schoolhouse loan . . .	1,100 00
Repairs on road near D. McDonnell's	150 00
Abatement of taxes . . .	200 00
Collection of taxes . . .	350 00
Fitting up High school . .	200 00
Relaying culvert, Harrison Ave.	75 00
Clock for M. E church tower .	500 00
	———— $26,536 49

From contingent fund . . $3,500 00
Town tax assessed . . 23,036 49

$26,536 49 $26,536 49

SPECIAL APPROPRIATIONS NOT ASSESSED.

Sand Hill road $1,600 00
Sidewalks 400 00

$2,000 00

SCHOOLS.

1897.
Mar. 22. Appropriation $6,200 00
          "   for overdraft 276 14
        Donation fund 12 00
1898.
Jan. 3. State treasurer, state school fund . . 256 28
Feb. 3. Dog license (one-half) 98 21
        State treasurer 300 00
        Town of Natick 2 20
        Overdraft 424 91

        Overdraft $276 14
        Expended 7,293 60

$7,569 74 $7,569 74

SUPPORT OF POOR.

Mar. 22. Appropriation $2,500 00
          "   for overdraft . . . 199 11
        Overseers of poor 1,351 25
        Overdraft $199 11
        Expended 3,664 91
        Unexpended balance . . . 186 34

$4,050 36 $4,050 36

INCIDENTALS.

Mar. 22.	Appropriation		$1,500 00
	" for overdraft, 1896 . .		462 89
1.	Overdrawn	$462 89	
26.	R. T. Lombard	30 70	
	J. E. Linnehan	25 00	
27.	J. E. Linnehan	25 00	
	H. G. Dudley	18 00	
	American Express Co. . .	1 20	
	C. H. Thing	2 00	
	G. M. Stevens	6 40	
	H. B. Phalen	25 00	
	N. A. Chessman . . .	8 00	
	R. T. Lombard	26 05	
Apr. 24.	W. W. Wight	75 00	
	Thomas Groom & Co. . .	13 00	
	A. F. Bliss & Co. . . .	32 00	
	L. H. McManus . . .	10 00	
	H. H. Rutter	18 02	
	Lakeview Press	87 60	
	J. M. Bent Hose Co . . .	6 50	
	Thomas Bryant	5 00	
	W. F. Garfield	1 00	
	W. F. Garfield	6 00	
May 29.	I. T. Moore	2 00	
	James Devine	1 38	
	P. B. Murphy	5 70	
	J. E. Linnehan	6 75	
	Darling & Russell . . .	1 50	
	H. F. Lee & Co. . . .	6 70	
	H. G. Dudley	7 25	
June 14.	M. Eagan	4 30	
	L. H. McManus . . .	10 48	
	E. R. Locke	1 50	
	A. S. Robbins	2 23	
26.	J. E. Linnehan	5 50	
	C. H. May	3 81	

June 26.	Wright & Potter	. . .	$14	75
	Howe & Co.'s Express	. .	1	04
.	A. S. Morse	. . .	2	00
	Fiske & Co.	. . .		90
	W. C. Neal	. . .	3	00
	Peter Gray	. . .	7	00
	American Express Co.	. .		95
July 31.	Edgar B. Loker .	. . .	250	00
	J. E. Linnehan .	. . .	30	00
	T. E. Glennon .	. . .	6	00
	A. F. Parmenter	. .	4	00
	W. C. Neal	. . .	1	50
	H. G. Hammond	. .	6	00
	Edward Carter .	. . .	4	00
	A. S. Morse	. . .	5	00
	G. M. Stevens .	. . .	12	92
	J. W. Jennison .	. . .	9	00
	W. C. Neal	. . .	9	00
	C. H. Boodey H. & L. Co.	.	8	75
	P. A. Leary	. . .	1	50
Aug. 28.	Hannah Mullen	. . .	16	45
	E. P. Butler	. . .	6	74
	Elbert Stevens .	. . .	1	25
	A. W. Mitchell Co.	. .	4	09
	L. H. McManus	. . .	16	00
	Thomas Groom & Co.	. .	19	50
	P. H. Cooney .	. . .	25	00
Sept. 25.	E. L. Barry	. . .	5	50
	J. W. Jennison .	. . .	14	00
	Wm. Stearns	. . .	20	00
	Arthur Hunting .	. . .	30	00
	W. C. Hunting .	. . .	6	20
	P. Andrews	. . .	4	23
	Washburn Moen Co.	. .		60
	Isaac Damon	. . .	15	20
	M. Rowan	. . .	50	00
	D. W. Mitchell .	. . .	4	30
Oct. 30.	J. E. Linnehan .	. . .	20	50

Oct.	30.	J. M. Forbush & Co. .	. .	$33 75
		Thomas Groom & Co.	. .	10 25
		H. G. Dudley .	. . .	2 70
		W. F. Garfield .	. . .	5 00
		H. F. Lee .	. . .	4 25
		L. H. McManus	. . .	14 00
		C. S. Williams .	. . .	1 50
		C. H. Thing .	. . .	1 50
		E. W. Marston .	. .	50 05
		C. H. Boodey H. & L. Co. .	.	11 50
		W. S. Haines .	. .	13 87
Nov.	27.	J. E. Linnehan .	. .	7 50
		C. H. Thing .	. . .	1 00
		G. M. Stevens . .	. .	39 08
		F. S. Earle .	. . .	4 00
		C. A. Roake	. . .	1 50
		W. C. Hunting .	. .	4 46
		J. H. Lee .	. . .	17 83
Dec.	23.	A. A. Williams .	. .	1 00
		J. M. Forbush & Co. .	. .	22 50
Jan.	3.	W. W. Wight .	. .	5 00
		Thomas Groom & Co.	. .	23 80
	29.	W. F. Garfield .	. .	1 50
		H. G. Dudley .	. .	1 60
		D. W. P. Loker .	. .	4 75
		A. S. Morse	. . .	1 75
		Dr. Wm. Richards	. . .	50
		Gilbert & Barker Mfg. Co. .	.	18 09
		B. & M. R. R. .	. .	42
		P. A. Leary	. . .	1 90
		J. E. Linnehan .	. .	14 00
		J. E. Linnehan .	. .	25 40
Feb.	26.	Wm. Howard .	. .	5 00
		L. K. Lovell .	. .	5 79
		H. G. Dudley .	. .	4 87
		E. A. Atwood .	. .	4 70
		E. P. Butler .	. .	2 09
		H. P. Sherman .	. .	9 25

Feb. 26.   W. D. Parlin $13 22
            John Everett 3 75
            J. H. Carroll 4 00
            A. F. Parmenter   .   .   .   3 50
            F. L. French 2 00
            E. W. Marston 16 79
            H. F. Lee 7 02
            W. C. Neal 6 92
            E. H. Atwood, American Express   50
            State treasurer 1 00
            L. H. McMannus   .   .   .   5 00
            Overdraft 58 79

                                         $2,021 68 $2,021 68

CLOCK FOR CHURCH TOWER.

Mar. 1. Appropriation $500 00
June 26 E. Howard Clock Co.   .   . $398 00
          E. W. Marston 102 00

                                          $500 00 $500 00

HIGHWAYS AND BRIDGES.

Mar. 1.   Unexpended balance $11 06
      22. Appropriation 3,000 00
           Overdraft 552 02
      27. Isaac Damon $165 66
           S. S. Dickey 6 85
           J. Woodworth 1 60
Apr. 24. M. W. Hynes 352 43
May   29.   "   " 1,009 46
June 14.   "   " 169 20
      26.   "   " 282 93
July 31.   "   " 69 89
                            .   .   .   .   4 55
Aug. 28.   "   " 66 03
Sept. 25.   "   " 151 71
Oct. 30.   "   " 347 89

Nov.	27.	Isaac Damon	.	.	.	.	$203 94	
Dec.	23.	M. W. Hynes	.	.	.	.	19 20	
1898.								
Feb.	26.	M. W. Hynes	.	.	.	.	666 83	
	28.	" "	.	.	.	.	44 91	

$3,563 08 $3,563 08

SALARIES OF TOWN OFFICERS.

Mar.	22.	Appropriation	.	.	.	.	.	.	$1,300 00
		" for overdraft, 1896,				.	.	55 31	
		Overdraft	.	.	.	.	.	.	122 56
Mar.	1.	Overdrawn	.	.	.	.	55 31	
	26.	T. W. Frost	.	.	.	.	125 00	
		T. W. Frost	.	.	.	.	100 00	
		R. T. Lombard	.	.	.	.	80 50	
		H. G. Hammond	.	.	.	8 75	
		T. L. Sawin	.	.	.	.	20 00	
		D. W. Mitchell	.	.	.	.	20 00	
		L. H. Sherman	.	.	.	.	20 00	
		Edward Carter	.	.	.	.	10 25	
		Wm. Stearns	.	.	.	.	5 00	
		C. H. Boodey	.	.	.	.	20 00	
		W. B. Ward	.	.	.	.	40 00	
		Geo B. Howe	.	.	.	.	50 00	
		Annie B. Bent	.	.	.	.	25 55	
		N. A. Chessman	.	.	.	2 50	
		Thos. Bryant	.	.	.	.	175 00	
		C. B. Williams	.	.	.	.	54 19	
		D. W. P. Loker	.	.	.	.	57 50	
Mar.	27.	H. P. Sherman.	.	.	.	5 00	
		L. A. Loker	.	.	.	.	5 00	
		J. H. Grady	.	.	.	.	5 00	
		H. B. Phalen	.	.	.	.	10 00	
		H. G. Dudley	.	.	.	.	3 00	
		H. G. Dudley	.	.	.	.	7 00	
		W. H. Campbell	.	.	.	5 00	

Mar.	27.	H. T. Lee	$200 00	
		Edward Carter	5 00	
Apr.	24	A. H. Bryant	50 00	
		Ralph Bent	10 00	
		H. G. Dudley	20 00	
July	31.	R. T. Lombard. . . .	38 50	
		Edward Carter	64 75	
		H. G Hammond . . .	43 75	
Aug.	28.	E. W. Marston	20 00	
Sept.	28	H. B. Phalen	8 32	
		D. W. P. Loker	20 00	
		Geo. B. Howe	25 00	
		Wm. Stearns	5 00	
Nov.	27.	W. C. Neal	5 00	
		H. E. Griffin	5 00	
		Thos. Bryant	5 00	
		H. P. Sherman	5 00	
		A. J. Lamarine	5 00	
		E. E Butler	5 00	
		C. S. Moore	3 00	
		E. F. Lee	5 00	
		E. B Smith	5 00	
Dec.	23.	M. W. Hynes	5 00	
1898.				
Jan.	29.	J. A. Draper	5 00	
		C. H. Sayen	5 00	

$1,477 87 $1,477 87

SCHOOL SUPPLIES.

Mar.	1.	Unexpended balance		$43 65
	22.	Appropriation		600 00
Jan.	24.	State treasurer		85 43
		Expended	$726 41	
		Unexpended balance . . .	2 67	

$729 08 $729 08

INTEREST ON TOWN DEBT.

Mar.	22.	Appropriation for overdraft . . .			$451 73
		Transferred from contingent fund . .			3,500 00
		" water commissioners . .			1,450 00
Mar.	1.	Overdrawn . . .	$451 73		
		Boston Safe Deposit & Trust Co.	3,635 00		
		Natick National Bank . . .	1,085 81		
		Puritan Loan & Trust Co. . .	396 00		
		Dwight B. Heard . . .	60 00		
		Donation fund	78 00		
		Allen fund	60 00		
		Loker fund	100 00		
		Library fund	66 00		
		Overdrawn			530 81
			$5,932 54		$5,932 54

WATER COMMISSIONERS.

1897.

Mar.	1.	Unexpended balance			$1 00
	11.	Water rates			675 86
Sept.	17.	" "			440 00
1898.					
Jan.	6.	Water rates			516 00
Feb.	26.	" "			565 74
		Transferred from hydrants . . .			384 00
	28.	Water rates			450 96
		" "			244 80
	11.	H. G. Dudley	$675 86		
Apr.	24.	" "	182 50		
Oct.	20.	D. F. Fiske	60 00		
		H. G. Dudley	46 00		
		Transferred to interest account .	1,450 00		
Feb.	28.	Wm. M. Fullick, Clerk . .	244 80		
		Balance due commissioners .	619 20		
			$3,278 36		$3,278 36

NOTE.—$288 50 of the above should have been drawn from appropriation for salaries, leaving the balance due the water commissioners $907.70.

STATE HIGHWAY LOAN.

1898.

Jan.	8.	State treasurer		$409 19
		Mass. Broken Stone Co. . .	290 35	
Feb.	26.	" " " . .	118 84	
			$409 19	$409 19

LIBRARY.

Mar.	22.	Appropriation		$300 00
Feb.	3.	Dog license, one-half		98 21
June	14.	H. D. Parmenter, treasurer .	$300 00	
Feb.	26.	H. D. Parmenter, treasurer .	98 21	
			$398 21	$398 21

HYDRANTS.

Mar.	22.	Appropriation		$384 00
		Trans. to Water Com. . .	$384 00	

SIDEWALKS.

Mar.	1.	Unexpended balance		$18 80
		Appropriation		400 00
1898.				
Feb.		Isaac Damon		2 83
Jan.	3.	D. J. Furguson	$120 17	
		J. C. Cloyes	83 30	
		W. C. Neal	47 10	
		W. Porter	43 96	
		John Hurley	23 46	
		C. C. Ward	16 00	
		Charles Morse	15 00	
		W. W. Wight	3 50	
		Isaac Damon	7 00	
		Transferred to Contingent . .	18 80	
		Unexpended balance . . .	43 34	
			$421 63	$421 63

FIRE DEPARTMENT.

Mar.	1.	Unexpended balance			$224 00
	22.	Appropriation			224 00
Apr.	24.	Ralph Bent, Chief . . .	$224 00		
		Unexpended balance . .	224 00		
			$448 00		$448 00

CEMETERY ACCOUNT.

Mar.	1.	Unexpended balance			$129 00
Nov.	11.	H. B. Phalen, Supt. Lakeview cemetery .			50 00
Feb.	28.	" "			25 00
		T. S. Sherman			5 00
		Unexpended balance . . .	$209 00		
			$209 00		$209 00

LAKEVIEW CEMETERY.

Mar.	11.	H. B. Phalen			$3 12
	22.	Appropriation			50 00
		" for overdraft . . .			3 12
	1.	Overdrawn	$3 12		
May	29.	H. B. Phalen	36 00		
July	31.	" "	14 00		
		Unexpended balance . .	3 12		
			$56 24		$56 24

NORTH AND CENTRE CEMETERIES.

Mar.	1.	Unexpended balance			$66 11
	22.	Appropriation			50 00
May	29.	T. S. Sherman	$66 11		
Jan.	29.	" "	22 41		
		Unexpended balance . . .	27 59		
			$116 11		$116 11

FENCE LAKEVIEW CEMETERY.

Mar. 11. H. B. Phalen		$19 46
Transferred to contingent . .	$19 46	

ELECTRIC LIGHTS.

Mar. 1. Unexpended balance		$62 43
22. Appropriation		340 00
Natick Gas & Electric Co. .	$379 21	
Unexpended balance . :	23 22	
	$402 43	$402 43

SUPERINTENDENT OF SCHOOLS.

Mar. 22. Appropriation		$600 00
" for overdraft . . .		52 30
1. Overdrawn	$52 30	
Superintendent	640 00	
Overdrawn		40 00
	$692 30	$692 30

REPAIRS ON SCHOOL BUILDINGS.

Mar. 22. Appropriation		$100 00
" for overdraft . . .		51 59
School committee		1 00
1. Overdrawn	$51 59	
Expended	67 70	
Unexpended balance . . .	33 30	
	$152 59	$152 59

ILLEGAL SALE OF INTOXICATING LIQUORS.

Mar. 1. Unexpended balance, ...		$235 80
1898.		
Feb. 28. Unexpended balance, . . .	$235 80	

STREET LIGHTS.

Mar. 1. Unexpended balance, ... $64 71
Transferred to Contingent, . . $64 71

FENCE AT COCHITUATE SCHOOL HOUSE.

Mar. 1. Unexpended balance, ... $100 00
Unexpended balance, . . . $100 00

HIGH SCHOOL TUITION.

Mar. 1. Unexpended balance, ... $450 00
. Transferred to Contingent acct., $450 00

TEMPORARY LOAN.

Mar. 1.	Notes outstanding, ...		$16,000 00
25.	Note to Natick National Bank, .	.	3,000 00
26.	" " " .	.	3,000 00
Apr. 24.	" " " .	.	2,000 00
June 1.	" .	.	3,000 00
29.	" " " .	.	2,000 00
Aug. 2.	.. .. .	.	2,000 00
Jan. 3.	" " " .	.	2,000 00
	Paid Natick National Bank,	$1,000 00	
Oct. 1.	" " "	1,500 00	
7.	" " "	3,000 00	
14.		2,000 00	
Feb. 28.	" " "	1,500 00	
28.	Notes outstanding, . .	. 24,000 00	
		$33,000 00	$33,000 00

TRANSPORTATION OF SCHOLARS.

Mar. 22. Appropriation, ... $1,500 00
" " overdraft, ... 20 50
Mar. 1. Overdrawn, ... $20 50
Expended, ... 1,335 25
1898.
Feb. 28. Unexpended balance, . . . 164 75

$1,520 50 $1,520 50

GRAVEL.

Mar. 22. Appropriation for overdraft, . . . $90 80

Mar. 1. Overdrawn, ... $90 80

OVERDRAFTS, 1895-6.

Mar. 1. Unexpended balance $58 39

      Unexpended balance . . . $58 39

CULVERT AND WALL NEAR HOUSE OF C. B. WILLIAMS.

Mar. 1. Unexpended balance $2 99

      Transferred to contingent . . $2 99

LIBRARY TABLET.

Mar. 1. Unexpended balance $50 00

    27. Expended . : . . . $54 00

      Overdrawn 4 00

                                $54 00 $54 00

MARKERS FOR REVOLUTIONARY SOLDIERS' GRAVES.

Mar. 1. Unexpended balance . . . $4 00

      Transferred to contingent . . $4 00

DECORATION DAY.

Mar. 22. Appropriation $150 00

June 26. C. H. May, chairman committee $150 00

PAINTING BUILDINGS AT TOWN FARM.

Mar. 1. Unexpended balance $3 65

      Transferred to contingent . . $3 65

HIGH SCHOOL HOUSE.

Mar. 1. Unexpended balance $35 19

    15. Francis Shaw $35 19

OVERDRAFTS, 1896-7.

Mar. 22.	Appropriation		$1,663 49
	Schools	$276 14	
	Support of poor	199 11	
	Incidentals	462 89	
	Salaries	55 31	
	Interest	451 73	
	Lakeview cemetery	3 12	
	Superintendent of schools	52 30	
	Repairs on school buildings	51 59	
	Transportation of scholars	20 50	
	Gravel	90 80	
		$1,663 49	$1,663 49

REPAIRS ON ROAD NEAR D. McDONNELL'S.

Mar. 22.	Appropriation		$150 00
June 26.	M. W. Hynes	$150 00	

SAND HILL ROAD.

	Appropriation		$1,600 00
	Levi S. Gould, County Com.	$1,549 94	
	Unexpended balance	50 06	
		$1,600 00	$1,600 00

FITTING UP HIGH SCHOOL.

Mar. 22.	Appropriation		$200 00
	Expended	$183 60	
	Unexpended balance	16 40	
		$200 00	$200 00

REPAIRS ON CULVERT, HARRISON AVE.

Mar. 22.	Appropriation		$75 00
Dec. 23.	Isaac Damon	$59 20	
	Unexpended balance	15 80	
		$75 00	$75 00

SCHOOL HOUSE LOAN.

Mar. 22.   Appropriation $1,100 00
          Puritan Loan & Trust Co. .   . $1,100 00

CONTINGENT FUND.

1897.

Mar. 1.   Unexpended balance $1,329 31

District court fines	61 90
Massachusetts cattle commission . .	175 00
District court fines	1 50
L. Anna Dudley, sale school furniture .	2 15
J. E. Linnehan	7 50
P. A. Leary	8 33
L. R. Lovell, Centre scales . . .	27 03
W. B. Ward, interest on tax title . .	13 10
J. E. Linnehan	20 00
M. W. Hynes, sale of gravel . . .	1 50
State treasurer, superintendent of schools .	200 00
" " corporation tax . . .	2,180 44
" " National Bank tax . .	785 84
" " military aid . . .	84 00
" " state aid . . .	996 00
J. E. Linnehan	7 50
W. B. Ward, interest on tax, 1896 . .	168 00
Additional assessments	112 08
Overlayings	3 55
Transferred from sidewalks . . .	18 80
" " street lights . . .	64 71
" " painting buildings at town farm	3 65
Transferred from culvert near Williams' .	2 99
" " markers for revolutionary soldiers graves	4 00
Transferred from fence, Lakeview cemetery	19 46
G. B. Howe, Cochituate scales . . .	21 93
Transferred from High school tuition .	450 00
W. B. Ward, interest on taxes . . .	276 73
" " $4-No. 8	12 00

Transferred to interest account . $3,500 00
State aid 1,127 00
Military aid 144 00
Needy soldiers 192 02
Union Snow Plow & Wagon Co. 85 00
G. L. Mayberry, Reaves vs. Way-
 land 447 58
State treasurer, tax refunded . 20 68
Unexpended balance . . . 1,542 72

$7,059 00 $7,059 00

W. B. WARD, TAX COLLECTOR.

Tax 1891.

1897.

Mar. 1. Due from collector . . . $366 80
Feb. 26. W C. Ward, abatement . . $370 80
 Cr. to contingent . . . 4 00

$370 80 $370 80

Tax 1892.

Mar. 1. Due from collector . . . $530 60
 W. B. Ward $112 00
 "   " abatement . . 345 60
 "   " 81 00
 Cr. to contingent . . . 8 00

$538 60 $538 60

Tax 1893.

Mar. 1. Due from collector . . . $355 12
 W. B. Ward $355 12

Tax 1894.

Mar. 1. Due from collector . . . $1,328 92
 W. B. Ward 963 96
 Balance due 364 96

$1,328 92 $1,328 92

TAX 1895.

Mar. 1.	Due from collector . .	.$5,791 34		
	W. B. Ward		4,329 75	
	Balance due		1,461 59	
			$5,791 34	$5,791 34

TAX 1896.

Mar. 1.	Due from collector . .	.$9,716 18		
	W. B. Ward		$3,311 68	
	Balance due from collector		6,404 50	
			$9,716 18	$9,716 18

TAX 1897.

Tax assessed . . .	$23,036 49		
Overlayings . . .	2 34		
State tax	1,102 50		
County tax . . .	1,491 95		
Additional assessments .	112 08		
Special tax, Marsh land .	330 51		
Overlayings . . .	1 21		
W. B. Ward, cash . .		$13,650 02	
Balance due from collector		12,427 06	
		$26,077 08	$26,077 08

ABATEMENT OF TAXES.

Mar. 1.	Unexpended balance			$17 39
22.	Appropriation.			200 00
July 31.	R. N. Jennison, cash . . .	$15 61		
Dec. 7.	Abatement tax, 1897 . . .	85 40		
Jan. 8.	" " 1896 . . .	4 68		
Feb. 26.	" " 1891 . . .	370 80		
	" 1892 . . .	345 60		

Abatement tax, 1893 . . . $20 00
" " 1894 . . . 108 77
" " 1895 . . . 40 96
" " 1892 . . . 81 00
Overdrawn 855 43

$1,072 82 $1,072 82

COLLECTION TAXES.

Mar. 22. Appropriation $300 00
27. W. B. Ward $300 00
" " 50 00

$350 00 $350 00

STATE TAX.

Tax $1,102 50
Dec. 13. State treasurer . . . $1,102 50

COUNTY TAX.

Tax $1,491 95
Dec. 7. J. O. Hayden, treasurer . . $1,491 95

SPECIAL TAX, CONCORD AND SUDBURY RIVERS.

Tax $330 51
Dec. 13. State treasurer $330 51

TAX TITLE.

Mar. 1. Tax title $97 94
Oct. 14. Cash, W. B. W. . . . $97 94

OUTSTANDING CLAIMS.

Town Debt.

Nov. 3, 1863.	Draper library fund, demand, 6% .	$500 00
Jan. 1, 1875.	Allen fund, demand, 6% . . .	1,000 00
Aug. 1, 1878.	Water bonds, due Aug. 1, 1898, 5% .	25,000 00
Oct. 1, 1878.	Town bonds, due Oct. 1, 1898, 5% .	44,500 00
Jan. 1, 1881.	L. Maria Child fund. demand, 6% .	100 00
Oct. 1, 1882.	Water bonds, due Oct. 1, 1902, 4% .	4,000 00
July 1, 1888.	" " July 1, 1898, 4% .	1,000 00
Jan. 1, 1889.	Donation fund, demand, 6% . .	1,300 00
Apr. 1, 1891.	Loker fund, demand, 5% . . .	2,000 00
Apr. 12, 1894.	Jas. S. Draper fund, demand, 6%. .	500 00
	High school house loan, $1,100, payable Nov. 1 of each year until paid in full	8,800 00

$88,700 00

Temporary loan notes outstanding . $24,000 00

Auditor's Report.

Henry F. Lee,

In account with the Town of Wayland.

RECEIPTS.			EXPENDITURES.		
Mar. 1, 1897.					
Cash balance .	.	$2,540 90	Selectmen's orders .	$33,783	89
Donation Fund	.	12 00	Water com. "	. 1,209	16
State Treas. schools		256 28	State highway	. 409	19
State fund, superin-			School house loan	. 1,100	00
tendent schools	.	300 00	Needy soldiers	. 192	02
Dog license	. .	196 42	State treasurer, tax		
Town of Natick	.	2 20	refunded	. . 20	68
Overseers of Poor	.	1,351 25	G. L. Mayberry	. 447	58
State treas., schools		85 43	Snow plow	. . 85	00
Water rates	. .	2,893 36	Military aid	. . 144	00
Isaac Damon .	.	2 83	State aid	. . 1,127	00
H. B. Phalen .	.	75 00	State tax	. . 1,102	50
T. S. Shuman .	.	5 00	County tax	. . 1,491	95
H. B. Phalen .	.	3 12	Special tax	. . 330	51
" "	. .	19 46	Temporary loans	. 9,000	00
L. Anna Dudley	.	1 00	Cash balance .	. 2,309	07
Temporary loans	.	17,000 00			
State highway loan .		409 19			
W. B. Ward, tax 1892		112 00			
" " " 1893		335 12			
" " " 1894		855 19			
" " " 1895		4,288 79			
" " " 1896		3,307 00			
" " " 1897		13,564 62			
Tax title .	. .	97 94			

District court fines .	63	40
State cattle com. .	175	00
Sale of school furni-		
ture . . .	2	15
Rent of town hall .	35	00
P. A. Leary . .	8	33
L. K. Lovell . .	27	03
Interest on tax title	13	10
M. W. Hynes . .	1	50
State treasurer, cor-		
poration tax .	2,180	44
State treasurer, Na-		
tional bank tax .	785	84
State treasurer, mil-		
itary aid . .	84	00
State treasurer, state		
aid . . .	996	00
Int. on taxes, 1896 .	168	00
State treasurer . ·	200	00
Geo. B. Howe .	21	93
Interest on taxes .	276	73

$52,752 55 $52,752 55

TRIAL BALANCE.

Cash	$2,309	07
Overdrawn schools .	424	91
Incidentals . .	58	79
Highways . .	552	02
Salaries . .	122	56
Interest . .	530	81
Supt. of schools .	40	00
Library tablet .	4	00
Abatement taxes .	855	43
Taxes due from collector . .	20,658	11
Appropriation at a special meeting to be assessed in 1898 . .	2,000	00
	$27,555	70

Unex. bal. poor .	$186	34
School supplies .	2	67
Water com'rs. .	619	20
Sidewalks . .	43	34
Fire department .	224	00
Cemetery acct .	209	00
Lakeview cem. .	3	12
No. & Centre cem.	27	59
Electric lights .	23	22
Repairs on school building . .	33	30
Illegal sale liquor	235	80
Fence schoolhouse	100	00
Sand iiill road .	50	06
Trans. scholars .	164	75
Overdrafts, 1895 .	58	39
Fitting up High school . .	16	40
Culvert . .	15	80
Contingent acct. .	1,542	72
Temporary loans .	24,000	00
	$27,555	70

ALFRED H. BRYANT,
Auditor.

INDEX.

OFFICIAL REPORTS

OF THE

WN OF WAYLAND,

FOR ITS

e Hundred and Nineteenth Municipal Year,

FROM

RCH 1, 1898, TO MARCH 1, 1899.

Lakeview Press:
TRIBUNE BUILDING, SOUTH FRAMINGHAM, MASS.
1899.

OFFICIAL REPORTS

OF THE

TOWN OF WAYLAND,

FOR ITS

One Hundred and Nineteenth Municipal Year,

FROM

MARCH 1, 1898, TO MARCH 1, 1899.

Lakeview Press:
TRIBUNE BUILDING, SOUTH FRAMINGHAM, MASS.
1899.

List of Town Officers

FOR 1898-99 AND WHEN THEIR TERMS EXPIRE.

CLERK.

RICHARD T. LOMBARD 1899

TREASURER.

HENRY F. LEE 1899

AUDITOR.

ALFRED H. BRYANT 1899

COLLECTOR.

WILLARD B. WARD 1899

TREASURER OF LIBRARY FUNDS.

HENRY D. PARMENTER 1899

SELECTMEN.

PATRICK A LEARY 1899
ALBION F. PARMENTER 1899
ELIJAH H. ATWOOD 1899

OVERSEERS OF POOR

GEO. B. HOWE 1899
DAVID P. W. LOKER 1899
WILLARD B. WARD 1899

4

SCHOOL COMMITTEE.

ERNEST E. BUTLER	1899
DELOSS W. MITCHELL	1900
L. ANNA DUDLEY	1901

ASSESSORS.

CHARLES H. MAY	1899
RICHARD T. LOMBARD	1900
EDWARD CARTER	1901

WATER COMMISSIONERS.

HENRY G. DUDLEY	1899
WILLIAM M. FULLICK	1900
CHARLES H. BOODEY	1901

TRUSTEES PUBLIC LIBRARY.

JAMES A. DRAPER	1899
CYRUS W. HEIZER	1899
JOHN CONNELLY	1900
CHAS. F. RICHARDSON	1900
ARTHUR G. BENNETT	1901
CHESTER B. WILLIAMS	1901

CONSTABLES.

MARSHALL C. BALDWIN	1899
JESSE W. JENNISON	1899
ERNEST F. LAWRENCE	1899
LAWRENCE H. MCMANUS	1899
ANDREW S. MORSE	1899
WILLIAM C. NEAL	1899
COLIN C. WARD	1899

TRUSTEES OF ALLEN FUND.

ISAAC DAMON	1899
DANIEL D. GRIFFIN	1899
WM. H. CAMPBELL	1899

FENCE VIEWERS.

ALBION F. PARMENTER 1899
ISAAC DAMON 1899
EDWARD CARTER 1899

FIELD DRIVERS.

IRA S. DICKEY 1899
CYRUS A. ROAK 1899

SEALER OF WEIGHTS AND MEASURES.

RICHARD T. LOMBARD 1899

MEASURERS OF WOOD AND BARK.

GEO. B. HOWE 1899
EDWARD CARTER 1899
WM. S. LOVELL 1899

SURVEYOR OF LUMBER.

FRANK HAYNES 1899

SUPERINTENDENTS OF CEMETERIES.

EDSON C. DAVIS 1899
ANDREW S. MORSE 1899

FINANCE COMMITTEE.

PATRICK A. LEARY 1899
RICHARD T. LOMBARD 1899
DAVID P. W. LOKER 1899
DELOSS W. MITCHELL 1899
CHAS. H. BOODEY 1899
HENRY F. LEE 1899
CHARLES H. MAY 1899

DECORATION DAY COMMITTEE.

EDSON C. DAVIS 1899
CYRUS A. ROAK 1899
PETER S. ZIMMERMAN 1899

ENGINEERS OF FIRE DEPARTMENT.

EDWIN W. MARSTON, *Chief* 1899
FRANK E. YEAGER 1899
ARTHUR J. RICKER 1899

SUPERINTENDENT OF STREETS.

CHARLES H. MAY 1899

REGISTRARS OF VOTERS.

JAMES H. CARROLL, *Chairman* 1901
CHARLES F. WHITTIER . . . 1899
THEO L. SAWIN 1900
RICHARD T. LOMBARD, *Town Clerk, ex-officio* . 1899

Annual Town Meeting, March 27, 1899.

WARRANT.

COMMONWEALTH OF MASSACHUSETTS.

MIDDLESEX, SS.

*To **Andrew** S. Morse, or either of the Constables of the Town of Wayland in said County,*

Greeting;

In the name of the Commonwealth of Massachusetts, you are directed to notify and warn the qualified voters of said Town of Wayland to meet at the Town Hall, Wayland, on Monday, March 27th, 1899, at 6.30 o'clock in the forenoon, then and there to act on the following articles, viz :

ARTICLE 1. To choose by ballot a Moderator to preside in said meeting.

ART. 2. To choose a Town Clerk, Treasurer, Collector of Taxes, Auditor, three Selectmen, three Overseers of the Poor, Treasurer of the Library Funds, and seven Constables, all for one year. One School Committee, one Assessor, one Water Commissioner, and two Trustees of the Public Library, all for three years. Also to answer the following question, "Shall licenses for the sale of intoxicating liquors be granted in the Town of Wayland for the year ensuing ? "

All names of candidates for the offices aforesaid and the said question must appear upon the official ballot, and be voted for in accordance with Chapter 548 of the Acts of the General Court of the year 1898.

For the purposes specified in this article the polls will be open immediately after the election of a moderator, and will remain open continuously until one o'clock P. M., when they may be closed, providing, the polls have remained open for not less than four hours at that time.

ART. 3. To choose all other necessary Town Officers, Agents, and Committees, and hear reports of Town Officers, Trustees, Agents and Committees, and act thereon.

ART. 4. To see how much money the town will grant for paying interest, existing debts, for roads and bridges, for support of poor, for support of schools, school supplies and repairs on school buildings and transportation of scholars, for the fire department, for abatement of taxes, and for all other necessary Town purposes, and order the same to be assessed, or do or act.

ART. 5. To authorize the Selectmen to consult counsel on important town cases.

ART. 6. To see if the town will authorize its Treasurer, with the approval of the Selectmen, to borrow money temporarily in anticipation of taxes for the municipal years 1899 and 1900, and if so how much, or do or act.

ART. 7. To see if the town will accept the list of Jurors as prepared by the Selectmen.

ART. 8. To appropriate the money received from the County Treasurer for dog licenses.

ART. 9. To see if the town will elect one surveyor of highways and that the names of candidates be placed on the official ballot, and accept Section 332 of Chapter 548 of the Acts of the General Court for the year 1898.

ART. 10. To see if the town will elect its Selectmen and Overseers of the Poor in accordance with Section 335 of Chapter 548 of the Acts of the General Court for the year 1898.

ART. 11. To see if the town will vote to place the names of candidates of Commissioners of Sinking Fund on the official ballot.

ART. 12. To see if the town will accept the bequest in the will of Mrs. Sarah M. Parsons, late of Brooklyn, N. Y., now deceased, of two hundred dollars, the income to be used as designated in said will, or do or act.

ART. 13. To see if the town will instruct its Treasurer to give a note for two thousand dollars, to replace the note given by the town for the "Loker Fund," which note has been lost,— or do or act.

ART. 14. To see if the town will appropriate money to fill and grade the west side of Main Street, in Cochituate village, and build a wall from Corman's Lane to Natick town line, so as to conform to that part of the street lying in Natick, or do or act.

ART. 15. To see if the town will vote to finish and fit up another room and its adjoining class room for school purposes, in the Wayland Centre school building, or do or act.

ART. 16. To see if the town will appropriate the sum of eleven hundred and fifty dollars for the purpose of finishing, furnishing and heating one of the unfinished rooms and its adjoining class room in the Wayland Center school building, or do or act.

ART. 17. To see if the town will accept the extension of Mitchell street as laid out by the selectmen, in accordance with plans and specifications on file with the Town Clerk, or do or act.

ART. 18. To see if the town will appropriate any money for Special Police, or do or act.

ART. 19. To see what action the town will take in reference to rebuilding "Baldwin's Bridge" so-called, or do or act.

ART. 20. To see if the town will instruct the Selectmen to petition the County Commissioners to widen and relocate that part of the road leading from Wayland to Cochituate, from near Johnson's lane, so-called, to the Boston road near the First Church, or do or act.

And you are directed to serve this Warrant by posting up true and attested copies thereof at the Town House, and each of the Post Offices in the town, seven days at least before the day for holding said meeting.

Hereof fail not, and make due return of this warrant, with your doings thereon, to the Town Clerk of said Town on or before the time appointed for holding said meeting.

Given under our hands this Seventh Day of March, in the year eighteen hundred and ninety-nine.

PATRICK A. LEARY,
ALBION F. PARMENTER,
ELIJAH H. ATWOOD,
Selectmen of Wayland.

A true copy.   Attest :

ANDREW S. MORSE,
Constable.

Jury List for 1899.

Fred P. Draper.

Jeremiah Lyons.

Arthur T. Felch.

John E. Linnehan.

James I. Bryden.

Frank Lupien.

Isaac S. Whittemore.

Warren B. Langmaid

Edward B. Smith.

Nathan S. Walton

Edgar B. Loker.

Andrew S. Morse.

Edward M. Partridge.

Harry H. Rutter.

John J. McCann.

Patrick A. Leary.

William H. Campbell.

Ernest E. Butler.

Andrew S. Norris.

Marcus M. Fiske.

Marshall C. Baldwin.

William S. Lovell.

Allen B. Sherman.

Paul Paradeau.

Edward F. Lee.

Randall W. Porter.

PATRICK A. LEARY,
ALBION F. PARMENTER,
ELIJAH H. ATWOOD,
Selectmen of Wayland.

March 9, 1899.

Report of the Selectmen.

WAYLAND, March 1, 1899.

The selectmen hereby submit their annual report as required by the By-laws of the town.

The following officers were appointed as required by statute :

Engineers of the Fire Department. Edwin W. Marston, Arthur J. Ricker, Frank C. Yeager.

Undertakers. Andrew S. Morse, David P. W Loker.

Inspector of Cattle and Provisions. Thomas Bryant.

Superintendent of Streets. C. H. May.

Truant Officers. A. F. King, T. S. Sherman.

Registrar of Voters. James Carroll.

Public Weighers. Geo. B. Howe, L. K. Lovell, A. W. Lombard.

Measurer of Wood and Bark. J. A. Draper.

Superintendent of Fire Alarm. Willard C. Hunting.

Fish and Game Warden. John J. Irwin.

Special Police. John Woodworth, John E. Linnehan, Charles Elms.

Janitor of Town Hall. John E. Linnehan

Election Officers. Precinct 1. Warden, W. C. Campbell ; Clerk, M. W. Hynes ; Inspectors, H. W. Parmenter, E. F. Lee, H. F. Haynes, J. J. Rowen ; Constable, A. S. Morse. *Precinct 2.* Warden, E. E. Butler ; Clerk, Willard C. Hunting ; Inspectors, E. M. Partridge, N. S. Walton, James Hannon, N. R. Gerald ; Constable, C. C. Ward.

According to the vote of the town, we settled the case of Susan Pierce for $350 paid from the contingent fund as ordered.

The town scales at Wayland Centre being unfit for use, new ones were purchased. No provision being made for insurance, we have been compelled to overdraw the account for incidentals, the insurance on all the town buildings being due this year. Premiums amounted to $1,163.50.

It was agreed with Mr. C. W. Dean to blow the Fire Alarm for $150 a year. At the end of the second month he presented his bill for $25 a month; and demanded payment or the removal of the Fire Alarm. We decided that the town could not afford to pay $300 a year and removed the Fire Alarm. Then we purchased a tapper for the bell on the Methodist church, at a cost of $256, this being satisfactory to the underwriters.

The section of road laid out by the highway commissioners has been completed and accepted by them. We have petitioned that the road be continued and have reason to expect that another section will be built this year.

We recommend that the town provide some means for lighting the streets at Wayland Centre.

In the case of Lupien vs. Town of Wayland, by the advice of counsel, we decided to defend the case, the amount of damage claimed being $4,000.

In June last, we received notice from Mr. C. W. Dean that the water fountain in Cochituate was in part situated on his land (about one foot) and if it was not removed at once, he should charge the town rent at the rate of $12 per month. We therefore promptly had the fountain moved at an expense of $13.75.

Early in the year, one of the arches of Baldwin's bridge gave way. The bridge was temporarily repaired, but will not long be safe.

In the case of Harriet Noyes vs. the Town of Wayland, we decided to defend the case.

> PATRICK A. LEARY,
> ALBION F. PARMENTER,
> ELIJAH H. ATWOOD,
> *Selectmen of Wayland.*

Report of Town Clerk and Registrar.

WAYLAND, January 1, 1899.

I hereby transmit the annual report of the clerk and registrar for the year ending December 31, 1898.

BIRTHS.

The number registered during the year was forty-two, being the same number recorded in 1897.

Males	24
Females	18
Born of native parents	20
" foreign parents	6
" native and foreign parents . . .	16

MARRIAGES.

The number registered during the year was twenty-seven, being three more than in 1897.

Native birth of both parties	22
" and foreign birth	4
Foreign birth of both parties	1
First marriage of both parties	22
Second marriage of both parties	2
First of one and second of the other party . .	3

DEATHS.

Whole number registered during the year was thirty-two, being three more than in 1897.

CONDITION.

Married	15
Widowed	4
Single	13
Native birth	25
Foreign birth	7
Males	17
Females	15

Names of persons deceased during the year who were over seventy years of age :

	Years	Months	Days
Henry Scott	70	4	
Joseph Bullard	93	10	4
Lucy Wilson	81	2	12
Sylvester E. Underwood	76	6	6
Lydia Loker	82	10	6
Mary E. Burnaby	74	1	14
Susan R. Rutter	87	6	
Celina G. Bennet	87	1	13
Susan L. Pierce	75	4	20
Henry W. Dean	77		
Francis X. Laconture	70	10	10

It appears that over one-third of the deaths were of persons over seventy years of age, and their average age was 79 years, 7 months and 15 days.

Nine deaths are recorded of children less than one year of age.

NOSOLOGICAL TABLE.

Paresis	1
Old Age	2
Inanition	2
Apoplexy	1

Influenza	1
Heart Disease	3
Paralysis	2
Meningitis	1
Pneumonia	2
Congestion of Lungs	1
Consumption	3
Convulsions	2
Bronchitis	1
Tuberculosis	2
Still Born	2
Cancer	1
Cholera Infantum	1
Tumor	1
Cerebral Hemorrhage	1
Disease of Brain	1
Bright's Disease	1

DOGS.

Number of dogs licensed

96 males, at $2 00	$192 00
15 females at $5 00	75 00
	$267 00
111 licenses at 20 cents	22 20
Amount received	$243 80

VOTERS.

Number registered November 7, 1898	482
Precinct 1	156
" 2	326
Ballots cast precinct 1	105
" " " 2	263
Total	368
Number of women voters	77
" who voted March 26, 1898	36

VOTE FOR GOVERNOR.

Alexander B. Bruce	109
George R. Peare	6
Winfield P. Porter	1
Roger Wolcott	244

VOTE FOR SENATOR.

William V. Hyde	121
Fred Joy	208

VOTE FOR REPRESENTATIVE IN THE 21ST MIDDLESEX DISTRICT.

	Elijah H. Atwood.	George Balcom.	William M. Brigham.	Frederick R. S. Mildon.	Blanks
Marlborough	884	1352	1310	919	513
Sudbury	111	21	109	19	290
Wayland	213	123	165	84	151
Totals	1,208	1,496	1,584	1,022	954

Respectfully submitted,

RICHARD T. LOMBARD,

Town Clerk.

Assessors' Report.

WAYLAND, March 1, 1899.

Value of real estate May 1, 1898 . . .	$1,311,360 00
" personal estate May 1, 1898 . . .	337,105 00
Total valuation May 1, 1898	$1,648,465 00
" " 1897	1,527,205 00
Increase	$121,260 00
Taxes assessed for town purposes . . .	$27,387 20
Overlayings	152 41
State tax	900 00
Special State tax (Marsh land) , . . .	330 52
County tax	1,492 93
Additional assessments	28 25
Additional polls assessed after May 1 . .	20 00
Total assessments committed to collector for collection	$30,311 31
Number of polls assessed May 1, 1898 . .	625
" " since May 1, 1898 .	10
Total polls assessed	635
Number of polls assessed May 1, 1897 . .	611
Increase	24
Number of persons assessed	956
" residents assessed on property . .	412
" non-residents assessed on property .	147

Total valuation of land $485,975 00
"   " buildings 825,385 00
Valuation of church property 32,040 00
Valuation of town property 122,382 00

Number of horses assessed 392
"   " Cows   " 737
"   " Sheep   " 28
"   " Swine   " 395
"   " Fowls   " 1,225
"   " Dwelling houses assessed . . . 426
"   " Acres of land   " . . . 9,021$\frac{9}{10}$
Rate of taxation for 1898, $17 60 per thousand.
"   "   "   " 1897, $16 00 ."   "

LIST OF ABATEMENTS GRANTED.

Taxes assessed in the year 1892.
Personal estate $80 00
    Total for 1892 . . . . . ———— $80 00

Taxes assessed in the year 1894.
Poll taxes $26 00
Personal estate 6 03
    Total for 1894 . . . . . ———— $32 03

Taxes assessed in year 1895.
Polls $132 00
Personal estate 42 41
Real estate 7 17
Special meadow tax, real estate . . . 2 25
    Total for 1895 . . . . . ———— $183 83

Taxes assessed in the year 1896.
Polls $4 00
Personal estate 6 68
Real estate 44 07
Special meadow tax, real estate . . . 8 49
    Total for 1896 . . . . . ———— $64 24

Taxes assessed in year 1897.

Polls	$2 00	
Personal estate . . . . : .	1,600 00	
Real estate	8 00	
Total for 1897 . . . . . ———		$1,610 00

Taxes assessed in the year 1898.

Personal estate	$253 44	
Real estate	81 40	
Total for year 1898 . . . . ———		$334 84

Total abatements granted during the year . . $2,304 94

Respectfully submitted,

RICHARD T. LOMBARD,
EDWARD CARTER,
CHARLES H. MAY,
Assessors of Wayland.

Collector's Report.

TAXES OF 1894.

Balance due March 1, 1898	$364 96
Paid treasurer	364 96

Interest, $249.04.

TAXES OF 1895.

Balance due March 1, 1898	$1,461 59
Paid treasurer	1,288 88
	$172 71

Interest, $100.00.

TAXES OF 1896.

Balance due March 1, 1898	$6,404 50
Paid treasurer	4,095 34
	$2,309 16

Interest $100.00.

TAXES OF 1897.

Balance due March 1, 1898	$12,427 06
Paid treasurer	5,272 78
	$7,154 28
Additional assessment	14 00
	$7,168 28

Taxes of 1898.

Taxes of 1898 . . . . $30,311 31
Paid treasurer 17,424 73

$12,886 58

WILLARD B. WARD,
Collector.

Report of the Overseers of the Poor.

FOR THE YEAR ENDING FEBRUARY 28, 1899.

Mr. M. Temple who has been superintendent of the almshouse for the past three years, has given general satisfaction and will remain another year, which is highly appreciated.

There is one inmate who is helpless and requires constant attention which has been given by the matron.

OUT DOOR POOR, PARTIAL SUPPORT.

Families aided	15	
Persons "	87	
		102

IN DOOR POOR, FULL SUPPORT.

Almshouse	4	
State Lunatic Hospital	4	
		. 8
Total number of persons aided. . . .		110

FINANCIAL STATEMENT SHOWING ACTUAL RECEIPTS AND EXPENDITURES FOR THE YEAR.

March 1st, 1898, unexpended balance . .	$186 34	
Appropriation . . .	2,500 00	
		$2,686 34

REIMBURSEMENTS.

From town of Lexington	$52 00	
Natick	236 74	
Southboro	160 45	
Framingham	23 50	
Commonwealth of Massachusetts .	5 90	
		$478 59

ALMSHOUSE RECEIPTS.

Sale of milk	$997 68	
Produce, eggs, poultry etc. . .	383 07	
Cows and calves	87 25	
For board of J. Mullen	53 90	
Laborers	74 10	
		$1,596 00

Total receipts	$4,760 93

EXPENDITURES OUT DOOR POOR.

Having a settlement in Wayland and residing elsewhere.

Themie Davis, Spencer	4 00	
Artemas Bond, Boston, now a state care .	72 00	
N. Normandin and family, North Brookfield .	14 40	
Wm. H. Mullin " " Boston . . .	5 50	
Frank Byron " " Natick . . .	6 50	
Henry Rust and family, Pittsfield, now a state case	85 48	
Alex L. Benoit and family, Brockton . .	9 98	
		$197 86

Having a settlement in Wayland and residing there.

John Chenett and family	$155 00
Annie Burrill, now a state case . - .	181 50
Lewis C. Maud and family	24 38
Frank X. Davieaux and family . . .	27 98
George Gayzette " " . . .	88 90
Ann Painter	52 00

Louis Cormier and family	$36 00	
George Chalmers	45 00	
Mrs. Nelson Latour and children . .	99 26	
James Foley	52 00	
Nelson Betmore, Jr., and family . . .	38 75	
		$800 77

Having a Settlement in Other Cities and Towns and Residing in Wayland.

Patrick Fay (Commonwealth of Mass.) .	$79 29	
J. F. Hawkins, Southboro	156 80	
H. W. Dean, Natick	96 10	
E. Haldwell, Lexington	52 00	
F. A. L. Towne, Natick	10 00	
		$394 19

In Door Poor in Insane Hospital.

Clara Davis, Westboro	$169 46	
J. A. Wing, Worcester	169 46	
James F. Loker, Worcester	87 71	
Ellen Stanton	169 46	
		$596 09

Almshouse Expenditures.

Paid warden's salary	$445 84	
Groceries	356 86	
Provisions	145 90	
Grain	350 61	
Cows	246 75	
Repairs	73 16	
Seeds	28 45	
Hay	74 52	
Tools	47 50	
Manure	79 23	
Repairs on house and barn . . .	47 37	
Clothing for inmates	11 50	
Labor	237 28	
Fuel	49 75	
Medical services for inmates . .	7 50	
Miscellaneous	67 47	
		$2,269 69

Miscellaneous.

Travelling expenses, settlement of cases,
stationery, order books, etc. $82 11

           $4,340 71

Unexpended balance 420 22

           $4,760 93

Outstanding Claims.

Town of Natick, bill not received.
City of Springfield, bill not received.
 " Waltham, " "
 " Brockton, case unsettled.
 " Boston, " "

Reimbursements Due.

From Commonwealth of Massachusetts . $89 29
 " Town of Southboro 29 60
 " " Lexington 52 00
              $160 89

Inmates at Almhouse During the Year.

Sarah Puffer, March 1, 1898, age 82 years
James Burke, " " " 71 "
Benj. Nealy, " " " 74 " now a State case.
One person, Oct. 10, " " 68 "

Inventory of Property at Almshouse.

Eleven cows $525 00
One horse 100 00
Two shoats 16 00
Forty hens 20 00
Twenty cords manure 100 00
Nine tons hay 126 00
Fuel 62 00

Potatoes	$15 00	
Provisions	15 00	
Farming implements and wagons . . .	240 00	
Furniture and utensils	220 00	
	————	$1,430 00
Real estate		5,800 00
Total		$7,239 00

Number of tramps lodged	336
Meals furnished	415

REMARKS.

The prospects in the fall of 1898 were not favorable for the overseers to take steps for building a wagon shed at the almshouse according to the vote of the town and therefore we respectfully ask for the same conditions to be granted from the appropriation this year as last.

An appropriation of twenty-five hundred dollars is asked for.

Respectfully submitted,

DAVID P. W. LOKER,
GEORGE B HOWE,
W. B. WARD,
Overseers of the Poor.

Report of Library Trustees.

In making our annual report, we wish to call your attention to a few facts. We find the books all in their proper places. We believe that there should be at least one hundred and fifty new books added to the library each year. The expenses the past year have been as follows :

Librarian's salary	$300 00
Asst. Librarian's salary at Cochituate	40 00
Expressing books to "	35 72
Fuel	38 37
Binding	11 64
Magazines	7 00
Janitor	5 00
New books	60 00
	$497 73

The running expenses for the coming year cannot consistently be reduced and we ask for an appropriation of $500.

C. W. HEIZER, *Chairman*
A. G. BENNETT,
JOHN CONNELLY,
C. B. WILLIAMS,
C. F. RICHARDSON,
J. A. DRAPER, *Clerk.*

Librarian's Report.

Statistical information for the year 1898-99 is respectfully submitted to the trustees.

ACCESSIONS.

	Books
By purchase	29
By gift	- 41
Bound and transferred from pamphlet department	12
Total	82

Whole number of volumes in the library	12,944
Pamphlets presented	446

CIRCULATION.

In Cochituate village	1,241
In Wayland Centre	4,378
Total	5,619

DONORS OF BOOKS AND PAMPHLETS.

	Books	Pamphlets
American Congregational society		1
American Library Commission		1
Bancroft Publishing company	1	
Beck, Mr. John E.	1	

	Books	Pamphlets
Brookline Public Library		4
Brooklyn " "		2
Chase, Mr. Walter G.		1
Coolidge, Miss Catherine		
Day, Rev. Wm. Y.		20
Dudley, Miss L. A.		67
Fowler, Mr. E. H.		
Heard, Misses M. & E.		13
Kettle, Mrs. E. M.	4	
London Athæneum		1
McGlennen, Mr. E. W.	1	
Palmer, Mrs.	1	
Sent to Reading Room		189
Rice, Mrs. Chas.		4
Root, Mr. L. Carroll		101
Salem Public Library		12
Sears, Rev. E. H., The family of . .	1	
State Government	15	10
United States Government	15	20

Library reports have been received as follows: Arlington, Brookline, Brooklyn, Concord, Fall River, Forbes Library (Northampton), Free Public Library Commission, Harvard College, Salem, Sudbury, Lawrence, Malden, Newton, Waltham, Weston and Watertown.

CLASSES OF READING.

Biography	.	.	.07	Literature	.	.	.05
Fiction	.	.	.55	Poetry	.	.	.04
History	.	.	.13	Religion	.	.	02
Juvenile	.	.	.13	Science	.	.	.02

The reading room has received regularly The Century Magazine, Good Roads, Harper's Monthly, Munsey's, The Land of Sunshine, The Woman's Journal, Traveller's Record and Cochituate Enterprize.

9690　　An Adventurer of the North.　Gilbert Parker.
9720　　Bell Ringer of Angells, The.　Brett Harte.
9739　　Birds of Village and Field.　Florence A. Merriam
9897　　Bradford's History of Plymouth Plantation.
9745　　Cathedral Courtship and Penelope's Experience.　Wiggin.
9815　　Coming People, The.　Chas. F. Dole
9827　　Cooking for Invalids　H. M. Spring and Catherine Coolidge.
9787　　Costume of Colonial Time.　Alice Morse Earle.
9836　　Dariel.　R. D. Blackmore.
9904-5　Deluge, The.　Henry Sienkiewicz.
9910　　English Composition.　Barrett Wendell.
9715　　Garden Making.　L. H. Bailey.
9684　　Garrison Tangle, A.　Capt. Chas King.
9903　　Harriet Beecher Stowe, Life and Letters.　Ed. by Annie Field.
9691　　In Kedar's Tents.　H. S. Merriman.
9902　　In Memoriam of Rev. and Mrs. Edmund Sears.
9820　　In Woods and Fields.　Augusta Larned.
9655　　Lochinvar.　S. R. Crockett.
9899　　Marble Faun, The.　Nathaniel Hawthorn.
9891-2　Old Virginia and Her Neighbors.　John Fiske.
9801　　Pan Michael.　Henry Sienkiewicz.
9808　　Phroso.　Anthony Hope.
9901　　Reminiscences of Wm. Wetmore Story.　Mary E. Phillips.
9721　　Rhyme and Reason.　Lewis Carroll.
9911　　Self Cultivation in English.　Geo. H. Palmer.
9719　　Seven on the Highway.　Blanche W. Howard.
9411　　Shrewsbury.　Stanley J. Weyman.
9672　　Stories for Boys.　R. H. Davis.
9744　　Story Hour, The.　Kate Douglas Wiggin.
9728　　Story of an Untold Love.　Paul Leicester Ford.
9893　　Westward Movements, The.　Justin Winsor.
9900　　Works of Wordsworth.

SARAH E. HEARD,
Librarian.

Feb. 27, 1899.

Report of Treasurer of Wayland Library Funds.

FOR THE YEAR ENDING MARCH 1, 1899.

HENRY D. PARMENTER, *Treasurer*,

In account with Library Funds.

1898.	DR.		
March 1.	To unexpended appropriation for 1897 .	$157	01
June 1.	Appropriation for 1898	300	00
July 1.	Cochituate Branch, fines collected and cards sold	1	70
Jan. 14.	Interest on Library Funds to Jan. 1, 1899 .	66	00
Feb. 28.	Town of Wayland dog licenses, one-half	74	38
		$599	09

1898.	CR.		
By Librarian's salary to Jan. 1	$300	00
Assistant Librarian's salary	40	00
American Express company	35	72
Books, magazines and binding bills . . .	46	60
Fuel and labor bills	46	25
	$468	57
Balance unexpended	130	52
	$599	09

Water Commissioners' Report.

WAYLAND WATER COMMISSIONERS,

In account with HENRY F. LEE, *Town Treasurer.*

1898.

Feb. 28.	Balance not drawn from town treasurer .	$907 70
July 30.	Paid from sinking fund	14,196 42
Aug 1.	Premium on bonds	784 85
1899.		
Feb. 28.	Transfer for hydrants	384 00
	By water rates, town treasurer . . .	1,917 51
	Interest on Bond not drawn, 1898-9 .	405 00
		18,595 48

1898.

Aug. 1.	Sinking fund	$14,000 00
	Transfer interest on bonds	1,450 00
1899.		
Feb. 28.	Order No. 1 Maintenance	220 53
	" " 2 H. G. Dudley, Supt. . .	150 00
	" " 3 " " " Com. . .	20 00
	" " 4 C. H. Boody " . .	20 00
	" " 5 W. M. Fullick " . .	20 00
	" " 6 " " " Clerk . .	32 50
	" " 7 For sinking fund . . .	1,454 48
	Balance not drawn	1,227 97
		$18,595 48

C. H. BOODY,
H. G. DUDLEY,
W. M. FULLICK,
Commissioners of Wayland Water Works.

WAYLAND, Feb. 28, 1899.

3

Report of Commissioners of Water Works Sinking Fund.

Amount deposited in Natick Five Cent
Savings Bank, Natick, Mass. .   .   . $3,694 74
Interest on above deposit May 1, 1898   .   2,390 15
Amount deposited in Suffolk Savings Bank,
Boston, Mass. 1,000 00
Interest on above deposit April 1, 1898   .   454 02
Amount deposited in Home Savings Bank,
Boston, Mass. 2,292 38
Interest on above deposit April 1, 1898   .   783 00
Amount deposited in North End   .   .   1,459 40
Interest on above deposit July 1, 1898   .   306 90
Amount deposited in Watertown Savings
Bank, Watertown, Mass 994 53
Interest on above deposit, April 1, 1898   .   121 16
Amount deposited in Farmers and Mechan-
ics Savings Bank, South Framingham,
Mass. 675 86
Interest on above deposit 27 28

$14,196 42

1898.
July 3.   Drawn from Sinking Fund   . $14,196 42

1898	Amount deposited in Framingham Savings Bank, South Framingham, Mass. .	. $1,205 21
	Interest on above deposit Nov. 1, 1897	. 263 94

$1,469 15

1899.
Feb. 28. Drawn from Framingham Savings
Bank $734 58

Deposited in Natick Five Cent Savings
Bank, Natick, Mass. $734 58

Amount in Framingham Savings Bank, Framingham, Mass 734 58

Amount deposited in Watertown Savings
Bank, Watertown,-Mass 1,000 00

Amount deposited in Home Savings Bank,
Boston, Mass. . . . . - 454 48

$2,923 64

C. H. BOODY,
H. G. DUDLEY,
W. M. FULLICK,
Commissioners Wayland Water Works Sinking Fund.

Report of the Superintendent of the Wayland Water Works.

GENTLEMEN —:

We have had a very wet year and for that reason the water has had more color than usual. The works are in as good condition as it is possible to put them under existing circumstances.

The maintenance account is,

1898.

April	1.	To Labor for March	$6 50
May	1.	Labor for April	14 50
	16.	Howe & Co.	75
	21.	R. W. Porter	5 00
June	1.	Labor for May	16 00
	16.	F. Ames	4 00
July	1.	Labor for June	21 00
	2.	J. B. McIroy	6 00
		James Devine	6 00
	18.	Walworth Mfg. Co.	30 27
Aug.	1.	Labor for July	18 00
Sept.	1.	Labor for August	17 50
Oct.	1.	Labor for September	12 00
Nov.	1.	Labor for October	11 50
Dec.	1.	Labor for November	10 25
	12.	R. W. Porter	3 00
	22	James Devine	3 00

1899.

Jan.	1.	Labor for December	. . . .	$5 50
	8.	J. B. McIroy .	. . . . .	3 00
	22.	E. P. Butlar .	. . . . .	2 28
Feb.	1.	Labor for January .	. . . .	6 50
	21.	Wm. F. Garfield .	. . . .	6 00
	28.	Labor for February	. . . .	7 25
		Postage for year .	. . . .	1 20
		Book . . .	. . . .	65
		Wm. M. Fullick .	. . . .	3 88

$220 53

The water at present is in use by the following :

Families	288
Manufactories	9
Public buildings	4
Miscellaneous	11
Horses	82
Cows	47

Respectfully submitted,

H. G. DUDLEY,
Superintendent.

WAYLAND, Feb. 28, 1899.

Report of Superintendent of Streets.

HIGHWAY PAY ROLL FOR THE MONTH OF APRIL, 1898.

	Per Day.	Days.	Hours.	Amount
M. W. Hynes . . .	$2 00	5	6½	$11 45
M. W. Hynes, horse . .	1 75	14	6½	25 75
T. L. Hynes . . .	2 00	4	6	9 34
T. L. Hynes, horse . .	1 75	3		5 25
A. B. Sherman . . .	2 00	16		32 00
A. B. Sherman, horse . .	1 75	16		28 00
Geo. E. Sherman . .	2 00	29		58 00
Geo. E. Sherman, horse .	1 75	25		43 75
James Fox	2 00	16		32 00
Henry Walker . . .	2 00	8		16 00
George B. Folsom . .	2 00	4		8 00
John Coughlin . . .	2 00	4		8 00
P. J. McLoughlin . .	2 00	4	6	9 34
Bill for lumber and nails				27 23
				$314 11
Cochituate				157 55
				$471 66

HIGHWAY PAY ROLL FOR THE MONTH OF MAY.

	Days.	Hours.		Days.	Hours.		
W. C. Neal . .	5		horse	10		$27	50
C. A. Roak . .	5	5	"	5	8	21	43
A. Moreau . .	5	1		.	.	10	22
F. Lemay . .	3	2		.	.	6	44
E. A. Carter .	5	8		.	.	11	76
C. W. Fairbanks .	2			4		11	00
C. H. May .	5	7	"	6		22	05
J. Hurley . .	4	7		.	.	11	95
P. Mathews .	4	5		.	.	9	10
W. E. Jennison .	5			.	.	10	00
						$141	45

HIGHWAY PAY ROLL FOR THE MONTH OF MAY.

	Per Day.	Days.	Hours.	Amount	
James Fox . . .	$2 00	8		$16	00
Harry Walker . . .	2 00	9		18	00
Geo. E. Sherman . . .	2 00	33		66	00
Geo. E. Sherman, horses .	1 75	30		52	50
T. L. Hynes . . .	2 00	5		10	00
T. L. Hynes, horse . .	1 75	10		17	50
A. B Sherman . . .	2 00	20		40	00
A. B. Sherman, horses .	1 75	8		14	00
M. W. Hynes, horses . .	1 75	8		14	00
G. N. Sherman . . .	2 00	13	$4\frac{1}{2}$	27	00
P. J. McLoughlin . .	2 00	5		10	00
J. J. Erwin	2 00	12	$4\frac{1}{2}$	25	00
J. J. Erwin, horses . .	1 75	9	7	17	08
M. C. Baldwin, hanging lanterns				4	00
Buttrick Lumber Co..				40	08
Rutter & Rideout, for spikes					90
Lawrence McManus, sharpening picks					60
James Knox, 203 loads gravel				20	30
				$392	96

Highway Pay Roll for the Month of June.

	Days.	Hours.		Days.	Hours.	
Geo. E. Sherman .	7	4½	horse	5		$23 75
Henry Sherman .	2			.	.	4 00
Butrick Lumber Co. .	.	.	.	.	. .	8 86
						$36 61

Highway Pay Roll for the Month of June

	Days.	Hours.		Days.	Hours.	
C. W. Fairbanks .	7	2	horse	14	4	$39 71
C. A. Roak . .			"	5		8 75
C. H. May . .	12	8	"	27		73 01
W. C. Neal .	15	2	"	20	6	66 61
W. E Jennison .	7	2		.	.	14 44
James Murphy .	6	1		.	.	12 22
Frank Brummett .	13	5		.	.	27 10
Frank Lemay .	1	6		.	.	3 30
Chas. Newton .	5			.	.	10 00
John Hurley .	12	6		.	.	28 68
Thomas Evans .	7	2		.	.	14 44
Levi Celorice .	1	3		.	.	2 66
E. A. Carter .	1	3		.	.	2 66
One and one-half barrels Portland cement				.	.	4 13
						$307 71

Highway Pay Roll for the Month of July.

	Days.	Hours.		Days.	Hours.	
G. E. Sherman .	16	1½	horse	8		$46 32
James Fox . .	2			.	.	4 00
Butrick Lumber Co., lumber	.	.	.	.	.	23 63
Rutter & Rideout, spikes .	.	.	.	.	.	90
J. H. Lee, lanterns, etc.	.	.	.	.	.	2 85
						$77 70

HIGHWAY PAY ROLL FOR THE MONTH OF AUGUST.

	Days.	Hours.		Days.	Hours	
Geo. E. Sherman	7		horse	4		$21 00
James Fox . .	2			.		4 00
Henry Walker .	2					4 00
Ed Eagen . .	2					4 00
P. J. McLaughlin	2			.		4 00
M. W. Hynes .	2			4		11 00
T. L. Hynes .	2		"	4		11 00
T. W. Frost, sign boards and lettering . . .						3 00
Geo.E Sherman, grading around scales and Town house						7 00

$69 00

HIGHWAY PAY ROLL FOR THE MONTH OF SEPTEMBER.

	Days.	Hours.		Days.	Hours.	
E. A. Carter .	11			.	.	$22 00
Wm. B. Underwood	9			.	.	18 00
H. F. Brummett .	14			.	.	28 00
J. H. Morrisey .	9	6½		.	.	19 46
John Hurley .	5			.	.	10 00
C. W. Fairbanks .	7		horse	14		38 50
W. C. Neal .	6	8½	"	12	8	36 45
C. H. May	12		"	24		66 00

$238 41

HIGHWAY PAY ROLL FOR THE MONTH OF SEPTEMBER.

	Days.	Hours.		Days.	Hours.	
J. S. Dickey .	3½		horse			$7 00
George E. Sherman	14		"	7		40 25
M. W. Hynes .	8	5	"	17	1	47 05
T. L. Hynes .	8	5	"	17	1	47 05
P. J. McLaughlin	8	5		.	.	17 11
Edward Egan .	8			.	.	16 00
James Linehan .	8					16 00
Isaac Whitemore, 45 loads of gravel						4 50
James Knox, 22 loads of gravel						2 20
Maynard Parmenter, 41 loads of gravel . . .						4 10

$201 26

Highway Pay Roll for the Month of October

	Days.	Hours.		Days.	Hours.		
Arthur Moreau .	3	6½		.	.	$7	50
E. W. Schleicher	1	2				2	44
E. A. Carter .	6			.	.	12	00
H. F. Brummett		5				1	11
James Morrisey .	5	8		.	.	11	72
W. C. Neal .	10	8	horse	10	8	40	86
C. H. May . . -	5	4	"	10	8	29	96
C. W. Fairbanks .	2	5	"	5	1	. 14	04
Isaac Whittemore, 266 loads of gravel . . .						26	60

$146 23

Highway Pay Roll for the Months of November and December.

	Days.	Hours.		Days.	Hours.		
M. W. Hynes .	5	6	horse	8	8	$26	68
T. L. Hynes .	4	1	"	8	2	22	62
John Linnehan .	6	4		.	.	12	89
Edw. Harrington	4	1		.	.	8	22
Albert Harrington	4	1		.	.	8	22
P. J. McLaughlin	4	3				8	68
James Linnehan .	2	7		.	.	5	56
Patrick Jennings.	2	7				5	56
Herbert Haynes .	2	6				5	34
John J. Rowan .	1	7				3	56
Chris. Saunders .	2					4	00
P. Zimmerman .	2	5				5	11
Kirby Whittier .	1					2	00
H. D. Lee .	1	5				3	11
Frank Immick .	1	1				2	22
John Coakley .	1					2	00
W. Dolan .	2	6½				5	47

$131 24

SNOW BILLS.

HIGHWAY PAY ROLL FOR THE MONTHS OF NOV. AND DEC.

	Days.	Hours.		Days.	Hours.	
A. B. Sherman .	7	4	horse	5	7	$24 98
Chas. Ellms .	1			.	.	2 00
George Campbell	1	3		.	.	2 66
Geo E. Sherman	7	2		7	2	27 05
Thomas Lane .	1	3			8	4 12
George W. Philbrick	5	3		.	.	10 66
G. N. Sherman .	4	5				9 10
James Fox . .	8	1½		.	.	16 30
George Folsom .	8			8	6	31 18
T. Coughlin .	8			.	.	16 00
John J. Coughlin	4					8 00
James McDonald	7			.	.	14 00
Frank Quinn .	3	5				7 10
Charles Quinn .		8½				1 88
S. S. Davidson .	3			.		6 00
M. C. Baldwin .	29			12		79 00
George A. Frost .	6			.	.	12 00
C. W. Bemis .	3			.	.	6 00
A. Randolph .	1	5				3 11
C. Homan .	1	1				2 22
C. A. Phillips .	2 .	2				4 44
J. H. Stephens .	2	4½				5 00
P. D. Gorman .	2	5½				5 22
E. W. Schleicher	1	3		.	.	2 67
A. T. Felch .	1					2 00
H. E. Griffin .	½			.	.	1 00
W. C. Neal .	1	7		2	4	7 83
Wilson Porter .		2			2	1 23
H. M. Mathews .	3	2			.	6 44
H. F. Brummett .		2		.	.	44
C. H. May .	6	1½	"	5	3	20 33
L. A. Loker .		7		.	.	1 55
Chas. Jacobs	.	.	.	.	.	3 20

W. G. Jessop	.	.	.	.	.	$2 40
E. S. Stone	.	.	.	.	.	1 00
Thomas Evans	.	.	.	.	.	2 00

$350 11

HIGHWAY PAY ROLL FOR THE MONTH OF FEBRUARY, 1899.

	Days.	Hours.		Days.	Hours.	
Joseph Tyrrell	3	½				$6 11
C. H. Carter	2			.	.	4 00
Thos. Evans	1	6		.	.	3 33
G L Baker	3	3		.	.	6 67
G. W. Videon	2			.	.	4 00
E. A. Carter	1	3		.	.	2 67
C. Homan	1	5	.	.	.	3 10
A. Randolph	2	7		.	.	5 55
W. E. Jennison	6	4½		.	.	13 00
M. J. Conway	2	2		.	.	4 45
H. M. Mathews	3	5		.	.	7 10
Chas. Newton	3	5		.	.	7 10
N. Tatro	3	1		.	.	6 22
Bert Tatro	1			.	.	2 00
Isaac Damon	3	8	horse	3	5	13 94
C. W. Fairbanks	2	4	"	4		11 88
C. H May	8	2	"	6	4	27 82
Charles Fiske	1	2½	"		4	3 34
A. L. Felch	1	7½	"	3		8 81
H. F. Brummett	3			.	.	6 00
Harry Bond	1			.	.	2 00
C. A. Roak	1	6		.	.	3 32
E F. Lawrence		8·		.	.	1 78
Wm. Coriner	2	5		.	.	5 10
L. Cormier		6		.	.	1 33
J. R Hawkins	⌐	6		.	.	3 33
L. A. Loker		4½		.	.	1 00
Wm. Bemis	1	5		.	.	3 10
J. Hawkins	1	4		.	.	2 89
Lewis Grant	3			.	.	6 00

	Days.	Hours.		Days.	Hours		
John E. Dolan	1			.	.	$2	00
P. J McLaughlin	7	8½		.	.	15	92
M. W. Hynes	6		horse	10	1	29	69
T. L Hynes	11	3½	"	8	4	37	54
A E. Adams	1		"	2		5	50
P. J Jennings	3	4½		.		7	00
John Alward	1				.	2	00
J. J. Rowan	6	7½	"		6	14	83
Thos. Maynard, Sr.	5				.	1	11
Philip Bradley	4	1½				8	33
Frank Buckley	4	1½				8	33
Thos. J. Dowey	4	1½				8	33
Thos. F. Maynard	3	1½				6	33
P. S. Zimmerman	2					4	00
John W Coakley	3					6	00
Ralph Morse	2	5				5	11
John Linnehan, Sr.		3½		.	.		78
James Linnehan	3			.	.	6	00
Herbert F. Haynes	3	8		.		7	78
J. F. Malloy	3	5	"	6		17	61
G. A. Frost	4			.	.	8	00
John McCann	4	1½				8	33
Anthony Imminck	2			.	.	4	00
Frank Imminck	2	2		.	.	4	44
Harry D. Lee	2	4		.	.	4	89
J. H. Lee ..		5				1	11
Frank C Moore	3			.	.	6	00
Geo. E. Sherman			"	14	5	25	44
James Fox	6			.	.	12	00
Martin Flynn	3					6	00
A. B. Sherman	2	7				5	56
C.. W. Ellms		8				1	78
G. N. Sherman	4	4				8	86
James McDonald	7			.	.	14	00
John J. Coughlin	3			.	.	6	00
Timothy Coughlin	4	5	".."	4	8	17	66
Leslie Sherman	3	4½		.	.	7	00

	Days.	Hours.		Days.	Hours		
George Campbell	2			.	.	$4	00
F. Bancroft .	1			.	.	2	00
Geo. W. Philbrick	4	6		.	.	9	32
J. J. Bryden .	4					8	00
Thomas Lane .	1					2	00
John E. Dolan .	3	6				7	37
Geo. G Jennison	3	4½				7	00
Michael Guilfoile	3	6½				7	43
Wm. T. Guilfoile	3					6	00
S. S. Davidson .	5			.	.	10	00
M. C. Baldwin .	36	5	horse	16	8	102	62
G. B. Folsom .	3		"	4	8	14	56
Frank Quinn .	2	7	,	.	.	5	55
Charles Quinn .		5½				1	10
A. S. Bowles as per bill	.	.	.	.	.	3	40
Alexander Sauer	.	.	.	.	.	3	40
Charles Jacobs	.	.	.	.	.	4	20
John M. Curtin	.	.	.	.	.	11	90
W. Spear	.	.	.	.	.	12	35
A. Spear	.	.	.	.	.	3	74
M. Temple	.	.	.	.	.	7	00
Daniel Fiske, 10 loads sand	.	.	.	.	.	1	00

$746 14

Report of Supt. of North and Centre Cemeteries.

Appropriation for 1898 . . . . $50 00
Unexpended, 1897 . . . . . . 27 59
                                                    $77 59

May 28. Order on Treasurer . . . $38 38
Aug. 27.   "   "   "   . . . 38 80
    Unexpended 41
                                                    $77 59

A. S. MORSE,
Superintendent.

Report of Engineers of Fire Department.

We beg to report the following fires for the year ending March 1, 1899 :—

1898.

Feb. 28. Alarm from box 34, at 9.15 a. m., for fire in Jos. Tyrrell's, Cochituate, caused by air-tight stove. Department responded promptly, but dwelling house was totally destroyed, it being beyond reach of hose. Small building in rear and most of the furniture was saved.

Mar. 13. Fire was discovered about 6 a.m. in barn of the Robie estate, Wayland, caused by incendiary ; extinguished with a loss of about $15.00

Evidences were also discovered of an attempt to fire the Congregational Church, at about the same time. Reported to, and investigated by, State Fire Marshall.

Mar. 19. Fire was discovered in barn on Elbredge Damon place (vacant) caused by incendiary, and extinguished by neighbors. Damage slight ; no alarm.

May 6. Alarm from box 36, at 10.30 a. m. for fire in Leonard Loker's house, Cochituate, caused by ignition of fat used in frying doughnuts. Department responded promptly, but this was also beyond reach of our hose. Excellent service was rendered. however, by the use of buckets and one chemical extinguisher, preventing a total loss.

-May 21. Alarm from box 34, at 10.15 a.m , for fire in Underwood's woods, near Dudley Pond, which was extinguished by the department.

May 27. Fire in premises of Jas. Devine, tin shop, Main St , Cochituate, was causud by dropping of large hanging lamp. Extinguished with slight damage. No alarm.

1899.

Jan. 3. Small fire discovered in house of Henry Neal, Pleasant St., Cochituate, caused by bursting of hall lamp. Small damage to building and contents. No alarm.

Jan. 24. Fire discovered in barn of D.C.Smith, on Rice road, Cochituate, at about 8 30 a. m., cause unknown. Total loss on barn ; partial on contents. No alarm. Reported to, and investigated by State Fire Marshal.

The Fire Department is in excellent condition, the membership of both companies being complete. The Hook & Ladder and Hose Carriages have been painted and put in first-class shape. We have added two chemical Extinguishers, which are carried on the Hook & Ladder truck. Also 600 feet of new hose ; 1 new Hart combination nozzle ; 35 new coats ; 1 new roof ladder ; 4 new helmets ; 4 new lanterns, and placed new curtains with proper lettering on windows. One new push button alarm box (No. 9) has been placed in front of Anthony Smeltz's house, Plain St.

The increase of fireman's pay, from $5.00 to $10.00, voted at the last March meeting, has been fully appreciated ; and an increased interest is taken by all in the department.

The $500 also appropriated at that meeting, for use of this department, has, we believe, been used to the very best of our ability, in securing the most necessary articles. Bids were solicited for hose, coats, painting of carriages, etc., from all and every reliable firm possible, and resulted in some very close figuring, so that we were enabled to secure bottom prices for the best goods.

We give below itemized account of expenditures :—

Boston Woven Hose & Rubber Co.

600 ft. knit hose and connections at 43 c. .	$258 00
35 army coats at $3.50	122 50
4 fire helmets at $3.50	14 00
	$394 50

Knight & Thomas.

2 chemical extinguishers at $18.00.	$36 00

Cleland & Underwood.

Curtains and lettering thereon	$9 00

J. D. Macewen.

Painting 2 hose carriages and H. & L. truck	$70 00	
Repairing and altering	17 00	
		$87 00

Incidentals.

S. K. Eaton, repairing buckets, and new straps	$6 60	
F. L. Penney, stencils, etc. . - . .	2 09	
Knight & Thomas, soda, acid, bottles, etc. .	2 43	
H. E. Auringer. ladder	2 00	
E. W. Marston, 1 day	3 00	
" " carfare	90	
" " 2 chemical boxes . .	2 00	
" " express on chemicals . .	50	
" " hose . . .	1 10	
" " coats . . .	65	
" " hats . . .	15	
		$21 42
		$547 92

Cr.

Sold condemned leather hose . . .	$60 00	
Rebated express charge on same .	2 55	
		$62 55
		$485 37
Appropriation	$500 00	
Unexpended		14 63
	$500 00	$500 00

We beg to recommend the following :—

That $100 be appropriated to put in foundations, and paint and repair engine house.

That the entire department, and all pertaining thereto, be placed under the jurisdiction of the board of engineers, as is the custom in other towns and cities, as we believe the best interests of both the department and town can be better served by placing the entire responsibility of the fire department with the board of engineers.

Respectfully submitted,

E. W. MARSTON, *Chief.*
A. J. RICKER, *1st Asst.*
F. E. YEAGER, *Clerk.*

Report of Library Building Committee.

To the Citizens of the Town of Wayland :—

The Library Building Committee respectfully submits the following report :—

On October 28, 1898, in pursuance of a vote of the town passed October 8, 1898, the gentlemen mentioned therein met and organized as "The Library Building Committee." Willard A. Bullard was chosen chairman, and Charles F. Richardson, clerk.

To familiarize your committee with the needs of a modern library, both as to construction, and as to administration, some of the best small libraries in this section of the state have been visited and carefully examined   Your committee found, however that as its investigations proceeded, questions arose that could not be properly solved without professional assistance of an architect; therefore it secured the services of Prof. F. W. Chandler, of the Massachusetts Institute of Technology, as a disinterested adviser, and who is of the highest standing in his profession.

From the first, your committee has regretted that the will of Mr. Roby restricts them in their choice of a library site.   The building, which, in itself, is hoped to be an architectural feature of the town, must of necessity be built upon a side hill and low, marshy land. A change in location seemed so desirable, that opinions of different lawyers and judges were taken, as to whether the terms of the will would permit such a change, but these opinions caused so much doubt in the minds of the committee that the idea of relocation was abandoned.

Your committee, with the assistance of Prof. Chandler, has invited competent architects to enter a competition for plans for the library building, and hopes to render a decision speedily. The work on the building will be begun as soon as the season will permit.

Respectfully submitted,

WILLARD A. BULLARD,
EDWIN W. MARSTON,
ALFRED W. CUTTING,
CHESTER B. WILLIAMS,
CHARLES F. RICHARDSON,

Library Building Committee.

Finance Committee.

To the Inhabitants of the Town of Wayland;

The Finance Committee of the town respectfully submits the following report, and recommends as follows : —

For schools, fuel and care of buildings	$7,600 00
School supplies	700 00
Transportation of scholars	2,000 00
Repair of school buildings	100 00
Superintendent of schools	750 00
Fitting High School	200 00
Overdrafts	3,930 22
Highways and bridges	3,000 00
Incidentals	1,500 00
Firemen's pay	448 00
Support of poor	2,500 00
Collection of taxes	350 00
Abatement of taxes	300 00
Hydrants	258 00
Lakeview cemetery	50 00
North and Center cemeteries	50 00
Library	500 00
Interest on town debt	3,000 00
Electric lights	357 00
Salaries	1,300 00
Schoolhouse loan	1,100 00
Decoration day	200 00
Repair Engine house	100 00
	$30,293 22

We recommend that the sum of six hundred and forty dollars be transferred from water rates to pay interest on water bonds.

That the selectmen be authorized to draw from contingent fund such sums of money as may be necessary, not exceeding five hundred dollars for assisting needy soldiers and their families.

That the overseers of the poor be authorized to build a wagon and tool shed at the poor farm from the money appropriated for support of poor, if in their judgment there is sufficient money for that purpose.

That the sum of three thousand dollars appropriated for interest be taken from the contingent fund.

That the sum of five hundred dollars be appropriated to repair and widen the road at the Willows if an electric railway is built from Cochituate village to Wayland, and that the same be drawn from the contingent fund.

That the money for removing snow be drawn from the contingent fund.

That for the year 1899 the collector's pay be four hundred dollars.

That the town should have the same reduction for hydrants that has been granted to water takers.

We feel that these appropriations are larger than the town should make with its present valuation, yet the necessities of the various departments seem to require them.

> P. A. LEARY,
> E. E. BUTLER,
> C. H. MAY,
> DAVID P. W. LOKER,
> HENRY F. LEE,
> RICHARD T. LOMBARD,
> *Finance Committee.*

March 11, 1899.

Treasurer's Report.

SCHOOLS.

1898.

Mar.	28.	Appropriation	$7,000 00
		" for overdraft, 1897 . .	424 91
	21.	State treasurer	500 00
1899.			
Jan.	1.	Donation fund	12 00
	16.	State treasurer	294 43
	28.	Town of Natick	18 50
		" " "	7 50
Feb.	7.	½ dog license	74 39

1898.

Mar.	1.	Overdrawn	$424 91	
		Expenditures . . .	7,628 08	
		Balance . . .	278 74	
			$8,331 73	$8,331 73

SCHOOL SUPPLIES.

1898.

Mar.	1.	Unexpended balance	$2 67
	28.	Appropriation	600 00
		Expenditures $629 22	
		Overdrawn	26 55
		$629 22	$629 22

SUPERINTENDENT OF SCHOOLS.

1898.

Mar. 28.	Appropriation		$600 00
	" for overdraft . . .		40 00
Mar. 1.	Overdraft	$40 00	
	Expenditures	653 00	
	Overdrawn		53 00
		$693 00	$693 00

TRANSPORTATION OF SCHOLARS.

1898.

Mar. 1.	Unexpended balance		$164 75
28.	Appropriation		1,500 00
	Expenditures	$1,569 77	
	Balance	94 98	
		$1,664 75	$1,664 75

REPAIRS ON SCHOOL BUILDINGS.

1898.

Mar. 1.	Unexpended balance		$33 30
28.	Appropriation		150 00
	Expenditures	$169 21	
	Balance	14 09	
		$183 30	$183 30

FITTING UP HIGH SCHOOL.

1898.

Mar. 1.	Unexpended balance		$16 40
28.	Appropriation		200 00
	Expenditures	$166 68	
	Balance	49 72	
		$216 40	$216 40

OVERDRAFTS, 1897.

1898.

Mar. 1.	Balance			$58 39
28.	Appropriation			2,598 20
	Transferred to schools . .		$424 91	
	" " incidentals . .		58 79	
	" " highways . ;		552 02	
	" salaries . .		122 56	
	.. " interest account .		530 81	
	" supt. schools .		40 00	
	" " library tablet .		4 00	
	" " abatement acct. .		855 43	
	Balance		68 07	
			$2,656 59	$2,656 59

HIGHWAYS AND BRIDGES.

1898.

Mar. 28.	Appropriation			$2,000 00
	" for overdraft . . .			552 02
1.	Overdrawn		$552 02	
	C. H. May, commissioner . .		2,093 46	
	Overdrawn			93 46
			$2,645 48	$2,645 48

FIRE DEPARTMENT.

1898.

Mar. 1.	Balance			$224 00
28.	Appropriation			448 00
Apr. 30.	E. W. Marston, Chief . .		$224 00	
	Balance		448 00	
			$672 00	$672 00

COLLECTION TAXES.

1898.

Mar. 28.	Appropriation		$350 00
.	Willard B. Ward . . .	$350 00	

HYDRANTS.

1898.

Mar. 28. Appropriation $384 00
          Transferred to Water acct. . . $384 00

LIBRARY ACCOUNT.

1898.

Mar. 28. Appropriation $300 00

1899.

Feb. 7. ½ Dog license 74 38

1898.

May 28. H. D. Parmenter . . . $300 00

1899.

Feb. 25. " " " 74 38

                                    $374 38 $374 38

CEMETERY ACCOUNT.

1898.

Mar. 1. Balance $209 00
Aug. 27. A. S. Morse 9 00

1899.

Feb. 21. E. C. Davis 55 00
          A. S. Morse 4 00

1898.

Oct. 29. E. C. Davis $71 43
          Balance 205 57

                                    $277 00 $277 00

SUPPORT OF POOR.

1898.

Mar. 1. Balance $186 34
Mar. 28. Appropriation 2,500 00
Mar. 1. Received from town of Natick . . . 95 06
          "   overseers 92 88
          "   " 91 26
          "   town of Lexington . . 52 00
May 28. "   overseers 81 75
June 5. " 80 00
July 30. " 75 00

Aug. 27.	Received from town of Southboro	.	.	$80 75
Sept. 24.	" overseers	.	. . .	137 00
	" town of Framingham	.	.	23 50
	" town of Natick	.	. .	10 00
Oct. 8.	" "	.	. .	131 68
Oct. 25.	" overseers	.	. . .	107 16
Nov. 26.	"	.	. . .	97 44
Dec. 31.	"	.	. . .	78 12
1899.				
Jan. 16.	"	.	. . .	26 40
	" state treasurer	.	. . .	5 90
Jan. 28.	" overseers	.	. . .	80 66
	"	.	. . .	19 00
	"	.	. . .	15 00
	" town of Southboro	.	.	79 70
Feb. 25.	" overseers	.	. . .	96 32
	" "	.	. .	12 50
	Expenditures . . .	$3,835 20		
	Balance	420 22		

$4,255 42 $4,255 42

SALARIES.

1898.

Mar. 28.	Appropriation . .	.	. .	$1,300 00
	" for overdraft	.	. .	122 56
1.	Overdrawn . . .	$122 56		
	Geo. B. Howe . . .	25 00		
	D. P. W. Loker . . .	20 00		
	C. H. Boodey . . .	20 00		
	W. B. Ward . . .	40 00		
	R. T. Lombard . . .	89 00		
	Isaac Damon . . .	75 00		
	A. F. Parmenter . . .	50 00		
	P. A. Leary . . .	50 00		
	H. F. Lee	200 00		
	Thomas Bryant V. S. .	250 00		
	A. H. Bryant . . .	50 00		
	A. W. Lombard . . .	5 00		

Mar.	1.	D. W. Mitchell	.	.	.	.	$42 00
		L. Flanders	.	.	.	.	25 00
		M. W. Hynes	.	.	.	.	5 00
		H. P. Sherman	.	.	.	.	5 00
		H. G. Dudley	.	.	.	.	20 00
		Wm. M. Fullick		.	.	.	20 00
		C. F. Whittier	.	.	.	.	˙20 00
		J. H. Carroll	.	.	.	.	20 00
		T. L. Sawin	.	.	.	.	20 00
		A. A. Lupien	.	.	.	.	5 00
		E. W. Marston	.	.	.	.	10 00
		F. E Yeager	.	.	.	.	5 00
		A. J. Ricker	.	.	.	.	10 00
		L A. Dudley	.	.	.	.	75 00
		Edward Carter	.	.	.	.	6 00
		" "	.	.	.	.	10 50
		H. G. Dudley	.	.	.	.	5 00
		H. G. Hammond		.	.	.	10 50
		C. H May	.	.	.	.	36 75
		Edward Carter	.	.	.	.	84 00
		W. H. Campbell		.	.	.	5 00
		Thomas Bryant	.	.	.	.	50 00
		N. R. Gerald	.	.	.	.	5 00
		A A. Lupien	.	.	.	.	5 00
		P. D. Gorman	.	.	.	.	3 00
		E. E. Butler	.	.	.	.	5 00
		H. W. Parmenter		.	.	.	5 00
		J. J. Hannon	.	.	.	.	5 00
		C. S. Williams	.	.	.	.	5 00
		N. S. Walton	.	.	.	.	5 00
		W. H. Campbell		.	.	.	5 00
		R. T. Lombard		.	.	.	87 50
		H. F. Haynes	.	.	.	.	5 00
		M. W. Hynes	.	.	.	.	5 00
		E. F. Lee	.	.	.	.	5 00
		Overdrawn	.	.	.	.	209 25

$1,631 81 $1,631 81

INTEREST ACCOUNT.

1898.

Mar.	28.	Appropriation from contingent fund . .		$3,500 00
		" for overdraft . . .		530 81
		Transferred from water account		1,450 00
Mar.	1.	Overdrawn	$530 81	
	26.	Boston Safe Deposit & Trust Co.	1,192 50	
Apr.	1.	Natick National Bank . .	588 75	
	30.	Puritan Trust Co. . . .	176 00	
May	11.	Natick Bank	36 56	
July	1.	Boston Safe Deposit & Trust Co.	625 00	
Aug.	27.	D. B. Heard	20 00	
Oct.	1.	Boston Safe Deposit & Trust Co.	1,192 50	
		Natick National Bank . .	756 48	
		" " " . .	1 99	
	29.	Puritan Trust Co. . . .	176 00	
		Jose Parker & Co. . . .	716 15	
1899.				
Jan.	1.	Trustees Loker Fund . . .	100 00 •	
		" Allen " . . .	60 00	
		" Donation " . . .	78 00	
		" J. S. Draper fund . .	60 00	
		" Childs fund . . .	6 00	
		Natick National Bank . .	120 00	
	18.	Boston Safe Deposit & Trust Co.	220 00	
		Overdrawn		1,175 93

$6,656 74 $6,656 74

ABATEMENT ACCOUNT.

1898.

Mar.	28.	Appropriation		$1,800 00
		" for overdraft . . .		855 43
Mar.	1.	Overdrawn	$855 43	
		Abatement tax 1894 . . .	32 03	
		" " 1895 . . .	183 83	
		" " 1896 . . .	63 24	
		" 1897 . . .	1,618 00	
		" 1898 . . .	334 84	
Overdrawn .		. . . . . .		431 94

3,087 37   3 087 37

LAKEVIEW CEMETERY.

1898.

Mar.	1.	Balance		$3 12
	28.	Appropriation		50 00
May	28.	E. C. Davis	$41 64	
July	30.	" " "	8 36	
		Balance	3 12	
			$53 12	$53 12

NORTH AND CENTRE CEMETERIES.

1898.

Mar.	1.	Balance		$27 59
	28.	Appropriation		50 00
		A. S. Morse	$38 38	
		" " "	38 80	
		Balance	41 00	
			$77 59	$77 59

ELECTRIC LIGHTS.

1898.

Mar.	1.	Balance		$23 22
	28.	Appropriation		357 00
		Natick Gas & Electric Co.	$360 28	
		Balance	19 94	
			$380 22	$380 22

ILLEGAL SALE OF INTOXICATING LIQUORS.

1898.

Mar.	1.	Balance		$235 80
Apr.	30.	J. B. Woodworth	$14 38	
May	28.	" "	15 23	
		W. C. Neal	6 50	
		J. W. Jennison	7 50	

June	25.	J. B Woodworth	.	.	.	$23 50
		" "	.	.	.	. 2 90
Aug.	27.	" "	.	.	.	18 75
Sept.	24.	"	.	.	.	15 00
Oct.	29.	" "	.	.	.	23 50
		C. W. Elms	.	.	.	19 97
Nov.	26.	C. C. Ward	.	.	.	6 25
Dec.	17.	J. B. Woodworth	.	.	.	3 85
		" "	.	.	.	14 75
		W. C. Neal	.	.	.	18 00
Feb.	25.	L. H. McMannus	.	.	.	15 38
		Balance	.	.	.	30 34

$235 80 $235 80

LIBRARY TABLET.

1898.

Mar. 28. Appropriation $4 00

1. Overdrawn $4 00

SCHOOLHOUSE LOAN.

1898.

Mar. 28. Appropriation $1,100 00

Puritan Trust Co. . . . $1,100 00

DECORATION DAY.

1898.

Mar. 28. Appropriation $100 00

E. C. Davis $100 00

NEW HOSE AND COATS FOR FIRE DEPARTMENT.

1898.

Mar. 28. Appropriation $500 00

E. W. Marston, Chief . . $500 00

TEMPORARY LOANS

1898.				
Mar.	1.	Notes outstanding		$24,000 00
Apr.	1.	" Natick National Bank . . .		3,000 00
	11.	" " " " . . .		3,000 00
May	10.	" " " " . . .		3,000 00
	11.	" " . . .		4,000 00
June	1.	" " " " . . .		2,000 00
	27.	" " " " . . .		2,000 00
Nov.	26.	" " " . . .		3,000 00
Apr.	27.	Paid " " "	$2,000 00	
May	11.		6,500 00	
Oct.	1.		5,000 00	
	29.		2,000 00	
1899.				
Feb.	28.	"	1,500 00	
		Notes unpaid . . .	. 27,000 00	
			$44,000 00	$44,000 00

STATE TAX.

State tax		$900 00
Marsh land tax		330 52
State treasurer	$900 00	
" "	330 52	
	$1,230 52	$1,230 52

COUNTY TAX.

County tax		$1,492 93
J. O. Hayden, treasurer .	. $1,492 93	

STATE HIGHWAY LOAN.

1898.				
Mar.	26.	State treasurer		$1,152 97
July	1.	" "		2,598 68
Oct.	22.	" "		799 60
May	26.	Mass. Broken Stone Co. .	. $1,152 97	
July	1.	" " "	. 2,598 68	
Oct.	25.	" " "	. 799 60	
			$4,551 25	$4,551 25

SIDEWALKS.

1898.
Mar. 1. Balance $43 34

Transferred to contingent acct. . $43 34

SAND HILL ROAD.

1898.
Mar. 1. Balance $50 06

Transferred to contingent acct. . $50 06

CULVERT HARRISON AVE.

1898.
Mar. 1. Balance $15 80

Transferred to contingent acct. . $15 80

WATER COMMISSIONER'S ACCOUNT.

1898.
Mar. 1. Balance $619 20
Aug. 1. Estabrook & Co. 784 85
          Transferred from T. & W. bonds . . 196 42
1899.
Feb. 28. Wm. Fullick 1,454 48
            " 463 03
          Transferred from hydrants . . . 384 00
1898.
Apr. 2. H. G. Dudley $150 00
          Wm. M. Fullick . . . 32 50
Aug. 27. H. G. Dudley 46 00
          Transferred to interest acct. . 1,450 00
1899.
Feb. 28. Wm. Fullick 463 03
            " 1,454 48
          Balance due commissioners . 305 97

                                    $3,901 98 $3,901 98

INCIDENTAL ACCOUNT.

1898.			
Mar. 28.	Appropriation	$1,500 00
	" for overdraft . . .	58 79
1.	Overdrawn	$58 79
Apr. 2.	C. H. Boodey, M.D. . . .	10 00
	R. T. Lombard	38 94
	T. E. Glennon	2 00
	M. W. Hynes	5 00
	W. F. Garfield	2 50
	M. J. Maloney	8 00
	J. W. Jennison	3 00
	" "	4 00
	C. H. Thing	2 00
	H. P. Sherman	5 00
	L. H. McMannus . . .	5 90
	H. H. Rutter	2 00
30.	F. E. Yeager	6 00
	T. Bryant	5 00
	W. W. Wight	22 50
	Thos. Groom & Co. . . .	44 72
	C. S. Williams	1 00
	G. M. Stevens	12 00
	C. A. Roak	1 00
	C. S. Williams	6 50
	W. E Hunting	17 07
	Fairbanks & Co. . . .	2 91
	Lakeview Press	134 40
	A. J. Ricker	20 00
	J. E. Linnehan	30 00
	J. W. Jennison	4 80
	H. P. Sherman	5 00
May 28.	J. E. Linnehan	3 00
	W. T. Howard	1 50
	H. P. Sherman	6 00
	C. A. Roak	2 00
	M. French	13 96
	J. M. Forbush	225 00

May 28.	C. W. Dean		$75 00·
	Wright & Potter Printing Co. .		13 00·
June 25.	Gilbert Paper Mfg. Co. . .		15 68·
	T. W. Frost		6 00·
	C. H. Thing		4 00·
	H. P. Sherman		4 50
	J. Breck & Sons		8 00
	C. H. Boodey, H. & L. Co. .		4 50·
	W. F. Garfield		6 00·
July 30.	E. E. Butler		22 50
	H. G. Dudley		13 75
	C. C. Ward		5 75·
	J. W. Jennison		9 00
	J. B. Woodworth . . .		11 75·
	E. H. Atwood		2 24
	C. S. Williams		1 50·
	" " & Co. . . .		2 10·
	J. E. Linnehan		25 00·
	" "		6 00
	Geo. C. Fairbanks . . .		4 00··
	J. H. Lee		7 96·
	H. F. Lee		5 10
	H. P. Sherman		2 75·
	Wright & Thomas . . .		27 00·
	J. B. Woodworth . . .		3 35·
Aug. 27.	F. E. Yeager		250 00
	E. E. Butler		200 00·
	A. Mudge & Son . . .		25 00
	F. Haynes		83 56·
	W. D. Parlin		16 79·
	G. M. Stevens		16 12
	H. P. Sherman		7 90·
	Wright & Potter . . .		1 07
	James Linnehan . . .		11 00
	C. H. May		3 00·
	Edward Carter		2 25·
	The Fairbanks Co. . . .		100 00
	Gilbert & Barker Mfg. Co. .		3 82·

Aug. 27.	I. Publishing Co.	. . .	$4 20
	Boston News Co.	. . .	7 50
	W. C. Neal	. . . .	1 00
	W. B. Ward	. . . .	7 80
	Hannah Mullen .	. . .	18 75
	G. S. Wyman & Co. .	. . .	8 25
Sept. 24.	H. H. Rutter	. . . .	2 50
	Martin Hall . .	. . .	2 50
	W. C. Neal	. . . .	3 00
	C. H. Thing	. . . .	2 00
	H. P. Sherman .	. . .	8 00
	W. C. Hunting .	. . .	6 35
	L. K. Lovell	. . . .	1 74
Oct. 29.	J. P. Lovell Arms Co.	. .	5 25
	T. W. Frost	. . . .	6 28
	J. W. Carey	. . . .	3 50
	Thomas Groom & Co.	. .	37 80
	J. W. Jennison .	. . .	10 00
	T. S. Sherman .	. . .	7 00
	Wm. Stearns	. . . .	35 50
	L. H. McMannus	. . .	19 00
	W. F. Garfield .	. . .	9 00
	J. J. McCann	. . . .	15 00
	Martin Hall	. . . .	2 50
	H. F. Lee .	. . . .	27 15
	A. Mudge & Son	. . .	50 00
	Waltham Publishing Co.	. .	3 50
	J. H. Lee .	. . . .	4 72
	S. D. Reeves	. . . .	3 00
Nov. 26.	W. W. Wight	. . . .	10 50
	W. F. Garfield .	. . .	1 50
	P. A. Leary	. . . .	6 40
	E. H. Atwood .	. . .	1 00
	F. M. Keefe	. . . .	2 50
	T. S. Sherman .	. . .	5 00
	J. W. Parmenter	. . .	22 00
	J. E. Linnehan .	. . .	28 72
	Fiske & Co.	. . . .	1 68

Nov.	26.	Howe & Co.	$1 40
		Gilbert & Barker Mfg. Co.	18 54
		F. E. Yeager	8 85
		R. T. Lombard	6 75
Dec.	31.	J. E. Linnehan	6 00
		M. J. Maloney	13 00
		C. C. Ward	5 00
		Robinson & Jones	14 25
		Wilson Porter	1 50
		E. P. Butler	8 37
		W. F. Garfield	3 00
		T. S. Sherman	4 75
		A. S. Morse	8 00
		D. P. W. Loker	3 75
1899.			
Jan.	28.	H. H. Rutter	3 40
		J. E. Linnehan	25 00
		W. F. Garfield	5 00
		W. D. Parlin	1 05
		Geo. M. Stevens	313 03
		Thomas Groom & Co.	10 00
		F. E. Yeager	230 00
		E. E. Butler	230 00
		A. S. Morse	2 00
		J. H. Lee	3 12
		D. P. W. Loker	25 00
		Martin Hall	5 75
		T. S. Sherman	8 25
		C. B. Felch	5 00
		Frank Haynes	5 51
		L. H. McMannus	4 00
		C. L. Logan	4 00

Overdrawn		1,535 00
	$3,093 79	$3,093 79

CONTINGENT ACCOUNT.

1898.

Mar.	1.	Balance	$1,542 72
	26.	Dist. Court Fines	2 30
		W. B. Ward	89 00
		Trans. from Fence C. School House . .	100 00
May	9.	J. E. Linnehan	10 00
	28.	S. Russell	1 00
June	13.	State Treas.	125 00
		" "	5 00
July	1.	Court fines	5 00
	30.	J. E. Linnehan	13 50
		Transferred from sidewalks . . .	43 34
		" " Sand Hill road . .	50 06
		" " culvert, Harrison avenue	15 80
Aug.	27.	L. K. Lovell	20 20
Sept.	24.	Gilbert & Barker	1 35
		W. B. Ward. Int. on tax 1894 . . .	160 04
Oct.	1.	Court fines	1 18
Nov.	30.	J. E. Linnehan	20 00
Dec.	10.	W. B. Ward. Int. on tax 1895 . . .	100 00
		State treasurer	1,752 55
		" "	729 64
		" "	72 00
		. . . . . .	1,125 00

1899.

Jan.	5.	N. R. Gerald	27 68
		Gilbert & Barker	1 35
Feb.	21.	E. H. Atwood	6 83
	28.	Overlayings on taxes	152 41
		Additional assessments	28 25
		" "	20 00
		" "	14 00
		Geo. B. Howe	19 77
		W. B. Ward, int. on tax	100 00
		C. B. Williams, sidewalks	149 83

Mar.	28.	Appropriation for interest .	$3,500 00	
Apr.	2.	Sidney Loker	9 06	

Apr.	2.	C. H. Boodey	$30	00
		W. F. Garfield, needy soldiers .	4	00
		J. B. Brigham, " " .	6	00
		M. W. Hynes, snow bill . .	61	52
		State aid	1,164	00
		Military aid	144	00
		Daniel Brackett, Susan Pierce claim	350	00
Apr.	30.	J. B. Brigham	6	00
May	28.	" " "	6	00
		J. Stevens	3	00
		W. A. Jessop	2	00
June	25.	A. Speare	11	88
		J. B. Brigham	6	00
		W. F. Garfield, needy soldiers .	12	00
July	30.	State treasurer	17	56
		W. W. Whitcomb . . .	10	00
		J. B. Brigham, needy soldiers .	6	00
		W. F. Garffeld " " .	8	00
Aug.	27.	J. B. Brigham " "	6	00
Sept.	24.	" " "	6	00
Oct.	29.	Wm. G. Webster . . .	10	00
		W. F. Garfield	8	00
		Wm. G. Webster . . .	10	00
Nov.	26.	Wm. F. Garfield . . .	4	00
		Sidney Loker	11	64
		J. B. Brigham	6	00
		" " "	6	00
Dec.	31.	C. H. May. Highways . .	480	35
		W. G. Webster	10	00
		W. F. Garfield	4	00
		C. H. Boodey	29	00
		J. B. Brigham	6	00
1899.				
Jan.	28.	W. F. Garfield	4	00
		J. B. Brigham . . .	6	00
		Thos Lane	10	00
		J. B. Howe. Poor . . .	26	40
		" " " " . . .	15	00

Feb. 25.	J. B Brigham	$6 00	
	W. F. Garfield	4 00	
	Sidney Loker	7 62	
	G. B. Howe. Poor . . .	12 50	
	Robinson & Jones . . .	7 00	
	Overseers of Poor, Boston . .	31	
	Wm. G. Webster . . .	10 00	
	C. H. May. Highways . .	746 25	
	Balance		$304 29
		$6,809 09	$6,809 09

TAXES 1894.

1898			
Mar. 1.	Balance due from collector .	$364 96	
July 14.	W. B. Ward		$75 00
Sept. 5.	" " "		239 96
1899.			
Feb. 28.	" " "		17 97
	Abatement		32 03
		$364 96	$364 96

TAXES 1895.

1898.			
Mar 1.	Balance due from collector .	$1,461 59	
26.	W. B. Ward		$53 99
June 16.	" " "		148 27
July 14.	" " "		100 00
Sept. 1.	" " "		145 06
30.	" " "		85 43
Nov 25.	" " "		65 00
30.	" " "		87 50
	Abatement		43 05
Dec. 10.	W. B. Ward		200 00
1899.			
Jan. 16.	W. B. Ward		100 00
Feb. 24.	Abatement		140 78
28.	W. B. Ward		119 80
	Balance due from collector .		172 71
		$1,461 59	$1,461 59

TAXES, 1896.

1898.				
Mar.	1.	Balance due . . .	.$6,404 50	
May	3.	W. B. Ward		$161 23
	17.	" "		100 06
June	16.	" "		100 00
July	11.	" "		123 76
	30.	" "		100 00
	18.	" "		118 93
Aug.	17.	" "		100 00
	27.	" "		140 08
Sept.	13.	" "		121 06
	22.	" "		288 73
	24.	" "		143 95
	30.	" "		463 85
Oct.	1.	" "		156 58
	11.	" "		188 62
	11.	Abatement		54 75
	14	W. B. Ward		233 26
	22.	" "		228 35
Nov.	2.	" "		300 00
	21.	" "		117 64
	25.	" "		100 00
	30.	" "		105 00
	30.	Abatement		8 49
1899.				
Jan.	1.	W. B. Ward		401 00
Feb.	28.	" "		240 00
		Balance due from collector .		2,309 16
			$6,404 50	$6,404 50

TAXES, 1897.

1898.				
Mar.	1.	Balance due . . .	$12,427 06	
		Additional tax	14 00	
	26.	W. B. Ward		80 00
		" "		140 94
May	3.	" "		1,032 46

May	3.	Abatements		$1,602 00
	7.	W. B. Ward		157 11
	17.	" "		535 65
July	7.	" "		145 56
	16.	" "		207 52
	30.	" "		251 07
Sept.	13.	" "		101 55
	30.	" "		100 00
Oct.	4.	" "		135 00
	6.	" "		200 10
	31.	" "		119 17
Nov.	12.	" "		135 12
		Abatement		8 00
1899.				
Jan.	5.	W. B. Ward		142 41
Feb.	1.	" "		171 12
	25.	Abatement		8 00
		Due from collector . . .		7,168 28

$12,441 06 $12,441 06

TAXES 1898.

1898.				
March		Levied and assessed . .	$30,291 31	
		Additional assessments . .	20 00	
Aug.	11.	W. B. Ward		$197 02
	15.	" " "		408 04
	22.	" " "		253 88
	27.	" " "		100 33
Sept.	1.	" " "		131 20
	5.	" " "		125 00
		. . . .		151 00
	15.	" " "		288 68
	17.	" " "		302 29
	22.	" " "		824 51
	24.	" " "		175 00
	27.	" " "		303 98
	30.	" " "		3,575 81

Oct	1.	W. B. Ward	. . . .		$1,726 55
	3.	" " "	. . . .		844 74
	4.	" " "	. . . .		526 00
	8.	" " "	. . . .		605 22
	11.	" " "	. . . .		1,175 82
		Abatement	. . . .		53 06
	14.	W. B. Ward	. . . .		186 40
	17.	" " "	. . . .		332 19
		Abatement	. . . .		35 38
	22.	W. B. Ward	. . . .		133 52
	25.	" " "	. . . .		290 00
	31.	" " "	. . . .		147 20
Nov.	2.	" " "	. . . .		103 00
	4.	" " "	. . . .		228 53
	12.	" " "	. . . .		265 56
	21.	" " "	. . . .		107 60
	25.	" " "	. . . .		331 11
	30.	" " "	. . . .		1,801 43
Dec.	2.	" " "	. . . .		334 19
	10.	" " "	. . . :		187 13
1899.					
Jan.	1.	W. B. Ward	. . . .	.	184 41
	5.	" " "	. . . .		141 05
	16.	" " "	. . . .		151 81
Feb.	7.	" " "	. . . .		200 93
	25.	Abatement	. ; . .		246 40
	28.	W. B. Ward	. . . .		338 76
					12,886 58

$30,311 31 $30,311 31

.

TOWN AND WATER BONDS.

1898.

Aug.	1.	Estabrook & Co.	. . . .	.	$11,000 00
		Wm. M. Fullick .	. . . .	.	14,196 42

Oct. 22. Jose Parker & Co. $44,500 00
Aug. 1. Boston Safe Deposit & Trust Co. 25,000 00
Oct. 22. Jose Parker & Co. . . . 44,500 00
          Trans. to Water Com. acct. . 196 42

                                $69,696 42 $69,696 42

LIBRARY FUND.
1898.
Oct.   Estate W. G. Roby $28,000 00
            Bal , cash in hands of Treas. $28,000 00

Auditor's Report.

HENRY F. LEE,

In account with the TOWN OF WAYLAND.

RECEIPTS.			EXPENDITURES.		
Mar. 1, 1898.					
Cash balance .	.	$2,309 07	Schools . .	.	$7,628 08
W. B. Ward, taxes	.	26,214 75	School supplies	.	629 22
Overseers of poor	.	1,090 49	" supt. .	.	653 00
Town of Natick	.	236 74	" transportation		1,569 77
" Lexington .		52 00	" repairs	.	169 21
" Southboro.		160 45	" fittings	.	166 68
" Framingham		23 50	Highways	.	2,093 46
State treasurer	.	5 90	Fire department	.	224 00
Water commissioners		1,917 51	Poor account .	.	3,835 20
Dog license .	..	148 77	Incidentals .	.	3,035 00
Cemetery account	.	68 00	Interest .	.	6,125 93
Court fines	.	8 48	Salaries . .	.	1,509 25
Tuition .	.	26 00	Collection of taxes .		350 00
Cattle committee	.	125 00	Library	.	374 38
State treasurer	.	799 43	Cemetery .	.	71 43
" corpo-			Lakeview cemetery .		50 00
ration tax .	.	1,752 55	North and Centre		
State treasurer, bank			cemeteries .	.	77 18
tax .	.	729 64	Electric lights	.	360 28
Military aid .	.	72 00	Illegal sale of liquor		205 46
State aid	.	1,125 00	Decoration day	.	100 00
Highway loan	.	4,551 25	New hose and coats		500 00
S. Russell	.	1 00	Contingent account .		1,633 53
Rent of hall .	.	43 50	Water commission-		
L. K. Lovell .	.	20 20	ers orders .	.	2,146 01

N. R. Gerald .	.	$27 68	State tax . .	$1,230 52
E. H. Atwood	.	6 83	County tax . .	1,492 93
G. B. Howe .	.	19 77	Schoolhouse loan .	1,100 00
W. B. Ward, interest		449 04	State highway .	4,551 25
Gilbert & Barker	.	2 70	" aid . .	1,164 00
Donation fund	.	12 00	Military aid . .	144 00
Est. W. G. Roby	.	28,000 00	Susan Pierce . .	350 00
Temporary loans	.	20,000 00	Town & water bonds	69,500 00
Water sinking fund.		14,196 42	Temporary loans .	17,000 00
Estabrook & Co.	.	11,000 00	State treasurer, cor-	
" "	.	784 85	poration tax .	17 56
Jose Parker & Co	.	44,500 00	Est. W G. Roby .	28,000 00
C. B. Williams	.	149 83	Cash . . .	2,573 02
		$160,630 35		$160,630 35

TRIAL BALANCE.

Feb. 28, 1899.			Temporary loans .	$27,000 00
Due from collector .		$22,536 73	Balance, schools .	278 74
Overdraft, school sup-			Transportation	94 98
plies . . .		26 55	Repairs school-	
Overdraft, superin-			house . .	14 09
tendent of schools		53 00	Fitting school	
Overdraft, highways		93 46	house . .	49 72
Salaries . .		209 25	Overdrafts .	68 07
Interest . .		1,175 93	Fire Dept. .	448 00
Incidentals .		1,535 00	Poor account .	420 22
Abatements .		431 94	Water account .	305 97
Contingent .		304 29	Cemetery acct.	205 57
Cash balance . .		2,573 02	Lakeview ceme-	
			tery . .	3 12
			North & Centre	
			cemeteries .	41
			Electric lights .	19 94
			Illegal sale of	
			liquor . .	30 34
		$28,939 17		$28,939 17

A. H. BRYANT, *Auditor.*

INDEX.

OFFICIAL REPORTS

OF THE

TOWN OF WAYLAND

FOR ITS

One Hundred and Twentieth Municipal · Year

FROM

March 1, 1899, to March 1, 1900.

Lakeview Press:
TRIBUNE BUILDING, SOUTH FRAMINGHAM, MASS.
1900.

OFFICIAL REPORTS

OF THE

OWN OF WAYLAND

FOR ITS

One Hundred and Twentieth Municipal Year

FROM

March 1, 1899, to March 1, 1900.

Lakeview Press:
TRIBUNE BUILDING, SOUTH FRAMINGHAM, MASS.
1900.

List of Town Officers

FOR 1899 AND 1900, AND WHEN THEIR TERMS EXPIRE.

Term Expires.

CLERK.

RICHARD T. LOMBARD 1900

TREASURER.

HENRY F. LEE 1900

AUDITOR.

ALFRED H. BRYANT 1900

COLLECTOR.

CHARLES F. RICHARDSON (By appointment) . 1900

TREASURER OF LIBRARY FUNDS.

HENRY D. PARMENTER 1900

SELECTMEN.

ALBION F. PARMENTER 1900
ELIJAH H. ATWOOD 1900
ELBRIDGE A. CARTER 1900

OVERSEERS OF POOR.

GEORGE B. HOWE 1900
DAVID P. W. LOKER 1900
THEO. S. SHERMAN 1900

4

SCHOOL COMMITTEE.

DELOSS W. MITCHELL	1900
L. ANNA DUDLEY	1901
ERNEST E. BUTLER	1902

ASSESSORS.

RICHARD T. LOMBARD	1900
EDWARD CARTER	1901
NATHANIEL R. GERALD	1902

WATER COMMISSIONERS.

WILLIAM M. FULLICK	1900
CHARLES H. BOODEY	1901
HENRY G. DUDLEY	1902

TRUSTEES PUBLIC LIBRARY.

JOHN CONNOLLY	1900
CHAS. F. RICHARDSON	1900
ARTHUR G. BENNETT	1901
CHESTER B. WILLIAMS	1901
HARRY E. CARSON	1902
FRANCIS SHAW	1902

CONSTABLES.

MARSHALL C. BALDWIN	1900
JESSE W. JENNISON	1900
ERNEST E. LAWRENCE	1900
LAWRENCE H. McMANUS	1900
ANDREW S. MORSE	1900
WILLIAM C. NEAL	1900
COLIN C. WARD	1900

TRUSTEES OF ALLEN FUND.

ISAAC DAMON	1900
WM. H. CAMPBELL	1900
DANIEL D. GRIFFIN	1900

FENCE VIEWERS.

ALBION F. PARMENTER	1900
ISAAC DAMON	1900
EDWARD CARTER	1900

FIELD DRIVERS.

IRA S. DICKEY	1900
CYRUS A. ROAK	1900

SEALER OF WEIGHTS AND MEASURES.

RICHARD T. LOMBARD	1900

MEASURERS OF WOOD AND BARK.

GEORGE B. HOWE	1900
EDWARD CARTER	1900
WILLIAM S. LOVELL	1900

SURVEYOR OF LUMBER.

FRANK HAYNES	1900

SUPERINTENDENTS OF CEMETERIES.

ANDREW S. MORSE	1900
(Vacancy)	

FINANCE COMMITTEE.

ALBION F. PARMENTER	1900
RICHARD T. LOMBARD	1900
DAVID P. W. LOKER	1900
DELOSS W. MITCHELL	1900
CHAS. H. BOODEY	1900
JOHN CONNOLLY	1900
HENRY F. LEE	1900
CHAS. H. MAY	1900
CHAIRMAN OF SINKING FUND COMMISSIONERS	1900

· COMMITTEE OF MEMORIAL DAY.

EDISON C. DAVIS	1900
ALFRED W. LOMBARD	1900
CLIFFORD A. BRYANT	1900
LORENZO R. LOVELL	1900
DAVID P. W. LOKER	1900

ENGINEERS OF FIRE DEPARTMENT.

EDWIN W. MARSTON, *Chief*	1900
FRANK E. YEAGER	1900
ARTHUR J. RICKER	1900

SUPERINTENDENT OF STREETS.

CHARLES H. MAY	1900

REGISTRARS OF VOTERS.

JAMES H. CARROLL, *Chairman*	1901
THEO. L. SAWIN	1900
CHAS. F. WHITTIER	1902
RICHARD T. LOMBARD, *Town Clerk, ex-officio*	1900

SINKING FUND COMMISSIONERS.

EDWIN W. MARSTON	1900
HENRY D. PARMENTER	1901
CHESTER B. WILLIAMS	1902

Annual Town Meeting, March 26, 1900.

WARRANT.

COMMONWEALTH OF MASSACHUSETTS.

MIDDLESEX, SS.

To Lawrence H. McManus, or either of the Constables of the Town of Wayland, in said County,

Greeting:

In the name of the Commonwealth of Massachusetts, you are hereby directed to notify and warn the qualified voters of said Town of Wayland to meet at the Town Hall, Wayland, on Monday, March 26th, 1900, at 6.30 o'clock in the forenoon, then and there to act on the following articles, viz. : —

ARTICLE 1. To choose by ballot a Moderator to preside in said meeting.

ART. 2. To choose a Town Clerk, Treasurer, Collector of Taxes, Auditor, Highway Surveyor, three Selectmen, one Overseer of the Poor, Treasurer of the Library Funds, and seven Constables, all for one year. One Overseer of the Poor for two years. One School Committee, one Assessor, one Water Commissioner, one Sinking Fund Commissioner, one Overseer of the Poor, and two Trustees of the Public Library, all for three years. Also to answer the following question, " Shall licenses for the sale of intoxicating liquors be granted in the Town of Wayland for the year ensuing? "

All names of candidates for the offices aforesaid and the said question must appear upon the official ballot, and be voted for in accordance with Chapter 548 of the Ácts of the General Court for the year 1898. For the purposes specified in this article the polls will be opened immediately after the election of a moderator, and will remain open continuously for at least four hours, when they may be closed.

ART. 3. To choose all other necessary Town Officers, Agents and Committees and hear reports of Town Officers, Trustees, Agents and Committees, and act thereon.

ART. 4. To see how much money the town will grant for paying interest, existing debts, for roads and bridges, for support of poor, for support of schools, school supplies, repairs of school buildings and transportation of scholars, for the fire department, for abatement of taxes and for all other necessary town purposes and order the same to be assessed, or do or act.

ART. 5. To authorize the Selectmen to consult counsel on important town cases.

ART. 6. To see if the town will authorize its Treasurer, with the approval of the Selectmen, to borrow money temporarily in anticipation of taxes for the municipal year 1900 and 1901, and if so how much, or do or act.

ART. 7. To see if the town will accept the list of Jurors as prepared by the Selectmen.

ART. 8. To appropriate the money received from the County Treasurer for dog licenses.

ART. 9. To see if the town will appoint a Committee or Agent to oppose the lease of the Fitchburg Railroad by the Boston & Maine R. R. Co., or do or act.

ART. 10. To see if the town will appropriate money to drain a portion of the Concord Road by a culvert near the entrance to the driveway of Frederick H. Fowler, or do or act.

ART. 11. To see if the town will sell the Town Farm, or any part of the same, and appoint a Committee to execute the deed or deeds of the same, or do or act.

ART. 12. To see if the town will add the name of the Chief Engineer of the Fire Department to the Finance Committee.

ART. 13. To see if the town will elect a Board of Health, and fix their pay, or do or act.

Art. 14. To see if the town will purchase two sidewalk snow plows, or do or act.

Art. 15. To see if the town will extend the Street Electric Lights to Fisk's Corner, or do or act.

Art. 16. To see if the town will appropriate money for sidewalks, or do or act.

Art. 17. To see if the town will appropriate the sum of two hundred dollars to repair Mitchell street, and its extension from Plain street to the Catholic cemetery, or do or act.

Art. 18. To see if the town will publish annually in the Town Report the names of all real and personal property owners with the amount of their valuation, or do or act.

And you are requested to serve the warrant by posting up attested copies thereof at each of the Post Offices and Town House in said Town, seven days at least before the appointed time for holding said meeting.

Hereof fail not and make due return of this warrant with your doings thereon to the Town Clerk at the time and place appointed for holding said meeting.

Given under our hands this sixth day of March, in the year of our Lord one thousand and nine hundred.

ALBION F. PARMENTER,
ELIJAH H. ATWOOD,
ELBRIDGE A. CARTER,
Selectmen of Wayland.

List of Jurors

AS PREPARED BY THE SELECTMEN FOR THE YEAR 1900.

Fred P. Draper.
Jeremiah Lyons.
Arthur T. Felch.
John E. Linnehan.
James I. Bryden.
Frank Lupien.
Samuel S. Davidson.
Warren B. Langmaid.
Edward B. Smith.
Nathan S. Walton.
Josiah W. Parmenter.
Andrew S. Morse.
Harry H. Rutter.

Elbridge A. Carter.
Patrick A. Leary.
William H. Campbell.
Ernest E. Butler.
Andrew S. Norris.
Marcus M. Fiske.
Marshall C. Baldwin.
Wm. S. Lovell.
Allen B. Sherman.
Paul Paradeau.
Chas. W. Ellms.
Edward M. Partridge.
Randall W. Porter.

ALBION F. PARMENTER,
ELIJAH H. ATWOOD,
ELBRIDGE A. CARTER,
Selectmen of Wayland.

Report of the Selectmen.

WAYLAND, March 1, 1900.

The Selectmen hereby submit their annual report as required by the By-laws of the town.

We have appointed the following officers as required by statute :

Undertakers. D. P. W. Loker, Andrew S. Morse.

Engineers of Fire Department. E. W. Marston, A. J. Ricker, Frank E. Yeager.

Inspector of Cattle and Provisions. Thos. Bryant, V. S.

Superintendent of Streets. Chas. H. May.

Public Weighers. Geo. B. Howe, L. K. Lovell, Alfred W. Lombard

Fish and Game Warden. John J. Irwin.

Special Police. Arthur F. Felch, C. C. Ward, M. W. Hynes, J. E. Linnehan, C. W. Ellms, Frank Jameson.

Registrar of Voters for three years. Theo. S. Sherman. Appointed C. F. Whittier to fill the unexpired term of T. S. Sherman, resigned.

We have appointed C. F. Richardson temporary tax collector to fill vacancy caused by the death of Willard B. Ward, who was elected tax collector at the annual town meeting, March 27, 1899.

Election Officers. Precinct 1. Warden, M. W. Hynes ; Clerk, Wm. H. Campbell ; Inspectors, A. W. Lombard, Edw. F. Lee, Wm. Stearns, H. W. Parmenter ; Constable, A. S. Morse. *Precinct 2.* Warden, C. S. Williams ; Clerk, E. E. Butler ; Inspectors, H. G. Dudley, L. A. Loker, P. A. Gormon, N. R. Gerald.

According to a vote of the town, the road at the willows has been widened at an expense of ($385.15) three hundred and eighty-five dollars and fifteen cents.

And a railing put up at an expense of ($26.00) twenty-six dollars.

In regard to Baldwin's bridge we have petitioned the county commissioners to rebuild the bridge and have reason to believe they will take the matter up in a short time.

The town lines were perambulated between Wayland and Weston, Sept. 28, 1899.

We have granted a franchise to the Waltham, Weston & Wayland Street R. R. Co. to build an electric road from Wayland Centre to the Weston line.

In the case of Lupien against the town of Wayland, the jurors disagreed nine in favor of the town and three in favor of Lupien.

We have petitioned the state highway commission to continue the state road from where it is already built to the centre of the town, and we have every reason to believe that it will be built this year.

We recommend that the town make a small appropriation for the maintenance of the fire department.

> ALBION F. PARMENTER,
> ELIJAH H. ATWOOD,
> ELBRIDGE A. CARTER,
> *Selectmen of Wayland.*

Report of Town Clerk and Registrar,

WAYLAND, January 1st, 1900.

I hereby transmit the annual report of the clerk and registrar for the year ending December 31st, 1899.

BIRTHS.

The births registered during the year were thirty-two, being ten less than in 1898.

Males	17
Females	15
Born of native parents	13
" foreign parents	8
" native and foreign parents . . .	11

MARRIAGES.

The number registered during the year was twenty-four, being three less than in 1898.

Native birth of both parties	14
Native and foreign birth	8
Foreign birth of both parties	2
First marriage of both parties	18
Second marriage of both parties	2
First of one and second of the other . . .	4

DEATHS.

The number registered during the year was twenty-seven, being five less than in 1898.

CONDITION.

Married	10
Widowed	8
Single	9
Native birth	18
Foreign birth	9
Males	13
Females	14

Names and ages of persons deceased during the year who were over seventy years of age :

	Years.	Months.	Days.
Rebecca J. Dickey	73	6	
Lafayette Dudley	74	5	25
Hannah Hyde	78		
Margaret E. Dolan	83		
Katharine Demers	78	7	20
Sarah A. Morse	83	8	12
David H. Pierce	84	9	21
Eustache Rasico	77		
Willard B. Ward	70	8	11
Hannah W. Pousland	75	7	
Margaret Egan	80		

NOSOLOGICAL TABLE.

Heart disease	2
Pneumonia	2
Bright's disease	1
Phthisis pulmonis	2
Cancer	1
Consumption	1
Blood clot	1
Old age	3
Inflammation of brain	1

Inflammation of liver 1
Dysentery 1
Hemorrhage 1
Tuberculosis 1
Gangrene 1
Paralysis 1
Meningitis 1
Typhoid fever 1
Cholera infantum 1
Apoplexy 1
Blood poison 1
Inanition 1
Accident 1

DOGS.

109 males at $2.00 . . . . . $218 00
16 females at $5.00 . . . . . 80 00

$298 00
125 licenses at 20 cents 25 00

Amount net $273 00

VOTERS.

Number registered Nov. 7, 1899 . . . 474
Precinct I 147
Precinct II 327

Ballots cast Precinct I 73
"   "   Precinct II 237

Total vote 310

Number of women voters 73

No women ballots were cast at the last annual town meeting.

VOTE FOR GOVERNOR.

Albert B. Coats	5
W. Murray Crane	176
Robert Treat Paine, Jr.	101
George R. Peare	13
Winfield P. Porter	3

VOTE FOR SENATOR.

Fred Joy	172
Frederic R. S. Mildon	108

VOTE FOR REPRESENTATIVES IN THE 21ST MIDDLESEX DISTRICT.

Names of towns.	Geo. Balcom.	Lucius P Bent.	Wm. M. Brigham.	Geo. A. Haynes.	Blanks
Marlborough	1089	841	1436	385	473
Sudbury	25	70	76	62	67
Wayland	81	207	86	82	164
Total	1195	1118	1598	529	704

Respectfully submitted,

RICHARD T. LOMBARD,
Town Clerk.

Assessors' Report.

WAYLAND, March 1, 1900.

To the Inhabitants of Wayland:

The present year marks the highest tax rate Wayland has ever had, and such a rate is alike a burden to the farmer, manufacturer, merchant and artisan ; in fact its baneful effect is injurious to all, especially to those who own small homesteads and depend on their daily manual labor to support their families.

Seemingly the time has come when appropriations should be small, and these disbursed with the greatest economy. Such a rate of taxation, to a large extent, prevents the sale of real estate, and is an effectual bar to incoming wealth.

As the manufacturers of the town did not bring in any "lists" to the assessors of the value of their machinery and stock, we were compelled to employ the best means at our command to make the assessment proportionate to both the large and small factories — the basis of such computation being the number of employees. While we could not hope, with the limited information furnished us, to make this assessment absolutely just or to please all, yet, as no applications for abatement have been made to the assessors, it would seem as if there were no grounds for complaint.

A large number of the tax payers have asked the assessors to recommend that the "valuation list" for the year 1900 be printed. It would seem to be desirable to have the list of the last year of the century prepared for circulation, no list having been printed since 1882.

Under Chap. 578, Acts of 1898, the Natick & Cochituate Street Railway Co. paid its first excise tax to the town on its four and nine-tenths miles of track within our limits. The tax amounted to $174.60.

STATISTICS.

Value of real estate May 1, 1899 . . .	$1,314,720 00
" personal estate May 1, 1899 . .	266,605 00
Total valuation	$1,581,325 00
" May 1, 1898	1,648,465 00
Decrease	67,140 00
Taxes assessed for town purposes . . .	$29,519 22
Overlayings	560 52
State tax	900 00
Special marsh land tax	330 52
County tax	1,626 24
Additional assessments	220 40
Omitted tax	7 20
Total taxes committed for collection . . .	$33,164 10
Number of polls assessed May 1, 1899 . .	655
" " " 1898 . .	635
Increase of polls	20
Whole number of persons assessed . . .	957
" " residents assessed on property	424
" " non-residents assessed on prop-	
erty	149
Total number assessed on property . . .	573
Total value of land	$480,190 00
" " buildings	834,530 00
Value of church property	31,040 00
" town property	138,923 00

Number of horses assessed 407
" " cows " 752
" " sheep " 26
" " swine " 606
" " fowls " 2,105
" " dwelling houses assessed . . . 428
" " acres of land " . . . 9,206 1-12

Rate of taxation for 1899, $20.00 per thousand.
" " " 1898, 17.60 " "

Taxes abated, assessed 1897 on real estate . $46 40
" " " 1898 " " . 63 36
" " " 1899 " " . . 106 00

No abatement of personal property tax has been made.

Respectfully submitted,

RICHARD T. LOMBARD,
EDWARD CARTER,
NATHANIEL R. GERALD,
Assessors of Wayland.

Collector's Report.

Concerning taxes collected by Willard B. Ward, from March 1, 1899, to Oct. 2, 1900, inclusive.

TAXES OF 1895.

Balance due March 1, 1899, as per last report . . $172 71.
Uncollected.
Interest, $164.59.

TAXES OF 1896.

Balance due March 1, 1899, as per last report . . $2,309 16
Paid treasurer 1,018 91

Balance uncollected Oct. 2, 1900 . . . . $1,290 25.

TAXES OF 1897.

Balance due March 1, 1899, as per last report . . $7,168 28
Paid treasurer 2,453 46

Balance uncollected Oct. 2, 1900 . . . . $4,714 82

TAXES OF 1898.

Balance due March 1, 1899, as per last report . . $12,886 58
Paid treasurer 3,849 34

Balance uncollected Oct. 2, 1900 . . . . $9,037 24

TAXES OF 1899.

Taxes assessed for 1899, as per warrants :

Town tax	$29,519 22	
Overlayings	560 52	
Additional assessments	23 40	
State tax	900 00	
Special (marshland) tax	330 52	
County tax	1,626 24	
Total taxes assessed to Oct. 2, 1900 . . ————		$32,959 90
Paid treasurer		10,524 00
Balance uncollected Oct. 2, 1900 . . .		$22,435 90

Respectfully submitted,

FRANK T. GERRY,
Administrator Estate of Willard B. Ward.

Report of Temporary Collector.

TAXES.

Amount of taxes in tax list for 1899 committed with
    warrant therefore to temporary collector . . $22,417 50
Additional assessments 204 20

                                                      $22,621 70

Abatements $106 00
Credit for tax paid former collector . . 10 00
                                             ————— $116 00

                                           $22,505 70

Total collection to March 1, 1900 :

    Paid treasurer $10,343 28
    Cash on hand 253 93
                                     ————— $10,597 21

Balance still due $11,908 49

Amount of taxes, in tax list for 1898 committed with
    warrant therefor to temporary collector . . $8,856 46

Abatements $49 28
Credit for taxes paid former collector . . 20 24
                                           ————— 69 52

                                         $8,786 94

Collections to March 1, 1900, and paid to treasurer . $2,016 09

Balance still due $6,770 85

Amount of taxes in tax list for 1897 committed with
    warrant therefor to temporary collector . . $4,660 86

Abatements $44 80
Credit for tax paid former collector . . 16 80
                                         61 60

                                 $4,599 26
Collections to March 1, 1900, and paid to treasurer . 1,068 21

    Balance still due $3,531 05

Amount of taxes in tax list for 1896 committed with
    warrant therefor to temporary collector . . $2,361 07
Credits allowed for taxes paid to former collector . 445 79

                                 $1,915 28
Collections to March 1, 1900, and paid to treasurer . 380 13

    Balance still due $1,535 15

Amount of taxes in tax list for 1895 committed with
    warrant therefor to temporary collector . . $367 97
Credits allowed for taxes paid former collector . . 25 83

                                 $342 14
Collections to March 1, 1900, and paid to treasurer . 55 86

    Balance still due $286 28

INTEREST.

Interest on taxes for 1899, collected and paid treasurer $72 71
Interest on taxes for 1898, collected and paid treasurer   142 52
Interest on taxes for 1897, collected and paid treasurer   124 33
Interest on taxes for 1896, collected and paid treasurer   152 99
Interest on taxes for 1895, collected and paid treasurer   13 35

    Total interest collected and paid treasurer . . $505 90

SUMMARY.

Total taxes committed to temporary collector .   . $38,868 06

Total collections .   .   .   , ... $14,117 50
Total abatements 200 08
Total credits 518 66
Balance to be collected 24,031 82

$38,868 06

Total taxes paid treasurer $13,863 57
Total interest paid treasurer 505 90
Taxes in cash on hand 253 93

$14,623 40

Total taxes collected $14,117 50
Total interest collected 505 90

$14,623 40

Respectfully submitted,

CHARLES F. RICHARDSON,

Temporary Collector of Taxes.

Report of the Overseers of the Poor

FOR THE YEAR ENDING FEB. 28, 1900.

The condition of the town farm remains about the same as last year. Mr. M. Temple resigned in October, 1899, and we engaged Mr. Norman W. Saunders to fill the vacancy, and he has given general satisfaction. We have engaged him for the ensuing year.

OUT OF DOOR POOR, PARTIAL SUPPORT.

Families aided	12	
Persons	42	
		54

IN DOOR POOR, FULL SUPPORT.

Almshouse	2	
State Lunatic Hospital	6	
		8

Total number of persons aided 62

FINANCIAL STATEMENT SHOWING ACTUAL RECEIPTS AND EXPENDITURES FOR THE YEAR.

March 1st, 1899, unexpended balance . .	$420 22	
Appropriation . . .	2,500 00	
		$2,920 22

Reimbursements.

From town of Lexington	$52 00	
Town of Southboro	159 20	
City of Everett	32 00	
G. B. Howe, guardian of S. E. Crofoot	169 93	
Commonwealth of Massachusetts .	36 14	
		$449 27

Almshouse Receipts.

Sale of Milk	$921 69	
Produce, eggs and poultry . .	133 92	
Cows and calves	114 25	
Pork	25 80	
Board of D. Mullen	52 50	
Commonwealth of Massachusetts . .	9 64	
Labor	44 70	
		$1,302 50

Total receipts	$4,671 99

Expenditures Out Door Poor.

Having a settlement in Wayland and residing elsewhere.

Mrs. Emily Sumpter, Hudson . . .	$68 21	
Alex. L. Benoit and family, Brockton . .	169 04	
Henry Benoit and family, Brookfield . .	92 05	
Rose Murphy, Boston	20 00	
Miss Bessie Stone, Boston	64 00	
		$413 30

Having a settlement in Wayland and residing there.

John Chenett and family	$77 60
Lewis C. Maud	7 00
Ann Painter	52 00
Louis Cormier	75 00
George Chalmers	36 00
Mrs. Nelson Leteur and family . . .	58 05

Napoleon Leteur	$98 35
James Foley. Died Feb. 17th, 1900 . .	68 50
Elijah Roberts and family	31 04
Mrs. Gayzette's boy	19 00
	$522 54

Having a settlement in other cities and towns and residing in Wayland.

Thomas Mead, Everett	$32 00
Mrs. H. C. McPherson, Commonwealth of Massachusetts	12 00
J. F. Hawkins, Southboro	161 35
E. Haldwell, Lexington	52 00
	$257 35

In Door Poor in Insane Hospitals.

Clara Davis, Westboro	$169 45
S. E. Crofoot, Geo. B. Howe guardian, Westboro, died Dec. 28, 1899 . . .	212 25
James A. Wing, Worcester	169 46
J. Frank Loker, Worcester, discharged .	86 58
Ellen Stanton, Taunton	169 46
Thomas N. Collins, Foxboro, discharged .	15 07
	$822 27

Almshouse Expenditures.

Paid Warden's salary	$435 30
Groceries	243 33
Provisions	184 12
Grain	521 50
•Horse (one)	100 00
Cows	147 00
Shoats	7 50
Repairs	9 89
Seeds	46 43
Hay	122 45
Tools	78 32

Paid Fertilizer	$52 35	
Clothing for inmates	13 67	
Labor	202 89	
Fuel	63 61	
Medical attendance for inmates . .	1 55	
Veterinary services	26 00	
Clothing and crockery	16 24	
Blacksmithing, etc.	62 65	
Miscellaneous	28 57	
		$2,363 37

MISCELLANEOUS.

Travelling expenses, settlement of cases, stationery, order books, etc. $41 09

$4,419 92
Unexpended balance 252 07

$4,671 99

OUTSTANDING CLAIMS.

Town of Hudson, bill not received.
City of Brockton " " "
" " Springfield, bill not received.
Commonwealth of Massachusetts, unsettled case.

REIMBURSEMENTS DUE.

Town of Lexington	$52 00	
" " Southboro	31 75	
Commonwealth of Massachusetts . .	12 00	
Estate of S. E. Crofoot	42 32	
		$138 07

INMATES AT ALMSHOUSE DURING YEAR.

Sarah Puffer, March 1, 1899, age 83 years
James Burke, March 1, 1899, age 72 years

Inventory of Property at Almshouse

Two horses	$200 00	
Nine cows	475 00	
Two shoats	10 00	
Forty-four hens	22 00	
Eight tons hay	130 00	
Corn fodder	8 00	
Twenty-five cords manure	125 00	
Potatoes	10 00	
Tools	365 50	
Coal	18 00	
Twenty-five cords wood	120 00	
Forty posts, rails, etc.	8 00	
		$1,491 50
Furniture and utensils (in house)		224 47
		$1,715 97
Real estate		5,800 00
		$7,515 97
Number of tramps lodged.	342	
Meals furnished	310	

Remarks.

We were obliged to purchase another horse this year, and owing to the severe drought of the past season the products of the farm were greatly reduced, also the rise in grain, etc., has effected the profits from the milk as milk did not materially advance in price.

An appropriation of twenty-five hundred dollars is asked for on same condition as last year.

Respectfully submitted,

DAVID P. W. LOKER,
GEORGE B. HOWE,
THEODORE S. SHERMAN,
Overseers of the Poor.

Report of Trustees of Public Library,

To the Citizens of the Town of Wayland:

The trustees respectfully submit the following report:

During the past year nothing out of the usual routine of the library has happened.

The annual inspection in October resulted in finding the books and furnishings in good condition, aside from the ordinary wear arising from use.

The trustees have paid all accounts to the first of March, in accordance with the town's by-laws, as will be seen in the report of their treasurer, under expressage, librarian's and assistant librarian's salaries. Heretofore the custom has been to allow the expressage, the three month's salary of librarian, and the whole year's salary of the assistant librarian to go over into the succeeding year. The unexpended balance in the treasurer's report is due to the dog tax received late in February. This has been applied to the spring books purchased early in March.

On August 7th, of this year, the first half century of the library's existence will be completed, and some fitting recognition of the fact seems worthy of the town's consideration.

Respectfully submitted,

JOHN CONNELLY, *Chairman.*
CHARLES F. RICHARDSON, *Clerk.*
ARTHUR G. BENNETT,
C. B. WILLIAMS,
HARRY E. CARSON,
FRANCIS SHAW.

Librarian's Report.

To the Board of Trustees :

The statistical information for the year 1899 to 1900 is respectfully submitted.

ACCESSIONS.

	Books.	Pamphlets.
By purchase	115	
By gift	182	
Bound and transferred from pamphlet department	33	
Total	330	

Whole number of volumes in the library .	13,274	
Pamphlets presented	231	

CIRCULATION.

In Cochituate village	1,695
In Wayland Centre	4,216
Total	5,911

DONORS OF BOOKS AND PAMPHLETS.

	Books	Pamphlets
American Congregational Society . .		1
American Library Commission . . .		1.
American Unitarian Association . . .	2	1

Bennett, Mrs. A. G.		24
Brookline Public Library		4
Brooklyn " "		2
Coolidge, Mr. James		4
Cutting, Mrs. Chas. A.	9	5
Cutting, Mr. Chas. A.	1	
Dorr, Mr. Morris	111	
Draper, Mrs. F. W.	8	
Dudley, Miss L. A.		13
Ford, Mr. A. E.	1	
Fowler, Mr. F. H	1	
Frost, Miss A.	4	
Heard, Misses M. and E.		16
Loring, The Misses	3	49
McGlennan	1	
Melville, Mr. Geo. W.		2
Rice, Mrs. Chas. A.		4
Richardson, Mr. Chas. F.		12
Reform Club, The		1
Rowe, Mr. G. H. M.		
Salem Public Library		10
Sent to the reading room		212
Shaw, Mr. Francis	2	
State Government	8	27
United States Government	28	83
Unitarian Association	2	1
Villafranca, Mr. R.		1

Library reports have been received as follows : Arlington, Brookline, Brooklyn, Concord, District of Columbia, Fall River, Forbes Library, Northampton, Free Public Library Commission, Harvard College and Harvard University, Institute of Technology, Indian Rights Reservation, Lowell Textile School, Malden Metropolitan Water Board, Newton, Public Reservation, Salem, Soldiers' Home, St. Louis Mercantile Library Association, Syracuse, University of Pennsylvania, Weston and Watertown.

CLASSES OF READING.

Art	.04	Juvenile	.12
Biography	.05	Poetry	.02
Fiction	.50	Science	.01
History	.23	Travels	.03

The reading room has received regularly The Century Magazine, Elliott's Magazine, Harper's Monthly, Munsey's, The Land of Sunshine, The Rhodosa, Woman's Journal, Woman's Home Companion, Traveller's Record and Cochituate Enterprise.

SARAH E HEARD,
Librarian.

Feb. 27, 1900.

9921	Adventures of Francois. S. W. Mitchell.
9876	American Revolution. Sir. Geo. D Trevelyan.
9986	Anglo Saxon Superiority. E. Demolius
9954	Associate Hermits, The. F. R. Stockton.
9964	Aunt Billy and Other Stories. A J. Keith.
856	Autumn. H. D. Thoreau.
9880–81	Ave Roma. F. M. Crawford.
9984	Awakening of a Nation. C. F. Lummis.
9931	Awkward Age, The. Henry James.
9933	Aylwin. T. W. Dunton.
9873	Barrack Room Ballads. R. Kipling.
9929	Battle of the Strong. Gilbert Parker.
9996	Bird Neighbors. N. Blanchan.
9970	Bird World. J. H Stickney and R. Hofman.
9884–5	Bismark's Autobiography. A. J. Butler.
9727	Bob Son of Battle. A. Olivant.
9976	Book of Folk Stories, The. H. Scudder.
9958	Boy I Knew and Four Dogs. L. Hutton.
9967	Boys of Fairport, The. N. Brooks.
9989	Boys of 98, The. J. Otis.
9973	Brave Little Holland and What She Taught Us. W. E. Griffins.

9878	Brunetiere's Essays in French.
9926	Caleb West Master Diver. F. H. Smith.
860	Cape Cod. H. D. Thoreau.
9412	Castle Inn, The. S. J. Weyman.
9955	Child Culture in the Home. M. B. Mashee.
9935	Children of the Ghetto. I. Zangwill.
9969	Child's World, A. J. W. Riley.
9898	Collection of Historical and Other Papers of Grindall Reynolds. A. R. Keyes.
9729	Concerning Isabel Carnaby. E. T. Fowler.
9966	Cruise of the Cachalot. F. T. Bullen.
9889	Cuban and Porto Rican Campaign. R. H. Davis.
9951	Cyrano DeBergerac. E. Rostand.
9942	David Harum. E. N. Wescott.
9870	Day's Work. R. Kipling.
9875	Departmental Ditties. R. Kipling.
9946	Dross. H. S. Merriman.
9982	Electricity for Everybody. P. Atkinson.
993	Evolution of Religion M. J. Savage.
858	Excursions. H. D. Thoreau.
9977	Fables. H. Scudder.
864	Free to Serve. E. Rayner.
9932	Gadfly, The. E. L Voynech.
9974	German Household Tales. Grimm.
9924	Gloria Mundi. H. Frederic.
9950	Great Love, A. C. L. Burnham.
9918	Heart of Denise. S. L. Yeats.
9705	Her Memory. M. Martens.
9988	Hero Tales from American History.
9919	Home Economics. M. Parloa.
9788	Home Life in Colonial Days. A. M. Earle.
9998	How to Enjoy Pictures. M. S. Emery.
9999	How to Know the Ferns.
9991	Interest of America in Sea Power. A. J. Mahan.
9972	Japanese Interior, A. A. M. Bacon.
9985	John Hancock, His Book. A. E. Brown.
9941	John Splendid Neil Munro.
9882-3	Letters of Robert and Elizabeth Barrett Browning.

9877 Letters of Thomas Carlyle.
9906-7 Letters of Victor Hugo. Paul Meurice.
9908 Life of Wm. Shakespeare. Sidney Lee.
861 Maine Woods, The. H. D. Thoreau.
9879 Manual of the History of French Literature, translated.
9872 Many Inventions. R. Kipling.
9934 Master, The. I. Zangwill
9990 Master of the Strong Hearts E. L. Brooks.
9909 Mastery of Books, The. H. L. Koopman.
859 Miscellanies H D. Thoreau.
9949 Mrs. Archer Archer. C. L. Burnham.
9886 Music and Musicians. A Lavingnac.
9912 My Sister Henrietta. E Renan.
9914 Myths and Legends Beyond Our Borders. C. M. Skinner.
9874 Naulahka. R Kipling.
9938 No. 5 John Street. R. Whiteing.
9961 On Many Seas. H E. Hamblin.
9940 Open Question, The. E. Robbins.
992 Our Unitarian Gospel. M. J. Savage.
9992 Outlines of the Earth's History. N. S Shaler.
9699 Patrius L: I. Guiney.
9956 Penelope's Progress. K. D. Wiggin.
9890 Phillipine Islands, The. Dean Worcester.
9927 Pride of Jennico, The. A. and E. Castle.
9716 Principles of Agriculture. L H. Bailey.
9922 Prisoners of Hope. M. Johnson.
9979 Ragged Lady. W. D Howells.
9920 Red Rock. T. N. Page.
863 Richard Carvel. Winston Churchill.
9944 Roden's Corner. H. S. Merriman.
9994-5 Romance of the House of Savoy. A. Weil
9923 Rupert of Hentzau A. Hope.
862 Santa Claus' Partner. T. N. Page.
9930 Scapegoat, The. Hall Caine.
9952 Second Thoughts of an Idle Fellow. J. Jerome.
9869 Shakespeare, The Boy. W. J. Rolfe.
9737 Sherburn Girls. A. M. Douglas.
9913 Siegfried and Beomelf. Z. A. Ragozin.

9953	Silence and Other Stories. M. E. Wilkins.
9888	Sketch of Life and Public Services of M. A. Richardson. F. W. Haskett.
9928	Soldier of Manhattan. J. A. Altsheler.
9871	Soldiers, Three. R. Kipling.
9987	Southern Soldier Stories. G. C. Eggleston.
9981	Span of Life, The. W. McLennan.
854	Spring. H. D. Thoreau.
9971	Starland. Sir R. S. Ball.
9948	Stories in Light and Shadow. B. Harte.
9960	Story of Marco Polo. N. Brooks.
9975	Story Mother Nature Told Her Children. J. Andrews.
9947	Strong Hearts G. W. Cable.
9993	Student's History of the United States. E. Channing.
855	Summer. H. D. Thoreau.
9959	Tales of the Enchanted Islands of the Atlantic. T. W. Higginson.
9963	Tales of the Maylayan Coast. K Wildman.
9915	Through Nature to God. J. Fiske.
9824	Liverton Tales. A. Brown.
9997	Trees of North Eastern America. C. S. Newhall.
9937	Trooper Galahad. Chas. King.
9965	Walter Sherwood's Probation. H. Alger, Jr.
9936	Warrior Gap Capt. King.
9957	What Shall Our Boys Do for a Living. C. F. Wingate.
9962	Wild Animals I Have Known. E S. Thompson.
9939	Wild Eelin. Wm Black.
857	Winter. H. D. Thoreau.
9916–17	Worker, The. Wyckoff.
9980	World's Rough Hand, The. H. P. Whitmarsh.
9887	Year Book of the Society of Colonial Wars.
9978	Young Folks History of Russia. N. H. Dole.
9943	Young Mistley. H S. Merriman.
9968	Young Puritans of Old. Hadley M. P. Welles.
9945	Zoeoaster. F. M. Crawford.

Water Commissioners' Report.

WAYLAND WATER COMMISSIONERS,

>In account with HENRY F. LEE, *Town Treasurer.*

Feb. 28, 1899.	Balance not drawn from town treasurer	$1,227 97
Feb. 28, 1900.	Transfer for hydrants	384 00
	By water rates, town treasurer . .	1,886 22
		$3,498 22

Transfer interest on bonds		$640 00
Mar. 27, 1899.	Order No. 1 For sinking fund . .	305 97
Feb. 28, 1900.	" " 2 H. G. Dudley, supt. .	150 00
	" " 3 H. G. Dudley, com. .	20 00
	" " 4 C. H. Boody, com. . .	20 00
	" " 5 W. M. Fullick, com. .	20 00
	" " 6 W. M. Fullick, clerk .	32 50
	" " 7 Sinking fund . . .	405 16
	" " 8 Maintenance . . .	1,238 59
		$2,832 22
Balance not drawn		666 00
		$3,498 22

>C. H. BOODEY,
>H. G. DUDLEY,
>W. M. FULLICK,
>*Commissioners of Wayland Water Works.*

Report of Commissioners of Wayland Water Works Sinking Fund.

Amount in Framingham Savings Bank, Feb.
28, 1899 . . . . . . $734 58
Amount drawn from above, Jan. 19, 1900 . 293 83

Amount in Framingham Savings Bank. Feb. 28, 1900 . $440 75

Amount deposited in Natick Savings Bank, Natick,
Mass , Mar. 2, 1899 . . . . . . $734 58
Interest on above to Nov. 1, 1899 . . . . 14 68
Deposited, Jan. 19, 1900 . . . . . . 293 83
Deposited, Mar. 7, 1900 . . . . . . 405 16

Amount deposited in Watertown Savings Bank, Watertown, Mass. $1,000 00
Interest on above deposit, Oct. 3 . . . . 20 00

Amount deposited in the Home Savings Bank, Boston,
Mass. . . . . ' . $760 45
Interest on above deposit 19 50

$3,688 95

C. H. BOODEY,
H. G. DUDLEY,
W. M. FULLICK,
Commissioners of Wayland Water Works Sinking Fund.

Report of the Superintendent of the Wayland Water , Works.

GENTLEMEN : —

We have this year taken up and replaced with larger pipe two thousand (2,000) feet, eleven hundred (1,100) feet of four (4) inch and nine hundred (900) feet of two (2) inch. We have also laid nine hundred (900) feet of new service pipe, so we have laid twenty-nine hundred (2,900) feet of pipe this year. We have also had a large amount of service pipe to clean out.

We believe the time has come to increase the supply of water by enlarging the basin, as we believe we are too near the limit of supply of the present basin for safety.

The maintenance account is :

1899.

April	1.	To Labor for March	.	.	.	.	$9 00
	3.	R. W. Porter	.	.	.	.	5 00
	7.	John Hurley .	.	.	.	.	1 50
	15.	W. C. Neal .	.	.	.	.	2 50
	28.	J. B. McIroy.	.	.	.	.	10 00
		J. F. Jones .	.	.	.	.	2 25
May	1.	Labor for April	.	.	.	.	32 50
	6.	J. N. Cunningham	.	.	.	.	26 65
	22.	Frank Brummett .	.	.	.	.	12 00
	25.	James Morrisey	.	.	.	.	16 00
	26	R. W. Porter	.	.	.	.	13 50

May	29.	T. B Haws		$12 00
		J. N. Cunningham		99 28
		Howe & Co.		2 15
		B. & A. R. R.		3 85
June	1.	Labor for May		42 00
	6.	J. B. McIroy		14 00
	30.	T. B. Haws		7 00
July	1.	Labor for June		26 00
	18.	Boston & Maine R. R.		41 18
Aug.	1.	Labor for July		16 50
	3.	James Devine		12 95
	7.	Walworth Mfg. Co.		107 61
	9.	B. & A. R. R.		51
	29.	R. O. Wood & Co.		266 29
	30.	Hinds & Comer		1 00
Sept.	1.	Labor for August		46 50
	4.	Ralph Neal		30 75
	5.	L. A. Loker		21 00
		Frank Brummett		36 65
		James Morrisey		36 65
		J. B. McIroy		17 00
		Conrad Homer		32 65
	16.	T. B. Haws		41 76
	19.	R. W. Porter		17 50
		Samuel Hobbs & Co.		4 37
	27.	Boston Lead Co.		50 25
Oct.	1.	Labor for Sept.		27 50
		Fiske & Co.		1 05
	10.	Walworth Manufacturing Co.		31 00
	19.	Robinson & Jones		2 00
Nov.	1.	Labor for Oct.		9 50
Dec.	1.	Labor for Nov.		8 50
1900.				
Jan.	1.	James Devine		4 70
		Labor for Dec.		10 50
Feb.	1.	Labor for Jan.		6 50
	19.	E. P. Butler		10 79

Feb. 27.	W. F. Garfield						$7 00
	Postage						1 25
							$1,238 59

The water at present is in use by the following :

Families	291
Manufactories	7
Public buildings	4
Miscellaneous	12
Horses	84
Cows	47

Respectfully submitted,

H. G. DUDLEY,

Superintendent.

WAYLAND, Feb. 28, 1900.

Report of Superintendent of Streets.

SNOW BILLS.

	Days.	Hours.		Days.	Hours.		
C. H. May . .	1	5	horse		4	$3	96
H. F. Brummett .					.		67
Joseph Tyrrell .				.	.		67
John Hurley . .		3		.	.	1	33
D. C. Smith . .	1			.	.	2	00
W. F. Smith . .	1			.	.	3	55
E. G. Stone . .	1			.	.	2	00
C. A. Rock . .		3		.	.		67
C. A. Phillips . .	1	¾		.	.	2	16
W. C. Neal . .				.	.	1	50
						$18	51

HIGHWAY PAY ROLL FOR THE MONTH OF APRIL.

	Days.	Hours.		Days.	Hours.		
Wilson Porter .	7		horse	14		$38	50
H. F. Brummett .	13			.	.	26	00
James Morrisey .	14	1		.	.	28	22
C. W. Fairbanks .	10	8	horse	21	7	59	86
C. C. Ward . .	4	8½		.	.	9	88
Joseph Corimer .	6	8½		.	.	13	89
Arthur T. Felch .	5			.	.	10	00

	Days.	Hours.		Days.	Hours.		
Chas Newton	12	5		.	.	$25	10
Wm G. Webster	10	4½		.	.	15	75
C. H. May	27	4½	horse	55	.	151	25
G. W. Whitney	4			.	.	6	00
Michael G. Hurley	10	3¼		.	.	25	98
John Hurley	10	3¼		.	.	31	17
Mrs. Thompson, 49 loads stone			.	.	.	12	25
E. A. Atwood, lanterns and oil	.	.	.	.	.	2	00
						$455	85
						154	00
						$609	85

HIGHWAY PAY ROLL FOR THE MONTH OF APRIL.

	Days.	Hours.		Days.	Hours.		
J. F. Malloy	4	7	horse	9	5	$26	28
J. W. Coakley	4			.	.	8	00
A. W. Lombard	5			.	.	10	00
James Linnehan	6			.	.	12	00
T. L. Hynes	6		horse	9	1	27	94
P. J. McLaughlin	6			.	.	12	00
M. W. Hynes	7	5½	horse	13	5½	39	03
Geo. E. Sherman	6	4¼		.	.	13	00
N. P. Rutter, 62 spikes	.	.	.	.	.	1	86
Butrick Lumber Co.	.	.	.	.	.	50	77
Geo. Tyler & Co., sections for road, March				.	.	8	75
						$209	63

HIGHWAY PAY ROLL FOR THE MONTH OF MAY.

	Days.	Hours.					
C. C. Ward	4			.	.	$8	00
Chas. Newton	1			.	.	2	00
John Hurley	2	4½		.	.	6	25
John Kelley	4			.	.	8	00
Wilson Porter	3		horse	6		16	50
W. C. Neal	4		horse	6		15	50
A. Felch	3		horse	6		16	50
C. W. Fairbanks	3		horse	6		16	50

	Days.	Hours.		Days.	Hours.		
C. H. May . .	9	2	horse	12	4	$40	22
H. F. Brummett .	3			.	.	6	00
James Morrisey .	3					6	00
E. W. Jennison .	3					6	00
Conrad Homer .	3					6	00
Wm. Webster .	3					4	50
Road tools						11	45
						$172	42

Highway Pay Roll for the Month of May.

	Days.	Hours.		Days.	Hours.		
Geo. E. Sherman .	6	4½	horse	13		$35	75
Geo. N. Sherman .	6	4½		.	.	13	00
John Fox . .	6	4½		.	.	13	00
Leslie Sherman .	6	4½		.	.	13	00
Henry Clark . .	6			.	.	12	00
Walter Randolph .	5			.	.	10	00
William Randolph .	5			.	.	10	00
John F. Malloy .	5	4½	horse	10		28	50
James Linnehan .	10	5½		.	.	21	22
P. J. McLaughlin .	10	3½		.	.	20	78
M. W. Hynes . .	12	8¼	horse	22		64	39
T. L. Hynes . .	9	5½	horse	12	6	41	38
Edward Harrington	3			.	.	6	00
William D. White, 116 loads of gravel . . .						11	60
						$300	62

Highway Pay Roll for the Month of June.

	Days.	Hours.		Days.	Hours.		
J. B. McElroy .	3			.	.	$6	00
H. F. Brummett .	16			.	.	32	00
J. Morrisey . .	15			.	.	30	00
C. Haman . .	9	5		.	.	19	12
A. T. Felch . .	15		horse	30		82	50
C. W. Fairbanks .	14	5	horse	29	1	79	87
Wilson Porter .	14		horse	28		77	00
W. C. Neal . .	7	4	horse	12	8	37	56

	Days.	Hours.		Days.	Hours.		
C. H. May . .	32	3	horse	42	6	$139	33
Wm. G. Webster .	10	¾		.	.	16	12
M. Guilfoile . .	3			.	.	6	00
A. Randolph . .	2			.	.	4	00
L. A. Loker . .	10		horse	4		27	00
Chas. Newton . .	15			.	.	30	00
C. C. Ward . .	14	2		.	.	28	44
E. P. Butler, paint . . . ✓						3	50
P. A. Leary, blacksmithing						39	73
E. W. Jennison						26	89
G. Nayler, Cr. to 105 loads gravel						5	25

$690 31

HIGHWAY PAY ROLL FOR THE MONTH OF JUNE.

J. F. Malloy . .	12		horse	24		$66	00
Walter Randolph .	8			.	.	16	00
William Randolph .	12			.	.	24	00
M. W. Hynes .	13		horse	26		71	50
T. L. Hynes . .	12	1	horse	24	2	66	60
P. J. McLaughlin .	11	1		.	.	22	22
James Linnehan .	13			.	.	26	00
P. S. Zimmerman .	6	4½		.	.	13	00
O. Woods, 2697 feet spruce 17 50-100 . . .						47	20

$352 52.

HIGHWAY PAY ROLL FOR THE MONTH OF JULY.

L. A. Loker . .	16	1½	horse	16	1½	$60	60
Wm. Ragan . .	15	3		.	.	30	66
C. A. Phillips .	14	8		.	.	29	78
John Hurley . .	6	4½		.	.	13	00
John E. Kelley −.	10	1		.	.	20	22
James Morrisey .	15	5		.	.	31	11
E. A. Carter . .	1	2		.	.	2	45
John B. McElroy .	11	4		.	.	22	87
Chas. Newton .	15	4½		.	.	31	00

	Days.	Hours.		Days.	Hours		
David Connell	12	7		.	.	$25	55
Wm. Randolph	8	5		.		17	10
Thos. Evans	20	4½	horse	15	4½	68	12
Michael Guilfoil	12	4½		.	.	31	25
Gilbert Wood	16	5		.	.	33	11
C. H. May	16	5	horse	14		59	36
Louis Champney	1	2		.	.	2	44
P. A. Leary, blacksmithing	.	.	.	.	.	15	84
Fiske & Co , dynamite and caps	.	.	.	.	.	25	63
E. P. Butler, lanterns	.	.	.	.	.	1	00
5 gallons of oil	.	.	.	.	.		45
L H. McManus, sharpening drills	.	.	.	.	.	7	95

$529 49

Hynes' bill 2 58

$532 07

Cr.   By cash from N. & C. R. R. 100 00

$432 07

HIGHWAY PAY ROLL FOR THE MONTH OF JULY.

M. W. Hynes	. .	5	horse	5		$2	08
T. S. Sherman, repairs on bridge	.	.	.	.			50

$2 58

HIGHWAY PAY ROLL FOR THE MONTH OF AUGUST.

	Days	Hours		Days	Hours		
Henry Smith	3			.	.	$6	00
Fred Marshall	8			.	.	16	00
P. Jennings	1					2	00
Geo. E. Sherman	4	4½		.		9	00
T. L. Hynes	6		horse	8	.	26	00
M. W. Hynes	11	1	horse	15	1½	49	54

$108 54

Highway Pay Roll for the Month of September,

	Days.	Hours.		Days.	Hours.		
John E. Kelley	7	4½		.	.	$15	00
Conrad Homer	4			.	.	8	00
C. C. Ward	2			.	.	4	00
Wilson Porter	3		horse			11	25
W. C. Neal	4	½	horse	3		22	10
C. H. May	7	4½	horse	11	4½	35	13
Frank Haynes, to lumber and labor	.	.	.	..		12	23
50 chestnut posts	.	.	.	.	.	5	00
						$114	46

Highway Pay Roll for the Month of September.

	Days.	Hours.		Days.	Hours.		
M. W. Hynes	9		horse	7	.	$30	25
Fred Marshall	11	1		.	.	22	22
T. L. Hynes	12	1	horse	5	5½	34	03
J. H. Lee, 76 spikes	.	.	.	.	.	2	28
						$88	78

Highway Pay Roll for the Month of October.

	Days.	Hours.		Days.			
M W. Hynes	1	6	horse	2		$6	84
T. L. Hynes	1	6	horse		6	4	50
Alfred Marshall	1			.	.	2	00
Buttrick Lumber Co., 1,320 feet spruce plank	.	.				26	40
						$39	74

Highway Pay Roll for the Month of November.

	Days.	Hours.		Days.	Hours.		
M. W. Hynes	3	2	horse	6	2	$17	34
Alfred Marshall	3			.	.	6	00
T. L. Hynes	3		horse	6		16	50
Patrick Jennings	3			.	.	6	00
P. S. Zimmerman	3			.	.	6	00
Thomas Evans	3			.	.	6	00
Joseph Breck & Sons, tree trimmer	.	.	.	.		1	75
						$59	59

SNOW BILL.

HIGHWAY PAY ROLL FOR THE MONTH OF FEBRUARY, 1900.

	Days.	Hours.		Days.	Hours.	
C. W. Fairbanks .	1	5	horse	3	1	$8 53
C. H. May . .	1	4	horse	2	8	7 95
Amos Dusseault .		5		.	.	1 11
James Morrisey .		4			.	88
W. C. Neal . .		2	horse		2	84
A. T. Felch . .	1		horse		1	3 75
M. Temple . .	1		horse		1	3 75
C. C. Ward . .		4½		.	.	1 00

$27 81

HIGHWAY PAY ROLL FOR THE MONTH OF FEBRUARY, 1900.

	Days.	Hours.		Days.	Hours.	
M. W. Hynes .	5	2	horse	9	3	$26 77
Alfred Marshall .	4	1		.	.	8 22
T. L. Hynes . .	4	1	horse	5	2	17 35
Alfred Lombard .		4½		.	.	1 00
John E. Dolan .	1			.	.	2 00
Henry Smith . .	2	5½		.	.	5 22
Geo E Sherman .	4		horse	6	5	19 42
S. S. Davidson .	2	2		.	.	4 44
Geo. E. Sherman, 15 loads gravel						1 50
Wm. Stearns, repairs on scraper, 39 bolts . . .						7 72

$93 64

HIGHWAY PAY ROLL FOR THE MONTH OF FEBRUARY, 1900.

	Days.	Hours.		Days.	Hours.	
Amos Dusseault .	1	2		.	.	$2 45
James Morrisey .	2	2½		.	.	4 55
John Morrisey .	2	2½		.	.	4 55
John E. Kelley .	2	6		.	.	5 33

	Days.	Hours.		Days.	Hours.		
W. E. Jennison .	4	1½	horse	5	1	$17	28
C. H. May . .	6		horse	12		33	00
E. W. Marston, lumber and labor			.	.	.	18	80
						$85	96
Snow						27	81
						$113	77
						93	64
						$207	41
Dis						1	75
						$205	66

Report of Supt. of North and Centre Cemeteries.

March 1, 1900.

Town of Wayland,

To A. S. Morse, Supt.

To labor	$91 95
" lock, hasps and bolts	1 50
	$93 45
Paid treasurer for hat	$1 00

A. S. MORSE,
Superintendent.

Report of Supt. Lakeview Cemetery.

Mar. 1.   Unexpended balance $3 12
    27.   Appropriation 50 00

                                             $53 12

May 27.   Order on town treasurer   .   . $34 00   ·
June 24.   "   "   "   "   .   .   9 35
       Unexpended balance .   .   .   9 77
                                    $53 12

E. C. DAVIS,
Superintendent.

Report of Engineers of Fire Department.

We beg to report the following fires, to which the department responded, for the year ending March 1, 1900 :

March 16. 7.50 A. M. Alarm from box 27, for fire in poultry house of Geo. Richardson, Happy Hollow road, which was extinguished with small loss by our chemical extinguishers, property being situated beyond reach of hose.

April 18. 7.20 P. M. Alarm given from engine house for woods fire, rear of O. Atwell's, Pleasant street.

April 20. 11.30 A. M. Alarm from box 25, for wo ;ds fire near the above.

May 12. 1.10 P. M. Alarm given from engine house for woods fire, in Bullard's woods, near Lakeview cemetery.

August 22. 6.30 P. M. Lightning struck barn of Chas. E. Fiske, Wayland road, setting same on fire. The electrical storm at the time having burned out our fire alarm system, no regular alarm could be given. Although this, also, was beyond reach of hose, the department succeeded in saving the house and contents, the barn, only a few feet away, being totally destroyed.

November 10. 9.50 P M. Alarm given from engine house, also from box 24, for fire in barn of Jos. Mathieu, Willard street, which was partially destroyed. Contents total loss.

The department also responded to a false alarm, rung in, supposedly, by some one maliciously inclined.

In accordance with our recommendation of last year, the select-men have turned all matters pertaining to the department over to the Engineers, and we appointed W. C. Hunting, superintendent of fire alarm.

The carriages and equipments, and hose and coats, also the fire alarm system, we consider are kept in the best of condition, con-sidering what we have to do with. The two chemical extinguishers purchased last year have proven their value at every fire, more particularly in brush fires, and beyond reach of hose. We are hampered, however, in cold weather by the liability of their freez-ing in the engine house; and would recommend that some system of heating the house be adopted for the coldest part of the year, at least.

We have received for firemen's pay, $448.00, and have turned over to the companies, $424.00, leaving an unexpended balance of $24 00 in our hands.

We have also received the $100.00 specially appropriated for re-pairs, etc, last year, to which we have added the $14.63, unex-pended from the $500.00 appropriation of a year ago, which we have expended as follows : —

E. W. Marston, labor and material on engine house	.			$29 31
W. D. Parlin	"	"	"	2 47
James Devine	"	"	"	2 85
Harry Pratt	"		.	40 00
Wesley Porter	"		.	40 00
				$114 63

There never having been a foundation under engine house, we have put in cellar wall and new sills, dug out cellar two feet, and properly drained the same ; also, made such other repairs as were absolutely necessary. The house has been blinded and painted two coats.

Respectfully submitted,

E. W. MARSTON, *Chief,*
A. J. RICKER, *1st Asst.,*
F. E. YEAGER, *Clerk.*

Report of the Library Building Committee.

To the Citizens of the Town of Wayland:

Your committee respectfully submits the following report:

Your committee, with the assistance of Prof. Chandler, held an architectural competition for plans for the library building; and decided in favor of Cabot, Everett & Mead, whose plans offered the best solution of the problems presented to your committee.

Proposals were submitted by numerous responsible contractors, and your committee awarded the entire contract to the lowest bidder, Fales & Co., of South Framingham, Mass.

The work on the building has proceeded satisfactorily, excepting an unavoidable delay caused by the assignment of Fales & Co, for the benefit of their creditors. However, your committee is assured by the assignee that the contract will be speedily and properly completed.

The town's interests in the building are thoroughly protected. Twenty per cent. of the money due Fales & Company has been withheld, and the Fidelity and Deposit Company of Maryland is surety on their bond of ten thousand dollars to ensure the performance of their contract.

Respectfully submitted,

WILLARD A. BULLARD,
E. W. MARSTON,
C. B. WILLIAMS,
ALFRED W. CUTTING,
CHARLES F. RICHARDSON.

Finance Committee.

The finance committee respecttully submits the following and
recommends that the same be appropriated and adopted, viz. : —

For schools, fuel and care of buildings	$7,000 00
School supplies	700 00
Transportation of scholars	1,500 00
Repair of school buildings	100 00
Superintendent of schools	750 00
Overdrafts	716 25
Incidentals	2,000 00
Salaries	1,300 00
Electric lights	350 00
Interest on town debt	3,000 00
Firemen's pay	400 00
Hydrants	384 00
Highways and bridges	2,000 00
Support of poor	2,500 00
Collection of taxes	350 00
Abatement of taxes	200 00
Library	500 00
Lakeview cemetery	50 00
North and Centre cemeteries	50 00
School house loan	1,100 00
	$24,950 25

We recommend that the sum of six hundred and forty dollars be transfered from water rates to pay interest on water bonds.

That the selectmen be authorized to draw from the contingent fund such sums of money as may be necessary, not exceeding five hundred dollars, for assisting needy soldiers and their families.

That the selectmen be authorized to draw from the contingent fund, not exceeding five hundred dollars, to pay back salaries.

That the overseers of the poor be authorized to build a wagon and tool shed at the poor farm from money appropriated for support of poor, if in their judgment there is sufficient money for that purpose.

That the sum of three thousand dollars be appropriated for interest on town debt to be taken from the contingent fund.

That the money for removing snow be drawn from the contingent fund.

We have carefully considered the needs of the various departments and find that the sums recommended, if adopted, will meet the needs of the departments and are as low as can be safely recommended.

> ALBION F. PARMENTER, *Chairman.*
> D. W. MITCHELL,
> DAVID P. W. LOKER,
> H. G. DUDLEY,
> C. B. WILLIAMS,
> HENRY F. LEE,
> RICHARD T. LOMBARD,
> CHARLES H. MAY,
> JOHN CONNELLY, *Clerk.*

March 3, 1900.

Treasurer's Report.

SCHOOLS.

1899.
Mar.	1.	Unexpended balance .	.	.	$278 74
	27.	Appropriation	.	.	7,600 00
Sept.	1.	School Board, for superintendent	.	.	625 00

1900.
Jan.	1.	Donation fund	.	.	12 00
	24.	State treasurer	.	.	294 38
Feb.	24.	One-half dog license . . .	.	.	110 29

Total expenditures . .	. $8,015 88	
Balance unexpended . .	. · 903 53	
	$8,920 41	$8,920 41

SCHOOL SUPPLIES.

Mar. 27.	Appropriation . . .	.	.	$700 00
	" for overdraft .	.	.	26 55

Overdraft	. $26 55	
Expended	. 707 50	
Overdrawn . . .	.	7 50
	$734 05	$734 05

TRANSPORTATION OF SCHOLARS.

Mar. 1. Unexpended balance $94 98
27. Appropriation 2,000 00

Expenditures $1,693 00
Balance unexpended . . . 401 98

$2,094 98 $2,094 98

SCHOOL REPAIRS.

Mar. 1. Unexpended balance $14 09
27. Appropriation 100 00

Expenditures $75 92
Balance unexpended . . . 38 17

$114 09 $114 09

SUPERINTENDENT OF SCHOOLS.

Mar. 27. Appropriation $750 00
"   for overdraft . . . 53 00

1. Overdrawn $53 00
Expenditures 750 00

$803 00 _ $803 00

FITTING UP HIGH SCHOOL.

Mar 1. Unexpended balance $49 72
27. Appropriation 200 00

Balance unexpended . . . $249 72

$249 72 $249 72

OVERDRAFTS.

Mar.	1.	Unexpended balance .	. . . .		$68 07
	27.	Appropriation .	. . . .		3,930 22

	1.	School supplies .	. . .	$26 55
		Superintendent, supplies	. .	53 00
		Highways and bridges	. .	93 46
		Salaries .	. . . .	209 25
		Interest account	. . .	1,175 93
		Abatements	. . . .	431 94
		Incidentals .	. . .	1,535 00
		Contingent account	. . .	304 29
		Balance .	. . . .	168 87

$3,998 29 $3,998 29

HIGHWAYS AND BRIDGES.

Mar.	27.	Appropriation		$3,000 00
		" for overdraft . . .		93 46
Apr.	18.	Transportation from contingent account .		198 41
Dec.	9.	Natick & Cochituate street railway . .		174 60
		State treasurer		209 53

Mar.	1.	Overdrawn	$93 46	
Apr.	29.	C. H May	609 85	
		" "	65 63	
May	27.	" "	463 04	
June	24	" "	690 31	
		. . . .	352 52	
July	29	" "	432 07	
Aug.	26.	" "	108 54	
Sept.	30.	" "	203 24	
Oct.	28.	" "	50 00	
		. . . .	4 12	
Nov.	25.	" "	59 59	
Dec.	30.	" "	9 50	
1900.				
Feb'y	24.	" "	205 66	
		Balance unexpended . . .	328 47	

$3,676 00 $3,676 00

INCIDENTALS.

Mar.	27.	Appropriation		$1,500 00
		" for overdraft . . .		1,535 00
		Overdrawn		563 82

Mar.	1.	Overdrawn . . .	$1,535 00	
	25.	R. T. Lombard	50 26	
April	1.	R. T. Lombard . . . ▾ .	22 55	
		J. J. Jennison . . . ⸝	9 00	
		Thos. Bryant	5 00	
		American Express Co. . .	3 15	
		H. F. Lee	12 00	
		Lakeview Press⸍. . . .	139 88	
		Robinson & Jones . . .	11 63	
		T. S. Sherman	4 75	
		,W. L. Doane . · . . .	5 00	
		W. F. Garfield	7 00	
		C. H. Thing ´	3 00	
		A. S. Morse	12 25	
		A. F. Parmenter . . .	4 00	
	29.	" " sundry bills .	219 36	
May	27.	" " " " .	417 48	
June	24.	" " " ∹ .	111 35	
July	29.	E. H. Atwood " " .	102 50	
Aug.	26.	A. F. Parmenter " " .	80 76	
Sept.	30.	E. H. Atwood " " .	92 92	
Oct.	28.	" " .	198 95	
Nov.	25.	E. A. Carter .	96 45	
Dec.	30.	E. H. Atwood " " ⟋.	139 66	
	1900.			
Jan'y	27.	E. H. Atwood " " .	116 44	
Feb'y	24.	" " .	198 48	

$3,598 82	$3,598 82

FIRE DEPARTMENT.

Mar.	1.	Unexpended balance		$448 00
	27.	Appropriation		448 00

April 29.	E. W. Marston, chief . .	$448 00	
	Unexpended balance . .	448 00	

$896 00	$896 00

COLLECTION OF TAXES.

Mar. 27.	Appropriation		$350 00
1900.			

Jan'y 27.	C. F. Richardson . . .	$75 00

HYDRANTS.

Mar. 27.	Appropriation		$384 00
	Transferred to water com. acct. .	$384 00

LAKEVIEW CEMETERY.

Mar.	1.	Unexpended balance		$3 12
	27.	Appropriation		50 00

May 27.	E. C. Davis	$34 00
June 24.	" "	9 35
	Unexpended	9 77

$53 12	$53 12

NORTH AND CENTRE CEMETERIES.

Mar.	1.	Unexpended balance		$ 41
	27.	Appropriation		50 00

April 29.	A. S. Morse	$13 90
May 27.	" "	36 51

$50 41	$50 41

LIBRARY ACCOUNT.

Mar. 27.	Appropriation			$500 00
	One-half dog license			110 29
April 29.	H. D. Parmenter . . .	$500 00		
	One-half dog license . . .	110 29		
		$610 29	$610 29

CEMETERY ACCOUNT.

Mar. 1.	Unexpended balance			$205 57
Dec. 30.	A. S. Morse			1 00
1900.				
Feb'y 24	E. C. Davis			15 00
May 27.	A. S. Morse	$9 79		
July 29.	" "	27 75		
Aug. 26.	B. F. Adams	10 77		
Oct. 28.	E. C. Davis	3 25		
Nov. 25.	E. H. Atwood	17 00		
Dec. 30.	A S. Morse	5 50		
	Balance unexpended . . .	147 51		
		$221 57	$221 57

SUPPORT OF POOR.

Mar. 1.	Unexpended balance			$420 22
27.	Appropriation			2,500 00
	Total receipts. See O. of P. report . . .			1,393 53
	Total expenditures . . .	$4,061 68		
	Balance unexpended . . .	252 07		
		$4,313 75	$4,313 75

DECORATION DAY.

Mar. 27.	Appropriation			$50 00
April 22.	"			100 00

Feb'y 24. E. C. Davis $7 62

May 27. " " $100 00
June 24. " " 43 82
Unexpended balance . . . 13 80

$157 62 $157 62

ABATEMENT OF TAXES.

Mar. 27. Appropriation $300 00
" for overdraft . . . 431 94

Mar. 1. Overdrawn $431 94
Oct. 2 Taxes of 1899 . . . . 4 00
Dec. 30. N. R. Gerald 12 32
Feb'y 28. Abatement taxes, 1899 . . 106 00
" " 1898 . . 49 28
" " 1897 . . 44 80
Balance unexpended . . . 83 60

$731 94 $731 94

ELECTRIC LIGHTS.

Mar. 27. Unexpended balance $19 94
Appropriation 357 00

Mar. 25. Natick Gas & Electric Co. . . $33 70
April 1. " " " " . . 32 09
June 24. " " " " . . 61 26
July 29. " " . . 30 63
Aug. 26. " " . . 30 63
Sept. 30. " " . . 30 63
Oct. 28. " " . . 30 63
Nov. 25. " " " . 30 63
Balance unexpended . . . 96 74

$376 94 $376 94

INTEREST ON TOWN DEBT.

Mar.	27.	Appropriation from contingent	.	.	$3,000 00
		" for overdraft	.	.	1,175 93
		Transferred from water com. acct.	.	.	640 00
		Overdrawn	.	.	162 31

Mar.	1.	Overdrawn . . .	.$1,175 93	
	25.	Natick National Bank	. .	25 94
		" " " .	. .	494 97
		Boston Safe Deposit & Trust Co.		220 00
		D. B. Heard . . .	.	20 00
	27.	Estabrook & Co. .	. .	34 61
April	27.	Puritan Trust Co. .	. .	154 00
June	1.	City Bank . . .	. .	280 00
	24.	Natick National Bank	. .	66 67
July	21.	Boston Safe Deposit & Trust Co.		220 00
Aug.	26.	D. B. Heard . . .	.	20 00
Sept.	1.	Boston Safe Deposit & Trust Co.		840 00
	9.	" " .' " "		80 00
	30.	Natick Bank . .	. .	420 00
Oct.	28.	Puritan Trust Co. .	. .	154 00
Dec.	9.	Natick Bank . .	. .	7 50
		" " .	. .	240 62
1900.				
Jan'y	1.	Trustees Loker Fund .	. .	100 00
		" Allen " .	. .	60 00
		" Donation Fund	. .	78 00
		" J. S. Draper Fund	.	60 00
		" Childs Fund	. .	6 00
	24.	Boston Safe Deposit & Trust Co.		220 00

$4,978 24 $4,978 24

SCHOOL HOUSE LOAN.

Mar.	27.	Appropriation . . .	.	..	. $1,100 00
Oct.	28.	Puritan Trust Co.	.	.	.$1,100 00

SALARIES.

Mar.	27.	Appropriation	.	.	.	.	.	.	$1,300	00
		" for overdraft			.	.	.		209	25
		Overdrawn	.	.	.	.	.	.	151	39

Mar.	1.	Overdrawn	.	.	.	$209	25
	8.	P. A. Leary	.	.	.	75	00
		A. F. Parmenter		.	.	50	00
		E. H. Atwood	.	.	.	50	00
		D. P. W. Loker	.	.	.	40	00
		T. L. Sawin	.	.	.	20	00
		W. B. Ward	.	.	.	40	00
		J. H. Carroll	.	.	.	20	00
		C. F. Whittier	.	.	.	20	00
		R T. Lombard	.	.	.	70	00
		Geo. B. Howe	.	.	.	50	00
		C. H Boodey	.	.	.	14	75
		E. W. Marston	.	.	.	61	14
		R. T. Lombard	.	.	.	17	50
		H. F. Lee	.	.	.	200	00
		Edward Carter	.	.	.	12	25
		C. H. May	.	.	.	10	50
April	1.	A. H. Bryant	.	.	.	50	00
		A. W. Lombard		.	.	5	00
		D. W. Mitchell	.	.	.	47	00
		E. E. Butler	.	.	.	30	00
		J. J. Roan	.	.	.	5	00
	29.	A. F. Parmenter		.	.	70	00
		L. Anna Dudley		.	.	50	00
July	29.	Board of assessors	.	.	.	199	50
Sept.	30.	E. H. Atwood	.	.	.	45	00
Oct.	28.	E. A. Carter	.	.	.	25	00
Nov.	25.	A. Parmenter	.	.	.	35	00
Dec.	30.	E. A. Carter, sundry salaries	.			133	75
	1900						
Jan'y	27.	C. S. Williams	.	.	.	5	00
						$1,660 64	$1,660 64

ILLEGAL SALE OF INTOXICATING LIQUORS.

Mar.	1.	Unexpended balance		$30 34
Apr.	1.	L. H. Wakefield . . .	$15 00	
June	24.	J. W. Jennison	2 00	
		Transferred to contingent account	13 34	
			$30 34	$30 34

STATE TAX.

July	29.	State tax		$900 00
		" " special		330 52
Dec.	9.	State treasurer	$900 00	
		" "	330 52	
			$1,230 52	$1,230 52

COUNTY TAX.

July	29.	County tax	$1,626 24
		J. O. Hayden, treasurer . . $1,626 24	

TEMPORARY LOAN.

Mar.	1.	Notes unpaid		$27,000 00
May	7.	Natick National bank		4,000 00
	27.	City bank		4,000 00
	28.	" "		6,000 00
July	31.	Natick National bank . . .		3,000 00
May		" " " . .	$10,000 00	
Oct.	28.	" " " . . .	3,000 00	
Nov.	25.	Shawmut " " . . .	6,000 00	
Dec.	9.	Natick " " . . .	3,000 00	
		" " . . .	2,000 00	
Feb.	28.	Notes unpaid	20,000 00	
			$44,000 00	$44,000 00

WATER COMMISSIONERS' ACCOUNT.

Mar.	27.	Due Water commissioners		$305 97
		Transferred from hydrants . . .		384 00
Feb.	28.	W. M. Fullick		1,886 25
		Overdrawn		640 00

		Transferred to interest account .	$640 00	
Mar.	27.	W. M. Fullick	305 97	
1900.				
Feb.	28.	W. M. Fullick	2,270 25	
			$3,216 22	$3,216 22

CONTINGENT ACCOUNT.

Mar.	27.	Appropriation for overdraft . . .		$304 29
		Estabrook & Co.		121 33
April	11.	E. W. Lamoine		2 00
	18.	State treasurer		198 41
		J. E. Linnehan		16 50
May	24.	John F. Foley		1,300 00
		W. B. Ward		164 59
June	26.	Court fines		4 50
July	21.	State treasurer		25 00
	29.	Geo F. Keep		5 00
	31.	Sam'l Russell		1 00
Sept.	30.	J. E. Linnehan		10 00
Oct.	2.	Court fines		23 21
	7.	Pool license		2 00
		Metropolitan water tax		30 00
	28.	J. E. Linnehan		8 00
Dec.	9.	State treasurer		2,121 97
		" "		704 06
		" "		72 00
		. . . . . .		1,116 00
		. . . . . .		20 00
1900.				
Jan'y	2.	Court fines		28 73
		J. E. Linnehan		7 50

Feb'y 13.	L. K. Lovell	$16 25
	Overlayings	560 52
	Additional assessments	23 40
	" "	197 00
	" "	7 20
	Transferred from illegal sale of liquor	13 34
	C. E. Richardson, interest on taxes	501 22
	G. B. Howe	19 11
Mar. 27.	Overdrawn	$304 29
	Transferred to interest account	3,000 00
April 1.	Mrs. Coakley	4 00
	Dennis Mullen	12 50
	J. B. Brigham	6 00
	C. H. May	18 51
	State aid	1,112 00
	Military aid	298 00
	W. G. Webster	20 00
29.	C. H. May	33 22
	" "	21 98
	Needy soldiers	20 00
May 27.	" "	10 00
	" "	4 00
		10 00
	" "	6 00
June 24.	M. C. Baldwin	243 40
	A. F. Parmenter	13 50
	State treasurer	325 00
July 29.	M. C. Baldwin	141 75
	W. G. Webster	20 00
	A. F. Parmenter	14 00
	Spanish war aid	10 00
Aug. 26.	E. H. Atwood	16 50
	Transferred to highways	198 41
Sept. 30.	Needy soldiers	93 85
Oct. 28.	" "	22 00
Nov. 25.	" "	46 00

Dec. 30. M. C. Baldwin $26 00
A. F. Parmenter, needy soldiers 26 31
1900.
Jan'y 27. " " 54 55
Feb'y 24. E. H. Atwood, " " 74 50
Balance unexpended . . . 1,427 86

$7,624 13 $7,624 13

LIBRARY FUND.

Mar. 1. Deposited N. E. Trust Co. . . . $28,000 00
Feb. 28. Interest 630 25

June 24. F. W. Chandler $150 00
July 13. Cabot, Everett & Meade . . 600 00
Sept. 30. Fales & Co. 1,000 00
Oct. 21. " " 700 00
Nov. 10. " " 1,955 00
Dec. 12. " 4,728 00
1900.
Jan. 9. Fales & Co. 2,377 00
24. " " 1,000 00
Feb. 9. Cabot, Everett & Meade . . 250 00
Balance unexpended . . . 15,870 00

$28,630 25 $28,630 25

REPAIRS ON ENGINE HOUSE.

Mar. 27. Appropriation . . -. . . . $100 00

E. W. Marston $100 00

NEW SCHOOL HOUSE, COCHITUATE.

Mar. 27. Appropriation $1,000 00

Unexpended balance . . . $1,000 00

FINISHING ROOM IN HIGH SCHOOL HOUSE.

Mar.	27.	Appropriation		$1,150 00
Oct.	28.	J. E. Warren	$300 00	
Nov.	1.	" "	69 76	
	7.	Wm. Lamb & Co. . . .	485 00	
		Paine Furniture Co. . . .	21 00	
		S. Homer Woodbridge . . .	20 90	
Feb.	28.	Francis Shaw	253 34	
			$1,150 00	$1,150 00

TOWN BONDS.

Mar.	27.	Estabrook & Co.		$445 00
		Estabrook & Co. . . .	$445 00	

SINKING FUND.

Mar.	27.	Estabrook & Co.		$2,691 20
		Balance	$2,691 20	

PARSONS FUND.

April 13.	. . . .		$200 00
	Balance	$200 00	

TAXES, 1895.

Mar.	1.	Balance due from collector .	$172 71	
Feb'y 28.		C. F. Richardson		$55 86
		Balance due		116 85
			$172 71	$172 71

TAXES, 1896·

Mar.	1.	Balance due from collector	. $2,309 16	
	27.	W. B. Ward, collector		$126 06
May	9.	" " "		130 97
July	10.	" " "		100 00
Aug.	3.	" " "		199 01
	19.	" " "		135 09
Feb'y	13.	C. F. Richardson		350 00
	28.	" "		34 81
		Balance due		1,233 22

$2,309 16 $2,309 16

TAXES, 1897.

Mar.	1.	Balance due from collector	. $7,168 28	
	27.	W. B. Ward, collector		$300 14
Apr.	18.	" " "		142 31
May	9.	" " "		229 29
	24.	" " "		100 58
June	24.	" " "		131 96
July	3.	" " " ·		132 12
	28.	" " ··		210 50
Aug.	3.	" "		174 55
		. . . . .		142 53
	26.	" " "		125 00
Sept.	26.	" " "		183 68
		" " "		120 00
	29.	" " "		193 00
Nov.	11.	C. F. Richardson, collector . . .		400 00
Dec.	9.	" " " . . .		400 00
1900.				
Jan.	30.	C. F. Richardson, collector . . .		253 72
Feb.	28.	" " "		14 49
		Abatement		44 80
		Estate W. B. Ward		267 80
		Balance due		3,602 81

$7,168 28 $7,168 28

TAXES, 1898.

Mar.	1.	Balance due from collector				$12,886 58	
	25.	W. B. Ward, collector	.	.	.	.	437 11
	27.	" " "	.	.	.	.	200 00
April	18.	" " "	.	.	.	.	116 53
	4.	" ", "	.	.	.	.	175 00
May	2.	" "	.	.	.	.	171 64
	9.	" "	.	.	.	.	115 29
	24.	" "	.	.	.	.	108 13
June	5.	" "	.	.	.	.	148 00
	24.	" "	.	.	.	.	252 99
July	3.	" "	.	.	.	.	203 35
	28.	" "	.	.	.	.	680 01
Aug.	3.	" "	.	.	.	.	309 53
	4.	" "	.	.	.	.	304 37
	23.	" "	.	.	.	.	103 33
Sept.	26.	" " "		.	.	.	96 00
Nov.	20.	C. F. Richardson	.	.	.	.	400 00
Dec.	12.	" "	.	.	.	.	1,000 00
Feb'y	24.	" "	.	.	.	.	600 00
	28.	" "	.	.	.	.	16 09
		Abatement	.	.	.	.	49 28
		W. B. Ward estate	.	.	.	.	428 06
		Balance due	.	.	.	.	$6,971 87

$12,886 58 $12,886 58

TAXES, 1899.

July	29.	Tax assessed	.	.	.	$29,519 22
		Overlayings	.	.	.	560 52
		Additional assessments		.	.	23 40
		" "		.	.	204 20
		State and county tax		.	.	2,856 76

Aug.	7.	W. B. Ward, collector			.	.	.	.	$246 00
	9.	"	"	"	.	.	.	.	440 20
	12	"	"	"	.	.	.	.	349 00
	23.	"	"		.	.	.	.	140 20
	26.	"	"		.	.	.	.	169 60
	31.	"	"		.	.	.	.	217 50
Sept.	11	"	"		.	.	.	.	192 88
	18.	"	"	..	.	.	.	.	1,204 70
	19.	"	"		.	.	.	.	919 70
	21.	"	"		.	.	.	.	130 00
	23.	"	"		.	.	.	.	476 50
	25.	"	"		.	.	.	.	226 00
	26.	"	"		.	.	.	.	1,843 80
	27.	"	"		.	.	.	.	270 00
	28.	"	"		.	.	.	.	554 36
	29	"	"		.	.	.	.	355 00
	30.	"	"		.	.	.	.	190 80
Oct.	2.	" _	"		.	.	.	.	1,926 10
					.	.	.	.	412 40
					.	.	.	.	4 00
		"	"	"	.	.	.	.	22 00
Nov.	1.	C. F. Richardson, collector			.	.	.	2,500 00
	4.	"	"	"	.	.	.	1,500 00
	11.	"	"	..	.	.	.	400 00
	25.				.	.	.	400 00
Dec.	12	"	..	..	.	.	.	400 00
					.	.	.	1,000 00
Jan'y	2.	"			.	.	.	1,500 00
	9.				.	.	.	1,500 00
	24.				.	.	.	300 00
Feb'y	28.	"	"		.	.	.	843 28
		Abatement			.	.	.	.	106 00
		W. B. Ward estate			.	.	.	.	233 26
		Balance due			.	.	.	.	12,190 82

$33,164 10 $33,164 10

APPROPRIATIONS.

1899.

Mar.

Schools, care of rooms and fuel	$7,600	00
School supplies	700	00
Transportation of scholars .	2,000	00
Repairs on school buildings .	100	00
Superintendent of schools . .	750	00
High school fittings . . .	200	00
Overdrafts	3,930	22
Highways and bridges . .	3,000	00
Incidentals	1,500	00
Fire department . . .	448	00
Support of poor . . .	2,500	00
Collection of taxes . . .	350	00
Abatement of taxes . . .	300	00
Hydrants	384	00
Lakeview cemetery . . .	50	00
North and Centre cemeteries .	50	00
Library	500	00
Interest on town debt . .	3,000	00
Electric lights	357	00
Salaries	1,300	00
Decoration day	50	00
Repairs on engine house . .	100	00
New school house, Cochituate .	1,000	00
Finishing and furnishing room high school house . .	1,150	00
School house loan . . .	1,100	00

Apr. 22. Decoration Day 100 00

$32,519 22

OUTSTANDING CLAIMS.

Town bonds, due March	1, 1919, 4%	$42,000	00
Water " " Aug.	1, 1913, "	11,000	00
" " " Oct.	7, 1902 "	4,000	00
" " " July	27, 1903, "	1,000	00

Draper Library Fund. 6%	.	.	.	.	$500 00
Allen " "	.	.	.	.	1,000 00
Childs " "	.	.	.	.	100 00
Donation "	.	.	.	.	1,300 00
Loker " 5%	.	.	.	.	2,000 00
James S Draper " 6%	.	.	.	.	500 00

School house loan, $1,100, payable Nov. 1,
    each year, until paid in full .   .   . 7,700 00

                                         ———— $71,100 00

Auditor's Report.

HENRY F. LEE,

In account with the TOWN OF WAYLAND.

TOTAL RECEIPTS.			TOTAL EXPENDITURES.		
Mar. 1, 1899.					
Cash balance .	.	$2,573 02	Schools . .	.	$8,016 88
W. G. Roby fund	.	28,000 00	School supplies	.	707 50
Estabrook & Co.	.	47,312 53	" transportation		1,693 00
Overseers of Poor	.	1,393 53	" repairs .	.	75 92
W. B. Ward, interest		164 59	" supt.	.	750 00
Pool licenses .	.	4 00	Highways	.	3,254 07
Parsons fund .	.	200 00	Incidentals	.	2,063 82
Street R. R. tax	.	198 41	Fire department	.	448 00
Rent of hall .	.	42 00	Coll. taxes	.	75 00
Temporary loans	.	17,000 00	Lakeview cemetery .		43 35
License .	.	1,300 00	N. & C. "	.	50 41
Court fines	.	56 44	Cemetery account	.	74 06
State treas.	.	944 38	Library . .	.	610 29
" " cor. tax .		2,121 97	Decoration day	:	143 82
" " bank tax		704 06	Poor account .	.	4,061 68
Military aid	.	72 00	Abatement (order)		12 32
State aid	.	1,136 00	Electric lights	.	280 20
Street R. R.	.	209 53	Interest . .	.	3,802 31
A. S. Morse .	.	1 00	School house loan .		1,100 00
Donation fund	.	12 00	Salaries . .	.	1,451 39
G. F. Keep .	.	5 00	Illegal sale of liquor		17 00

S Russell	. .	$1 00	State tax . .	$1,230 52
Met. water tax	.	30 00	County tax . .	1,626 24
Excise tax	. .	174 60	Temporary loans .	24,000 00
County treasurer	.	220 58	Water com. orders .	2,576 22
L. K. Lovell	. .	16 25	Contingent . .	2.693 57
E. C. Davis	. .	22 62	Library fund .	12,760 00
Int. on taxes, C.F.R.		501 22	Engine house . .	100 00
Water Rates	. .	1,886 25	High school . .	1,150 00
G. B. Howe	. .	19 11	Town bonds . .	44,500 00
Int on library fund		630 25	Cash balance . .	18,966 95
Taxes	. .	31,382 18		
		$138,334 52		**$138,334 52**

TRIAL BALANCE.

March 1, 1900.

Unexpended balances :

Cash . . .	$18,966 95	Schools . .	$903 53
Due from collector .	24,114 57	Trans scholars .	401 98
Overdrafts :		School repairs .	38 17
School supplies .	7 50	Fitting high school	249 72
Incidentals .	563 82	Overdrafts . .	168 87
Salaries . .	151 39	Highways . .	328 47
Interest account .	162 31	Fire department .	448 00
Water commis'rs	640 00	Collection taxes .	275 00
		Lakeview ceme'ry	9 77
		Cemetery acct .	147 51
		Decoration day .	13 80
		Poor account .	252 07
		Abatements .	83 60
		Electric lights .	96 74
		Contingent acct .	1,427 86
		Library fund .	15,870 25
		New school house	1,000 00
		Sinking fund .	2,691 20
		Parsons fund .	200 00
		Temporary loans .	20,000 00
	$44,606 54		**$44,606 54**

A. H. BRYANT, *Auditor.*

INDEX.

OFFICIAL REPORTS

OF THE

Town of Wayland

FOR ITS

One Hundred and Twenty-first Municipal Year

FROM

MARCH 1, 1900, TO MARCH 1, 1901

CAMBRIDGE, MASS.
PRINTED BY J. FRANK FACEY
1901

TOWN OFFICERS AND COMMITTEES.

Term Expires

ASSESSORS.

EDWARD CARTER, Chairman	1901
NATHANIEL R. GERALD	1902
MARCUS M. FISKE	1903

WATER COMMISSIONERS.

WILLIAM M. FULLICK	1903
CHARLES H. BOODEY	1901
HENRY G. DUDLEY	1902

TRUSTEES PUBLIC LIBRARY.

CHESTER B. WILLIAMS	1901
ARTHUR G. BENNETT	1901
FRANCIS SHAW	1902
HARRY E. CARSON	1902
JOHN CONNELLY	1903
ALFRED C. BRYANT	1903

CONSTABLES.

MARSHALL C. BALDWIN	1901
WILLIAM C. NEAL	1901
COLON C. WARD	1901
CYRUS W. HEIZER	1901
LAWRENCE H. McMANUS	1901
ANDREW S. MORSE	1901
ERNEST F. LAWRENCE	1901

TRUSTEES ALLEN FUNDS.

ISAAC DAMON	1901
CHARLES H. BOODEY	1901
JAMES A. DRAPER	1901

FENCE VIEWERS.

ALBION F. PARMENTER	1901
ISAAC DAMON	1901
EDWARD CARTER	1901

FIELD DRIVER.

Vacancy

CYRUS A. ROAK 1901

SEALER OF WEIGHTS AND MEASURES.

DANIEL W. RICKER 1901

MEASURERS OF WOOD AND BARK.

GEORGE B. HOWE 1901
EDWARD CARTER 1901
WILLIAM S. LOVELL 1901

SURVEYOR OF LUMBER.

JAMES H. LEE 1901

SUPERINTENDENTS OF CEMETERIES.

ANDREW S. MORSE 1901
RANDALL W. PORTER 1901

FINANCE COMMITTEE.

Chairman of SELECTMEN 1901
    "   ASSESSORS 1901
    "   OVERSEERS OF POOR 1901
    "   SCHOOL COMMITTEE 1901
    "   WATER COMMISSIONERS . . . 1901
    "   SINKING FUND COMMISSIONERS . 1901
    "   TRUSTEES PUBLIC LIBRARY . . 1901
          TREASURER 1901
          SURVEYOR OF HIGHWAYS . . . 1901

MEMORIAL DAY COMMITTEE.

ELBRIDGE A. CARTER   CHARLES H. THING
CHARLES H. MAY

TREE WARDEN.

FRANCIS SHAW 1901

Term Expires

ENGINEERS OF FIRE DEPARTMENT.

EDWIN W. MARSTON	1901
ARTHUR J. RICKER	1901
WILLIAM L. KING	1901

SURVEYOR OF HIGHWAYS.

WILLIAM C. NEAL	1901

REGISTRARS OF VOTERS.

THEODORE L. SAWIN, Chairman . . . :	1903
JAMES H. CARROLL	1901
FRANK HAYNES	1902
DANIEL BRACKETT	1901

SINKING FUND COMMISSIONERS.

EDWIN W. MARSTON	1903
HENRY D. PARMENTER	1901
CHESTER B. WILLIAMS	1902

BOARD OF HEALTH.

CYRUS W. HEIZER	1903
PHILIP S. IDE, M. D.	1902
ALFRED A. CARTER	1901

SPECIAL POLICE (Without Pay).

MICHAEL W. HYNES
WILLIAM L. KING
CHARLES M. MAGORTY
PATRICK J. BEATTY
ALONZO S. CARSON

SCHOOL-HOUSE BUILDING COMMITTEE (Cochituate).

WILLIAM M. FULLICK	CHARLES W. DEAN
LLEWELLYN FLANDERS	EDWIN W. MARSTON
RICHARD T. LOMBARD	

LIBRARY BUILDING COMMITTEE.

WILLIARD A. BULLARD EDWIN W. MARSTON
ALFRED W. CUTTING CHESTER B. WILLIAMS
CHARLES F. RICHARDSON

STOCKING PONDS.

HENRY G. DUDLEY

ANNUAL TOWN MEETING, MARCH 25, 1901.

WARRANT.

COMMONWEALTH OF MASSACHUSETTS.

MIDDLESEX, SS.

To either of the Constables of the Town of Wayland, in said County,
Greeting :

In the name of the Commonwealth of Massachusetts, you are commanded to notify and warn the qualified voters of said Town of Wayland, to meet at the Town Hall in said Wayland, on Monday, March 25th, 1901, at 6.30 o'clock in the forenoon then and there to act on the following articles, viz :

ARTICLE I. To choose by ballot a Moderator to preside in said meeting.

ART. 2. To choose a Town Clerk, Treasurer, Collector, Auditor, three Selectmen, Treasurer of the Library Funds, Highway Surveyor and seven Constables, all for one year. One School Committee, one Sinking Fund Commissioner, one Assessor, one Water Commissioner, one Overseer of Poor, and two Trustees of the Public Library, all for three years. Also to answer the following question, "Shall licenses for the sale of intoxicating liquors be granted in the Town of Wayland for the year ensuing?"

All names of candidates for the offices aforesaid and the said question must appear upon the official ballot, and be voted for in accordance with Chapter 548 of the Acts of 1898. For the purposes specified in this article the polls will be open immediately after the election of a moderator and will remain open continuously till 1.30 o'clock P. M. when they may be closed.

ART. 3. To choose all other necessary Town Officers, Agents and Committees, and hear reports of Town Officers, Trustees, Agents and Committees, and act thereon.

ART. 4. To see how much money the town will grant for paying interest, existing debts, for roads and bridges, for support of poor, for support of schools, school supplies and repairs on school buildings, and transportation of scholars, for the fire department, for abatement of taxes, and for other necessary town purposes and order the same to be assessed, or do or act.

ART. 5. To authorize the Selectmen to consult counsel on important town cases.

ART. 6. To see if the town will accept the list of jurors as prepared by the Selectmen.

ART. 7. To appropriate the money refunded by the County Treasurer for dog licenses.

ART. 8. To see if the town will authorize the Treasurer, with the approval of a majority of the Selectmen, to borrow money temporarily in anticipation of taxes of the municipal year 1901 and 1902, and if so how much, or do or act.

ART. 9. To see if the town will drain the Concord road in front of the residence of Frederick H. Fowler, by a culvert with proper outlet, at a cost not exceeding $75, the money to be drawn from the appropriation for highways and bridges, or do or act.

ART. 10. To see if the town will appropriate a sum of money to paint the Town Hall, place wires therein for electric lighting, and to renovate the room formerly used by the Public Library, or do or act.

ART. 11. To appropriate the money received, known as the Parsons' Fund, and fix the rate of interest to be paid thereon.

ART. 12. To see if the town will order the names of candidates for Board of Health and for Tree Warden, to be hereafter placed on the official ballot.

ART. 13. To see if the town will extend the electric lights to Fiske's corner on Main street, and Simpson's corner on Plain.

ART. 14. To see if the town will vote to build a school-house in Cochituate, the cost of same including land, not to exceed $25,000, or do or act.

ART. 15. To see if the town will vote to sell the land in Cochituate occupied for school purposes, and buildings thereon and authorize the Treasurer to sign deeds for the same, or do or act.

ART 16. To see what action the town will take in reference to the sum of $1,000 appropriated March 27, 1899, for school building in Cochituate.

ART. 17. To see what action the town will take in reference to the preservation of town records and original papers, or do or act.

ART. 18. To see if the town will direct the auditor to examine the books of the Town Treasurer and Collector of Taxes once each month, and on or before the 20th day of March in each year notify each person or corporation whose tax appears unpaid of that fact, or do or act.

And you are required to serve this warrant by posting attached copies hereof at the Town Hall, and at each of the Post Offices in said town, seven days at least before the time appointed for holding said meeting.

Hereof fail not, and make due return of this warrant, with your doings thereon, to the Town Clerk, on or before March 23rd, 1901.

Given under our hands this ninth day of March in the year of our Lord one thousand nine hundred and one.

ELIJAH H. ATWOOD,
ELBRIDGE A. CARTER,
N. C. GRIFFIN.

LIST OF JURORS

AS PREPARED BY THE SELECTMEN FOR THE YEAR 1901.

Fred P. Draper.
Jeremiah Lyons.
Arthur T. Felch.
John E. Linnehan.
James I. Bryden.
Frank Lupien.
Samuel S. Davidson.
Edward B. Smith.
Josiah W. Parmenter.
Harry H. Rutter.
Marcus M. Fiske.
Marshall C. Baldwin.
Allan B. Sherman.

Napoleon Paradeau.
Alfred A. Carter.
George B. Howe.
Charles H. Fiske.
Edwin W. Marston.
Henry F. Imminck
Patrick Nolan.
Michael W. Hynes.
Cyrus A. Roak.
Roscoe C. Dean.
Elijah H. Atwood.
Clarence S. Williams.
James H. Lee.

> ELIJAH H. ATWOOD,
> ELBRIDGE A. CARTER,
> N. C. GRIFFIN,
> *Selectmen of Wayland.*

March 4, 1901.

REPORT OF SELECTMEN.

WAYLAND, February 28, 1901.

We have made the following appointments as required by statute :

Engineers of Fire Department. Edwin W. Marston, Arthur J. Ricker, Frank E. Yeager. December 3, Mr. Yeager resigned and William L. King was appointed.

Undertakers. Andrew S. Morse, D. W. P. Loker.

Inspector of Animals. Thomas Bryant, V. S., resigned October 1, and Marshall C. Baldwin appointed.

Registrars of Voters. Theodore L. Sawin, 3 years. Frank Haynes vice Chales F. Whittier, resigned.

Auctioneers. George E. Sherman, Jacob Reeves.

Public Weighers. George B. Howe, Alfred W. Lombard, Lorenzo K. Lovell.

Special Police (to serve without pay). Frank E. Bailey, (resigned August 6.) Charles W. Ellms, Michael W. Hynes, and on petition of Metropolitan Water Commissioners, Patrick J. Beatty and Alonzo S. Carson were appointed special officers, without pay.

Fish and Game Warden. John J. Erwin.

Burial Agent for Indigent Soldiers. Charles H. May.

Election Officers. Precinct 1. Warden, Michael W, Hynes; Clerk, William H. Campbell; Inspectors, William Stearns, Herbert F. Haynes; Edward F. Lee, Howard W. Parmenter. *Precinct* 2. Warden, Williard C. Hunting; Clerk, Ernest E. Butler; Inspectors, Patrick A. Gorman, Nathaniel R. Gerald, Leonard A. Loker, Roscoe C. Dean.

Janitor. Joseph C. Vincent.

We granted two liquor licenses of the sixth class, (druggist).

Also two licenses to keep billiard and pool tables, and one inn-holder's license.

Permission was granted to the New England Telephone and Telegraph Company to extend its lines along Pond street from Natick line to Main street. And permission was also given the Weston Electric Company to extend its lines from Bigelow's corner to Tower Hill.

We petitioned the county commissioners to re-locate the high-way over Baldwin's bridge and for assistance from the county in building a new bridge. The petition was granted and the county assumes two-thirds of the cost, provided the whole cost does not exceed $3,000. Bridge is to be completed on or before July 1, 1901.

The Massachusetts Highway Commission allotted $13,000 to this town, and it has been expended under the direction of the Commission on the Boston and South Sudbury roads. A further small allotment next year will enable the contractor to finish the state highway to the Sudbury line.

The suit of Lupien against the town remains undecided.

The lines between this town and Sudbury, Lincoln and Natick were perambulated as by law required.

As authorized, we have made a final settlement with the estate of W. B. Ward on account of his salary as collector and for all taxes collected by him.

We have purchased two sidewalk snow plows at a cost of $130.

The unusually large expenditure on account of salaries was occasioned by the payment of salaries of officers for the year end-ing February 28, 1900, as well as for the present year, it having been the custom heretofore to pay the salaries of the outgoing officers from the appropriation of the succeeding year. The salaries of all town officers are now paid, with the exception of that of the auditor.

> ELIJAH H. ATWOOD,
> ELBRIDGE A. CARTER,
> N. C. GRIFFIN,
> *Selectmen of Wayland.*

REPORT OF TOWN CLERK AND REGISTRAR.

WAYLAND, January 1, 1901.

The following is the annual report of the clerk and registrar for the year ending December 31, 1900 :

BIRTHS.

Whole number registered during the year is forty-six, being eleven more than in 1899.

Males, ...	16
Females	30
Born of native parents	18
Born of foreign parents, ...	10
Born of native and foreign parents . . .	18

MARRIAGES.

Whole number registered during the year is twenty-four, being the same as in 1899.

Native birth of both parties	16
Native and foreign birth	3
Foreign birth of both parties	5
First marriage of both parties	20
Second marriage of both parties	1
First of one and second of the other . . .	3

DEATHS.

Whole number registered during the year is thirty-two, being five more than in 1899.

Married	9
Widowed	14

Single	. . . .	9
Native birth .	. . . .	24
Foreign birth .	. . . .	8
Males	. . . .	14
Females	. . . .	18

Names of persons deceased during the year who were over seventy years of age.

	Years.	Months.	Days.
Phebe A. Jennison. . . .	76	5	20
Ann Moran	86		
Kimball Lovejoy	87	8	21 .
Jerusha C. Cotting. . . .	97	3	19
Sarah A. Puffer	84	11	14
Jefferson Loker	93		25
Lucy A. Giles	78	10	26
William Ward	79	11	
Gilbert Bent.	80		
Hodijah B. Braman . . .	80	4	
Eliza R. R. Drew	71	7	18
Mary Byron	76		
Helene Lupien	85	3	26
Ellen Hynes	70	8	7
Samuel D. Reeves	82	6	21
Adeline Adams	73	7	
George J. Marston . . .	80	10	19

NOSOLOGICAL TABLE

Pneumonia .	. . . .	3
Paralysis .	. . . .	4
Old age .	. . . .	4
Heart disease	. . . .	5
Bronchitis .	. . . .	1
Stricture of intestines .	. . . . .	1
Failure of respiration .	. . . . .	1
Senile Dementia .	. . . . . .	1
Premature birth .	. . . . . .	3

Drowning 1
Inflammation of liver 1
Pernicious anenmia 1
Myocarditis 1
Pythisis 1
Carcimona of kidneys 1
Bright's disease 2
Grippe 1

DOGS.

114 males at $2.00	$228 00
15 females at $5.00	75 00
	$303 00
129 licenses at 20 cents	25 80
Amount net	$277 20

VOTERS.

Number of voters registered November 6, 1900		534
Precinct I.	153	
Precinct II.	381	
Ballots cast precinct I. . . .	129	
Ballots cast in precinct II. . . .	348	
Number of women voters		73
Number of women voting at annual meeting		13

VOTE FOR PRESIDENT.

Bryan	160
Debs	7
Malloney	1
Woolley	2
McKinley	244

VOTE FOR GOVERNOR.

Berry, Socialistic Labor	23
Bradley, Democrat Social	10
Crane, Republican	232
Fisher, Prohibition	4
Paine, Democrat	150

VOTE FOR SENATOR.

Bendroth, S. L.	10
Daley, Democrat	157
Williams, Republican	260
George E. Sherman	1

VOTE FOR REPRESENTATIVES, 21st Middlesex District.

Names of towns.	Brigham.	Hunter.	Plunkett.	Balcolm.	Blanks.
Marlboro . . .	1534	1280	984	1	1241
Sudbury . . .	118	111	42		121
Wayland . . .	230	203	149		372
Totals . .	1882	1594	1175	1	1734

DANIEL BRACKETT,

Town Clerk.

ASSESSORS' REPORT.

At the annual town meeting held March 26, 1900, the following vote was passed, to wit, "That the assessors be authorized to make a general valuation of all the taxable property in the town and publish the same in pamphlet form for distribution to the voters of the town."

In compliance with the said vote we have taken the general valuation and had the same printed and a copy left at each house in town.

We have abated taxes as follows:

Taxes assessed in the year 1895.

. On real estate	$67 70
On polls	8 00
Taxes of 1897.	
Real estate	11 60
Taxes of 1898.	
Real estate	17 60
Taxes of 1899.	
Real estate	30 00
Polls	4 00
Taxes of 1900.	
Real estate	87 47
Personal estate	10 29
Polls	14 00
Total abatement for the year	$250 66

EDWARD CARTER,
NATHANIEL R. GERALD,
MARCUS M. FISKE,
Assessors.

WAYLAND, February 28, 1901.

REPORT OF THE OVERSEERS OF THE POOR

FOR THE YEAR ENDING FEBRUARY 28, 1901.

The Almshouse has been in charge of Norman W. Saunders, and he has given general satisfaction.

OUT-DOOR POOR, PARTIAL SUPPORT.

Families aided	12	
Persons	61	
		73

IN-DOOR POOR, FULL SUPPORT.

Almshouse	2	
State Insane Hospitals . . . ·	4	
		6
		79

FINANCIAL STATEMENT.

March 1, 1900. Unexpended balance . .	$252 07	
March 26, 1900. Appropriation . .	2,500 00	
April 2, 1900. Received from State . .		
Treasurer ·	12 00	
November 3, 1900. Received from . .		
Town of Southboro	84 10	
November 3, 1900. Received from . .		
Town of Lexington	52 00	
		$2,900 17

ALMSHOUSE RECEIPTS.

Sale of milk	$217 63	
Cows	263 00	

Pork	37 61	
Poultry and eggs	57 22	
Produce	26 00	
Received for work	110 32	
Received for wagon	25 00	
Received for wood	5 00	
	——	741 78

$3,641 95

EXPENDITURES, OUT-DOOR POOR.

Having a settlement in Wayland and residing elsewhere.
Malvina C. Benoit and children, Brockton.

Groceries	$81 16	
Fuel	21 85	
Clothing	13 00	
	——	$116 01

Nelson Normandin and family, North Brookfield.

Groceries	$20 55	
	——	$20 55

Mrs. E. Roberts and family, North Brookfield.

Groceries and provisions . .	$81 68	
Coal and wood	15 80	
Shoes	3 55	
Medical aid and medicine . .	11 75	
	——	$112 78

J. Frank Loker and family, Natick.

Groceries	$34 35	
	——	$34 35

Mrs. Emily Sumpter, Hudson.

Board	$64 00	
Medical attendance and medicine .	58 00	
Nurse	10 00	
Burial. Died, August, 1900 . .	15 00	
	——	$147 00

Miss Bessie Stone, Boston.

Hospital	$36 32	
	——	$36 32

Henry Benoit and family, Springfield.

Provisions	$111 18	
Fuel	21 49	
Medical aid and medicine . .	12 20	
	———	$144 87

Adrian Cormier, Boston.

Carney Hospital	$15 00	
	———	$15 00

W. H. Mullin and family, Boston.

Groceries	$3 50	
	———	$3 50

Mrs. Andros C. Anderson, Westminister.

Board	$5 00	
	———	$5 00
		$635 38

Having a settlement in Wayland and residing there.

Ann Painter.

Board	$52 00	
	———	$52 00

George Chalmers.

Board	30 00	
Rent	51 00	
Medical aid and medicine . .	5 25	
	———	$86 25

Joseph Cormier and family.

Moving	$11 57	
Groceries and provisions . .	3 00	
	———	$14 57

Francis Weber.

Board	$18 50	
	———	$18 50

Ralph Smith.

Clothes	$6 75	
	———	$6 75

John Chenett and family.

Groceries	$34 00
Provisions and milk	20 95
Rent	48 00
Coal and wood	17 88
	$120 83

Frank Davieu, Jr., and family.

Groceries	$12 00
Provisions	8 00
Rent	16 00
Clothes	10 33
	$46 33

Mrs. N. Latour and family.

Rent	$19 00
Coal and wood	6 18
Groceries	8 00
	$33 18

Louis Cormier.

Coal and wood	$6 75
Medicine	6 00
	$12 75

John B. McElroy.

Coal and wood	$4 13
	$4 13

	$1,030 67

In Insane Hospitals.

J. A. Wing, Worcester	$169 46	
Ellen Stanton, Taunton	169 46	
Clara Davis, Westboro	169 46	
Hannah Naylor, Westboro	61 29	
		$569 67

	$1,600 34

Having a settlement in other towns and residing in Wayland.

E. Holdwell, Lexington.

Board	$52 00	
		$52 00

J. Hawkins and family, Southboro

Rent						$48 00	
Groceries						80 87	
Coal and wood						34 33	
Medical aid and medicine						27 55	
							$190 75

Charles H. Morse and family, Southboro.

Rent						$8 00	
Groceries						4 50	
Provisions						4 50	
							$17 00

$1,860 09

ALMSHOUSE EXPENDITURES.

Paid Warden's salary	$400 00	
Paid provisions	166 19	
Paid groceries	194 42	
Paid grain	273 39	
Paid fish	20 74	
Paid work	28 00	
Paid wagon	12 50	
Paid pigs	4 00	
Paid ice	8 46	
Paid pump	22 63	
Paid medical aid	4 00	
Paid miscellaneous	4 00	
Paid auctioneer	6 50	
Paid pasturing	5 00	
Paid lumber	9 36	
Paid clothing	21 15	
Paid blacksmithing	13 40	
Paid hardware	13 12	
Paid seeds	5 17	
		$1,212 53

Traveling expenses, settlement of cases,
    stationery and postage stamps .   . $41 02
                                      ———— $41 02

                                            $3,113 64

Unexpended balance, February 28, 1901 $528 31

                                            $3,641 95

OUTSTANDING CLAIMS.

City of Brockton, Bill not rendered.
City of Springfield, Bill not rendered.
Commonwealth of Massachusetts, unsettled case.

REIMBURSEMENTS DUE.

Town of Lexington $52 00
Town of Southboro 145 40
                                   ———— $197 40

INMATES AT ALMSHOUSE DURING YEAR.

James Burk, March 1, 1900, age 84 years.
Francis J. Weber, July 18, 1900, age 59 years.

Tramps lodged   292
Meals furnished   145

INVENTORY OF PROPERTY AT ALMSHOUSE.

Real estate $2,500 00
Two horses $200 00
One cow 50 00
One calf 10 00
Four pigs 30 00
Seventy-five hens 37 50
Mowing machine 25 00
Double harness 25 00
Single harness .   .   .   10 00
Three ploughs .   .   .   15 00

Harrow	. . . . . .	1 00
Wheel harrow	. . . . .	5 00
Hay wagon	. . . . . .	30 00
Light wagon	. . . . . .	15 00
Sled	. . . .	15 00
Hay rake	. . . . . .	10 00
Horse cart	. . . . . .	10 00
Manure	. . . . . .	30 00
Two tons hay	. . . . .	40 00
Oat fodder	. . . . . .	10 00
Sleigh	. . . . . .	30 00
Potatoes	. . . . . .	10 00
Hay cutter	. . . . . .	3 00
Wood	. . . .	60 00
Milk cooler	. . . . . .	3 00
Tools	. . . .	33 75

$708 25

Furniture and utensils in house . . $166 90

$3,375 15

An appropriation of $2000 is asked for the ensuing year.

Respectfully submitted,

DAVID P. W. LOKER, *Chairman,*
DANIEL W. RICKER, *Clerk,*
THEODORE S. SHERMAN.

REPORT OF TRUSTEES OF PUBLIC LIBRARY.

The two important events of the last year in the history of the library were the fifteenth anniversary of the opening of the library, which occurred August 7, and moving into the new library building in November.

We now have a beautiful library home, artistic, modern, and up-to-date in all its appointments, thanks for which are due not only to the munificence of the late Warren G. Roby, but also to the efficient and tireless work of the building committee.

When the time came for moving, the Trustees went before the town at a special meeting, asking for an extra appropriation of $300. This was cheerfully given, and under the direction of one of the trustees the moving was accomplished at the minimum of expense.

The books, as a whole, are in good condition, although many of the standard sets are sadly in need of replacing. Owing to the shortness of funds during the past, we found ourselves completely out-of-date, few books having been purchased of late years. This we have been somewhat enabled to remedy by the purchases just made, and as far as current literature is concerned we are in better shape. We are still woefully in need of up-to-date books of reference, and those books which are needed by the scholars of the public schools, as well as others of our townspeople, who desire to pursue special lines of research and study, and books which they have a right to expect to find in the library. We are endeavoring to get into closer touch with the schools. With the cordial assistance that we are now receiving from the superintendent and teachers we are accomplishing much. One of the first steps taken in the new building was to procure a file of magazines for the reading room, and this now seems to be the most attractive feature of the library to many.

A need of the most urgent nature is a classification of the library, bringing it up to the modern ideas and thus fully doubling its usefulness.

The interest taken and the increased circulation since the first of January are noticed with gratification by the Trustees, and the many calls for more open hours at the library we hope to meet within a few weeks.

The rules and regulations appended we have adopted after careful consideration.

Herewith is also the Librarian's report containing statistical information, also a catalogue of the last year's accessions. The Treasurer of Library Fund's report shows an unexpended balance, which is somewhat misleading from the fact that necessary expenses consequent upon moving have been voted, bills for which have not been presented.

In recommending the appropriation of $800 for next year we have taken into consideration the desire of the town to keep the tax-rate down as low as possible, and have asked only for that which is absolutely necessary.

Respectfully submitted,

JOHN CONNELLY, *Chairman*,
ARTHUR G. BENNETT, *Clerk*,
CHESTER B. WILLIAMS,
HARRY E. CARSON,
FRANCIS SHAW,
A. S. BRYANT.

BY-LAWS AND REGULATIONS OF PUBLIC LIBRARY.

ARTICLE I.

The library shall be known as the Wayland Town Library, and shall be kept undivided, in some suitable room or building in the central village of Wayland.

ARTICLE II.

There shall be a board of six trustees, two of whom shall be elected by ballot annually at the annual town meeting, to hold office for three years thereafter, or until a successor or successors shall be chosen.

ARTICLE III.

At the first regular meeting of the board in April its officers shall be elected and shall continue in office until their successors are appointed.

ARTICLE IV.

A majority of the board shall constitute a quorum for transaction of business.

ARTICLE V.

The Board of Trustees shall hold a regular monthly meeting, except during the months of July and August, the date of such meeting to be determined by the board at its annual meeting in April.

ARTICLE VI.

The Board of Trustees shall select and purchase books for the library; shall appoint a Librarian with such other agents as may be necessary, and fix their salaries; provide catalogues; exercise a general control of the library; order all necessary repairs and alterations of the building and its appurtenances; make a special examination of the books during the week ending with the last Saturday in October.

ARTICLE VII.

The Librarian shall keep the books and appurtenances of the library in proper order. He shall record in a record, called " Catalogue of Accessions," the title of each book placed therein, with the date of its purchase, and also the title of all books or other property given to the library with the donor's name and date of presentation. He shall prepare such catalogues, books and forms as the Trustees may direct. He shall report to the Trustees all gifts of funds to the library and shall, if accepted by the board, send an acknowledgement of the same to the givers. He shall keep a record of all such books as are asked for, and are not in the library, with the names of the persons asking for them, and submit the record to the Trustees. He shall cause a book plate to be attached to each volume belonging to the library, and shall note on it the date of the receipt of the book; if a gift, the name of the giver; and the number it bears in the Catalogue of Accessions. He shall permit no book to be used until it shall be properly prepared for entry in the catalogues. He shall charge to each borrower the books delivered, with the dates of their delivery and of their return. He shall, on the first day of February in each year, present to the Board of Trustees a detailed report of the condition and the circulation of the library, including an alphabetical list of the previous year's accessions, with catalogue numbers, to be printed in annual town report, together with such other facts and suggestions as he may deem of importance. He shall perform such other duties as may be required of him by the Trustees.

ARTICLE VIII.

No book, pamphlet, work of art or other property whatsoever, offered by any person to the library shall be accepted and placed therein except by express vote of the board. A notice of acceptance shall then be sent to the giver with suitable acknowledgement.

ARTICLE IX.

All duplicate books, pamphlets and articles belonging to the library may be exchanged at any time at the discretion of the Board of Trustees.

ARTICLE X.

The library shall be open for delivery and return of books every Wednesday and Saturday (except legal holidays) from 3 to 5 and 6.30 to 9 P. M., provided, however, that no books shall be delivered during the week ending with the last Saturday in October; and provided further that the library may be closed by order of the Board of Trustees when deemed necessary for any special purpose.

ARTICLE XI.

Any resident (in town) twelve years old and over may take from the library not exceeding two books at one time; and children under that age may take one book each; the parents or guardians of minors being responsible for their wards or children. Minors and strangers may use the library on the same conditions as residents, provided they furnish satisfactory reference or deposit with the Librarian the value of the book desired.

ARTICLE XII.

The library card of the person wishing for books, with the shelf number of the books wanted written thereon, must be presented to the Librarian as the only method of obtaining books.

Note. — Cards to be furnished by the Librarian at one cent each.

ARTICLE XIII.

Borrowers may take two books at the same time. No books shall be kept out more than four weeks, except by the permission of the Trustees; and the Trustees may limit the time during which any book may be kept one week. "New books" cannot be renewed, and all others can be renewed but once.

ARTICLE XIV.

" New books " kept from the library more than one week, and all others kept more than four weeks at a time, will subject the borrower to a fine of six cents per week per volume for each week's delay in returning.

N. B. Books are considered "new" until one year after the date of their purchase or presentation. The date of their purchase or presentation will be found on the book plate inside the cover of each book.

ARTICLE XV.

All books must be returned to the library on or before the last Saturday but one in October. Subject to a fine of twenty-five cents per volume.

ARTICLE XVI.

Books kept from the library more than three months shall be deemed lost, and must be replaced by other copies, or paid for by the borrower.

ARTICLE XVII.

All penalties named under these articles and also those incurred under the State laws (see below) if remaining unpaid more than four weeks will forfeit the library privileges to the defaulter until settlement is made.

ARTICLE XVIII.

Teachers of the public schools may take from the library at one time not exceeding ten books, for school use and may hold same not over four weeks subject to recall by Librarian after two weeks, and same fines as regular takers after four weeks. Any person pursuing a special study may, by obtaining a signed permission of two Trustees take out not exceeding ten books for a period of two weeks.

ARTICLE XIX.

Books of reference and those deemed unsuitable for general circulation shall not be taken out of the library except by an order signed by at least two Trustees.

ARTICLE XX.

Persons may always receive books for reading, consultation or study in either the reading or waiting room, by making written application on special slips furnished at the library desk. All such books must be returned to the desk before the borrower leaves the library. Books, magazines and papers belonging to the reading room may be used in the building but cannot be taken out.

ARTICLE XXI.

All persons visiting the library building will be required to conduct themselves quietly and avoid all unnecessary conversation. Any person abusing the privilege of the library by improper or offensive conduct may be denied admission to the building for such period as the Trustees may determine.

ARTICLE XXII.

The Trustees from time to time may make any new or special permanent or temporary regulation for the management and preservation of the library, and for penalties for injury thereto, or the books therein, or for violation of the regulations which they may deem expedient, provided that such regulations do not conflict with those adopted by the town.

ACTS AND RESOLVES, MASSACHUSETTS, 1883.

CHAPTER 81, SECTION 1.

"SECTION 1. Whoever wilfully and maliciously or wantonly and without cause writes upon, injures, defaces, tears or destroys a book, plate, picture, engraving, map, newspaper, magazine, pamphlet, manuscript, or statue belonging to a law, town, city or other public or incorporated library, shall be punished by a fine of not less than $5.00 nor more than $50, or by imprisonment in the jail not exceeding six months."

ACTS AND RESOLVES, MASSACHUSETTS, 1883.
CHAPTER 77, SECTION 1.

"SECTION 1. Whoever wilfuly and maliciously or wantonly and without cause detains any book, newspaper, magazine, pamphlet or manuscript belonging to a law, town, city or other public incorporated library for thirty days after notice in writing, from the librarian of such library, given after the expiration of the time which by the regulations of such library such book, newspaper, magazine, pamphlet, or manuscript may be kept, shall be punished by a fine of not less than $1 nor more than $25, or by imprisonment in the jail not exceeding six months."

LIBRARIAN'S REPORT.

To the Board of Trustees :

The statistical information for the year 1900-1901 is respectfully submitted.

ACCESSIONS.

	Books.	Pamphlets
By purchase	217	
By gift	140	
Bound and transferred from pamphlet department	23	
Total	390	
Whole number of volumes in the library . .	13,664	
Pamphlets presented	766	

CIRCULATION.

In Cochituate village	1,457
In Wayland Centre	4,444
Total	5,901

DONORS OF BOOKS AND PAMPHLETS.

Balch, Mr. T. W.	1
Brookline Public Library	4
Campbell, Miss C. H.	2
Cutting, Mrs. Charles A.	93
Cutting, Mr. Charles A.	1
Clement, Mr. Hazen	

	Books.	Pamphlets
Draper, Mr. Wallace		12
Esty, Mr. C. C.		1
Fowler, Mr. F. H.	1	
Free Public Library Commission . . .	1	1
Heard, Misses M. and E.		5
Howe, Mrs. Oscar F.	48	360
Joseph Burnett Co.	1	
Loring, the Misses	56	173
McGlenan, Mr. E. W.	1	
Richardson, Mr. C. F.		14
Salem Public Library		5
Shaw, Mr. Francis	2	
Smith, Mr. Elbridge	1	
State Government	9	6
Stockwell, Mr. J. W.	1	
United States Government	13	27
Underwood, Mr. Herbert	1	
Wilson, Mrs. M. C. C.	1	
Sent to the Reading Room	1	62

Library reports have been received as follows : Arlington, Brookline, Brooklyn, Concord, Fall River, Forbes Library, Northampton, Harvard College and Harvard University, Hyde Park, Lawrence, Institute of Technology, Lawrence, Newton, State Library, Theological Library, Winthrop, also from Young Men's Christian Union, Board of Agents, Bronson Library Fund, Adams Nervine and St. Louis Mercantile.

CLASSES OF READING.

Art	.05	Juvenile . . .	.13
Biography . . .	.05	Poetry . . .	.01
Fiction . . .	.49	Science . . .	.02
History . . .	.24	Travels . . .	.01

SARAH E. HEARD,
Librarian.

February 15, 1901.

BOOKS ADDED SINCE JANUARY, 1900.

6720	Alice of Old Vincennes. Maurice Thompson.
6956	Along French Byways. C. Johnson.
6952	Alps From End to End. W. M. Conway.
6700	Amateur's Garden Book. L. H. Bailey.
6651	American Fights and Fighters. C. T. Brady.
6673	American in Holland, The. William E. Griffis.
6972	Among The Farmyard People. C. D. Pierson.
6940	Among The Forest People. C. D. Pierson.
6659	An American Anthology. Clarence Stedman.
6696	Anglo-Boer Conflict, The. A. Ireland.
6732	Anneke. E. M. Champney.
6769	Ars Et Vita. R. S. Sullivan.
6691	Art of Living, The. Robert Grant.
6751	As Seen By Me. Lilian Bell.
6698	As We Go. Charles Dudley Warner.
6699	As We Were Saying. Charles Dudley Warner.
8225T	Austria. Sydney Whitman.
6704	Autobiography of a Quack. S. Weir Mitchell.
6703	Banker and the Bear, The. H. K. Webster.
6749	Bennett Twins, The. Grace M. Hurd.
6942	Biography of a Grizzly, The. E. S. Thompson.
6937	Bird Homes. A. R. Dugmore.
6971	Black Rock. R. Connor.
6620	Black Wolf's Breed, The. H. Dickson.
6634	Bonaventura. George W. Cable.
6946	Book For All Readers. A. R. Spofford.
6695	Book Lover, The. James Baldwin.
6752	Cardinal's Rose, The. S. Van Tassel.
6725	Cardinal's Snuff Box. H. Harland.
6784	Century Book of the American Colonies. E. S. Brooks.
6785	Century Book of the American Revolution. E. S. Brooks.
6678	Century of Science, A. John Fiske.
6786	Century Book For Young Americans. E. S. Brooks.
6603	Children of The Mist. E. Phillpotts.

6736	Children of the Sherburn House. A. Douglas.
6655	China, The Long Lived Empire. E. R. Skidmore.
6962	China's Only Hope. Chang C. Tung.
6658	Concerning Cats. H. M. Winslow.
6683	Contemporaries. T. W. Higginson.
6963	Crises in China. G. B. Smith and Others.
6648	Crittenden. John Fox.
6618	Dionysius, The Weaver's Heart's Dearest. B. W. Howard.
6763	Divine Comedy, Hell. Charles E. Norton.
6764	Divine Comedy, Purgatory. Charles E. Norton.
6765	Divine Comedy, Paradise. Charles E. Norton.
6629	Dorothy Deane. E. O. Kirk.
6630	Dorothy and Her Friends. E. O. Kirk.
6633	Dorothy Dracot's To-morrow. V. Townsend.
6743	Double Thread, A. E. A. Fowler.
6654	Dr. North and His Friends. S. Weir Mitchell.
6679–80	Dutch Quaker Colonies. John Fiske.
6771	Eastover Court-House, The. B. Boone and K. Brown.
6722	Eben Holden. Irving Bacheller.
6647	Ednah and Her Brothers. E. Orne White.
6950	Educational Reform. Charles W. Elliot.
6935	Eccentricities of Genius. Major J. B. Pond.
6706	Eleanor. Mrs. Humphrey Ward.
6608	Elizabeth and Her German Garden.
6685	European History. Arthur Hassal.
6964	European Travel for Women. M. C. Jones.
6750	Expatriates. Lilian Bell.
6742	Farringdons, The. E. T. Fowler.
6938	Field, Forest and Wayside Flowers. M. Going.
6687	First Book of Birds. O. T. Miller.
6609	Fisherman's Luck. H. Van Dyke.
6776	For Freedom of the Sea. C. T. Brady.
6775	For Love of Country. C. T. Brady.
6714	Friend of Cæsars, A. William Stearns.
6755	From the Land of the Shamrock. J. Barlow.
6756	Gateless Barrier, A. Luces Malet.

6675   Land of the Long Night. P. Da Chaellu.
6708   Lane Which Had No Turning, The. G. Parker.
6668—9 Letters of R. L. Stevenson. S. Colvin.
6973   Letters to the Farm Boy. H. Wallace.
 994   Life Beyond Death. M. J. Savage.
6948   Life of Francis Parkman. C. H. Farnham.
6670   Life and Letters of Lewis Carrol. S. D. Collingwood.
6623   Lion and the Unicorn, The. R. H. Davis.
6945   Literary Friends and Acquaintances. W. D. Howells.
6660   Literary History of America. Barrett Wendell.
6635   Lost Man's Lane, The. A. K. Green.
6628   Loveliness. E. S. Phelps.
6636   Love of Parson Lord, The. M. E. Wilkins.
6746   Maid of Maiden Lane, The. A. Barr.
6622   Main Travelled Roads. H. Garland.
6631   Manifest Destiny, A. J. Magruder.
6712   Mantle of Eliza, The. I. Langwill.
6686   Manual of Mineralogy and Petrography. J. D. Dana.
6624   Man with the Hoe, The. E. Markham.
6616   Market Place, The. H. Frederic.
6710   Master Christian, The. Marie Corelli.
6625   Meg Langholme. Mrs. Molesworth.
6753   Meloon Farm, The. M. L. Pool.
6951   Men Who Made the Nation, The. E. E. Sparks.
6960   Mexican Vistas. H. W. Sherrat.
6947   Modern Reader and Speaker. G. Riddle.
6653   Mooswa and Others of the Boundaries. W. A. Fraser.
6759   Monsieur Beaucaire. B. Tarkington.
6637   Mr. Dooley in the Hearts of His Countrymen.
6640   My Journal in Foreign Lands. J. H. Newell.
6627   Nannie's Happy Childhood. C. L. Field.
6936   Nature's Garden. Mellje Blanchau.
6684   Old Cambridge. T. W. Higginson.
6949   Oliver Cromwell. Theodore Roosevelt.
6757   On the Wings of Occasions. J. C. Harris.
6619   Other Fellow, The. F. H. Smith.

6690	Search Light Letters. R. Grant.
6733	Senator North. G. Atherton.
6777	Shadowings. L. Hearn.
6735	Sherburn Romance, A. A. Douglas.
6773	Simon Dale. A. Hope.
6615	Sir Patrick, the Puddock. L. B. Walford.
6970	Sky Pilot, The. R. Connor.
6745	Soft Slide, The. Henry James.
6715	Solitary Summer, The.
6709	Sophia. Stanley Weyman.
6976	Squirrels and Others. The Bearers. John Burroughs.
6626	Square Pegs. A. D. T. Whitney.
6657	Stage Coach and Tavern Days. A. M. Earle.
6676	Story of Magellan. H. Butterworth.
6652	Story of the Ninteenth Century. E. S. Brooks.
6646	Stories. Polly Pepper Sold the Peppers. M. Sidney.
6766	St. Philips. M. C. Harris.
6747	Stringtown on the Pike. J. W. Lloys.
6607	That Fortune. Charles D. Warner.
6601—2	Their Silver Wedding Journey. W. D. Howells.
6692	Theology of Civilization, The. C. F. Dole.
6606	To Have and To Hold. Mary Johnston.
6711	Tommy and Grizel. J. M. Barrie.
6943	Trail of the Sandhill Stag. E. S. Thompson.
6610	Translations of a Savage. Gilbert Parker.
6730	Uncle Terry. C. C. Mann.
6729	Unleavened Bread. Robert Grant.
6639	Venetian June, A. Annie Fuller.
6605	Via Crusis. F. M. Crawford.
6740	Voice of the People. Ellis Glasgo.
6611	When Knighthood was in Flower. E. Caskoden
6739	Whilomville Stories. Stephen Crane.
6719	Who Goes There? B. R. Benson.
6697	Wireless Telegraphy. Richard Kerr.
6689	Wisdom and Destiny. M. Masterlinck
6663	With Buller in Natal. G. A. Henty.

6614 With Edged Tools. H. S. Merriam.
6738 Wounds in the Rain. Stephen Crane.
6941 Woman Tenderfoot. G. G. and S. Thompson.
6934 Wood Working for Beginners. C. G. Wheeler.
6772 Young April. Egerton Castle.

REPORT OF THE TREASURER OF WAYLAND PUBLIC LIBRARY FUND

FOR THE YEAR ENDING MARCH 1, 1901.

	Dr.
To unexpended Appropriation for the year 1899 . .	$129 75
To Appropriation for the year 1900	500 00
To additional Appropriation	300 00
To Interest on Library Funds	66 00
To one-half Dog Tax Money	131 67
To Fines collected by N. R. Gerald	6 66
	$1,134 08

	Cr.
By Salary of Librarian	$300 00
By Salary of Assistant Librarian	40 00
By American Express Co., carting books . . .	35 72
By Books, Periodicals, etc., ...	284 23
By Book-Binding	25 77
By Fuel	83 08
By Albert B. Franklin, bills for Carbide . . .	17 40
By F. Knight & Son, bill for moving Library . .	33 60
By L. K. Lovell, bill for Sundries	5 74
By J. H. Lee, bill for Sundries	1 75
By Thomas Groom & Co.	2 00
By Stone & Forsyth	3 80
By Janitor's Salary, etc., to March, 1901 . . .	52 75
	$885 84
Balance unexpended	248 24
	$1,134 08

HENRY D. PARMENTER,
Treasurer of Wayland Library Fund.

REPORT OF THE BOARD OF HEALTH.

The Board of Health of the town of Wayland herewith present their report for the year 1900-1901.

This has been the first year when a regularly organized Board of Health has existed, and necessarily there has arisen a countless number of things, some of which have required careful considera- tion. It has been the desire of the board not to interfere, unless it seemed to them necessary, in any matter coming under their control, but in several instances where some measures were needed for protection to the public health, action has been taken. We have received numerous complaints from different sources, princi- pally about cesspools, and in some cases, though notified, the parties at fault have neglected to abate such nuisances.

Of course, during the cold weather the average nuisance would be concealed, but whenever a written complaint, which is required by the board, has been handed in, it has been taken up and con- sidered. We have been fortunate in not having many contagious diseases in our town the past year, which speaks well for it as a residential place, but in some sections of the town it will be neces- sary in the near future to take action, if possible, and in unison with one or two neighboring towns, see what can be done relating to the basins at the southerly part of the town. We have kept informed concerning them and at a meeting soon to be held we hope some favorable move will be made by the Metropolitan Water Board.

A bill has already been introduced into the Legislature and referred to the Committee on Public Health, having reference to the meadow basins of Lake Cochituate.

Attention of the board has been called to the condition of several piggeries in the north end of the town. These have been visited and the law relating to the same explained to the owners. The board has taken no action further than to notify the parties complained of of their intention to abate all such nuisances, preferring that the parties themselves should conform to the requirements of public health.

LICENSES.

Undertaker 1

CONTAGIOUS DISEASES REPORTED

Diphtheria 1
Scarlet Fever 1
Measles 4
Deaths from causes independent of disease 1

For deaths not specified above, we would respectfully refer you to the report of the Town Clerk.

Respectfully submitted,

C. W. HEIZER,
P. S. IDE,
A. A. CARTER.

WATER COMMISSIONERS' REPORT.

WAYLAND WATER COMMISSIONERS,

In account with HENRY F. LEE, *Town Treasurer.*

February 28, 1900.	Balance not drawn from town treasurer	$666 00
February 28, 1901.	Transfer for hydrants . . .	384 00
February 28, 1901.	By water rates, town treasurer .	1,888 02
		$2,938 02

Transfer interest on bonds		$640 00
February 28, 1901. Order No. 1 Maintenance . .		362 56
" " 2 H. G. Dudley, sup't.		150 00
" " 3 H. G. Dudley, com. .		20 00
" " 4 C. H. Boodey, com. .		20 00
" " 5 W. M. Fullick, com.		20 00
" " 6 W. M. Fullick, clerk		32 50
" " 7 Sinking Fund . .		1,282 96
Balance not drawn		410 00
		$2,938 02

C. H. BOODEY,
H. G. DUDLEY,
W. M. FULLICK,
Commissioners of Wayland Water Works.

Wayland, February 28, 1901.

REPORT OF COMMISSIONERS OF WATER WORKS SINKING FUND.

February 28, 1901.

Amount in Framingham Savings Bank, South Framingham, Mass.	$440 75
Amount deposited in Natick Five Cent Savings Bank, Natick, Mass.	1,433 58
Interest on above deposit November 1, 1900 . .	43 82
Amount deposited in Watertown Savings Bank, Watertown, Mass.	1,000 00
Interest on above deposit October 3, 1900 . .	61 20
Amount deposited in Home Savings Bank, Boston, Mass.	771 65
Interest on above deposit March 1, 1900 . .	29 80

March 7, 1801.

Amount deposited in Natick Five Cent Savings Bank, Natick, Mass.	1,282 96

$5,063 76

C. H. BOODEY,
H. G. DUDLEY,
W. M. FULLICK,
Commissioners of Water Works Sinking Fund.

Wayland, February 28, 1901.

REPORT OF THE SUPERINTENDENT OF THE WAYLAND WATER WORKS.

We have passed through another very dry year, and the water in the basin was quite low for about three months.

We had enough rain in the fall to fill the basin, and it has remained so all winter.

We did not enter into any new work or extensions this year, simply doing the work that was necessary to keep the works in as good shape as possible.

The maintenance account is as follows:

1900.

April	1.	To Labor for March	$10 50
	21.	Howe & Co.	70
May	1.	Labor for April	24 00
	9.	Samuel Hobbs & Co.	10 50
	14.	B. & A. R. R. and Howe & Co.	75
	28.	Harry G. Dudley	7 00
June	1.	Labor for May	28 00
	25.	Andrew J. Morse & Co.	12 00
	26.	Barrett M'f'g Co.	2 50
July	1.	Labor for June	21 50
	1.	Wayne Post	20 00
Aug.	1.	Labor for July	25 50
	14.	Walworth M'f'g Co.	10 18
	22.	Samuel Hobbs & Co.	75
	22.	A. Whelan	1 10
	24.	Howe & Co.	1 45

Sept.	1.	Labor for August	$24 50
	17.	Robinson & Jones	1 65
	20.	P. A. Leary	6 35
	22.	James Devine	5 00
Oct.	1.	Labor for September	17 50
	15.	Wayne Post	8 67
Nov.	1.	Labor for October	9 50
	7.	R. W. Porter	6 00
Dec.	1.	Labor for November	4 50
	12.	Walworth M'f'g Co.	61 28
1901.			
Jan.	1.	Labor for December . . - .	2 50
Feb.	11.	E. P. Butler . . , . .	2 46
	28.	Labor for February	10 50
	28.	W. F. Garfield	5 00
	28.	John Hurley	2 00
	28.	Postage	1 85
	28.	Stock and Labor, W. M. Fullick . .	15 87

$362 56

The water at present is in use by the following :

Families	288
Manufactories	5
Public Buildings	4
Miscellaneous	14
Horses	80
Cows	46

Respectfully submitted,

H. G. DUDLEY.
Superintendent.

Wayland, February 28, 1901.

REPORT OF SUPERINTENDENT OF STREETS.

Highway Pay Roll for the Month of March.

		Days.	Hours.		Days.	Hours.	Amount.
C. H. May	. .	10	2	horse	6	.	$29 48
Henry Smith	. .	1			.	.	2 00
M. W. Hynes	. .	2			1	2	5 80
							$37.28

Highway Pay Roll for the Month of April.

		Days.	Hours.		Days.	Hours.	Amount.
William C. Neal	. .	23	5½	horse	38	3	$113 66
C. W. Fairbanks	. .	9	8	horse	19	8	54 44
John Hurley	. .	9	4½		.	.	19 00
Joe Lemoine	. .	10	4½		.	.	21 00
John Kelly	. .	11	3		.	.	22 65
R. W. Neal	. .	16	5		.	.	33 10
Arthur Bartlett	. .	7	4		.	.	14 88
L. A. Loker	. .	3	7				7 50
Stephen Comier	. .	4	6				9 34
Con. Collins	. .	4	6				9 34
H. T. Tyrell	. .	5	3½		.	.	10 76
Mat. Temple	. .	6	3		.	.	12 71
Mat. Temple	. .	1					1 95
Peter Foster	. .	3					7 12
Bert Ward	. .	4	5				9 11
Nelson Mathews	. .	4	6				9 27
M. G. Hurley	. .	5					10 00

	Days.	Hours.		Days.	Hours.	Amount
Herbert Bond . .	5	7		.	.	$11 56
Wilson Porter . .	2	7		-	-	5 55
Alvin Neale . .	2	5				5 33
T. B. Hawes . .	4	5				9 11
Joseph Mathews . .	1	7½				3 66
H. E. Griffin . .		5				1 11
Henry Mathews . .	1					2 00
H. G. Dudley . .		2				.44
W. Post . . .	1					2 00
C. C. Ward . .	11	3		.	.	22 66
Geo. E. Sherman .	5		horse	2	6	14 65
S. S. Davidson . .	3	4½		.	.	7 00
M. W. Hynes . .	14		horse	28	.	77 00
T. L. Hynes . .	16		horse	30	.	84 50
Henry Smith . .	6	4½		.	.	13 00
John B. McManus .	13			.	.	26 00
Lewis J. Bemis . .	11	4½	horse	23	.	63 25
P. S. Zimmerman .	7	4½		.	.	15 00
M. C. Baldwin . .	1	4½	horse	4	4½	8 50

Robinson & Jones, piping						3 80
Union Lumber Co., lumber						8 22
Joseph Breck & Sons, shovels						5.40
American Express, expressage						.25
Frank Haynes, lumber						5 10

$760.82

HIGHWAY PAY ROLL FOR THE MONTH OF MAY.

	Days.	Hours.		Days.	Hours.	Amount.
W. C. Neal . .	21	8	horse	48	.	$115 81
John Morrissy . .	1			.		2 00
James Morrissy . .	14			.	.	28 00
T. B. Hawes . .	7	3½		.	.	14 76
A. Bartlett . . .	5			.	.	10 00
W. E. Jennison . .	2	4	horse	2	4	12 23

	Days.	Hours.		Days.	Hours.	Amount.
John Hurley	5	7		.	.	$11 55
E. Sayers	2	7				5 55
M. G. Hurley	17	7½		.	.	35 64
Alvin Neal	1					2 00
John Curtin	1		horse	1	.	5 00
John Kelly	4	3				8 66
Joseph Lemoine	7	5½		.	.	15 19
N. Temple	3		horse	3	.	15 00
C. H. May	6	2	horse	6	2	30 89
R. Neal	9	8		.	.	19 76
Wilson Porter	15	6		.	.	31 29
W. Post	8	3		.	.	16 66
C. C. Ward	11	1		.	.	22 21
John Bowles	1					2 00
Edward Harrington	4					8 00
Henry Smith	1	4½		.	.	3 00
M. W. Hynes	11	5	horse	19	1	52 08
T. L. Hynes	10	7½	horse	13	.	41 17
John B. McManus	8	3		.	.	16 67
James Eagan	2		horse	4	.	10 00
Frank Moore	16	5		.	.	33 11

						Amount.
H. Huntley, 30 perch of stone	.	.	.	.	.	7.50
Frank Quinn, 4 perch of stone	.	.	.	.	.	1 00
Car fare — Wayland	.	.	.	.	.	2 50

$581 22

HIGHWAY PAY ROLL FOR THE MONTH OF JUNE.

	Days.	Hours.		Days.	Hours.	Amount.
W. C. Neal	17	7	horse	25	7	$74 00
Town of Wayland	3	4	horse	3	4	17 23
T. Evans	5			.	.	10 00
E. Jennison	3		horse	3	.	15 00
M. G. Hurley	17	7		.	.	35 54
C. C. Ward	14			.	.	28 00

	Days.	Hours		Days.	Hours.	Amount.
John Morrissy	13			.	.	$26 00
J. Lemoine . . .	10	8		.	.	21 48
L. A. Loker . .	1		horse	1	.	3 50
R. Neal . . .	9	3		.	.	18 65
Nat. Temple . .	2		horse	7	.	25 00
J. Kelly . . .	13			.	.	26 00
N. Mathews . .	3					6 00
T. B. Hawes . .	1			.		2 00
C. Fairbanks . .	1		horse	1	.	5 00
W. R. Porter . .	11	5		.	.	23 11
James Eagan . .	.13		horse	26	.	65 00
John B. McManus .	14	4½		.	.	29 00
M. W. Hynes . .	13		horse	28	.	68 00
T. L. Hynes . .	11		horse	24	.	58 00
Edward Harrington .	13	4½		.	.	27 00
Henry Smith . .	2			.	.	4 00
John J. Rowan . .	6	2	horse	6	2	21 78
G. E. Sherman . .	2		horse	4		10 00
John Bowles . .	6			.	.	12 00
Henry Zimmerman .	3					6 00
G. W. Hancock, 240 loads gravel	.	.	.	·		24 00
E. P. Butler, 210 loads gravel	.	.	.	.		21 00
Frank Haynes, carpenter -	.	.	.	.		4 78
Union Lumber Co. .	.	.	.	.	.	10 51
						$697.58

HIGHWAY PAY ROLL FOR THE MONTH OF JULY.

	Days.	Hours.		Days.	Hours.	Amount.
W. G. Neal . .	9	4	horse	17	7	$44 61
M. G. Hurley .	9	1		.	.	18 22
W. Porter . . .	5	5		.	.	12 11
R. Neal . . .	6	2		.	.	12 44
C. C. Ward . . .	3				.	6 00
W. Spear . . .	1	6	horse	.	6	4 13
L. Loker . . .	2				.	4 00
						$100 51

Highway Pay Roll for the Month of August.

	Days.	Hours.		Days.	Hours.	Amount.
F. Haynes . . .	Labor			.	.	$4 77
W. C. Neal. . .	4	2	horse	5	4	16 57
M. G. Hurley . .	1	3		.	.	2 67
R. Neal . . .	5			.	.	10 00
Jos. Lemoine . .		4				.89
John Plass . . .		4				.89
						$35 79

Highway Pay Roll for the Month of September.

	Days.	Hours.		Days.	Hours.	Amount.
W. C. Neal . .	4	1	horse	7	6	$19.73
M. G. Hurley . .	2	3		.	.	4 66
C. C. Ward . .	2			.	.	4 00
W. Post	2			.	.	4 00
R. Neal . . .		3		.	.	.66
M. W. Hynes . .	2	3	horse	4	3	11 17
T. L. Hynes . .	1	8	horse .	3	7	9 44
J. B. McManus . .	1			.	.	2 00
P. S. Zimmerman .	1	7½		.	.	3 67

W. C. Neal, 8 posts	1 20
Robinson & Jones	17 15
W. D. Parlin, sewer grates and mail	18 58
William Stearns, 3 sign boards	2 00
	$98 26

Highway Pay Roll for the Month of October.

	Days.	Hours.		Days.	Hours.	Amount.
J. F. Burke . .	½			.	.	$1 00

Highway Pay Roll for the Month of November.

	Days.	Hours.		Days.	Hours.	Amount.
Lewis J. Bemis . .		2		.	.	.45
M. W. Hynes . .	5	2	horse	3	.	14 95
T. L. Hynes . .	4	5	horse	3	5	14 44

	Days.	Hours.		Days.	Hours.	Amount.
M. W. Hynes .	5	3	horse	10	6	$26.67
M. Smith . . .	5	3		.	.	10 67
T. L. Hynes . .	7	1	horse	12	4	33 38
Henry Smith . .	6	2		.	.	12 25
						$112 81

HIGHWAY PAY ROLL FOR THE MONTH OF DECEMBER,

	Days.	Hours.		Days.	Hours.	Amount.
W. C. Neal . . .	5	½	horse	10	1½	$25 35
C. Fairbanks . .	1	6	horse	1	6	8 90
W. R. Porter . .	2	6			.	5 34
M. G. Hurley . .	2	6		.	.	5 34
T. B. Hawes . .	2	1¼				4 24

S. R. Adams, stone . .	. . . .	1 00
L. H. McManus, repairing .	. . . .	2 70
E. P. Butler . . .	. . . .	2 39
T. W. Frost . .	. . . .	5 00
4 posts . . .	. . . .	.60
		$60 86

HIGHWAY PAY ROLL FOR THE MONTH OF JANUARY.

	Days.	Hours.		Days.	Hours.	Amount.
W. C. Neal . .	1	2½	horse	1	5	$4 87
C. Fairbanks . .	1		horse	1	3	4 00
M. Temple . .		6	horse	1	3	3 33
T. B. Hawes . .		8			.	1 78

P. A. Leary . . .	. . . .	2 32
Mrs. Thompson, load of stone	. . . .	.25
		$16 55

HIGHWAY PAY ROLL FOR THE MONTH OF FEBRUARY.

W. C. Neal, labor and lumber on bridges . . .	$12 11
Total	$2,514 79

REPORT OF SUPERINTENDENT OF NORTH AND CENTRE CEMETERIES.

March 1, 1900. Appropriation $50 00
Expended . . . $50 00
——— $50 00

A. S. MORSE,
Superintendent.

REPORT OF SUPERINTENDENT OF LAKE-VIEW CEMETERY.

March 1. Unexpended balance $9 77
Appropriation 50 00
——— $59 77
May 7. Wilson Porter $37 10
June 4. Wilson Porter 8 00
Unexpended balance . . . 14 67
——— $59 77

WILSON PORTER,
Superintendent.

NEEDY SOLDIERS AND FAMILIES.

March 26, 1900. Appropriated		$500 00
John B. Brigham, six dollars per month .	$72 00	
J. H. Tyrrell, board for J. M. Pierce . .	48 00	
J. M. Pierce	27 00	
E. M. Partridge, rent for Mrs. Coakley .	48 00	
William Webster	128 00	
J. P. Keevan, board for Ed. Lemoine . .	60 00	
F. L. Howe, milk for Mrs. H. Butterfield .	15 90	
Waltham Hospital, care of Rockwood .	6 42	
F. E. Wellington, ambulance for Rockwood .	5 00	
Robinson & Jones, coal	11 38	
Ellen Coakley, board for Dennis Mullen .	68 00	
Dennis Mullen, ticket to Ireland . . .	59 33	
D. W. Ricker, putting Mullen on steamer .	2 00	
C. H. May, burial of indigent soldiers .	70 00	
J. A. Dupuis, board for Ed. Lemoine . .	26 00	
E. B. Loker, milk for Mrs. H. Butterfield .	4 60	
T. S. Sherman, shoes for Dennis Mullen .	3 00	
C. M. Keay	20 00	
B. W. McKeen, M. D., professional services for Mrs. H. Butterfield . .	3 50	
C. H. Boodey, M. D., professional services for Mrs. H. Butterfield . . .	11 00	
Mrs. H. C. Butterfield	10 00	
	$699 13	

ELIJAH H. ATWOOD,
ELBRIDGE A. CARTER,
N. C. GRIFFIN,
Selectmen of Wayland.

REPORT OF THE ENGINEERS OF FIRE DEPARTMENT.

We beg to report the following fires to which the department responded for the year ending March 1, 1901 :

March 1, 12.50 P. M. Alarm from box 24 for fire in Loker building, Main street, in that part occupied by George Chalmers, caused by explosion of kerosene lamp; owing to the location of the building had it not been for the prompt response of the fire department the loss might have been great.

April 6, 7.05 P. M. Alarm from box 36 for fire in H. E. Hammond's woods.

June 1. Alarm from box 23 for a fire in out building of Sarah Stone, German Hill street, cause unknown. Slight damage.

June 20, 3.30 A. M. Alarm from engine house for fire in Puritan Color Works, North Natick. Did not respond, it being thought unnecessary.

June 22, 7.25 P. M. Alarm from box 34 for fire in Edgar Loker's ice house; extinguished by chemicals.

September 21, 3 A. M. Alarm from box 30 for fire in Colburn Dean's shoe factory, occupied by Rosco Dean. Fire probably incendiary. Loss, total.

We appointed W. C. Hunting, Superintendent of the fire alarm, but he would not accept, the salary being so small.

Mr. Hunting had also notified us he wanted the battery jars removed from his place as they gave his family so much uneasiness during electrical storms.

As we had no place for them we conferred with the Selectmen in regard to the matter, and it was decided to put an addition on the rear of the engine house at an expense of $115.67.

September 28, batteries were removed to new room in engine house since which time they have been taken care of by engineers, and they have been much improved by putting in the new system of wiring, there being much less danger of being burned out by electrical storms, or by getting crossed by electric wires.

We have been over the fire alarm district resetting poles where needed, cutting out all limbs of trees where resting on wires, and putting on new insulators where needed, there being a great many broken, at an expense of $9.00.

Mr. N. C. Griffin gave a furnace for the engine house which he put in November 2; this is one of the long-needed and great improvements, as before it was necessary to take the chemical extinguishers from the house to prevent freezing during cold weather.

We appreciate the generous gift of Mr. Griffin, as also do the firemen and townspeople.

After the furnace was put in we found it necessary for some one person to look after it, and to avoid a continual expense we have fitted up a small room in the engine house at an expense of $34, the rent of which is given to a fireman for taking care of the furnace. This we believe to be a great advantage to the fire department, as it gives us one fireman in the engine house every night.

There has been a Hopper closet and cesspool put in at an expense of $12.80. Also a smoke heater to heat the battery room at an expense of $8.00. As this is heat that would otherwise escape up the chimney, it is no additional expense to heating the room.

The engine house, carriages and equipment, battery room and fire alarm system are all in good condition.

December 3, W. L. King was appointed on the Board of Engineers to fill a vacancy caused by F. E. Yeager's resignation.

We have received for firemen's pay $400, and added the unexpended balance of last year, $24.00, and have turned over to the companies $424.00. The engineers recommend that the sum of $700.00 be appropriated for the firemen's pay, superintendent of fire alarm, and general maintenance of fire department and fire alarm.

Respectfully submitted,

E. W. MARSTON, *Chief*,
A. J. RICKER, *First Assistant*,
W. L. KING, *Clerk*.

REPORT OF LIBRARY BUILDING COMMITTEE.

To the Citizens of the Town of Wayland :

Your committee has completed the Wayland Public Library building, and turned it over to the town.

The disposition of the fund of $28,000, with its accumulation of interest with which the library was built, appears from the account below :

Fund,		$28,000 00
Interest,		866 43
Prof. Chandler, professional advice to committee	$150 00	
Architects, fees	1,254 66	
Fales & Co., contractors	25,689 43	
Soundings for foundation	48 10	
Water pipe and laying	60 53	
P. P. Caproni, plaster casts, " Dancing boys "	115 00	
J. Evans & Co., cutting inscriptions	35 00	
Mats and matting	48 51	
Granolithic walks	119 32	
Furniture	515 75	
W. B. Whittier & Co., shrubs and plants	57 38	
Gas plant	170 00	
Insurance	100 00	
Hardware	121 25	
Gas and electric fixtures	245 75	
Windows and door screens	68 00	

Stationery, telegrams, etc.   .   .   . $11 00
A. A. Applebee, coloring mortar .   .   56 75

                                        $28,866 43 $28,866 43

Respectfully submitted,

    WILLARD A. BULLARD,
    CHARLES A. RICHARDSON,
    ALFRED WAYLAND CUTTING,
    CHESTER B. WILLIAMS.
    E. W. MARSTON.

FINANCE COMMITTEE.

The finance committee respectfully submits the following and recommends that the same be appropriated and adopted, viz : —

For schools, fuel and care of buildings	$7,500 00
School Supplies	800 00
Transportation of scholars	1,200 00
Repair of school buildings	100 00
Superintendent of schools	750 00
Overdrafts	1,783 87
Incidentals	2000 00
Salaries	1,300 00
Electric lights	365 00
Fire department, including fire alarm	700 00
Hydrants	384 00
Highways and bridges	2,000 00
Culverts and sidewalks	500 00
Support of poor	2,000 00
Collection of taxes	350 00
Abatement of taxes	200 00
Library	800 00
Lakeview Cemetery	50 00
North and Centre Cemeteries	50 00
School-house loan	1,100 00
Memorial day	100 00

$24,032 87

We recommend that the sum of six hundred and forty dollars be transferred from water rates to pay interest on water bonds.

That the Selectmen be authorized to draw from the contingent fund such sums of money as may be necessary, not exceeding six hundred dollars, for assisting needy soldiers and their families.

That the sum of three thousand dollars be appropriated for interest on town debt to be taken from the contingent fund.

That the money for removing snow be drawn from the contingent fund.

That the sum of three thousand dollars be appropriated from the contingent fund to build Baldwin's bridge as ordered by the county commissioners.

We have carefully considered the needs of the various departments and find that the sums recommended, if adopted, will meet the needs of the departments and are as low as can be safely recommended.

> ELIJAH H. ATWOOD, *Chairman.*
> JOHN CONNOLLY,
> WILLIAM C. NEAL,
> NATHANIEL R. GERALD,
> E. W. MARSTON,
> DAVID P. W. LOKER,
> HENRY F. LEE,
> C. H. BOODEY,
> ERNEST E. BUTLER, *Clerk.*

March 6, 1901.

REPORT OF THE COMMISSIONERS OF THE SINKING FUND OF THE TOWN OF WAYLAND.

Your Commissioners would respectfully report that they have
received from the Town Treasurer $5,927 44
Interest on Bonds purchased 100 00

$6,027 44

And have invested this sum as follows : —
Town of Wayland Bonds purchased . . . $5,589 61
Deposited in Cambridgeport Saving Bank . . 437 83

$6,027 44

E. W. MARSTON,
C. B. WILLIAMS,
HENRY D. PARMENTER,
Commissioners Wayland Sinking Fund.

TREASURER'S REPORT.

SCHOOLS.

1900.

March 1.	Unexpended balance		$903 53
26.	Appropriation		7,000 00
Sept. 28.	State treasurer		625 00
1901.			
Jan. 1.	Donation fund		12 00
24.	State treasurer		328 59
Feb. 1.	County, one-half Dog license . . .		131 67
	Total expenditures .	$8,390 48	
	Balance unexpended . .	610 31	
		$9,000 79	$9,000 79

SCHOOL SUPPLIES.

March 26.	Appropriation		$700 00
	Appropriation for overdraft . . .		7 50
	From school board		2 80
	Overdrawn		2 30
	Overdraft	$7 50	
	Expended	705 10	
		$712 60	$712 60

TRANSPORTATION OF SCHOLARS.

March 1.	Balance unexpended		$401 98
26.	Appropriation		1,500 00
	Expenditures . . .	$1,422 68	
	Balance unexpended . .	479 30	
		$1,901 98	$1,901 98

SCHOOL REPAIRS.

1900.

March 1.	Unexpended balance		$38 17
26.	Appropriation		100 00
	Expenditures . . .	$44 82	
	Balance unexpended . .	93 35	
		$138 17	$138 17

SUPERINTENDENT OF SCHOOLS.

1900.

March 26.	Appropriation		$750 00
	Expended	$750 00	
		$750 00	$750 00

FITTING UP HIGH SCHOOL.

1900.

March 1.	Balance unexpended		$249 72
1901.			
March 1.	Balance unexpended . .	$249 72	
		$249 72	$249 72

OVERDRAFTS.

1900.

March 1.	Balance unexpended		$168 87
	Appropriation		1,638 15
	Expended	$1,525 02	
	Balance	282 00	
		$1,807 02	$1,807 02

HIGHWAYS AND BRIDGES.

1900.

March 1.	Balance unexpended		$328 47
26.	Appropriation		2,000 00

1901.

Jan. 1. Excise Tax $187 05
      Expended $2,514 79
      Balance 73

                              $2,515 52 $2,515 52

INCIDENTALS.

1900.

March 27. Appropriated $2,000 00
      27. Appropriated for overdraft . . . 563 82
1901.
Feb. 28. Overdrawn 1,070 57

                                          $3,634.39

EXPENDED.

1900.

April 2. M. J. Maloney, rent of K. of L.
         Hall, caucus . . . $8 00
      2. Thomas Bryant, horse and .
         carriage, (registrars of voters) 1 00
      2. Natick Gas and Electric Co., .
         lighting 4 30
      2. A. N. Bryant, distributing town
         reports 5 00
      2. C. H. Thing, distributing town
         reports 5 00
      2. T. S. Sherman, lighting street .
         lamps 5 00
      2. Gilbert Barker & Co., gasoline 2 32
May 7. A. S. Morse, election officer, .
         March 27, 1900 . . . 5 00
      7. A. S. Morse, printing and serving
         two town warrants . . 13 50
      7. P. A. Leary, temporary registrar
         of voters 5 00
      7. R. T. Lombard, recording births,
         marriages and deaths . . 7 00

May	7.	R. T. Lombard, preparing voting lists, postage stamps . .	$11 00
	7.	R. T. Lombard, fare and services, district clerks' meeting .	4 00
	7.	R. T. Lombard, stationery .	4 00
	7.	R. T. Lombard, two days' service as assessor . . .	7 00
	7.	R. T. Lombard, conveyance as registrar	1 50
	7.	R. T. Lombard, clerical service for selectmen . . .	5 00
	7.	R. T. Lombard, professional services at State House . .	10 00
	7.	R. T. Lombard, cash paid . express	75
	7.	Lake View Press, printing town and school reports . .	142 24
	7.	G. F. Marston, use of tower, M. E. Church, for fire alarm .	50 00
	7.	G. F. Marston, care of clock and oil	20 65
	7.	W. L. King, labor . . .	1 50
	7.	E. E. Butler, insurance . .	22 50
	7.	Wright & Potter, official ballots	14 25
	7.	H. M. Dolbear, dog licenses and posters	2 10
	7.	J. E. Linnehan, janitor and cash paid, gasoline . . .	27 30
	7.	C. M. Magorty, police service .	29 99
	7.	C. C. Ward, police service .	30 47
	7.	Thomas Groom & Co., list of voters and posters . .	24 00
	7.	M. C. Baldwin, conveying ballot box to Cochituate . .	2 00
	7.	M. C. Baldwin, temporary registrar	1 50

May	7.	F. E. Yeager, postage and stationery, (fire department) .	$1 00
	7.	Natick Gas and Electric Co., lighting	8 17
	7.	T. S. Sherman, lighting street lamps	5 00
	7.	Edward Carter, stationery (assessors) . . .	1 28
	7.	J. H. Lee, oil, (postage and stationery for treasurer) .	7 71
	7.	P. B. Murphy, posters and books (assessors) . . .	4 00
	7.	R. E. Frye, damage to wagon (fire department) . .	5 00
June	4.	Masury & Young, modusto (oil)	1 50
	4.	Breck & Sons, lawn shears .	2 70
	4.	H. G. Dudley, moderator .	5 00
	4.	H. G. Dudley, labor and cash on drinking fountain . .	5 05
	4.	T. S. Sherman, lighting street lamps	5 00
	4.	H. G. Goldwaite, supplies, (board of health)	27 40
	4.	M. J Maloney, rent K. of L. Hall, (town meeting) . .	8 00
	4.	A. F. Parmenter, services in Boston, 4 days . . .	10 00
	4.	A. F. Parmenter, car fare and postage	1 46
	4.	P. S. Ide, M. D., vaccinating 108 children	54 00
	4.	P. S. Ide, M. D., printing, express and telephone . .	3 40
	4.	Daniel Brackett, examining book town collector . . .	10 00
	4.	Daniel Brackett, obtaining release of abutters on State road	10 00

June	4.	Charles M. Magorty, police service	$39 17
July	2.	L. H. McManus, service as constable	3 00
	2.	L. H. McManus, printing and posting two warrants	14 00
	2.	J. H. Lee, oil and lamp chimneys	1 75
	2.	T. S. Sherman, lighting street lamps	5 00
	2.	Thomas Bryant, disinfecting Videon house	2 50
	2.	Gilbert Barker & Co., gasoline and repairs	13 80
	2.	F. E. Bailey, police service	8 00
	2.	C. W. Dean & Co., fire alarm service	50 00
	2.	A. J. Ricker, engineer	10 00
	2.	C. M. Magorty, police service	30 50
	2.	Natick Gas and Electric Co., lighting	4 65
	2.	B. W. McKeen, M. D., vaccinating 59 children	29 50
Aug.	6.	J. C. Vincent, janitor, town hall, 3 months	25 00
	6.	H. F. Lee, printing tax bills and postage	4 85
	6.	Natick Gas and Electric Co., lighting	8 76
	6.	Wilson Porter, work on drain (school yard)	9 33
	6.	John Ploss, labor on drain (school yard)	5 77
	6.	W. C. Neal, labor on	13 57
	6.	R. Neal, labor	8 33
	6.	Frank Haynes, stock and labor on	20 72

Aug.	6.	J. A. & W. Bird, vitriol, (fire department) . . .	$28 38
	6.	Fire Extinguisher Co., (fire department)	4 50
	6.	Martin & Hall, printing letter heads (fire department) .	4 50
	6.	Puritan Color Works, oil (fire department) . . .	7 91
	6.	Thomas Groom & Co., stationery	3 69
	6.	T. S. Sherman, lighting street lamps	5 00
	6.	E. Moody Hennessy, dinners, (county commissioners) .	8 00
	6.	C. C. Ward, police duty .	2 50
	6.	F. E. Bailey, police duty .	19 61
	6.	C. M. Magorty, police duty .	46 00
	6.	Daniel Brackett, cash paid, postage stamps . . .	5 00
Sept.	3.	E. W. Marston, use current breaker one year . .	5 00
	3.	Knight & Thomas, hose (fire department)	1 00
	3.	W. D. Parlin, one-half dozen axe handles (fire department)	1 20
	3.	J. D. McCuwin, painting axe handles (fire department) .	75
	3.	G. M. Stevens, labor and supplies (fire department) . .	5 62
	3.	T. W. Frost, paint, paper and labor (fire department) .	1 91
	3.	C. & G. W. Underwood, (fire department) . . .	4 12
	3.	C. E. Coakley, services, H. and L. Co., No. 1, fire in woods .	3 75
	3.	Hannah Mullen, envelopes and stamps (treasurer) . .	13 23

Sept.	3.	T. S. Sherman, lighting street lamps	$5 00
	3.	E. F. Lawrence, police duty	4 00
	3.	C. H. Boodey, vaccinating children	40 00
	3.	Edward Carter, horse and carriage (assessors)	8 00
	3.	N. R. Gerald, horse and carriage (assessors)	6 00
	3.	E. S. Draper, printing tax bills	6 50
	3.	C. M. Magorty, police service	37 14
	3.	L. H. McManus, printing and serving warrant	7 00
	3.	L. H. McManus, service as constable	11 50
Oct.	1.	C. M. Magorty, police service	33 26
	1.	E. W. Marston, stock and labor, engine house	122 19
	1.	Albert Stevens, stock and labor	4 30
	1.	T. S. Sherman, lighting street lamps	5 00
	1.	Thomas Bryant, horse and carriage (selectmen)	1 75
	1.	Natick Gas and Electric Co. lighting	4 41
	1.	M. W. Hynes, police service	6 00
	1.	William Stearns, care of clock, one year	20 00
	1.	Gilbert Barker & Co., gasoline	10 60
	1.	B. W. McKeen, M. D., vaccinating 7 children	3 50
	1.	A. S. Morse, police service	5 00
	1.	P. S. Ide, M. D., vaccinating 14 children	7 00
	1.	W. N. Sharp. M. D., return of birth	25

Oct.	1.	Barry Printing Co., posters, (registrars of voters) . .	$1 50
	1.	Daniel Brackett, examining collector's book . . .	75 00
	1.	Daniel Brackett, services before State board of health . .	10 00
	1.	Daniel Brackett, mailing town warrant to voters . . .	3 00
	1.	Thomas Bryant, inspector of animals	125 00
Nov.	5.	S. Bowles, (fire department) .	1 50
	5.	E. P. Butler, supplies and lunch	3 82
	5.	Pettingill & Andrews (fire department)	24 51
	5.	C. M. Magorty, police service .	35 00
	5.	H. G. Dudley, water for engine house, one year . . .	12 00
	5.	J. C. Vincent, janitor 3 months	25 00
	5.	Natick Gas and Electric Co., lighting	6 73
	5.	P. S. Ide, M. D., antitoxine (board of health) . .	5 50
	5.	Alfred Mudge, valuation report	107 20
	5.	L. H. Wakefield, professional services	5 00
	5.	E. F. Lawrence, collecting fees (dog licenses) . . .	10 00
	5.	Thomas Groom & Co., list assessed polls and stationery .	30 85
	5.	Mitchell Manufacturing Co., badges for firemen. . .	6 10
	5.	T. S. Sherman, lighting street lamps	5 00
	5.	J. H. Lee, oil for street lamps .	2 25
	5.	J. F. Burke, labor on drain .	
	5.	W. C. Hunting, superintending fire alarm and labor . .	14·50

Nov.	5.	Daniel Brackett, cash paid postage special meeting . .	$6 00
Dec.	3.	Charles M. Magorty, police service	26 50
	3.	William Hall & Co., opening vault	7 00
	3.	L. K. Lovell, supplies for janitor ,Town Hall	6 82
	3.	F. E. Yeager, insurance, library building . . ,	360 00
	3.	L. E. A. Smith, carriage, (selectmen)	6 50
	3.	A. S. Morse, printing and pasting warrants . . .	15 50
	3.	A. S. Morse, election officer, November 6 , . .	5 00
	3.	T. S. Sherman, lighting street lamps.	5 00
	3.	T. W. Frost, stock and labor on clock	7 81
	3.	A. S. Morse, police service .	5 65
	3.	Gilbert Barker & Co., gasoline	18 20
	3.	E. A. Carter, perambulating town lines	2 50
	3.	James W. Carney, police service	11 99
	3.	Daniel Brackett, cash paid postage (town meeting) . .	5 00
	3.	Daniel Brackett, perambulating town lines and mailing warrants	6 50
	3.	L. H. McManus, conveying ballot box to Cochituate . .	3 00
	3.	L. H. McManus, collecting license fee on dogs . .	10 00
Jan.	7.	E. A. Atwood, perambulating town lines	7 50

Jan.	7.	E. A. Atwood, sundries.	$7 12
	7.	C. M. Magorty, police service	28 39
	7.	P. S. Ide, return six births.	1 50
	7.	Gilbert Barker & Co., gasoline.	10 30
	7.	Daniel Brackett, cash paid postage	5 00
	7.	Daniel Brackett, mailing copies	6 00
	7.	F. F. Hyde, return of three births	75
	7.	T. S. Sherman, lighting street lamps	5 00
	7.	E. A. Carter, perambulating town lines	2 50
	7.	Natick Gas and Electric Co., lighting	19 44
	7.	W. F. Garfield, team (selectmen)	3 00
	7.	Thomas Groom & Co., stationery	27 40
	7.	D. P. W. Loker, return eight deaths	2 00
	7.	J. H. Lee, oil and lamp chimneys	1 40
	7.	L. R. Lovell, supplies, (janitor, Town Hall)	1 36
	7.	Emerson Bill, 17 rolls paper (fire department)	3 37
	7.	James Devine	2 85
	7.	G. & C. W. Underwood, stock and labor	13 29
	7.	Albert Stevens	5 23
	7.	Ernest F. Lawrence, conveying ballot box	1 00
Feb.	4.	A. S. Morse, posting and printing warrants	11 50
	4.	J. W. Parmenter, 2 cords wood	13 00
	4.	J. C. Vincent, janitor 3 months	25 00
	4.	Treasurer, Sudbury, marking line monument	1 75

Feb.	4.	Natick Gas & Electric Co., lighting	$9 83
	4.	G. F. Marston	5 25
	4.	G. M. Stevens . . .	2 22
	4.	Pettingill & Andrews . .	1 50
	4.	C. M. Magorty, police service	21 75
	4.	T. S. Sherman, lighting street lamps	5 00
	4.	E. A. Carter, stationery and postage	7 25
1900			
March	8.	Robinson & Jones, coal and wood (fire department) . .	10 25
	8.	E. W. Marston, (fire department.	53 25
1901			
March	4.	Robinson & Jones, coal (fire department) . . .	33 75
	4.	Cleland & Underwood (fire department)	12 60
	4.	Albert Stevens, labor on fire alarm	1 50
	4.	W. D. Partin, labor on fire alarm	16 21
	4.	E. W. Marston, labor on fire alarm	49 94
	4.	J. H. Lee, labor on fire alarm .	5 85
	4.	H. G. Dudley, labor on fire alarm	7 15
	4.	American Express, express .	1 60
	4.	T. S. Sherman, lighting street lamps	5 00
	4.	C. H. Boodey, return of births	3 75
	4.	D. W. Ricker, sealer of weights and measures . . .	5 00
	4.	N. R. Gerald, express . .	95

March 4. C. M. Magorty, police service $27 35
     4. D. Brackett, express, postage,
        recording 61 64
     4. E. A. Carter, service for Board
        of Health and returns to State   10 79
     4. L. R. Gerald, distributing
        assessors' report . . .   10 00
     4. E. P. Butler, pail for the lockup   30

                                      $3,634 39

FIRE DEPARTMENT.

1900.
March 1. Balance unexpended $448 00
    26. Appropriation 400 00
May   7. Expended $400 00
1901.
March 1. Balance unexpended . . 448 00

                                  $848 00 $848 00

COLLECTION OF TAXES.

1900.
March 1. Balance unexpended $275 00
    26. Appropriation 350 00
April   2. C. F. Richardson . . . $125 00
June   4. C. F. Richardson . . . 69 00
1901.
Feb.   28. Henry F. Lee 335 00
           Balance 96 00

                                  $625 00 $625 00

HYDRANTS.

1900.
March 26. Appropriation $384 00
           To Water Commissioners . . $384 00

                                  $384 00 $384 00

LAKEVIEW CEMETERY.

1900.

March 1.	Balance unexpended	. . . .		$9 77
	Appropriation .	. . . . .		50 00
May 7.	Wilson Porter .	. . .	$37 10	
June 4.	Wilson Porter .	. . .	8 00	
1901.				
March 1.	Balance .	. . . .	14 67	
			$59 77	$59 77

NORTH AND CENTRE CEMETERIES.

1900.

March 26.	Appropriation	. . . . .		$50 00
May 7.	A. S. Morse .	. . .	$7 50	
June 4.	A. S. Morse .	. . .	42 50	
			$50 00	$50 00

LIBRARY ACCOUNT.

1900.

March 26.	Appropriation	. . . . .		$500 00
Nov. 16.	Appropriation	. . . . .		300 00
	One-Half Dog License	. . . .		131 67
May 17.	H. D. Parmenter	. . .	$500 00	
1901.				
Jan. 7.	A. E. Adams .	. . .	71 08	
	H. D. Parmenter	. . .	228 92	
	H. D. Parmenter	. . .	131 67	
			$931 67	$931 67

CEMETERY ACCOUNT.

1900.

March 1.	Unexpended balance	. . . .		$147 51
July 2.	A. S. Morse .	. . . . .		11 00
1901.				
Feb. 4.	A. S. Morse .	. . . . .		5 00

1900.

June	4.	A. S. Morse	$19 15	
Sept.	3.	J. C. Butterfield . . .	18 90	
Dec.	3.	H. G. Dudley	7 85	

1901.

Feb.	28.	A. S. Morse	6 00	
		Unexpended balance . .	111 61	
			$163 51	$163 51

SUPPORT OF POOR.

1901.

March	1.	Unexpended balance	$252 07
	26.	Appropiation	2,500 00
		Total receipts. See O. of P. report . .	758 10
		Total expenditures . . . 2,981 86	
		Balance unexpended . . 528 31	
			$3,510 17

$3,510 17 $3,510 17

DECORATION DAY.

1900.

March	1.	Unexpended balance	$13 80

1901.

March	1.	Unexpended balance . . $13 80	
			$13 80

$13 80 $13 80

ABATEMENT OF TAXES

1900.

March	1.	Balance unexpended	$83 60
	26.	Appropriations	200 00

1901.

Feb.	28.	Taxes of 1895	$75 77
		Taxes of 1897 . . .	16 40
		Taxes of 1898 . . .	17 60
		Taxes of 1899 . . .	32 00

Feb.	28.	Taxes of 1900 . . .	$107 02	
		Balance	34 81	
			$283 60	$283 60

ELECTRIC LIGHTS.

1900.

March	1.	Unexpended balance		$96 74
	26.	Appropriation		350 00
1900.				
March	1.	Overdrawn		14 74
May	1-7.	Natick Gas and Electric Co. .	$155 18	
July	2.	Natick Gas and Electric Co. .	30 63	
August	6.	Natick Gas and Electric Co. .	61 26	
Sept.	3.	Natick Gas and Electric Co. .	30 63	
Nov.	5.	Natick Gas and Electric Co. .	61 26	
Dec.	3.	Natick Gas and Electric Co. .	30 63	
1901.				
Jan.	7.	Natick Gas and Electric Co. .	30 63	
Feb.	28.	Natick Gas and Electric Co .	61 26	
			$461 48	$461 48

INTEREST ON TOWN DEBT.

1900.

March 26.	Appropriation from contingent . . .	$3,000 00
	" for overdraft . . .	162 31
	Transferred from water commissioners' account	640 00
1900.		
March 1.	Overdrawn	642 74

1900.

March	1.	Overdraft	$162 31
	1.	Boston Safe Deposit and Trust Co.	840 00
	20.	Boston Safe Deposit and Trust Co.	80 00
	30.	Natick National Bank . .	231 48
	30.	Estabrook & Co. . . .	369 40
April	23.	D. B. Heard	20 00
	23.	Puritan Trust Co. . . .	132 00

May	14.	Natick National Bank . .	$16 88	
July	2.	Estabrook & Co. . . .	114 71	
	2.	D. B. Heard	20 00	
	17.	Boston Safe Deposit and Trust Co.	220 00	
Aug.	18.	Boston Safe Deposit and Trust Co.	840 00	
Oct.	1.	Boston Safe Deposit and Trust Co.	80 00	
	1.	Estabrook & Co. . . .	195 44	
	1.	Natick National Bank . .	292 50	
	1.	Sinking fund . . - .	23 54	
	21.	Puritan Trust Co. . . .	132 00	
	27.	Boston Safe Deposit and Trust Co.	4 54	
1901.				
Jan.	1.	Natick National Bank . .	146 25	
	1.	Trustees of Loker fund . .	100 00	
	1.	Trustees of Allen fund . .	60 00	
	1.	Trustees of Donation fund .	78 00	
	1.	Trustees of J. S. Draper fund .	60 00	
	1.	Trustees of Childs fund .	6 00	
	16.	Boston Safe Deposit and Trust Co.	220 00	

$4,445 05 $4,445 05

SCHOOL HOUSE LOAN.

1900.

March 26.	Appropriation		$1,100 00
Oct. 21.	Puritan Trust Co. . . . $1,100 00		

$1,100 00 $1,100 00

SALARIES.

1900.

March 26.	Appropriation	$1,300 00
	From Contingent fund	500 00
	For overdraft	151 39
	Overdrawn	435 52

$2,386 91

EXPENDED

1900.

March	1.	Overdrawn	$151 39
	1.	A. F. Parmenter, selectman, 1899-1900	75 00
	1.	T. S. Sherman, overseer of poor 1899-1900	20 00
	1.	E. A. Carter, balance, selectman, 1899-1900 . . .	25 00
	1.	G. B. Howe, overseer of poor, 1899-1900	25 00
	1.	D. P. W. Loker, overseer of poor, 1899-1900 . . .	20 00
	1.	R. T. Lombard, balance clerk, 1899-1900	35 00
	1.	J. H. Carroll, registrar of voters, 1899-1900	20 00
	1.	E. E. Butler, school committee, 1899-1900	25 00
	1.	E. H. Atwood, selectman, 1899-1900	50 00
	1.	T. L. Sawin, registrar of voters, 1899-1900	20 00
	1.	D. W. Mitchell, school committee, 1899-1900 . .	35 00
	1.	C. F. Whittier, registrar of voters, 1899-1900 . .	10 00
	1.	Estate, W. B. Ward, overseer of poor, 1899-1900 . . .	20 00
	1.	H. F. Lee, treasurer, 1899-1900	200 00
April		M. W. Hynes, election officer, 1899-1900	5 00
		A. H. Bryant, auditor, 1899-1900	50 00
		W. C. Hunting, election officer .	5 00
		F. E. Yeager, election officer .	10 00
		C. F. Williams, election officer	5 00

Willard C. Hunting, superintendent fire alarm . . .	$25 00
Edward Carter, election officer .	5 00
N. R. Gerald, assessor . .	132 00
M. M. Fiske, assessor . .	122 50
Edward Carter, assessor . .	135 00
E. W. Marston, . . .	10 00
D. P. W. Loker, overseer of poor	20 00
William Stearns, election officer	5 00
William H. Campbell, election officer, 1899 . . .	5 00
F. E. Yeager, election officer, 1899	5 00
R. C. Dean, election officer, 1900	5 00
William H. Campbell, election officer, 1900 . . .	5 00
P. D. Gorman, election officer, 1900	5 00
H. W. Parmenter, election officer, 1900	5 00
Thomas Bryant, election officer, 1900	2 00
Willard C. Hunting, election officer, 1900 . . .	5 00
E. F. Lawrence, election officer, 1900	5 00
C. M. Keay, election officer, 1900	2 50
E. E. Butler, election officer, 1900	5 00
Albert Stevens, election officer, 1900	2 00
C. E. Gerald, election officer, 1900	2 00
E. F. Lee, election officer, 1900	5 00
L. A. Loker, election officer, 1900	5 00

Dec.	N. R. Gerald, election officer, 1900	$5 00
1901.		
March 4.	E. H. Atwood, selectman, 1900-1901.	75 00
4.	E. A. Carter, selectman, 1900-1901	50 00
4.	D. W. Ricker, overseer of poor, 1901-1901 . . .	50 00
4.—D.	P. W. Loker, overseer of poor, balance 1900-1901 .	20 00
4.	T. S. Sherman, overseer of poor 1900-1901	40 00
4.	J. H. Carroll, registrar of voters, 1900-1901	20 00
4.	T. L. Sawin, registrar of voters, 1900-1901	20 00
4.	Edward Carter, assessor, 1900-1901	3 50
4.	Marcus M. Fiske, assessor, 1900-1901	17 50
4.	N. R. Gerald, assessor, 1900-1901	21 00
4.	Frank Haynes, registrar of voters, 1900-1901 . .	20 00
4.	Herbert Haynes, election officer, 1900-1901	5 00
4.	C. H. Boodey, school committee, 1900-1901	25 00
4.	B. C. Wood, school committee 1900-1901	35 52
4.	Daniel Brackett, town clerk and registrar of voters, 1900-1901	70 00
4.	Henry F. Lee, treasurer, 1900-1901	200 00
4.	William Stearns . . .	10 00
4.	A. H. Bryant, auditor . .	25 00

March 4. Thomas Bryant, U. S. inspector
of animals $250 00
4. E. E. Butler, school committee 50 00
4. N. C. Griffin, selectman . 50 00

$2,386 91

STATE TAX.

1900.
Aug. 1. State Tax $900 00
State, Special 330 52
Dec. 11. State Treasurer . . . $1,230 52

$1,230 52 $1,230 52

COUNTY TAX.

1900.
Aug. 1. County Tax $1,605 93
Nov. 5. J. O. Hayden, Treasurer . . $1,605 93

$1,605 93 $1,605 93

TEMPORARY LOAN.

1900.
March 1. Notes unpaid $20,000 00
29. Estabrook & Co. 12,000 00
July 2. Estabrook & Co. 3,000 00
Oct. 1. Estabrook & Co. 5,000 00
1900.
March 29. National Shawmut Bank . . $6,000 00
May 14. Natick National Bank . . 3,000 00
Sept. 28. Boston Safe Deposit and Trust Co. 6,000 00
1901.
Feb. 18. Natick National Bank . . 2,000 00
March 1. Notes unpaid $23,000 00

$40,000 00 $40,000 00

WATER COMMISSIONERS' ACCOUNT.

1900.

March 1.	Appropriation	$640 00
	Transferred from hydrants . . .	384 00
1901.		
Feb. 28.	W. M. Fullick	1,888 02
	Overdrawn	256 00

	Overdraft . . .	$640 00	
	Transferred to interest account .	640 00	
Feb. 28.	W. M. Fullick	1,888 02	

$3,168 02 $3,168 02

NOTE. There is a decrepancy of $666.00 between the Town Treasurers' account and the Water Commissioners' account, upon which some action should be taken by the town.

CONTINGENT ACCOUNT.

1900			CR.
March 1.	Unexpended balance		$1,427 86
8.	J. E. Linnehan, rent of hall . . .		8 50
April 23.	F. C. Bean, license		1 00
23.	C. E. Thayer, license		1 00
23.	Middlesex South District Court (fines) .		24 91
May 10.	Paul T. Draper, proceeds from sale at town farm		3,212 70
10.	C. F. Richardson, interest on taxes . .		249 44
10.	E. H. Atwood		60
July 2.	Middlesex South District Court (fines) .		9 10
2.	A. L. Moore, license		2 00
2.	L. Russell, license		1 00
2.	J. C. Reeves, license		2 00
Aug. 4.	Fred E. Perkins, license		8 00
4.	Middlesex South District Court (fines) .		12 41
4.	G. R. Scott, license		2 00
4.	J. C. Vincent, rent of hall . . .		25 00
4.	State Treasurer, cop. tax. . . .		2,301 25

Aug.	4.	State treasurer, national bank tax . .	$747 78
	4.	State treasurer, military aid . . .	102 00
	4.	State treasurer, Spanish war aid . .	37 00
	4.	State treasurer, State aid, ...	1,130 00
	4.	William Remick, license	2 00
	4.	Court fines	2 70
	4.	James M. Forbush, returned insurance premiums	48 60
	4.	State treasurer, street railway tax . .	549 21
	4.	J. S. Estabrook, one half expense town meeting	8 00
	4.	Underwood or bearer	4 12
	4.	J. C. Vincent, rent of hall . . .	20 00
	4.	Overlayings on taxes	16 09
	4.	Additional assessments	9 93
	4.	Additional assessments	19 11
	4.	Additional assessments	104 37
	4.	Additional assessments	30 00
	4.	Additional assessments	27 00
	4.	Additional assessments	12 00
	4.	W. B. Ward estate, interest on taxes .	967 87
	4.	F. L. Smith, one half expense town meeting	8 00
	4.	George Howe, Cochituate scales . .	16 00
	4.	L. K. Lovell, Centre scales . . .	15 18
	4.	Henry F. Lee, interest on taxes . .	831 07

$11,996 80

1900.			DR.	
March 26.		Appropriation for interest .	$3,000 00	
		Metropolitan Water Tax . .	30 00	
Aug.	1.	Transferred to Town Tax .	100 00	
Oct.	1.	To Henry D. Parmenter, treasurer	3,212 70	
Nov.	16.	Appropriation for Library .	300 00	
1901.				
Jan.	7.	F. W. Pousland . . .	1 58	
		A. B. Black, agent . . .	130 00	

Feb.	18.	W. B. Ward, estate	.	.	$800 00
	28.	W. C. Neal . . .	.		1,028 07
		Transferred to salaries	.	.	500 00
		Needy soldiers	.	.	699 13
		Military and State aid	.	.	1,274 00

| | | | | $11,075 48 |
| March 1. | Balance unexpended | . | . | 921 32 |

| | | | | $11,996 80 |

W. G. ROBY LIBRARY FUND.

1900.

March 1.	Balance unexpended .	.	.	.	$15,870 00
Dec. 25.	Interest . . .	.	.	.	234 94
	Paid to Library Committee	$16,104 94	

| | | $16,104 94 | $16,104 94 |

NEW SCHOOL HOUSE, COCHITUATE.

1900.

| March 1. | Balance unexpended . | . | . | . | . | $1,000 00 |

1901.

| March 1. | Balance unexpended . | . | . $1,000 00 | |

| | | $1,000 00 | $1,000 00 |

SINKING FUND.

1900.

March 1.	Balance on hand	.	.	.	.	. $2,691 20
Oct. 1.	Interest due .	.	.	.	.	23 54
	From contingent	.	.	.	.	3,212 70
	To Henry D. Parmenter, treasurer	.	.	. .	. $5,927 44	

| | | $5,927 44 | $5,927 44 |

PARSONS FUND.

1900.

March 1.	Balance on hand	.	.	.	.	.	$200 00
Oct. 1.	A. S. Morse, Superintendent	.	$8 00	
	Balance unexpended .	.	.	192 00	

| | | $200 00 | $200 00 |

TAXES OF 1895.

Balance due, March 1, 1900		$165 00
From C. F. Richardson, collector . . .	$3 18	
From Henry F. Lee, collector . . .	86 05	
Abatements	75 77	165 00

TAXES OF 1896.

Balance due, March 1, 1900		$1,291 24
From C. F. Richardson, collector . . .	$301 47	
From Henry F. Lee, collector . . .	185 12	486 59
Balance uncollected, March 1, 1901 . .		$804 65

TAXES OF 1897.

Balance due, March 1, 1900		$3,542 29
From C. F. Richardson, collector . .	$417 47	
From Henry F. Lee, collector . . .	1,641 82	
Abatements	16 40	$2,075 96
Balance uncollected, March 1, 1901 . .		$1,466 33

TAXES OF 1898.

Balance due, March 1, 1900		$6,825 24
From C. F. Richardson, collector . .	$650 82	
From Henry F. Lee, collector . . .	2,399 89	
Abatements.	17 60	3,068 31
Balance uncollected, March 1, 1901 . .		$3,756 93

TAXES OF 1899.

Balance due, March 1, 1900		$12,029 02
From C. F. Richardson, collector . .	$2,106 76	
From Henry F. Lee, collector . . .	2,500 37	
Abatements	32 00	4,639 13
Balance uncollected, March 1, 1901 . .		$7,389 89

TAXES OF 1900.

Taxes assessed for 1900 as per warrant.

Town Tax	$22,872 15	
Overlayings	16 09	
Additional assessments	163 41	
State Tax	900 00	
Special (marsh land) tax . . .	330 52	
County Tax	1,605 93	$25,888 10

Total taxes assessed to October 1, 1900.

Paid treasurer	$17,282 99	
Abatements	107 02	$17,390 01
Balance uncollected, March 1, 1901 .		$8,498 09

INTEREST.

Interest on taxes for 1895, collected and paid treasurer	$28 10
Interest on taxes for 1896, collected and paid treasurer	33 82
Interest on taxes for 1897, collected and paid treasurer	257 94
Interest on taxes for 1898, collected and paid treasurer	249 19
Interest on taxes for 1899, collected and paid treasurer	148 80
Interest on taxes for 1900, collected and paid treasurer	113 22
Total interest collected and paid treasurer . . .	$831 07

APPROPRIATIONS.

1900.

March 26.	Schools, care of rooms and fuel . .	$7,000 00
26.	School supplies	700 00
26.	Transportation of scholars . . .	1,500 00
26.	School repairs	100 00
26.	Superintendent of schools . . .	750 00
26.	Overdrafts	1,638 15
26.	Incidentals	2,000 00
26.	Salaries	1,300 00
26.	Electric lights	350 00
26.	Interest on town debt	3,000 00

March 26.	Firemen's pay	. . . . .	$400 00
26.	Hydrants	. . . . . .	384 00
26.	Highways and bridges	. . . .	2,000 00
26.	Support of poor	. . . . .	2,500 00
26.	Collection of taxes	. . . . .	350 00
26.	Abatement of taxes	. . . . .	200 00
26.	Library	. . . .	500 00
26.	Lake View Cemetery	. . . .	50 00
26.	North and Centre Cemeteries	. . .	50 00
26.	School house loan	. . . . .	1,100 00
Nov. 16.	Library	. . . .	300 00

$26,172 15

OUTSTANDING CLAIMS.

1901

March 1.	Town bonds due March 1, 1919, 4% .	. $42,000 00
1.	Water bonds due August 1, 1913, "	. . 11,000 00
1.	Water bonds due October 7, 1902, "	. . 4,000 00
1.	Water bonds due July 27, 1903, "	. . 1,000 00
1.	Draper Library fund, 6%	500 00
1.	Allen fund, "	1,000 00
1.	Childs fund, "	100 00
1.	Donation fund, "	1,300 00
1.	Loker fund, 5%	2,000 00
1.	James S. Draper fund, 6%	500 00
1.	School house loan, $1,100 payable November 1, each year, until paid in full . .	5,500 00

$68,900 00

AUDITOR'S REPORT.

Henry F. Lee,

In account with the town of Wayland.

TOTAL RECEIPTS.

March 1, 1901

Cash Balance, March 1, 1899 . . .	$18,966 95
Overseers of Poor	758 10
Temporary Loans	20,000 00
Excise Tax	187 05
Water Rates	1,888 02
Interest on Library Fund	234 94
Back Taxes received, Ward Estate . . .	299 78
Contingent	3,205 96
Taxes	27,546 21
	$73,087 01

Total Expenditures.

Schools	$7,293 22
School Supplies	702 30
" Transportation	1,422 68
" Repairs	44 82
" Superintendent	750 00
Highways	2,514 79
Incidentals	3,070 57
Fire Department	400 00
Collection of Taxes	529 00
Lakeview Cemetery	45 10
North and Centre Cemeteries	50 00
Cemetery Account	35 90
Poor Account	2,981 86
Electric Lights	461 48
Interest	4,259 20
School-House Loan	1,100 00
Salaries	2,235 52
State Tax	1,230 52
County Tax	1,605 93
Temporary Loans	17,000 00
Water Commissoners' orders	1,888 02
Library Fund	16,105 19
Sinking Fund	2,714 74
Parsons Fund	8 00
Library Account	800 00
Cash	3,838 17
	$73,087 01

TRIAL BALANCE.

Cash on hand	.	$3,838 17	Schools . .	$610 31
Due from Collector			Transportation of	
of Taxes .	.	21,815 89	Scholars . .	479 30
OVERDRAFTS.			School Repairs .	93 35
School Supplies	.	2 30	Fitting High School	249 72
Incidentals .	.	1,070 57	Overdrafts . .	282 00
Salaries	. .	435 52	Highways and Bridges	73
Electric Lights	.	14 74	Poor . . .	528 31
Interest	. .	642 74	New School House	1,000 00
Water Commissioners		256 00	Parsons Fund .	192 00
			Fire Department .	448 00
			Collection of Taxes	96 00
			Lakeview Cemetery	14 67
			Cemetery Account	111 61
			Temporary Loans	23,000 00
			Abatements . .	34 81
			Contingent Account	921 32
			Decoration Day .	13 80
		$28,075 93		$28,075 93

INDEX.

Lightning Source UK Ltd.
Milton Keynes UK
UKHW020623120219
337137UK00005B/548/P